THE
MYSTERY
OF
U-33

Hitler's Secret Envoy

Nigel Graddon

Other Books by Nigel Graddon:

*OTTO RAHN AND THE SEARCH
FOR THE HOLY GRAIL*

THE
MYSTERY
OF

U-33

Adventures Unlimited Press

The Mystery of U-33

by Nigel Graddon

Copyright 2010

ISBN 13: 978-1-935487-10-4

Published by:
Adventures Unlimited Press
One Adventure Place
Kempton, Illinois 60946 USA
auphq@frontiernet.net

www.adventuresunlimitedpress.com

The Mystery of U-33

U-33

Hitler's Secret Envoy

Though the seas threaten, they are merciful;
I have cursed them without cause.

(All section and chapter heading quotations are from William Shakespeare's *The Tempest*.)

Contents

And how does your content
Tender your own good fortune?

Acknowledgements   vii
Preface   x
Introduction   1
Part 1 ON RECORD
U-33: the Official Story   8
The First Questions   46
Survivors and Deceased   58
Part 2 OFF RECORD
August 1985—the story breaks   74
The Carradale U-boat   82
The Tail of the Bank Event   91
In the wake of U-33   100
"We, the people..."   108
Wrecks   130
The Greenock Lairs   137
The Mystery Men   158
"Brass Bounders at the Admiralty"   167
Captain's Log   176
Max Schiller through the Lens   180
Part 3 U-BOAT SPECIAL MISSIONS
Neu-Schwabenland and Station 211   196
Mercury Rising   205
The Holy Lance   209
U-boats in Scotland—Fact in Fiction   215
Part 4 ENDGAME
What happened...?   228
...when U-33 went through?   240
...and why?   253
U-33: Argo of the Grail   285
The Female Pope   309
Appendix   318
Bibliography   334

By kind permission of the Schiller family of Annan I dedicate this book to Max Schiller, the youngest survivor from U-33. Without help from remarks and hints that Max dropped here and there the real story of U-33 could never be told.

Scotland

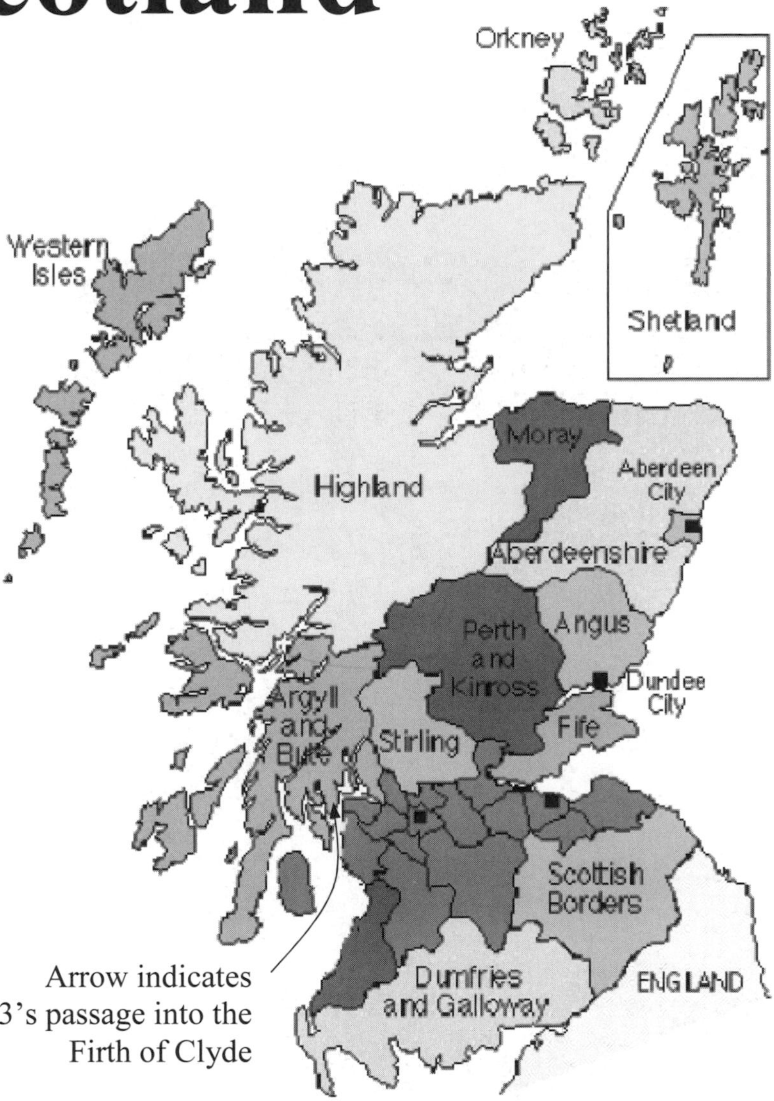

Orkney

Shetland

Western
Isles

Highland

Moray

Aberdeen
City

Aberdeenshire

Perth
and
Kinross

Angus

Dundee
City

Argyll
and
Bute

Stirling

Fife

Scottish
Borders

Dumfries
and Galloway

ENGLAND

Arrow indicates
U-33's passage into the
Firth of Clyde

The area of U-33's Scottish patrols in detail

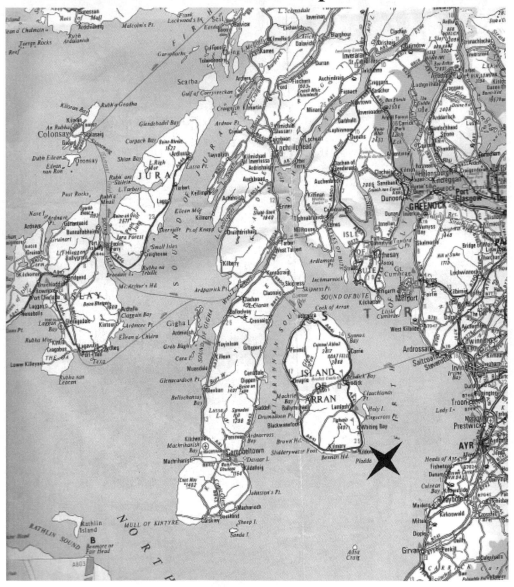

The star marks the position where U-33 was reported as sunk off Pladda by the Isle of Arran 12 February 1940. The map also incorporates other key locations for U-33's activities (both known and unrecorded) including Rathlin Island, the Isles of Islay and Bute, the Kintyre Peninsula and the Clyde Anchorage (the "Tail of the Bank" above Greenock-Dunoon).

U-boat pen at Lorient, Brittany (photographed by the author)

Acknowledgements

My library
Was dukedom large enough

I owe a big thank you to all those who have contributed to the development of this present work since I set out in 2001 to raise U-33 into the open waters of discovery.

To say that I am indebted to the many Scots who wrote to me describing their memories of the Cloch Point-Dunoon Boom Defence event and other associated incidents in the Firth of Clyde is a gross understatement. In attesting to extraordinary events in late 1939-early 1940, denied then and now by officialdom, an impressive number of citizens have been enormously free and giving with their personal experiences. Their very substantial contributions are the heart and foundation of this book, which I trust will satisfy their patient desire to see truth prevail.

Amongst these correspondents I would like to make mention of two in particular. The boyhood recollections of Glasgow resident Mr William Magee about both the Tail of the Bank U-boat "picnic" and the subsequent *Maillé Brézé* disaster at Gourock have been invaluable. Mr Magee is singularly unimpressed with the "brass bounders at the Admiralty" who in their persistent refusal to accept the stalwart opinions of firth citizens relegate these views into the category of daydreaming.

I was very grateful, too, to hear from Harry Young whose grandfather Horace Oakes was a reporter for *The Greenock Telegraph* at the time the events here described were taking place. Interested in the enigmatic story of German Grail explorer Otto Rahn,[1] Harry was kind enough to send me the relevant extracts from his grandfather's diary. Its pages reveal in no small degree that the events surrounding U-33 are far more convoluted than appear on the surface.

I was delighted to receive the blessing of Ray and Edna Schiller, Max Schiller's son and daughter, for the publication of this work and

---

[1] Graddon N., *Otto Rahn and the Quest for the Holy Grail: the Amazing Story of the Real "Indiana Jones,"* Adventures Unlimited Press, Kempton, 2008

for the opportunity to dedicate it to their father. I am especially thankful for their kind permission to reproduce photographs featuring Max Schiller with family, friends and boatmates.

Having no specific interest in U-boat history and, hence, no technical expertise when I embarked on the project, I am grateful for the help that so many offered to ensure accuracy of detail. It is hard to single out individual contributors but I wish to thank Horst Bredow, Ron Young, Howard Cock, Hubertus Weggelaar and, especially, Pamela Armstrong for permission to draw on her excellent analysis of U-33's three patrols and its encounter with minesweeper HMS *Gleaner*.

In the early days of my U-33 research I received first-rate help from the Naval Historical Branch (NHB) of the United Kingdom's Ministry of Defence (MoD). In particular, I would like to thank Kate Tildesley and Captain C.L.W. Paige RN, both for their expert contributions and for their patience in reviewing and responding to questions from an enquirer who clearly did not know one end of a submarine from another!

British U-boat expert Lawrence Paterson was a tremendous asset in the early days of the research and I am grateful for his time, knowledge and patience in the many exchanges with this shameless rooky.

I should give warm mention to Alistair Alexander who trod the U-33 research trail with me in the earlier days. His contribution was much appreciated.

Hazel Menzies of the Vennel Local and Family History Centre in Irvine performed a superb task in locating the *Largs and Millport Weekly News* articles between 1984 and 1986. In so doing, Ms Menzies turned up the most definitive eyewitness testimony on the Cloch Point-Dunoon U-boat incursion on record.

As ever, Eric Baxter of *The Greenock Telegraph* provided terrific support along the U-33 trail. The *Telegraph* has been an enthusiastic champion of my work since the early days of the Otto Rahn research in the late 1990s. It remains an ideal vehicle for two-way information exchanges and for the gathering of invaluable recollections from citizens around the Clyde. Long may our friendship continue!

Last, but not least, I give thanks (in no particular order) to: Deutsches U-Boot Museum-Archiv for providing a wealth of high quality material for background and reproduction, Greenock Crematorium personnel for friendly expert advice and key documents, Scotland Library & Information Service, General Register Office for Scotland (Extract Services), Commonwealth War Graves Commission, MacLean Museum and Art Gallery, Royal Naval Museum Library, Co-operative Funeral Service Greenock, Paul Bevand for the logs of HMS *Hood* in February 1940, Harry Cooper, Iain Crosbie, Lesley Schiller, Peter Moir, James Taylor, Eileen Rombach, Matthew Lafferty, Angus Martin, Donald Kelly, Robert Graham, W.J. Bannatyne, Elizabeth Brown, Harry Young, Reverend Mel Coogan, Robert Brown, T.E. McKillop, Katherine Kurtz, David Hendry, Elizabeth Redwanz, Patti Duncan, Jak P. Mallmann Showell, Richard Hampo, Jonothon Boulter, Dr. M. Nelson, Charlie Bass, Cdr. Bill Jones (Staff of Flag Officer Scotland, Northern England & Northern Ireland), Ken McCoy, Fred Wallace, George Bradley, Paul Bristow, Archie McKenzie, Leslie Couperwhite, David Mayo, M.S., the Magic Torch Inverclyde history group and Arthur "Penry" Warr, an avid U-33 enthusiast who sadly passed away while this work was in preparation.

Preface

Like one,
Who having, into truth, by telling of it,
Made such a sinner of his memory,
To credit his own lie

Otto Rahn pointed a finger at the wake of U-33. By 2001 I had been researching the fabled German Grailhunter for six years, gingerly scraping away the accumulated cavern dust that had concealed his treasure seeking activities in the South of France and ancient European power centres since the early 1930s.

Then, out of the blue, I heard a whisper from an informed source overseas that Rahn's disappearance and the activities of U-33 in the early stages of World War II were linked. That was the full extent of the lead but in 2001, never one to dismiss a potential line of enquiry, I made a tentative start in reviewing the records of U-33, not seriously imagining that there would be any worthwhile return from the effort invested in the exercise.

One of my first actions was to contact the U-Boot-Archiv[1] in Cuxhaven (Altenbruch) in Germany, a superb resource and museum run with the help of unpaid volunteers by its founder Herr Horst Bredow who served as Watch Officer on U-288. Not long afterwards I received a package of material from Herr Bredow. It contained a sheaf of items on U-33 and a trove of additional supporting material including various maps, charts, photos and Kriegsmarine records.

I learned that U-33 had met its nemesis in HMS *Gleaner* on 12 February 1940, having spent the preceding six months wreaking havoc in two successive excursions in British waters, sinking eleven ships in the process. These were interesting facts of historical record but none provided any clue to aspects of U-33's operations that one might term out of the ordinary. Certainly there were none that would widen one's eyes to see better the figure of treasure seeker Otto Rahn waving from the conning tower.

Nevertheless, there were two items in the package that did grab my

---

[1] In 2007 the archive changed its name to the Deutsches U-Boot Museum-Archiv

attention and which drove a more strenuous programme of research in a subsequent nine-year period.

Herr Bredow had included copies of newspaper articles published in 1985 by the *Largs and Millport Weekly News*, a provincial newpaper serving those two North Ayrshire towns and surrounding areas, Largs being situated on the Firth of Clyde mainland faced by Millport across the water on the island of Great Cumbrae.

Editor John McCreadie had written two articles, published a few weeks apart, in his "Out and About" column concerning an event he dated as February 1940. Local (Firth of Clyde) residents claimed it had taken place at the mouth of the Clyde Anchorage (the "Tail of the Bank").

Max Schiller (right) on HMS *Cromer* reflected in a sonar image of U-33 off Pladda

More precisely, the *Largs and Millport Weekly News'* claims stipulated that the Tail of the Bank event took place in mid-February of that year, a time period closely proximate to the date of the 12th when U-33 was sunk by HMS *Gleaner*, thirty-five miles to the southwest by Arran. This was unexpected and exciting news.

The circumstances surrounding this alleged event and one of like nature and location reported by various parties to have occurred in

November 1939 are the foundation for this present work.

One does not have to labour to marshal the facts about U-33. In time they present themselves—but in ways surprisingly far removed from the direction an incoming researcher might anticipate having reviewed just the classic features of the story.

In some ways the riddles surrounding U-33 can be described as a provocative footnote to the account of Otto Rahn's life but the story (or rather U-33's untold story) is a page-turner in its own right and deservedly so.

The receipt of Herr Bredow's package dropped a depth charge upon my growing indifference to U-33's relatively minor placement in WWII history. Its arrival kindled a sense of passion and purpose for a task not felt since embarking upon the Otto Rahn research in the mid-nineties. Every instinct told me that there was a headline story about U-33 that would not see the light of day until repeated dives brought it piece by piece to the surface.

Naturally, there is interest in U-33 among many other parties. One thing that struck me right at the start of my investigations was the global, intense interest in U-boat lore and history. It is a hugely important topic for countless enthusiasts. Many of these fans and aficionados were enormously helpful to me, a U-boat novice, in providing information, thoughts and opinions about countless questions. That help was invaluable.

But as the research expanded into new tributaries of enquiry, revealing aspects about U-33 that increasingly shocked and excited in equal measure, I noticed a growing trend among some quarters to adopt a policy of "radio silence" upon further commentary or assistance.

Like morning mist upon the Clyde an air of reluctance fell upon U-33 and its apparent determination to reveal its secrets. Had it been ruefully observed, perhaps, that long concealed facts about the boat and its final mission, which had been supposed would remain hidden were coming to light?

But to one standing back, with a sense of detachment, what did it matter if an enthusiastic naïf had stumbled across a few facts about U-33 unrecorded by history? So what, for example, if there were more people buried from U-33 than was evident from the crew list? Were not side-stories such as these little more than insubstantial geegaws of fact, adding little or nothing to an understanding of Second World War naval history? What possible harm could come from presenting a more complete story about U-33 for public debate and scrutiny?

Nevertheless, seven decades after the event there still appears to be a distinct nervousness in some circles about public dissemination of the true circumstances surrounding events in the Firth of Clyde in the early months of the war. The question bubbles to the surface and floats uncomfortably. Just what is the nature of the threat in the twenty-first century posed by exorcising the elderly ghost of U-33?

In the Rahn biography I offered the opinion that the medievalist's ultimate destiny was intrinsically connected with international political and esoteric activity during and after WWII. Having reflected upon it at length, I believe that U-33 occupies a key nodal point along these geopolitical pathways. I believe, too, that it is linked in ways not yet fully understood with other significant subsequent events in Scottish twentieth century wartime history, principally Rudolf Hess' flight to Scotland in May 1941 and the Sunderland seaplane crash on Eagle's Rock, Caithness, in August 1942. These synergies are explored in this present work.

In the following pages we shall review U-33's beginnings and its first incursions into British waters, before moving on to make a forensic investigation of the submarine's forays into Scottish waters and their truly remarkable consequences.

Introduction

I'll break my staff,
Bury it certain fathoms in the earth,
And deeper than did ever plummet sound
I'll drown my book

There are no features of the historical account of U-33's final voyage which, at first glance, warrant the "mystery" tag in its re-telling in the twenty-first century.

U-33 came to the lower reaches of the Firth of Clyde in February 1940 intent on laying mines to destroy British shipping. Sinking enemy vessels was precisely what U-boats did. It was their operational imperative.

In keeping with this prime directive, U-33's Commandant, Kapitänleutnant (Kplt) Hans-Wilhelm von Dresky, was under orders from Konteradmiral (Rear Admiral) Karl Dönitz to inflict maximum damage upon the enemy. Von Dresky and his crew, forty-two dedicated professional fighting men, were loyal to that objective. On this occasion, the aura of impermeability that had protected the submarine while sinking eleven ships during two prior patrols in British waters since August 1939 drained into the freezing cold depths of the Clyde.

U-33's practice of *veni, vidi, vici* stopped short of completing the third action on 12 February 1940. Instead, it was the British who did the conquering and twenty-five brave men of the Kriegsmarine (the name given to the German Navy between 1935 and 1945) lost their lives.

The only factor of note surrounding the sinking of U-33 was the recovery of parts from the boat's Enigma code machine. Had von Dresky's order been obeyed faithfully Obermaschinensmaat (Chief Mechanic) Friedrich Kumpf would not have reportedly stuffed three Enigma rotors in his trouser pockets to be found by the British after his rescue from the Firth of Clyde.

But the fine silt around U-33's hull that denies curious divers today clear visibility of the wreck has also served to mask other tantalising features of its Scottish travails for seventy years.

In the mid-1980s Firth of Clyde citizens began to express beliefs that activities identical to but quite distinct from the Isle of Arran U-boat episode took place thirty-five miles to the northeast in the closely packed and heavily defended Clyde Anchorage.

Enigma machines

These opinions, running contrary to the official record, were aired extensively in the *Largs and Millport Weekly News* championed by its enthusiastic editor, John McCreadie.

In 2001 I obtained copies of two invaluable articles written by McCreadie on the topic in which the main bodies of text were verbatim eyewitness accounts of the U-boat that had passed through the boom defences. These two pieces, in turn, referred to other associated articles but initial enquiries were unsuccessful in tracking them down.

McCreadie prefaced his reports about the U-boat that tricked its way through the boom by dating its occurrence in mid-February 1940. This date was incorrect. Evidently, the journalist was fixating on the well known and documented U-33 story, reporting reactively, insufficiently engaged with his correspondents. Had McCreadie enquired further they would have confirmed that the event they were describing in arresting detail had actually taken place during the previous autumn.

Perhaps it never occurred to McCreadie that the sinking of U-33 in February 1940 was the final part of a two-act play whose curtain rose in the late autumn of 1939. To him, all the colourful stories eagerly narrated by his readers were exciting embellishments that merely enhanced the *known* record of U-boat activities in the Clyde in the first months of WWII, culminating in the sinking of U-33 by Arran.

The stories his readers told were true; the impression conveyed by McCreadie to his newspaper's readership as to when they took place was false. It was a falsity that was to pose as fact for many years and, in consequence, would shroud the true nature and import of U-33's activities in Scottish waters until recent times.

Due to this perpetuating error, made all the more credible because McCreadie's introductory remarks refer to a dating for the event that appears to have come from informed local sources, my researches sought vainly to reconcile the irreconcilable. Fruitlessly, I struggled for many years to square the apparent certain probability that while on the same night in February 1940 when U-33 was sunk off Arran another enemy submarine was making mischief up at the boom between Dunoon and Cloch Point. In hindsight, it was a Sisyphean task.

McCreadie's articles came and went. The story fell into renewed slumber. But another forty-five years would not have to pass before it was re-awakened.

Finally, in October 2008, I obtained copies of the remaining articles in the complete series on the U-boat incursion and related matters, which were published in the *Largs and Millport Weekly News* by John McCreadie between 1984 and 1986.

The new material established two very important facts, namely that the audacious U-boat incursion into the Clyde Anchorage had truly taken place (according to very strongly held opinions from time-witnesses) and that it had done so in late 1939.

A number of previously contradictory factors fell quickly into place, allowing me to join up more dots in the bigger picture than at any time since embarking upon the U-33 journey in 2001.

It would be unwise for hindsight to insist that U-33's Scottish adventures wholly belong to the month of February 1940. The events in the Firth of Clyde of November 1939 and February 1940 are profoundly and directly connected. A great number of the gaps about what may be discovered about them are now filled.

The whole canvas does retain a few patches of white here and there. Nevertheless, it has advanced well beyond the sketch stage to a level of detail and insight where all that is required are a few brush strokes to bring to life the Firth of Clyde U-boat episodes in their entirety, seventy years after the event. Even so, the picture that presently confronts the onlooker is bold and astonishing.

Maybe one or more of those who are drawn to this work will pick up their brush and, equipped with more knowledge, more interconnectedness with "those that know," will complete the canvas and hang it up for all to see.

In essence, this book is a call to arms to those who, moved by the tale, are stirred to dive deeper upon the wreck of U-33 and bring its log book gingerly to the surface, wherein all may be revealed.

A U-boat on patrol during the First World War

PART ONE

ON RECORD

We are such stuff
As dreams are made on, and our little life
Is rounded with a sleep

Chapter ONE

U-33: the Official Story

I would fain die a dry death

The Firth of Clyde forms a large area of coastal water sheltered from the Atlantic Ocean by the Kintyre Peninsula, which encloses the outer firth in Argyll and Ayrshire.

At its entrance the firth is some 26 miles (42km) wide. Its upper reaches include an area where it is joined by Loch Long and the Gare Loch. The area includes the large Clyde Anchorage off Greenock, known locally as the Tail of the Bank in reference to the sandbar that separates the firth from the estuary of the River Clyde. The Clyde is still almost 2 miles (3km) wide at the sandbar and its upper tidal limit is at the tidal weir adjacent to Glasgow Green.

The cultural and geographical distinction between the firth and the River Clyde is vague. People will sometimes refer to Dumbarton as being on the Firth of Clyde while the population of Port Glasgow and Greenock frequently refer to the firth to their north as "the river."

In Scottish Gaelic the landward end of the Firth of Clyde is called Linne Chluaidh while the area of the firth around the south of Arran, Kintyre and Ayrshire-Galloway is called An Linne Ghlas, which simply means a long narrow estuary.

The area's defences included the Cloch Coast Battery in Inverkip Parish, which formed a part of the Clyde defence system in both World Wars. It was originally fitted with 6-inch guns from Portkil in 1916. The Coast Battery was decommissioned in 1956. Today the site has been partly demolished with two gun emplacements filled in.

One of the most important beacons on the Clyde is the Cloch Lighthouse situated two miles south of Gourock. Erected at a point where the firth suddenly changes direction, the lighthouse is a circular tower eighty feet high. The jurisdiction of the water-baille of Glasgow terminates at this point. Here there is a regular ferry to and from Dunoon on the opposite shore. Above and beyond Dunoon are the peaks of the Argyllshire Mountains.

During the war years on a hill high above Cloch Lighthouse was a naval station operated by members of the Women's Royal Naval Service (WRENS). Their task was to send and receive messages to and from vessels as they came through the boom. The blinking "dot-dot-dot-dash" of the WRENS' Aldis lamps must have been one of the last sights for many sailors leaving the Clyde.

At the beginning of September 1940 Greenock was a part of the Clyde Sub Command of the Rosyth Command. The Flag Officer in Charge, Clyde (Rear Admiral J.D. Campbell), was based in Glasgow with an Extended Defence Officer and Boom Defence Officer at Greenock.

Consequent to the sinking of HMS *Royal Oak* in Scapa Flow naval authorities decided in October 1939 to remove the armed merchant cruisers of the Northern Patrol and base them on the Clyde, which also became an alternative base for ships of the Home Fleet.

After visiting Greenock in HMS *Nelson* in December 1939 the Commander-in-Chief Home Fleet decided that Flag Officer in Charge, Clyde, was too far from the scene in Glasgow to keep in regular touch with operational matters. Consequently, the Sub Command was divided into a Glasgow Sub Command and a Greenock Sub Command.

Rear Admiral J.A.G. Troup was appointed as Flag Officer in Charge, Glasgow, and was responsible for all fitting out, repair and maintenance work in the Clyde area.

Rear Admiral B.C. Watson was appointed Flag Officer in Charge, Greenock, responsible for seaward defences, Anti-Submarine (A/S) patrols, control of traffic in port, berthing at Greenock, issue of sailing orders and local administrative work at the Greenock base. In Chapter 9 we shall return briefly to Rear Admiral Watson when we examine the burial details of the deceased from U-33 in Greenock Cemetery.

The £1,000,000 defence boom installed in the early autumn of 1939 between Cloch Point, Renfrewshire and Dunoon, Argyllshire protected the Clyde Anchorage during WWII. The massive A/S defence, comprising two lines of torpedo nets constructed in 12-foot square mesh and laced with depth charges, was supported by a twin row of floats. It spanned the whole width of the firth except for a small gap near the Dunoon shore left open to allow river steamers and shallow-draught local traffic to come and go. The boom was patrolled constantly by a fleet of seven hastily conscripted A/S Guard ships: two trawlers, three armed motor yachts and two motor boats.

Nearby gun towers were built with bevelled frontages to support the revolving actions of the guns. Officially, the coastal gun sites never saw

The Cloch Lighthouse-Dunoon defence boom in WWII

action against any U-boats but, interestingly, the history books do record the successful penetration of the boom in 1943 by a top-secret British midget submarine. Its crew was practising for raids on ships like the Bismarck battleship *Tirpitz*, which they carried out successfully later that year. Its undetected passage through the netting meant that the lookout men of the Cloch battery subsequently had a lot of explaining to do. It will be necessary to recall this operational carelessness when we review in later chapters the successful passage of a U-boat through the boom in November 1939.

Standing today on Millport pleasure beach in the southeastern corner of Great Cumbrae, looking out over the sparkling waters of the Clyde, it is difficult to recall that during WWII this great Scottish river saw much of the violent events of the time.

Convoys assembled in the Clyde Anchorage before setting out on the hazardous voyage to America, Gibraltar, Africa or India—indeed anywhere in the world where the war was being fought—while hundreds of ships bringing vital cargoes from the U.S.A. unloaded their precious burdens at the ports that lined its banks. In turn, other large convoys of men and supplies set out through the Cloch-Dunoon boom on many notable operations, including the invasion of Africa (Operation Torch) and the invasion of Europe.

Between May 1942 and the end of 1944 more than 1,200,000 American GIs had been been delivered safely to the Clyde by various troop ships.

Exiled governments also set up bases and billets in Greenock, including the Poles, Czechs and Free French. A memorial to the latter, erected in the form of a Cross of Lorraine on a hill above Greenock (reproduced in Chapter 10), commemorates the members of the Free French Navy who lost their lives during the hostilities.

Nine miles northeast of Millport is Largs, the Ayrshire town where so many top-secret plans were laid by Britain's senior wartime administrators away from the glare of London. Not least among these covert operations was the occasion when Largs hosted at the Vanduara and Hollywood Hotels the major planning conference for D-Day (Operation Overlord) in June 1943 on behalf of Lord Mountbatten, Chief of Combined Operations. The gathering of Britain's top brass also planned the fake D-Day operation, "Fortitude," which was leaked to the Germans to fool them into thinking the offensive would take place from Kent and the Pas de Calais.

For the D-Day landings pier-heads for the "Mulberries" (artificial harbours still seen scattered around the Normandy beaches today) were made by Clydesiders. Fresh water for the troops was taken from Loch Thom behind Greenock.

RAF Coastal Command was also based in Largs. The base housed a large number of Catalina flying boats and two Sunderland flying boats fitted out for U-boat killings. U-33 would be heading for very dangerous waters.

In December 1939 ten thousand Canadian troops arrived in Greenock in an assortment of well known liners escorted by a great assembly of battleships and cruisers. They were welcomed by Colonial Secretary (later Prime Minister and Earl of Avon) Anthony Eden. In 1942 twelve thousand American troops arrived on the liner RMS *Queen Elizabeth*.

On 1 December Greenock residents were treated to the startling spectacle of five officers and thirty-eight ratings from U-35 being led along Hamilton Street, at that time the town's main shopping thoroughfare. In front and behind these officers was a Royal Navy jeep, each carrying three or four British servicemen. Behind the rear jeep followed the U-boat ratings. Both groups of POWs were smartly attired in their uniforms. The 4 December edition of *The Scotsman* reported that the men were rescued after their vessel had been destroyed. U-35 was sunk in the North Sea on 29 November in position 60.53N 02.47E by depth charges from the British destroyers HMS *Kingston*, HMS *Icarus* and HMS *Kashmir*. All forty-three men on board survived.

The officers and ratings were given a remarkably friendly send-off by Greenock folk. The briefest of official Admiralty communiqués said:

"A number of U-boat prisoners were landed last night at a Scottish port, the result of recent naval operations.

"The crew were brought in by two destroyers, which berthed at the wharf alongside each other. When the prisoners went down the gangway they were cheered by the sailors who lined the rails and decks of the warships. One little fairheaded German, a fluent English speaker who made himself popular with his captors, was greeted by the British sailors as 'Blondie' and given a special cheer.

*"The U-boat commander (*Werner Lott*), a strongly-built young man, was the last to go ashore and as he stepped across the gangway there was clapping and cheering. An officer in charge of the military armed guard on the quay remarked to him, 'I suppose you will be glad to be out of it,' and the German replied, 'Yes.'*

"Before landing the submarine commander shook hands with the officers of the warship. Cigarettes were distributed to the prisoners by British sailors. As the Germans drove away in motor buses to an

internment camp there was more cheering and the members of the U-boat crew, who were all scantily attired, replied by waving their hands." The crew of U-35 were transported by train to London on the night of 2-3 December 1939.

Winston Churchill made many visits to Greenock during the war. Other distinguished dignitaries who came to the town included King George VI and Queen Elizabeth, General de Gaulle and other members of both the British and Norwegian Royal Families. British celebrities of the day such as Gracie Fields and Harry Lauder made public appearances. Later, Hollywood stars Douglas Fairbanks Jr. and Robert Montgomery serving in the U.S. Navy came to Greenock.

When the decision was made early in the war to relocate Britain's gold reserves (Operation Fish) one of the consignments was transported to Greenock where it was loaded onto HMS *Revenge* for removal to Halifax in Canada. Security was extremely tight in the July of 1940. Boxes containing either four gold bars or bags of coins arrived in Greenock harbour in railway box wagons. One naval officer checked the boxes coming off the wagons while another checked them going into the boat. A third officer checked them being lowered to the bomb room and a fourth checked them arriving in the room. The procedure was reversed in Halifax.

By far the biggest story of the war in the locality was the blitz on Greenock and district on the nights of 5, 6 and 7 May 1941. The towns in what is now Inverclyde suffered almost 1,000 casualties, including nearly 300 dead. Between 8,000 and 10,000 houses were destroyed or damaged. Industrial centres were decimated, including the destruction of a distillery storing thousands of gallons of industrial alcohol.

The banks of the Clyde were the birthplace of a great armada of ships. Shipbuilding yards literally lined the river. The Royal Navy had secure and formidable bases here. The Clyde echoed to the noise of riveting and metal forging. The very air was acrid with welding fumes and diesel exhausts from the host of small vessels engaged in servicing the frantically busy shipbuilding industry. While out in protected anchorage areas ships were marshalled together in preparation for their next dangerous journey.

On 24 September 1939, just three weeks after the commencement of hostilities, the Admiralty requisitioned the Clyde Steamers for war service. The turbines *King Edward, King George V* and the *Duchess of Hamilton* and the paddlers *Waverley, Jeannie Deans, Mercury, Juno, Jupiter, Caledonia, Duchess of Fife, Duchess of Rothesay, Queen Empress* and *Eagle III* were all withdrawn from sailings, leaving only the *Marchioness of Graham* to carry on the Clyde ferry services.

And so it was that steamers, paddlers, tugs and battle cruisers passed downriver into the firth then out into the open sea. All too often they struggled back savaged and battle damaged to the places on the Clyde where they had been given life. Mostly they were repaired as quickly as possible then set off again to keep their next appointment with the enemy. Some died facing fearful odds. Others would fall victim to sly torpedo attacks. These "Daughters of the Clyde" were proud ships, constructed by craftsmen who made the words "Clyde Built" an international benchmark for the best.

With 1939 drawing to a close and the likelihood that the war would continue for some time there was also great concern about moving the Cunard liner RMS *Queen Elizabeth* out of the Clyde danger area as soon as possible.

Across the North Sea Germany had fifteen yards building U-boats (Unterseebootes) of the VII (often wrongly called the VIIA) and VIIB types. U-33 was a VII type. The type VII boasted four torpedo tubes in the bow and one in the stern, which, together with a highly efficient 88mm deck gun, made this easily manoeuverable boat a dangerous opponent. In addition to its other qualities it could with relative ease be used for minelaying if the torpedoes were removed and replaced with twenty-two TMA mines.

The presence of so many ships made the Clyde a most desirable target for Rear Admiral Karl Dönitz of the German Navy and his U-boats. It was brutally savaged by air raids. Right through until May 1940 U-boats operated around the coasts of Britain and in the North Sea attacking with both torpedoes and magnetic mines. Mines were also laid by surface ships and aircraft. In January 1940 U-32 was the first enemy submarine to be detailed with mining the Firth of Clyde but her commander Kplt Paul Büchel laid a small minefield south of Ailsa Craig instead. Dönitz quickly dismissed Büchel for taking what he considered the easier option.

According to the book *Black May* by Michael Gannon, on 3 September 1939 Germany was equipped with between 39 and 51 operational U-boats, of which between 22 and 26 were Type VII-IX vessels. Additionally, there were training boats, new boats in workup for duty and boats on the builders' ways. Taking these facts together, German U-boats in commission on 3 September 1939 were:
- ➢ 2 x Type IA: U-25 and U-26
- ➢ 6 x Type IIA: U-1 to U-6
- ➢ 18 x Type IIB: U-7 to U-24

> ➤ 6 x Type IIC: U-56 to U-61
> ➤ 10 x Type VII: U27 to U-36 (including U-33)
> ➤ 8 x Type VIIB: U-45 to U-49 and U-51 to U-53
> ➤ 7 x Type IXA: U-37 to U-43

All the other types came along after the war started so the total commissioned fleet in September 1939 was 57 boats of which 40 were out at sea, namely:

> ➤ 18 on patrol in the North Atlantic (1 x Type I, 12 x Type VII, 5 x Type IX)
> ➤ 18 on patrol in the North Sea (17 x Type II, 1 x Type VII)
> ➤ 4 on patrol in the Baltic Sea (4 x Type II)
> ➤ 3 x Type VII previously patrolling in the Baltic from 1 September, then patrolling in the Atlantic in the second week of September
> ➤ 14 U-boats were schoolboats or in training

Apart from minelaying the only other activity that is often missing from the BdU[1] War Diary and even the U-boats' logbooks (Kriegstagebücher abbreviated to KTB) is the landing of agents. We will return to this topic.

There was a certain amount of deliberate hysteria whipped up by Churchill regarding the U-boat menace, quite justified with their early war minelaying programme when the magnetic mine became more successful than early torpedo patrols.

The story of U-33, a VII type, Feldpost # M28 962, began quite typically at the construction yard of F. Krupp Germaniawerft AG, Kiel-Gaarden for Kriegsmarine, Kiel. Every German naval unit had their own Feldpost (German military mail service) number. Those allocated to U-boats were preceded by the letter M for Kriegsmarine. Feldpost numbers had other uses apart from that of postal address. For example, in the case of individual crewmembers being called out in a public place to report back to base the Feldpost number would be used instead of the U-boat number in the interests of security.

She was ordered on 25 March 1935 within the batch of U-33 to U-36. Her keel was laid in Yard No. 556 on 1 September 1935. The Baubelehrung[2] took place at Marinelehr-und Reporaturwerkstatt, Kiel. The Type VII could accommodate a 45-man crew, a distinctly cramped

---

[1] *Befehlshaber der Unterseeboote* Commander-in-Chief for submarines, Karl Dönitz from 19 September 1939.
[2] The familiarisation visit for a U-boat crew on the construction of the vessel—it took place 6-8 weeks before completion under the supervision of the KLA (the Kriegsshiftbandehrabteilung—warship construction training detachment).

experience in a space 142 feet long and a mere 10 feet wide, compared with the U-boat's 210 by 19 feet outer shell.

The 500-ton U-boat was launched on 11 June 1936. U-33 was commissioned by Kplt Ottoheinrich Junker on 25 July 1936 and formally assigned to Germany-based U-Flottille "Saltzwedel" at Wilhelmshaven as a frontline boat from that date until 31 December 1939.

Junker, born 12 July 1905 in Freiburg im Breisgau, joined the German Navy in 1924. He commanded U-33 until 2 June 1937 except for a four-week period from 21 November to 20 December 1936 when Kplt Kurt Freiwald took the helm. Freiwald resumed command for seven weeks from June 1937 before Junker once more took over the post of Commanding Officer, remaining in charge until 29 October 1938. Junker then passed command of U-33 to Kplt Hans-Wilhelm von Dresky, the man who would be at the helm on U-33's night of disaster in February 1940.

Von Dresky was born in Halle an der Saale 27 January 1908. He joined the Kriegsmarine in 1929, serving as Watch Officer on U-20 between February 1936 and September 1937. He then took command of the small "duck" U-4 on 30 Sept 1937. He was promoted to Kapitänleutnant on 1 August 1938.

Kplt Hans-Wilhelm von Dresky

Over a nine-month period von Dresky led the crew of U-33 in continual practice runs, including trimming practices, balancing the boat, radio and torpedo drills and anti-aircraft procedure.

On 19 August 1939 U-33 went to war. She set out from her home-port on what was to be the first war patrol for all on board, including von Dresky. She proceeded to an operational area southwest of Ireland.

Nine days later U-33 reached the Western Approaches where she waited to receive news of the commencement of hostilities with England and France.

At 14:55 GMT[3] on 7 September U-33 found a British vessel, the steamer SS *Olivegrove* (4,060 tons), 420 miles southwest of Land's End

---

[3] All times of the clock reported throughout this book are expressed as GMT.

in the Atlantic and sunk her with a torpedo. The *Olivegrove* was sailing independently from Puerto Padre, Cuba, to London with 4,500 tons of sugar. She sank at position 49:05N 15:58W. The crew abandoned ship in two lifeboats.

Von Dresky's subsequent actions showed him to be a chivalrous foe. He brought *Olivegrove's* master Captain James Barnetson on board U-33 for questioning. After being returned to the lifeboat Barnetson decided to head for Fastnet, which was almost 300 miles away. Von Dresky courteously sent a radio message to the 24,289-ton American liner SS *Washington*, giving the position of the lifeboats. During the nine hours it took for the ship to arrive on the scene U-33 slowly circled the two boats and actually fired Very lights to guide the *Washington* to the scene before sailing off to the west. The survivors were landed at Southampton on 9 September 1939.

At 06:00 on 16 September the 1,567-ton British steamer SS *Arkleside* (Smith, Hogg Co. Ltd., West Hartlepool) was steaming from the Tyne to Gibraltar with 2,500 tons of coal and coke when U-33 sent her to the bottom. Von Dresky sank her with gunfire off the Scilly Isles, 150 miles southwest from Land's End at position 48:00N 09:30W. Two French fishing smacks rescued the master Captain Robert William Edmondson and his crew and landed them at Concareau 60 miles south of Ushant.

Von Dresky repeated this performance on 24 September. U-33 was south of the Faroe Isles and making her way home when she sank the 287-ton Fleetwood fishing vessel *Caldew* by gunfire at 07:00 at position 60:47N 06:20W. The crew of the *Caldew* was later picked up by the Swedish steamer *Kronprinsessan Margareta*. (The steamer was subsequently intercepted by the German destroyer *Friedrich Ihn* and the crew landed at Kiel.)

U-33 then made a triumphant return to Wilhelmshaven on 28 September 1939 and was visited by no less a V.I.P. than Adolf Hitler, a clear indication of the success of their first wartime patrol and of the high esteem in which elite U-boat crews were held by the Nazi leadership. In commendation 10 Iron Crosses 2nd Class were awarded.

Carrying twelve TMB mines and six torpedoes, U-33 departed Wilhelmshaven with von Dresky on 29 October for its second excursion and sailed for a minelaying operation in the Bristol Channel area, travelling via the north of Scotland.

However on the outbound voyage across the North Sea both diesel engines broke down and U-33 had to lie on the seabed for three days while engineers made repairs. One crewman later remarked that the boat was not really seaworthy and that the men were nervous, so much so that many of them were reluctant to go back to sea in her.

A mine laid by U-33 around this time sank the 2,473-ton British steamer *Stanholme* (ex *Goleta*, Stanhope Steamship Co. Ltd) at 06:45 on Christmas Day. She was sailing from Cardiff to London with 4,300 tons of coal and sank in grid AM9947, position 51:20N 03:39W. The 3,068-ton Norwegian vessel *Liv* rescued the master Captain David Llewellyn Hook and eleven men and landed them at Cardiff. Twelve crewmen were lost.

The final toll of U-33's 2nd patrol came at 15:19 on 16 January 1940 when the 9,456-ton British motor tanker *Inverdargle* (Inver Tankers Ltd., Liffey Transport & Trading Co. Ltd.) detonated one of U-33's mines southwest of Nash Point in the Bristol Channel. She was on passage from Trinidad for Avonmouth via Halifax (Nova Scotia) with 12,554 tons of aviation spirit and sank at position 51:16N 03:43W. The master Captain Evan Murdock Skelly, one RN Gunner and forty of the crew were lost.

While at sea von Dresky received a signal (Instruction Number 154) sent by Admiral Dönitz to all U-boat Commanders. It stated: *"Rescue no one and take no one with you. Have no care for the ships' boats. Weather conditions amd proximity of land is of no account. Care only for your own boat and strive to achieve the next success as soon as possible. We must be hard in this war. The enemy started this war in order to detroy us, therefore nothing else matters."*

Admiral Karl Dönitz in 1943

The uncompromising tone of Dönitz's command signal does not square logically with von Dresky's gentlemanly actions in assisting the captain and crew of the *Olivegrove* during U-33's first patrol, a kindly deed that did not appear to have evoked higher level criticism. Nor does it sit comfortably alongside the Führer directive of October 1939 (reviewed in Chapter 2), which forbade the inflicting of civilian casualties during attacks made on HMS *Hood*. One might draw the conclusion that gung-ho signals such as Dönitz's were an official requirement in a period of wartime conflict but that, in practice, a less bombastic line prevailed, at least in the war's early stages.

After laying his mines von Dresky searched for torpedo and gun-targets. On 20 November U-33 sank three Fleetwood steam trawlers by gunfire: the 276-ton *Thomas Hankins* at 13:30, 14 miles northwest of Tory Island, all of the crew were saved; the 250-ton *Delphine* at 15:00, 18 miles northeast of Tory Island with no casualties; and the 329-ton *Sea Sweeper* at 16:05, 25 miles northwest of Tory Island, no casualties.

Two more Fleetwood boats were sunk with gunfire the next morning, Tuesday 21 November, 75 miles northwest of Rathlin Island: the 287-ton *Sulby* at 07:30 with the loss of the five crewmen and the 276-ton *William Humphries* sunk at 08:20. Lloyd's War Losses state that thirteen crewmen were lost.

Even on her way home on 23 November, northwest of the Orkneys, fate handed U-33 a parting gift in the shape of a German steamer: the 3,670-ton *Borkum* (Norddeutscher Lloyd). The ship had been on passage from Rosario for Hamburg with grain when the British captured her on the 17th. A prize crew was taking her to Kirkwall in the Orkneys. U-33 encountered the *Borkum* at 14:30 northwest of the islands at position 59:33N 03:57W. Presumably believing it to be unoccupied, U-33 torpedoed and shelled the *Borkum* which nevertheless made it to Papa Sound two days later where it was beached and written off. Unknown to von Dresky U-33's attack killed five captive German sailors who were on board. (On 18 August 1940 the vessel was re-floated, towed to Rosyth and broken up.)

U-33 made her way home through Fair Isle Channel, arriving at Wilhelmshaven on the 26 November 1939. Dönitz commended von Dresky for a "well conducted patrol."

The design problems with U-33's diesels meant she had to be returned to Germania Werft for an overhaul and the crew went home on well-deserved leave. U-33 formally transferred to Salzwedel Flotille (2.U-Flotille), Wilhelmshaven, on 1 January 1940 as a frontline boat.

The official reports of U-33's departure from Wilhelmshaven on Monday 5 February 1940 for her 3rd (and final) patrol record that Admiral Dönitz made a point of being on hand to bid the submarine's Captain and crew a personal "bon voyage." We now know that this description of events is dramatically incorrect.

Max Schiller, at eighteen years of age U-33's youngest crewmember in February 1940, told Scottish researcher David Hendry that Dönitz came to Wilhelmshaven for one reason only—to try to *stop* U-33's departure. The admiral was fearful for U-33's safety on a mission that he had not sanctioned. Indeed, Dönitz stated in his memoirs: "*At first the idea of thus operating in the very jaws of the enemy* [the heavily populated Firth of Clyde] *was regarded generally as a very bold and hazardous enterprise. The operation orders in the subject, which I had drafted in peace time as part of our mobilization scheme, were held by most U-boat Commanders to be very difficult, if not impossible to carry out. "*

Despite the Admiral's remarks, he had few qualms about his submarines engaging in high-risk enterprises and was bullish about what he expected his Kriegsmarine officers to deliver once U-boats were at sea and undertaking their operational directives. Korvettenkapitan Büchel wrote in his U-32 War Diary: "*...the weather, the navigational difficulties of the Firth and the strength of the naval forces watching over the area made it impossible for U-32 to lay her mines any further up the Firth of Clyde.*" Dönitz did not go along with his officer's assessment and, as noted, dismissed Büchel for taking an overly cautious approach. Moreover, it was Dönitz who ordered Von Dresky to plant 8 TMC mines at the British naval base in the Firth of Clyde. So what was it that made Dönitz uncharacteristically fearful about U-33's operational remit during its 3rd patrol?

Kplt Hans-Wilhelm von Dresky and fellow officers

According to Schiller, Hitler personally overruled Dönitz and ordered U-33 to embark on a journey from which it would not return— precisely the grim fate that the Admiral feared would come about. Hitler's decision must have been extremely testing for Dönitz who was known for his total loyalty to the Reich leader. Described as the mouthpiece of his Führer, Dönitz was known in Kriegsmarine circles as "Hitlerjunge Quex," the devoted Nazi youth in a popular propaganda film of the day.[4]

Just what were Hitler's additional overriding objectives, which had to take precedence above all other considerations, the safety and wellbeing of the crew of U-33 included? Hitler's strategic thinking behind U-33's mission cannot today be clarified. Schiller did not subsequently elaborate further but he did state on more than one occasion that it was U-33's task to sink HMS *Hood*, an attack plan that contradicted Hitler's October 1939 directive. Nevertheless, we have sufficient facts and clues by which to make intelligent assessments of the true nature of the U-boat's covert activities. By and by, we will examine these extraordinary circumstances.

The 42-man crew came smartly to the salute as the submarine slipped away from the quay where Admiral Dönitz stood in grim repose while a military band played martial music. On the quayside were the tin boxes containing the sailors' civilian clothes, personal belongings, family contact details and Last Wills and Testaments.

On this patrol the boat was charged with the duty of laying mines in the Firth of Clyde, a mission fraught with danger for a number of reasons, which shall be presently addressed.

U-33 firstly made for Helgoland to undergo minor repairs. Owing to the shortage of U-boats, U-33 sailed before the repairs were properly completed. The crew were very nervous on this account. They would have every reason to be. They could not forget the occasion during their first war cruise when U-33 spent the best part of three days lying on the bottom repairing her diesels. (It has been suggested that in the course of U-33's stopover at Helgoland she may have embarked "special" personnel.)

U-33 set off again on 7 February. An icebreaker had run interference for them through the white fields floating off Helgoland then U-33 was on its own. Von Dresky did not disclose their exact destination until U-33 had almost reached it.

Proceeding west and then due north, mainly on the surface, U-33's passage across the North Sea seems to have been uneventful. Only an aircraft and some destroyers were sighted.

For six days and nights U-33 headed north, then once again south, steering well clear of known British convoy routes. It seems probable that U-33 passed through Fair Isle Channel between Orkney and Shetland during the night of 9-10 February. It is on record that she was in the Atlantic on the 10th.

On this date three aeroplanes were sighted, estimated to be flying

---

[4] Beevor A., *Berlin: the Downfall 1945*, Penguin, London, 2002

at about 1,300 feet, three miles distant, causing U-33 to submerge to periscope depth. One of the Petty Officers stated that during the morning two torpedoes were fired at the U-boat but as no surface craft could be seen he concluded that a British submarine must have been in the vicinity.

Despite steering clear of Cape Wrath off the North Highlands coast, U-33 encountered a mounting gale to the west. When the storm reached Force Eight von Dresky reluctantly gave the order to dive to calmer water below.

On Sunday the 11th von Dresky surfaced to take a star-sight to correct U-33's position. The star-sight revealed that the foul weather had worked in U-33's favour. Gratefully, von Dresky found the boat to be ten miles closer to the Isle of Mull than expected.

Von Dresky spoke of his plan to Chief Engineer (Kplt) Friedrich-Ernst Schilling, a second engineer on board for training to meet Dönitz's requirement that all his submariners should quickly experience war patrols. Schilling subsequently told his interrogators that von Dresky's plan was to ensure that U-33 was in the optimum tactical position before sunrise on the 12th. He would then submerge and lay U-33 on the seabed until the relative safety of the evening. The boat would then surface and lay its mines on Sunday evening and early Monday morning while proceeding on its electric motors. On this reckoning, U-33 would then make a dash into the open Atlantic and be in relative safety before dawn on Tuesday the 13th.

Skirting west of the Hebrides U-33 proceeded down but well away from the Scottish coast, making her way into the North Channel between Scotland and Ireland, the gateway to the Clyde Estuary.

U-33 bottomed for five hours at noon, removing four torpedoes and reloading with eight TMC mines. TMC mines had been brought in to replace the less efficient TMB mine at the end of 1939. The TMB mine had a length of 2.31 metres and a total weight of 740kg. The TMC mine had a length of 3.39 metres and a total weight of 1,115kg. The first U-boat to patrol using TMCs was U-32.

U-33 then proceeded to her minelaying area (which included the narrowest part of the firth half a mile south of the boom) as fast as possible on the surface. The U-boat crept into the Firth of Clyde in the early hours of Monday the 12th at periscope depth.

For the crew it was a nervewracking affair. The Firth of Clyde swarmed with A/S vessels, some of them equipped with searchlights. Survivors later remarked that there were so many searchlights that the landward side seemed to glow with light.

U-33 had been ordered to mine firstly the approaches to the Clyde, an area where fast shoaling water made things very dangerous for a submarine. Nevertheless, von Dresky and his crew had shown great determination in carrying out their previous war patrols. They had struggled to address defects in the boat, persevering in their efforts rather than aborting missions and returning home. Their attempt to mine the area, having wrestled with engine problems and then operating just five miles from the Scottish shore showed considerable courage and resourcefulness.

The Royal Navy was not to be caught napping again and certainly not in its own "backyard." Von Dresky would have to be extremely skilful in carrying out U-33's mission while avoiding detection, especially in waters where the surface waves broke only 35-40 metres over the seabed. Escape by diving deep was not an available option, a fact that further imperilled the safety of the on-board Enigma cipher machine. Von Dresky must have known that the Navy patrols in this area were aggressive, vigilant and experienced. Nevertheless, he had his orders (from Dönitz to plant mines at the British naval base in the Firth of Clyde and, by Schiller's account, from Hitler to perform other unspecified tasks).

Von Dresky would have been acutely aware that Büchel in U-32 had failed a few weeks earlier to carry out the same mission, opting for discretion over valour when he had seen the very large volume of A/S defences in the Clyde Anchorage. Observing these, Büchel elected to lay his TMC magnetic mines in deeper water, an act which triggered his curt dismissal.

Whatever the circumstances that U-33 might encounter in its Firth of Clyde mission, reprising Büchel's playsafe action was not among the available options on von Dresky's charts table. It was "do or die." Von Dresky pressed on with his mission and, in so doing, was to meet his nemesis in the shape of HMS *Gleaner*, a Royal Navy minesweeper commanded by an equally determined captain. Minelaying in the seemingly impregnable Tail of the Bank, the local term for the upper Clyde Anchorage encompassing Gourock, Greenock, Port Glasgow and Glasgow was not the least of von Dresky's operational considerations. He was also acutely mindful of the glaring fact that the 83,673-ton liner RMS *Queen Elizabeth* was lying at anchor upriver.

Von Dresky did not know it but the *Queen Elizabeth* was preparing for a fast dash to New York. The Royal Navy was fully aware of her presence and, equally, of its duty to protect this valuable ship for which any enemy submarine commander would give his eye teeth to send to the bottom. The Royal Navy's keen sense of duty was also heightened by the painful memory of the devestating attack made by U-47 on the naval base at Scapa Flow in October of the previous year.

In these early morning hours of the 12th in the firth U-33 spotted Ailsa Craig ("Paddy's Milestone") over to starboard just before an Atlantic gale gathered momentum, making the prospect of minelaying deep in enemy territory highly perilous. With nose now submerged at periscope depth in the southern maw of the Firth of Clyde U-33 approached the tip of Arran.

Suddenly, the lookouts on the bridge saw a ship emerge from the darkness. It was coming their way. With a sigh of relief von Dresky watched as the blacked out vessel passed them by.

As 03:00 approached, Schilling, like his crewmates unaware of the fast approaching threat from *Gleaner*, made an inspection of U-33 and then went up to the bridge. It was a dark night. Visibility was poor, less than 800m. Von Dresky was in a good mood and told Schilling that at 01:00 the sub had passed a large vessel, possibly an anchoring cruiser.

From remarks made by survivors after the sinking of U-33 von Dresky's short-sightedness convinced him he had seen a cruiser when in fact it had been the *Gleaner*, which he had observed for several hours before attempting to pass her. Accordingly, von Dresky assumed that the vessel would go by and head for open waters.

But of course the "cruiser" did not move away and nerves were stretched taut when at 03:30 a searchlight-equipped vessel was seen from U-33 to emerge from the gloom ahead. Von Dresky shouted: "Alarm!" and jumped down from the conning tower. The crew prepared for an emergency dive. When the alarm was called Schilling went back down below. Later Schilling recalled Paul Anger, U-33's coxswain, saying in an agitated manner: "Better go as deep as possible 'cause I reckon they have found us." However, at at this point the captain and crew of U-33 were not completely certain of what had appeared out of the darkness.

In fact the oncoming vessel was not a destroyer. Moments later the ASW patrol boat, the converted surveyor ship HMS *Gleaner* patrolling a triangular line south of the Isle of Arran with the patrol apex on the Island of Pladda, detected U-33 and turned its searchlight on the sub, which went down to periscope depth.

HMS *Gleaner*, a Halcyon class minesweeper, 245 feet 6 inches overall with a standard displacement of 815 tons, was a sloop launched in 1937 as a surveying vessel and converted to a minesweeper in 1939 armed with two 4" guns. She also carried four 20mm guns, two Lewis guns and forty depth charges. When her conversion was completed she was sent to join the 1st Antisubmarine Striking Force based in Belfast and operated in the Northwestern Approaches under the command of Lieutenant-Commander Hugh Perceval Price, R.N. Her patrols also ranged across the Irish Sea between Belfast and Liverpool, a vital sea-lane for allied vessels, making the Atlantic crossing an area of considerable U-boat activity.

In November 1939 *Gleaner* joined the 2nd Anti-Submarine Striking Force operating between the Clyde and Loch Ewe. In January 1940 she became part of the 3rd Anti-Submarine Striking Force concerned with the protection of the Firth of Clyde and its approaches.

In Lieutenant-Commander Price *Gleaner* was assured of a command by an experienced and skilful captain. The ship carried an equally experienced crew of eighty who had spent their war to date hunting submarines in these waters and who were fully aware of the damage a U-boat could do if it penetrated the Clyde. It was not going to happen on *Gleaner*'s watch.

A report in the *Scottish Daily Express* of 18 February 2000, the day that BBC Scotland televised Max Schiller's commemoration on HMS *Cromer* by Arran for his fallen boatmates, stated that the *Gleaner* had been shadowing U-33 for several days, a fact not previously reported. If the claim is true it invites serious consideration as to the source of *Gleaner*'s prior intelligence. As we make speed into the deepening tale of U-33 we shall see why Lieutenant-Commander Price may have been so well prepared for the U-boat's arrival.

On the night of 11 February 1940 *Gleaner* was ordered to maintain Outer Patrol in the approaches to the Firth of Clyde, in particular to the north and westward of Ailsa Craig. Also operating in the region were Home Fleet vessels the battlecruiser *Hood*, the battleship *Warspite* and the 8th Destroyer Flotilla, each of which had sailed from the Clyde on 9 February 1940 for operations in the North Sea and would return to the Clyde on the 18th.

During the small hours of the 12th *Gleaner* was about her business searching diligently for any enemy U-boat that might have crept into her patrol area. It was a typically cold winter's night with the wind lashing the surface of the sea into a strong chop, stinging the faces of the men on watch with hard driving gusts of rain. It was the kind of weather when men wished they were tucked up warm in their beds. It was also the kind of weather when every man strained his eyes to watch the water on dark nights and when poor visibility favoured a determined enemy.

Suddenly at 02:50 *Gleaner* picked up a hydrophone effect from a submarine bearing about two points on the starboard bow, three miles from Pladda. (In the early stages of the war radar was only fitted to a few very large ships.)

The source of the noises was too distant for an echo to be obtained by asdic. The Officer of the Watch, Sub-Lieutenant E.L. Reade, took instant action in bringing guns and depth charges to the ready and called the Captain who ordered the ship to be turned around. On board U-33 Chief Engineer Schilling was making an inspection of the boat before making his way up to the bridge.

Asdic, named after the Anti-Submarine Detection Investigation Committee, was a sonar device, highly secret at the time, for locating submarines by using sound waves. It consisted of an electronic sound transmitter and receiver accommodated in a dome beneath the ship's hull. High-frequency beams, audible "pings," were sent out and bounced back when they hit a submarine. The interval of time that passed before an echo was received indicated the range of the submarine. The pitch of the echo revealed if it was approaching or moving away.

Ayrshire undertaker and U-33 researcher, David Hendry, helped to introduce Max Schiller to the BBC in the late 1990s. Subsequently, the BBC produced in 2000 a fascinating programme in which the well-known broadcast personality and political commentator, Kirsty Wark, interviewed Schiller about his time on U-33 (Max's rank was Matrose - Ordinary Seaman), his life as a POW and his post-war years as a family man resident in Dumfriesshire, southwest Scotland. Schiller told Wark that because of the threat posed by underwater detection systems U-33 always travelled as much as possible upon the surface while on its missions.

Wark asked Schiller how much of each day was spent underwater. Schiller said that there was no hard and fast routine but generally they would go down every morning first thing to see that everything was all right. He remarked drily that it did not matter how many times they went down; that is what they were paid to do and they could only be paid once. Schiller said that roughly speaking U-33 would dive to about fifty metres when travelling beneath the surface but that the actual depth would vary according to circumstance.

Despite its precautions U-33 was shortly to become the first submarine in WWII to be sunk with the aid of this powerful new asdic detection device.

Able Seaman Mellor, keeping middle watch on *Gleaner*, reported to

Lieutenant-Commander Price that contact had been lost; the object was probably out of range. Course was slightly altered to bring the telltale hydrophone noises more to the starboard side. *Gleaner*'s speed was increased to 16 knots.

At 02:57 *Gleaner* made its first asdic contact at about 3,000 yards, using hand transmission. The target was crossing the bow from starboard to port at high speed and was therefore suspected of being a surface vessel. Reade altered course to close upon the unknown craft.

When the bearing of the target had altered to 55 degrees left the hydrophone effect became very loud and was thought to be a diesel engine giving about two distinct "tonks" per second. A check on the Royal Navy records of allied submarines on operations in home waters indicated that none were in the vicinity. Price concluded that *Gleaner* had picked up the sounds of a U-boat.

Initially, the sound came from astern on U-33's starboard side and then crossed to the port bow. Reade altered course to intercept and speed was increased gradually until at 03:16 the range was about 3,200 yards. *Gleaner* then maintained its increased speed of 16 knots. The screws were audible at medium speed as the ship criss-crossed around looking for the U-boat.

At 03:30 *Gleaner*'s searchlights were switched on and picked out a white object, which could have been spray made by a periscope coursing through the waves. The object disappeared rapidly.

A little later, fearing the vessel would escape, *Gleaner* sheered off to port to bring the searchlight to bear. At about the same time the U-boat must have turned to starboard as the bearing drew aft rapidly. The searchlight swept round and once again illuminated an object that looked white and was possibly the spray of a periscope. It disappeared almost at once but not before *Gleaner* had glimpsed a huddle of figures in the conning tower. Seeing *Gleaner*'s searchlight sweeping the water, the myopic von Dresky was still weighing his first instinct that she was a heavy cruiser.

At 03:36 *Gleaner*'s wheel was put over and the ship swung rapidly to starboard to close the object, telegraphs being put to full ahead. *Gleaner* turned towards after accurately locating the submarine, which had now gone towards the bottom.

Schiller told the BBC that in these moments before submerging he was in the conning tower on lookout duty with three other shipmates. Four people were needed in the tower because in order to ensure 360-degree all-round observation the seascape was divided into quarters and each person was responsible for their allotted quarter. The officer in front of Schiller saw the shadow of something. It left his quarter and the officer handed the shadow to Max who tracked it until he reported its disappearance from his section. The next thing they knew was that *Gleaner* was right behind them. Its light went on. The conning tower lookouts made to dash below and U-33 immediately submerged.

The *Scottish Daily Mail* of 18 February 2000 carried a statement reportedly made by Max Schiller that when this order was given for U-33 to submerge there were just seconds available for the lookout men to clamber below. Schiller said he made it down by the skin of his teeth but that other companions were not so lucky. They drowned at that spot. This account highlights a particularly tragic aspect of the U-33 story that does not appear to have been recorded in historical works covering the topic.

Schilling asked von Dresky: "What depth?" The commander replied: "Go to 40m." Schilling was aghast. He wanted to go as deep as possible. The helmsman exclaimed: "He's got us!"

Gleaner was over the target at 03:40 before sufficient asdic data had been collected to initiate a successful attack. Price ran about 800 yards past the sub, turned, regained contact and then carried out a deliberate attack at 03:53. *Gleaner* fixed the submarine on sonar and dropped four depth charges. These exploded directly about 25 feet above U-33, which had got as far as 75 feet, pounding the sub and causing severe leaking.

Dropping the charges at a relatively shallow setting caused *Gleaner* to experience some difficulty with its electrics. Its dynamo failed as did temporarily all of the ship's lights and electrical equipment. The carbons in its searchlight were also damaged and attempts to get the light burning continued at least for the next hour. Contact with the submarine was briefly lost.

There is uncertainty about the precise number of charges dropped in this first attack. Friedrich-Ernst Schilling told researcher Klaus Peter Pohland that five "wabos"[5] exploded close to U-33's starboard beam. Schilling's account of the attack enjoys credibility in U-boat research circles. Irrespective of the exact number, the wabos inflicted serious damage.

The crew were thrown violently onto the floor as a very loud bang cannoned throughout the sub. At first Oberleutnant Heinz Rottman thought that one of his boatmates, in panic, was firing a revolver and then realized that the fearsome noise was that of ruptured rivets ricochetting inside U-33 with incredible velocity.

---

[5] A contraction of Wasserbomben: "water bombs"

Max Schiller, the youngest seaman on board, was asked by one of the more experienced officers to sit with him and talk. The officer was a married man with children and he told Schiller that at that point he needed comfort to help divert his thoughts.

Von Dresky ordered: "Prepare to hit the bottom, silent routine, get the tauchretter sets[6] ready."

The boat settled in a depth of 56m and Schilling tried to assess the damage. U-33 had taken on about 500 litres of water, which caused the port motor to spark. The sub crept along the bottom on the port motor, reasoning that if it kept underway there was always the possibility it might give its attacker the slip.

The lights were smashed but the crew managed to rig the emergency set. The helmsmen reported that the hydroplanes were loose in their hands. Repairs were made to the port side electrical circuit but it soon became clear that the hydroplane motor was damaged. U-33 was reduced to manual operation.

The wabos had also ruptured the portside trim tank seams, resulting in a steady ingress of water. The pumps could barely keep pace with the flow. All the depth gauges were damaged with the exception of a gauge attached to the starboard trim tanks.

Schilling's examination of the starboard motor revealed that its switchboard was burned out and likely to remain inoperable. The driving shafts were bent. Schilling's men managed to repair the cracked battery cells. The noisy engine room valves were shut down. All thoughts were on the best options for making an escape.

The attack had caught von Dresky by complete surprise. Believing the attacker to be a destroyer, his men urged him to lift U-33 off the bottom, 170 feet below the surface, and evade to sea but von Dresky appeared to be paralyzed.

By now the high pressure air was nearly exhausted but Schilling was not overly concerned and told his skipper that there was nothing to stop the U-boat getting home. His plain advice was that U-33 should slip away under the water. Von Dresky, though, decided to keep the boat quietly on the bottom. Surviving officers criticised him for this decision but it is not clear how he could have attacked *Gleaner* because there was only one torpedo in U-33's stern tube.

Fifteen minutes had elapsed since *Gleaner*'s first round of attack. Lieutenant-Commander Price was worried. His men were doing their level best to keep the U-boat pinned down, while at the same time trying to keep stable 250lbs of high explosives stacked upon the boat's

---

[6] Bag-on-back rebreathers for self-rescue of submarine crews

slippery deck.

At 04:12 *Gleaner* made a second attack, this time firing only one charge (a charge that had hung up on the stern rails during the first round of attack), and then began to circle at twelve knots while combing the area with her searchlight.

Inside the U-boat the replacement light bulbs shattered and the lights went out again. The drive shaft glands that had been leaking since the first attack now allowed water to cascade into the stern. Exterior valves were also leaking badly. The sub was stuck on the seabed.

The commander considered his options and asked Schilling what he thought should be done. By this stage the boat was shipping so much water that it would never be able to regain the surface unless the pumps were restarted immediately. The boat had a negative buoyancy of about two tons, even without the drop keel.

It was obvious to the first engineer that U-33 would be unable to regain the surface with just the propellers and he wanted to pump out 1,000 litres in order to get the boat off the bottom. Schilling advised von Dresky of this course of action so that U-33 could crawl away just above the seabed.

Von Dresky half-heartedly agreed with Schilling's plan, believing that with dawn just hours away escape in British waters would be nigh impossible. He objected, however, to the deployment of the pumps, arguing that the noise would serve to attract the enemy. Von Dresky ordered the men to switch them off then came into the conning tower issuing orders: "Both engines, low speed ahead."

Gleaner's second attack had caused further electrical trouble, damaging the minesweeper's delicate asdic gear, putting it out of action. The first attack had also smashed the carbons of its searchlight and efforts were being made to get the light burning again in case the U-boat should surface. Meanwhile two Aldis signalling lamps were used to comb the surface whilst the ship circled at 12 knots around the position of the first strike.

Had the men on U-33 been aware of *Gleaner*'s asdic difficulties they could have taken the necessary steps to bring their boat to the surface and then submerge again immediately. Their subsequent chances of getting away scot-free, in the absence of sweeping sonar beams, would have been reasonably fair.

It was not to be. Minutes later *Gleaner* regained contact. Price brought his ship around and at 04:40 ran over U-33 again, this time making a drop of five charges set between 100 and 150 feet. His target lay on the bottom 177 feet below *Gleaner*'s keel.

The ferocity of this third and final round of attack damaged *Gleaner*'s radio and gyro and prolonged its asdic difficulties. While efforts continued to repair *Gleaner*'s searchlight the minesweeper used the Aldis signalling lamps to scan the surface while the ship circled the attack position.

Masked by the noise of the attack, Schilling ordered his men to start the main bilge pump but again von Dresky countermanded his Chief Engineer's instructions.

"Water is pouring in astern!" was the shout from the rear compartments but the commander stopped Schilling from returning to locate the cause. It transpired there was a leak in the connecting pipe between the trim tanks and the torpedo compensation tank causing water to run into the bilges. Schilling's team immediately set to work stopping up the pipe.

Meanwhile, von Dresky told Schilling that he wanted the boat off the seabed. Orders were given. The first watch officer was to get the mines ready for laying while the second watch officer was to prepare to destroy confidential papers.

The crew got the main bilge pump working until a huge flame shot out of the starter motor. Feverishly, the men had to dismantle then reassemble it, succeeding in nursing the pump back to life. The emergency bilge pump was switched on, too. Unfortunately, it made such a loud racket that it had to be turned off right away.

There was no option now but to blow tanks to get U-33 off the bottom. No one on board was more aware than Schilling that any trip through shallow water with a damaged boat would be a tough proposition. As tanks were vented a shout came from astern: "Strong sound of leaking air!"

Shutting off the diesel exhaust valves did not work. A crewmember was ordered to vent momentarily tank number 1 to discover whether the noise was coming from the compressed air cylinders, which had been damaged during the first attack. Sure enough, the noise was only audible during the venting process.

Although the gauges measured just three tons of water in the bilges, despite best efforts the boat hardly budged from the bottom. Two thirds of its compressed air supplies had already been expended. Tank 2 was then blown and that finally got U-33 off the seabed.

The commander was once again considering the next step. Coxswain Anger thought escape was impossible and that U-33 should surrender to the British. Schilling disagreed. When von Dresky asked if the boat could make it home, Schilling replied: "Yes, I believe I am capable of doing anything as long as the boat is afloat."

He made this confident claim in the knowledge that although tanks 1 and 3 were ruptured beyond repair the boat's fuel leaks were not a serious problem. From the technical and military point of view surrendering the boat seemed to Schilling to be totally absurd. The commander appeared to agree with Schilling at this stage but from a navigational perspective the situation was critical. In a couple of hours dawn would break.

U-33 survivor records indicate that the sub was lying in a narrow channel with strong currents. The Royal Navy had several bases thereabouts and the men on board the U-boat could expect their ships to come out and hunt them down. They had also not yet shaken off the enemy ship. Indeed a cry came from the radio office: "Next run starting." The commander made up his mind and ordered: "Blow all tanks." At 05:22 the U-boat boat popped up to the surface about one mile from *Gleaner*.

By now *Gleaner* had got its searchlight working and fire was immediately opened. Five rounds of 4" were fired and one of them whizzed past very close to the conning tower. *Gleaner* turned to ram with engines full ahead.

When the searchlight's fierce carbon glare, enhanced by the beams from the bridge sponsons' signalling projectors, picked out in the conning tower a group of men with arms raised in surrender, Price checked fire. The wheel was put hard to starboard until the ship was parallel with U-33 about one cable away (200 yards).

"Cease fire. Stop engines and get a boat into the water," ordered Price as he swung his command around the stricken U-boat and got on with the business of rescue for the submarine was sinking quickly.

Von Dresky opened the hatch and went out onto the bridge. Whatever he saw made him shout down: "Everybody up. Scuttle the boat. Send the radio message." Before taking this irrevocable step von Dresky could have opted to order the boat's gun to be manned and the torpedo in the after tube fired. Why then did he he choose the more drastic action? Armstrong and Osborne, authors of *The Clyde at War*, claim that Hitler ordered the scuttling. If this is true then one is left to speculate on why Hitler would have intervened in the matter.

Was it purely possession of the Enigma parts that the Fuhrer wanted to deny the enemy? Or were there other items on board that had to be destroyed at all costs, perhaps plans or documents of some description? As the following chapters unfold the basis for the decision may become better understood.

Schilling repeated his Captain's order but did not understand the change in circumstances that had led to it. The diesel engines were still working. He tried to tell his commander that the engines were in order and that the boat was ready to go but by this stage men were making their way out and he could not get the message to von Dresky.

The Chief Engineer joined the men on the bridge and told his superior about the feasibility of U-33 making a successful escape. Von Dresky did not want to listen and merely repeated the order to scuttle the boat.

Schilling glanced over to the starboard bow and saw the minesweeper heading towards U-33 at a distance of 400m. Searchlights were trained on them and shells were being fired. Perhaps it was at this point that Schilling understood why the captain had issued his orders.

There was no option now but to scuttle the U-boat. Since U-33 carried an Enigma and could be salvaged von Dresky distributed its rotors among his officers and instructed them to swim well away from the boat before discarding them. He then ordered fuses for the explosives to be placed at strategic points inside U-33. Schilling got on with the task of setting the scuttling charges. His first attempt failed but after a delay of eight minutes Schilling was able to set the fuses. However, a quick-witted engineer realised that the fuses would blow before the crew had vacated the boat. Max Schiller explained that the crewman who had set the dynamite fuses asked if there were still men to come out of the sub (Schiller must have been one of the last to make his escape). When Schiller said that to his knowledge there were still more to follow the engineer went back down to extinguish the fuses.

Schiller told the BBC that he and his crewmates were standing on deck in rising water while *Gleaner* was firing its live rounds at U-33. Consequently, the men ran pell-mell around the conning tower to avoid the bullets. The firing stopped, as did the men who were waiting for the order from the captain to abandon ship. All the while the water level was rising ever higher as the stricken submarine began its descent. Eventually, given the order, the crew jumped from the boat yelling for help. All were wearing lifebelts fitted with oxygen apparatus and carrying small electric lamps on their foreheads. Schiller saw von Dresky climbing back down into the boat.

It appears that when the fuses were subsequently re-set Schilling, possibly von Dresky too, was not told because when the explosives failed to go off quickly the Chief Engineer, followed by the commandant, hurried down from the bridge to ensure that the fuses were lit and that all the vents and hatches were opened. This was the moment when Max Schiller saw his captain re-enter the sub. Schilling opened the valves beside the ammunition lockers, while von Dresky tried to open valve No.2. But still U-33 would not slip below the waves.

Fuses were burning in the radio room ready to blow the boat apart. Suddenly water surged in; that was good enough for Schilling who ran to report the situation to the commander. Von Dresky asked his Engineer to go down one last time to see if something could be done to speed up the sinking of U-33. Before Schilling could voice his intended refusal the explosives went off.

The build up of pressure was so great that a wall of flame rocketed out of the conning tower and shot to a height of thirty metres into the dark pre-dawn sky. The shock tore the conning tower's iron ladder from its casing narrowly avoiding U-33's stoker MaschOGfr Puchta who, being one of the tail-end seamen abandoning ship, had a narrow escape.

Schilling felt something strike his left shoulder, discovering only later that it had been the conning tower ladder.

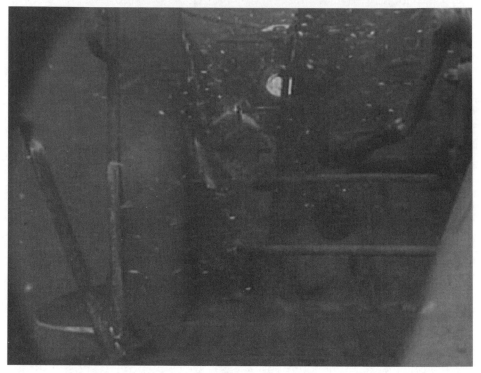

Scuttling underway!

Weber later stated that the pressure hull inside the radio office had been ruptured by the explosion of the charges, detonating the signal grenades and the ready-use ammunition.

The U-boat began a dive at an angle of about 40 degrees. Shortly, the boat hit bottom and there was another explosion.

Survivor records indicate that von Dresky, having re-emerged from the sub, jumped into the sea with Schilling to join the other crewmen waiting to be picked up by the *Gleaner*. At this moment, so the story goes, von Dresky realised that he had lost the mouthpiece of his Tauchretter set. The Second Watch Officer was wearing a life saving vest so he gave the commander his own mouthpiece.

Contemporary reports state that as the stern of the boat went down, three times the commander shouted a rousing: "Hurrah for U-33!" and Schilling heard the commander urge the men to keep together in the water.

Max Schiller's BBC account flatly contradicts this version of events. According to Schiller von Dresky did not die among his men in the freezing waves.

Interviewer Kirsty Wark sought clarification both on Max's remark that he had seen his captain go back into U-33 and on the latter's decision to abandon ship:

Wark: "*So you think... Did he (*von Dresky*) go down with the U-boat then?*"

Schiller: "*Yes, yes.*"

Wark: "*So he's still... his body is still on the U-boat?*"

Schiller: "*Yes, if you find any bones on the boat, they'll be his. He'll be the only person. Every...everyone from us that was accounted for, except the Captain.*"

Wark: "*What made the Captain decide to abandon ship?*"

Schiller: "*Ah, there was no point in us going on, you see, and we had laid on dynamite and they went off and the boat started to sink. I was standing in water, still on the boat – that much – then waiting for the order to abandon ship. So...the Captain gave the orders to abandon ship, so...and we all left the boat and when I looked back and the Captain, he went back down in it, through the hatch, you see. Everybody from the boat was accounted for, but no for the Captain, for the simple reason, he went down with the boat.*"

One may only speculate upon the reporting differences between the time-witnesses' accounts and Schiller's testimony. Max's memory was sharp. There was no reason why he should have been confused about the sequence of events.

The Monthly Anti Submarine Report[7] for March and April 1940 states: "*At 05:30 sparks were seen arising from the conning tower and the crew abandoned ship. It was learned that the Commanding Officer had placed a small explosive charge among the confidential matter and parts of the enciphering machine were distributed amongst the officers with instructions to throw them away when clear of the U-boat. The Senior Engineer Officer (Schilling) who had been ordered to ensure the destruction of the vessel by blowing her up had not time to make his escape before the explosion took place and was blown some considerable distance into the air. U-33 at once trimmed down by the bow to an angle of 40° and disappeared without listing.*"

The position of sinking was about 4.8 miles S.E. by S. of Pladda Lighthouse, off the southeastern corner of the Isle of Arran. The number one task was to rescue survivors. Other men on *Gleaner* tried to wreck-buoy the exact point of the enemy's position, dropping a sea

---

[7] ADM 199/ 2034 - ADM 199/123 NARA T-1022, Roll 3103, PG30030, PG33325

tombstone to guide Naval Intelligence later. Sub-Lieutenant Reade took a bearing—Pladda 150 degrees, distance 4.8 miles, position about 55:25N 05:07W. Captain Price also instructed HMS *Scott*, which arrived on the scene later to locate and buoy the wreck. Elsewhere in Admiralty document ADM 199/123, a succinct report on the attack by HMS *Gleaner*, the position is given as 55:21:50N 05:02:08W.

Having radioed the Admiralty with the news of U-33's sinking Lieutenant-Commander Price received the message: *"With large convoys arriving and departing from the Clyde every week the sinking of the U-33 has prevented a major disaster in home waters. Well done! The U-33 is the 13th U-boat to be destroyed since the commencement of hostilities! Repeat, well done!* " On arrival at HMS *Fortitude*'s land base at Ardrossan Harbour, the captain and crew of Gleaner were given a heroes' welcome. The Enigma rotor parts were sent on to the British code breaking centre at Bletchley Park for detailed study.

HMS *Gleaner*

Lieutenant-Commander Price was awarded the Distinguished Service Order for his "outstanding readiness, proficiency and skill in destroying an enemy submarine." Sub-Lieutenant Edward Perry Reade, the Watch Officer when contact was made, was awarded the Distinguished Service Cross with the same citation. Able Seamen Harold Thomas Rhodes, Bernard Duncan Winstanley and William John Trevethan Mellor were each awarded Distinguished Service Medals.

From U-33's listed crew complement of 42 only 17 men, including

3 officers lived to become POWs. Steiner was dead. Kampert had died from exposure.

Von Dresky had urged his men through the hatch as the seawater swirled around the bank of batteries, pouring off chlorine gas, until the final explosions. The compilers of the Interrogation of Survivors report make reference to a notebook they had obtained from an engine room Petty Officer, which went some way to corroborate testimony from survivors.

Oberleutnant zur See Karl Vietor had saluted Lieutenant-Commander Price at the first opportunity. In excellent English he explained that he knew Fleet class minesweepers did not carry doctors. They did however have a Petty Officer trained in First Aid. Could he check over the survivors? And would warm clothing be supplied immediately?

Price had given the necessary orders before the first survivor had been lifted to the deck. There was concern for Heinz Rottman; he had been in the sea longer than the others. They fed him brandy and hot coffee.

Hitler, Dönitz at his side, congratulates Kplt von Dresky on a successful patrol

In return Rottman volunteered the information all waited to hear. No mines had been launched in the area of the running battle. The British understood that U-33 had intended to lay mines off Pladda Lighthouse. The five in the first lay were far to the westward.

Once again, Max Schiller's testimony to BBC Scotland appears to contradict the contemporary report. Rottman is on record as saying that no mines had been laid off Pladda. On the other hand, Schiller said that their orders were that after laying the TCM mines they were to re-load the tubes with the four torpedoes they had removed the day before in the North Channel. He went on to say that it was during the operation to reload the tubes that *Gleaner*'s depth charging of U-33 commenced.

One can only interpret Schiller's statement as a confirmation that all eight mines had been laid: five laid far westward, according to Rottman, and three laid more locally thereby triggering compliance with the order to reload the torpedoes. Evidently, there had been time to load only one of the four torpedoes: the one in the after tube which could still have been turned to U-33's advantage, together with the deployment of the boat's guns, had von Dresky not been obligated to comply with Hitler's reputed order to scuttle the vessel.

Schiller's statement is also supported by the content of the BdU log for 16 February 1940, which notes: *"It seems more and more likely that U-33 has been lost. Several radio intelligence reports show that she was in action with an English minesweeper and then surrendered. Assistance was requested to rescue survivors. The English authorities assumed that mines had been laid. This is not improbable as these events took place in the early morning hours. The boat would certainly not have chosen this time to penetrate into the Clyde and she then at latest would have been on her way out. If she really did lay the mines, the high price paid will have been worth it."*

Later HMS *Tedworth* with a party of naval divers was sent to examine the sunken U-boat in thirty fathoms of water and recovered various articles from the conning tower, amongst them a Nazi Ensign.

StObMasch Friedrich Kumpf was rescued by the trawler *Bohemian Girl*. Official record has it that during the passage to Greenock his pockets were searched and the British recovered three Enigma rotors—wheels VI, VII and VIII.

These were helpful to the codebreakers at Bletchley Park (especially wheels VI and VII used only by the Kriegsmarine for which the wiring was then unknown), but not sufficiently so to penetrate naval Enigma (the vital "Dolphin" signals). In the next chapter Max Schiller tells the Kumpf Enigma story very differently.

Chief Engineer Schilling also hid Enigma parts on his person. Like Kumpf he, too, did not dump them in the sea straightaway. He knew that navy divers would be making strenuous efforts to recover Enigma parts dropped in the sea at U-33's sinking position. It was a dangerous gamble but luck was on his side. For reasons unknown Schilling was not searched after being picked up out of the water. He waited until his Greenock-bound rescue boat was as far away as possible from U-33 before he pulled them from his jacket and, unseen, ditched the parts out of a porthole by Skelmorlie Bank, a few miles south of Greenock. Schilling's action ensured that at least the Enigma parts in his possession would not be recovered by the naval team which would shortly be scouring the seabed off Pladda. (One might ask, however, how Schilling knew that he was ditching the parts by Skelmorlie. Perhaps he casually asked a helpful British sailor where they were in the firth.)

Dönitz knew at once that U-33 was lost but, as evidenced by the content of the BdU log, held on to a slim degree of hope that minelaying in the Firth of Clyde had succeeded where U-32 had previously failed. His source was B-dienst, which intercepted three signals from *Gleaner*. The first was an alarm at 05:25 reporting U-33 to be on the surface. The second at 05:30 was a notice stating that the U-33 crew was surrendering. The third at 05:45 was a request for assistance in rescuing the crew. It should be noted that none of these signals appears to have highlighted U-33's precise geographical position at time of sinking.

Shortly after the sinking of U-33 minelaying operations were broken off in this area. Henceforth, Dönitz's small U-boat force was deployed in supporting the German invasion of Norway. When minelaying operations were resumed the Clyde was avoided with U-boats concentrating on the East Coast and the Channel where they were likely to affect more shipping. U-boats did not begin to target the Clyde area again until late in the war when, for example, U-482 made a successful patrol in the North Channel between August and September 1944.

Survivors from U-33 were immediately transported to London for interrogation. Senior officers Schilling, Vietor, Rottman, Becker and Kumpf passed through the interrogation centre in Kensington—the "London Cage" to Intelligence men—before they landed up at Grizedale Hall (known as the "U-boat Hotel") No. 1 Prisoner-of-War camp in the Lake District.

Galilea, Masanek, Marticke, Siegert, Puchta, Krink, Weber, Lingscheidt, Scherer, Ehrhardt, Krampe and Schiller went to a prison camp until all seventeen were reunited at Bowmanville Camp in Canada in early 1942. Schilling was repatriated via the Red Cross in 1943 because of serious illness.

Max Schiller was interned in Lockerbie Camp in Dumfriesshire, southern Scotland, sharing a hut with thirty other prisoners. Each day captives were transported by truck to various places for work. The option to volunteer for work detail on neighbouring farms was popular as the men could supplement their meagre rations with home-cooked, homegrown farm produce. Max opted for dairyhand duty at the large Barrasgait Farm in Cummertrees, thirteen miles south of the camp and just six miles from the English border as the crow flies.

As soon as Max arrived at Barrasgait and set eyes on dairymaid Jessie Grearson he knew he had seen the girl he was going to marry. Petite, with a ready smile and dark curly locks, Jessie had been a maid at the big house since leaving school. She stepped out of the front door, busying herself with household chores and took Max's breath away. It was love at first sight for both. "I knew from the first moment, the very first moment," Max would say. Max resolved to see Jessie as much as possible and was willing to take risks to see his sweetheart.

A fellow prisoner in charge of the bicycles owned by the Lockerbie camp guards was persuaded to let Max smuggle a bike under his bed. Max, a man of slight stature and build, would squeeze under the camp's perimeter wire after evening lock-up and cycle back to Cummertrees to see Jessie. He was never caught.

Max was also an enthusiastic football fan both as a player and and a spectator. Barrasgait farmhands lent Max civilian clothes and money for the bus so he could sneak off to Dumfries and watch Queen of the South, the team he followed all his life.

When Max was released from custody from Bowmanville Camp he refused to be repatriated to Germany, insisting that he wished to return to Scotland—to Barrasgait and to Jessie.

He returned briefly to Germany to tell his family of his decision. They were not happy but Max's mind was made up. He returned to the life of a dairyhand at Barrasgait Farm and married Jessie on Boxing Day 1947. Jessie's enlightened parents raised no objections to the match.

The couple were given accommodation in a bothy—a tiny rudimentary shelter typically used to house farm workers. Theirs had one room serving as living area and kitchen with an open-hearth fire, one bedroom and a toilet. The family lived in these cramped conditions until 1955, Ray coming along in 1948 and Edna in 1952. They were then given the use of the three-bedroom farm cottage. Jessie died in 1991, Max in 2002.

Max was only one among a number of Germans who settled in Scotland after being held there as POWs, many of whom worked on the farms around Dumfries and Galloway, an area today with a large German population and an active German Society.

The Wrecks Section of the U.K. Hydrographic Office records that U-33, Kriegsmarine U-boat, is located at Map Reference 55:21:48.3N 05:01:75.2W, 5 miles south of Pladda, off Turnberry Point, in the Firth of Clyde, at depth 57m. The wreck is orientated in an east by south / west by north (100° / 280°) direction and lies on a firm seabed of sand, mud and stones in a general depth of 57m (187ft), the lowest astronomical depth. She is upright, in reasonable condition, standing 4.6m from the seabed.

The conning tower hatch is open and divers peering into it have seen what they describe as a sort of "milk-bottle crate," which contained about four or six ready-use shells for the boat's deck gun. The deck casing is showing signs of deterioration but the whole wreck is covered in marine growth and fine silt. The wreck is a war grave, last officially surveyed by HMS *Herald* in 1976.

The day after the sinking of U-33 HMS *Reclaim*, which had been assisting in repairs to the battleship HMS *Nelson* severely damaged by a TMB mine from U-31 near Loch Ewe in November 1939, arrived at the scene. Her divers recovered discarded Enigma parts.

Scottish historian Donald Kelly has told of a story that a heavy lifting operation was mounted to move U-33 from its seabed position. Other local Scots have told a similar tale. The plan was to send divers down to try and retrieve what they could from around the wreck site. There is no certainty that such an operation was undertaken and there are some doubts that it was viable in that area of the Firth of Clyde. Nevertheless, there were suitable heavy lifting ships in the Gareloch that were capable of making the attempt. It will be a fact worth recalling when we come to review the true circumstances surrounding U-33's Firth of Clyde activities.

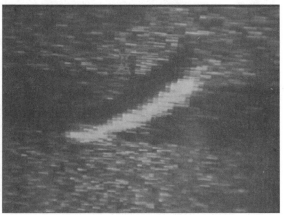

Sonar image of U-33 by Arran, February 2000

What has been laid out in these opening pages is U-33's imprint upon the wreck-bed of WWII maritime action, unadorned with questions about the whys and wherefores surrounding it. One might say so far, so good…but is it truly?

Later we shall learn of an entirely different version of events, one that fundamentally challenges the official history of the sinking of U-33. In the correspondence of reporter Horace Oakes we shall read that HMS *Gleaner* was not alone among the British attack force in the early hours of 12 February 1939. By Oakes' account the *Gleaner* was not even the ship that delivered the *coup de grâce* upon U-33.

As the following pages peel away we will increasingly have cause to question not only the circumstances that prevailed on the night of the 12th but the wide array of other significant elements in U-33's history.

We will quickly recognise that to do honour to the staunch beliefs of the folk of the Firth of Clyde a new, unvarnished truth must emerge.

Two years before he died, on the 60th anniversary of the sinking of U-33, Max Schiller sailed out of Campbeltown Loch on 12 February 2000 on board HMS *Cromer*. He was accompanied by his daughter Edna and David Hendry. The trip had been planned so that Max could toss a wreath on the waters over the resting place of his former boat. HMS *Cromer* was joined by German minesweeper, the *Weider*, which was on exercise in the Clyde.

U-boat officers at Gravenshurst POW camp, Ontario, Canada,
Kplt Friedrich-Ernst Schilling from U-33 is standing 3rd from the right.

It was intended that an unmanned midget sub should be sent down to take detailed pictures of the wreck for Max's benefit but Cromer's captain explained that, disappointingly, the bad weather ruled this out. Instead, Max was shown a series of ghostly, sodium-orange sonar images of U-33. At one moment during the trip Max, standing overlooking the Firth of Clyde, said quietly and emotionally that U-33 had been on a "suicide mission." In making this remark it was evident that the nature and finale of U-33's 3rd patrol had weighed heavily in Max's memories for more than 60 years. A few minutes later, in a short ceremony, Max tossed the wreath onto the waves

After the ceremony the *Weider* sailed away but returned some time later. When the men on the German minesweeper saw that Max was still standing on the deck of HMS *Cromer* looking out to sea they stood to their feet as one and saluted the elderly survivor from U-33. The BBC cameramen, professionals who had doubtless filmed all kinds of challenging action and emotional situations in the past, paused filming, moved to tears by the intensity of the scene, which probably explains why the *Weider*'s wonderful homage to Max was not included in the broadcast documentary.

In the next chapter Max Schiller, a man who by now can be trusted at every turn to prick the hallowed balloons of U-33 history, will tell a far different story as to the location of the wreck of his former billet under the waves. We will then begin the interrogation process, starting with the first layer of questions that have been posed by various comentators about apparent operational inconsistencies surrounding U-33's last mission. Subsequently, we will take meticulous note of the questions thrown up by the mass of comments from Firth of Clyde citizenry.

Both the first level review and the far deeper investigation at local level will highlight more doubts and questions about U-33's final cruise in February 1940 than can be even remotely attributable to random statistical chance.

Chapter TWO

The First Questions

The fringed curtains of thine eye advance
And say what thou seest yond

Certainly, there are elements in U-33's putative story that neither stand up to brief nor logical scrutiny. Various authors have highlighted these issues, which indicate that U-33's mission was not what it seemed. In this chapter we will examine a number of factors about the official record that continue to vex investigators. In conducting this initial review, we will be doing no more than peeling away the top layer of hull metal that conceals the marked extent of U-33's many mysteries.

Researchers have offered the view that German naval officials regarded U-33's February 1940 mission as being especially dangerous. In making this claim, writers such as Hugh Sebag-Montefiore[1] have described the unusual, even unique circumstance in which senior Nazi officials hosted a banquet in a forest hut for the crew of U-33. Giggling girls were laid on for the banquet. Junior crewmembers broke with etiquette, one rating picking up a chicken leg and tearing into it with his teeth. A sympathetic officer rescued what could have been an embarrassing gaffe by the younger man by repeating the action, which encouraged everyone to join in good-humouredly and do the same.

The crew was honoured by a personal visit from Hitler while they were still in Wilhelmshaven and Admiral Dönitz saw them off personally. U-boat crews were certainly viewed as an elite force and were pampered accordingly. In early 1940 the Admiral was stationed in Wilhelmshaven and on the spot to see U-33 out of harbour. Nevertheless, in the BBC2 Scotland documentary Max Schiller emphasised how unusual it had been that Dönitz came personally to bid them a safe journey, a comment contradicting Kriegsmarine historians who claim that the Admiral was on hand whenever possible to see off

---

[1] Sebag-Montefiore H., *Enigma: The Battle for the Code*, Weidenfeld & Nicolson, 2000

his crews and to welcome them home.

Experts have also observed that the banquet held for U-33, although not customary practice was not unique. Certainly, there were occasions when U-boats crews were hosted by people as diverse as the shipyard owner, the Organisation Todt (a Third Reich civil and military engineering group that project-managed a vast range of engineering projects in this period), the local Gauleiter or Nazi officials of a sponsoring city.

Max Schiller speaks fondly of the "power of a woman"—his wife Jessie

For example, Jürgen Oesten and the crew of U-61 were treated to a week at a ski resort in Bavaria, a trip that was organised by the local Bavarian Gau. Nevertheless Sebag-Montefiore, no lightweight in research circles, has highlighted the particulars of the U-33 forest banquet as evidence to indicate that the submarine's voyage to the Firth of Clyde was out of the ordinary.

We have seen that the presence of Hitler and Dönitz on the occasion of U-33's departure for its third patrol was not as it appeared. When Max spoke "off-line" with David Hendry he confided that Dönitz's purpose in coming to Wilhelmshaven was to attempt to persuade Hitler to rescind his order that U-33 must make its journey to the Clyde, for undisclosed purposes.

It has also been suggested that Hitler's visit to Wilhelmshaven in February 1940 could have been related to U-29, which had recently sunk the British aircraft carrier HMS *Courageous*, a noteworthy feat of arms. On this occasion Hitler inspected the crew of both U-33 and U-29 and spoke at the HQ of 2nd U-Flotilla. However, Max Schiller's remark to David Hendry about Hitler's express orders for U-33's mission, in face of stiff opposition from Dönitz, would appear to rule out the suggestion that the Führer's visit on that occasion was predominantly related to U-29.

While in Wilhelmshaven harbour the bow of U-33 briefly dropped in the water while supplies were being loaded. In consequence, ice and feeezing seawater poured into a torpedo hatch. A quick-thinking crewmember blew all the water out of the diving tanks and averted disaster.

En route to Helgoland two holes were discovered: one in a torpedo hatch and another in a copper pipe seemingly caused by clumsy hand drilling. These holes were the probable cause of the water ingress back in Wilhelmshaven. Both holes were roughly fixed, hastily botched with bits of rubber and wooden wedges until better repairs could be made in Helgoland. U-33 was definitely not seaworthy yet the order was given to press ahead with its mission.

Expert opinion is more relaxed on this charge of carelessness. The early Type VIIs such as U-33 did suffer under the rigours of operational use. Several had been forced to abort patrols and return with mechanical difficulties. A professional like von Dresky could feasibly have ordered makeshift repairs rather than shirk the decision to proceed with an operational voyage. Von Dresky and his Chief Engineer, Schilling, were not on good terms. There were many curtailed voyages in the war's early stages and Dönitz expected the most from his men. The ability to press on in trying circumstances would have been favourably viewed by him. Von Dresky's action in ordering U-33 out to sea with unfinished repairs may have been no different to a decision that would have been made by fellow Commandants in similar circumstances.

The Navy interrogated the survivors from U-33. The summary of the interrogation begins by pointing out that U-boat crews had been warned to refuse all information in the event of capture and so the prisoners may have deliberately misled their captors. There was one part of the report, however, that was surprising, viz:

"The morale of the crew was distinctly bad. The state of discontent may be in some respect due to the unpopularity of the Commanding Officer, Kplt von Dresky. He seems to have been domineering and distant in his manner. The crew bitterly resented the fact that they were never informed of the objective of their cruises. This was contrary, for example, to the practice of the Captain of U-35, Kplt Lott, one of the most popular of Commanders, who always paraded his men on deck before leaving harbour and informed them of his intentions and of the probable length of their cruise...The crew was unanimous in criticising the Captain for not giving them any information about his intentions. They had expected to be told the objective and duration of the cruise."

This lack of respect for the U-33 Commander stretched back to prior missions. When U-33 had been in the Bristol Channel the previous November and had sunk a number of British ships von Dresky responded to a request from the commander of a ship under attack to hold talks. Von Dresky was agreeable to this and ordered one of his officers, Hans Heidtmann, to stop the gunners on the upper deck from firing. Heidtmann believed the request was a ruse and, in direct contravention of his superior's orders, told the gunners to resume firing. Immediately, von Dresky sought to countermand his officer's order but did not succeed in restoring his authority until he had put a gun to Heidtmann's head. Heidtmann then obeyed but the crew of U-33 had seen their captain lose control.

Present day U-boat authorities concede that the Heidtmann incident is an extreme example of poor captain-crew relations, with no examples on record of similar accounts. The event may say more about Heidtmann's personality than von Dresky's when one factors in other opinions that show the Commander in a more favourable light.

Max Schiller told the BBC that von Dresky *"really was a nice person, a human being, he wasn't one of them shouting about and what have you. He was a human being, he was well-liked, really...a father-figure...an exceptionally nice man...he was fair, he was human."*

Schiller gave the example of the time during the Bristol Channel cruise when the 17-year old had been steering the boat and having difficulty maintaining course. Von Dresky had observed this from his cabin but not knowing who was steering shouted out that the boat was too far off-course. He then came along, saw that it was young Schiller at the helm, apologised and stayed with him to supervise and give advice.

Sebag-Montefiore claims that operational rules were blatantly ignored. After the earlier U-26 scare an order was issued that U-boats must, henceforth, leave their Enigma code machines behind. This order was not enforced by Dönitz for U-33. Sebag-Montefiore suggests that this had something to do with U-33's official status as a torpedo strike boat rather than as a dedicated mine layer.

Experts' views have been far more equivocal on this point of operational non-compliance, concluding that the decision was odd and illogical. Whatever the reason for non-enforcement the ruling was to cost Germany dear. Friedrich Kumpf was one of the survivors of U-33. He panicked and did not follow the order to dump into the water the Enigma rotor wheels VI, VII and VIII that he had been given to dispose of at the time of abandoning ship. He told Lieutenant Heinz Rottman he had forgotten to dump them and that this, therefore, was the moment when Rottman knew the rotor parts had been captured by the British. This account, however, conflicts with that from Max Schiller who told Sebag-Montefiore that he had undressed Kumpf before the latter was searched by the British and found his trouser pockets empty.

The precise circumstances were told to me by Ray and Edna Schiller. A tale often repeated is that when Max was pulled aboard the rescue boat *Bohemian Girl* he grabbed a teakettle from a stove and poured the contents over his freezing cold feet. Max told his family that the shivering crewman who doused himself with hot water was actually Kumpf. Straightaway, Max helped strip him of his wet clothes, which explains precisely when and why he undressed the officer and why also he knew with certainty that there were no heavy (Enigma parts sized) objects in the Chief Mechanic's pockets.

In light of the real story how did the Navy obtain Kumpf's rotor and how could the mechanic have made a statement to Rottman that he had failed to discard it? Lawrence Paterson, a U-boat expert who provides consultative services on behalf of the British Royal Navy's Historical Branch, has considered the circumstance and can offer no definite answer, other than suggesting that the rotor wheels *were* still in Kumpf's pocket, accepting in offering this explanation that it conflicts squarely with Schiller's account. There is no reason why Schiller should have fabricated the story he imparted to his family. Paterson's position is therefore untenable, which is why he has consigned this puzzling factor into the "another unknown" category concerning the unresolved issues surrounding U-33's final excursion.

In his 1960 book *A River Runs to War* John Drummond reported that Schiller, like all other members of the crew of U-33, had been puzzled and worried by the security precautions before sailing. The new TMC mines were bigger than any they had seen during training: two to each torpedo tube instead of the usual three. The crew of U-33 shared a heavy foreboding that something was not right. Sebag-Montefiore says: "So it was that U-33 was sent on what amounted to a suicide mission with an Enigma machine aboard." Max Schiller made identical remarks during his interview at home with BBC television and while he was on board HMS *Cromer* for the wreath-laying ceremony.

Grossadmiral Erich Raeder, Dönitz's superior, subsequently rounded on Hitler, saying that the operational order (on U-33) was "utter madness, sheer suicide!" Raeder acknowledged that the Clyde was vital to the enemy and therefore a prime target for U-boat offensives. Nevertheless, he emphasized to Hitler that for as long as he was Commander-in-Chief he would not allow another U-boat to attempt the impossible in those waters. In 1943 Raeder asked Hitler to relieve him of his duties "on the grounds of ill-health."

HMS *Hood*

At this time Raeder was unhappy at Hitler's desire to push more funding towards the U-boat building programme at the expense of the surface Navy. Dönitz then assumed command at OKM,[2] a move

---

[2] Oberkommando der Kriegsmarine (High Command of the German Navy, WWII)

favoured by Hitler who preferred Dönitz's more down-to-earth (and more compliant?) approach to the haughty, aristocratic mannerisms of the "Blue Tzar" Admiral Carls, the other of Raeder's choice of possible successors.

For what other reasons could the "utterly mad"operational order have been made upon U-33? There are many theories concerning the reason why the boat was operating in the Firth of Clyde in February 1940 including one, revealed more than sixty years later by Max Schiller to the BBC, that she had been sent on a mission to sink battle cruiser HMS *Hood*. Responding to the question as to who had given the order to sink the *Hood* Schiller said it had been Dönitz, not von Dresky.

Although the British Navy, having completed its investigation, concluded that the evidence indicated U-33 was simply laying mines Schiller spoke confidently to his BBC interviewers about the *Hood* mission. He stated that after laying the mines U-33 was to go underwater and reload the tubes with the four torpedoes, which would be targeted at the *Hood*. Schiller went on to claim that it was the noise they were making in trying to pick up the torpedoes for reloading that attracted *Gleaner*. After that, depth charging started "left, right and centre. But none of them near enough."

Photographs of U-33 show that she had "boom defence" cutting equipment mounted at her bow. The serrated steel-cutter was well supported and fixed in position. Despite Admiral Dönitz's War Diary remarks that U-boats could not attack the Clyde anchorages because access was closed by a boom, the presence of U-33's cutting gear indicates that there was no hard and fast rule prohibiting attempts at high risk activity should operational necessity demand.

Nevertheless, the *Hood* story poses many questions. An examination of the *Hood*'s logs for 5-8 February 1940 show that she was berthed in Greenock during this 4-day period but then set out to sea several days before U-33's arrival in the Firth of Clyde. But did U-33 really have permission to attack the *Hood* (regardless of the fact that U-33's intelligence was evidently poor and that it missed the battle cruiser by such a wide time margin)? On 16 October 1939 German JU 88s from the island of Sylt attacked naval ships in the harbour at Rosyth, Scotland. HMS *Hood* was about to enter dry dock for repairs but the pilots on the German boats had strict orders not to attack. Hitler had issued a personal order stating: "Should the *Hood* already be in dock, no attack is to be made, I won't have a single civilian killed."

It is not immediately obvious, therefore, how Max Schiller's statement about U-33's operational objective and the abundantly clear

Führer directive isssued just weeks before sit comfortably together. If Hitler's views had not changed then it is barely conceivable that U-33 would have risked invoking his anger to go it alone in sinking the *Hood* while it was in a place (the densely packed Clyde Anchorage) where a number of civilians would likely have died in the course of the attack. It is possible, of course, that the intervening five months of wartime activity had hardened Hitler's attitudes, making him more responsive to an attack in circumstances which he had previously embargoed.

HMS *Hood* log of 8 February 1940 showing her berthed at Greenock

Hood's log for the 10th showing her at sea well before U-33's arrival

Curiously, the content of Admiral Dönitz's entry in the War Diary [3] conflicts with the views of Grand Admiral Raeder. Dönitz clearly believed that the loss of U-33 was an acceptable cost, writing that it was not improbable that mines had been laid seeing that the events took place in the early morning hours.

The stark contradiction between Raeder's spitting anger about the "utter madness" of U-33's orders and the fatalistic, almost *laissez-faire* tone of Dönitz's Diary text begs the question as to whether the two men were actually talking about the same thing. Raeder's remarkably brave and vehement remarks suggest that he knew Hitler had overruled Dönitz in ordering U-33 to embark on its final patrol against naval advice.

Was the Grand Admiral referring to an operational order for U-33 quite distinct from the minelaying imperative under which the crew believed they were sailing? Was Raeder saying, in effect, that U-33 had been charged with carrying out covert orders, the undertaking of which amounted to "utter madness, sheer suicide"? If this was the case, might this help to explain why von Dresky was so reluctant to impart to his crew the true circumstances of U-33's mission to the Firth of Clyde in February 1940?

A reading of the interrogation report[4] indicates that an objective of U-33's cruise was to lay mines somewhere to the north of The Cumbraes in the lower Firth of Clyde. This is in line with von Dresky's objective to mine the British Naval base in the Clyde Anchorage. According to Max Schiller, U-33 not only reached The Cumbraes but it advanced further, a fact flatly denied by the British Navy then and now.

The northen tip of Great Cumbrae (the larger of the two islands: Great and Little Cumbrae, comprising The Cumbraes) is just seven miles south from a midway point between Wemyss Bay and Skelmorlie (six miles south of the Clyde Anchorage—the Tail of the Bank), which Schiller confirmed, to his knowledge, was the resting place of U-33 in an interview he gave to *The Sunday Post*'s Glasgow office during the 1960s.

By the time of the press interview Schiller had been living in Scotland for nearly twenty years and so one can rule out unfamiliarity with his adopted country's geography as a convenient explanation, from the perspective of officialdom, as to why his statement should have been regarded as wrong or unsafe.

Thirty-five years later Kirsty Wark asked Max Schiller if he was

---

[3] War Diary Flag Officer U-boats 16 February 1940
[4] U-33 Interrogation of Survivors, BR1907 (103) March 1940

aware of exactly where his boatmates and he were in the Clyde at the time of the sinking of U-33. Schiller replied that they knew their approximate position. Wark went on to ask if he roughly knew where the U-boat finally went down, to which Schiller said "yes," the broad answer one would expect from any of his crewmates seeing that they did not jump into the water with charts and compass.

It is clear, however, that the crew of U-33 were not wholly ignorant of the submarine's more precise position prior to sinking. In answer to Wark's subsequent questioning, Schiller confirmed that "the *Hood* was in there (Tail of the Bank) as well, so… that's what we really were after…after that (minelaying) we had to go right up the Clyde and try and get the *Hood*…try to do the same as what happened at Scapa Flow.[5] It works once, not twice!" The reality is that the *Hood* was *not* in the Anchorage on 12 February 1940, a fact one puzzles to understand was not known to Dönitz's planners. In the circumstances, one could justifiably deduce that the *Hood* story was a concoction from first to last, that U-33 had no intention of going for it (and incurring Hitler's wrath) but, instead, travelled beyond The Cumbraes in pursuit of an entirely different mission-critical objective.

(U-47's success at Scapa Flow merited four pages in Dönitz's diary while U-33 filled just one. Why, one might ask, was Dönitz so uncomfortable or reluctant to add more information about the detailed circumstances surrounding the sinking of U-33?)

Perhaps in the Wark interview Schiller went as far as he thought wise in telling the world about U-33's actual resting place. At the same time he evidently felt compelled to give a steer towards the truth. Throughout the interview it is abundantly clear that Schiller had his wits about him and that he had no difficulty recalling the events of February 1940.

The remark about U-33 and The Cumbraes in the interrogation report and Max Schiller's later, unequivocal statements about: HMS *Hood*, U-33 having "to go right up the Clyde," and U-33's wreck position placing it more than thirty miles northeast of Pladda are crucially pertinent facts to bear in mind as we undertake a rigorous review of the idiosyncratic and largely untold circumstances of U-33's Scottish excursions. It will quickly become evident in the following pages that Schiller's statements, which appear to contradict directly the official position on U-33's movements and resting place are, in fact,

---

[5] Scapa Flow is a body of water in the Orkney Islands. On 14 October 1939 U-47, under the command of Günther Prien, penetrated Scapa Flow and sank the battleship HMS *Royal Oak* anchored in Scapa Bay. Of the 1,400-man crew, 833 were lost.

being made about two wholly separate cruises which U-33 made into the Firth of Clyde—the first in November 1939 and the second in February 1940.

In phrasing his statements in such fashion for newspapers and television cameras, it suggests that Schiller was being smart and circumspect, taking care not to give so much away that he contravened any secrecy undertakings that may have been imposed on him by British security services, while at the same time peppering his statements with seemingly out of context remarks alluding to more than one Firth of Clyde episode directly involving U-33.

Evidently, Schiller did not want history to remain in ignorance of the complete picture of U-33's Scottish travails in the first few months of the war. His various remarks indicate that Schiller knew that U-33's operational imperatives for these two outings were a mixture of the norm and the remarkable. When we come to stand back and review all the facts here presented we may conclude that the covert aspects of U-33's activities were indeed so remarkable that they should deservedly be assigned to that rare category of events, undertaken no doubt by both sides in WWII, in which frantic efforts were made at the highest levels to find a peaceful solution to the conflict before it gained an unstoppable momentum.

My book on language scholar and historian Otto Rahn referred to some of these activities undertaken from the beginning of the war. The British factions involved conducted these initiatives largely outside official channels and pursued them contrary to the express wishes of Britain's political leadership.

The difficulty faced by leaders such as Churchill (who was seen as an impediment to peace by many leading Establishment figures) was that those backing these covert activities were extremely well connected and, in many cases, extraordinarily powerful, their position and reach even extending into the inner circle of the British Royal Family. British secrecy rules demand that in cases relating to controversial or questionable activities directly involving the Royals the information can be kept under lock and key for up to one hundred years.

As we shall shortly observe there are substantial indications that U-33 carried or chaperoned non-operational personnel for undisclosed purposes. Taking all the facts and circumstances together, it is entirely feasible that these were top-rank Nazi emissaries seeking on behalf of the highest figures in the Reich to sue, *sub rosa*, for an early peace. It is the objective of this present work to investigate these remarkable diversions from U-33's historical record.

Hitler salutes Hans-Wilhelm von Dresky and crew of U-33 at Wilhelmshaven 27 September 1939

Chapter THREE

Survivors and Deceased

Full fathom five thy father lies;
Of his bones are coral made;
Those are pearls that were his eyes:
Nothing of him that doth fade
But doth suffer a sea-change
Into something rich and strange.

There could hardly be more confusion than that which clouds the rescue details and statistics for the survivors and decedents from U-33. Besides HMS *Gleaner* a number of other vessels were party to the task of rescue and retrieval.

A logical starting point for analysis and reconciliation purposes is the official record confirming the number of persons on board U-33. In 2002 the NHB stated in response to my letter of enquiry that: *"3 officers and 14 men survived out of a total complement of 42."* This official statement serves perfectly well as the springboard for our detailed deliberations. 42 persons are therefore our start and end points in seeking to reconcile the number of survivors and deceased. The NHB's letter goes on to give a more detailed account of the rescue operation.

Gleaner's port whaler was lowered and sent away for survivors but as the ship was drifting fast to leeward the starboard whaler and both motor skiffs were not lowered until the ship had steamed slowly ahead to the centre of the largest group of men. The sea was very choppy and pulling boats could hardly make any headway. One officer and eight ratings were picked up by *Gleaner*'s boats.

First Enginer Friedrich Schilling later told his interrogators:[1] *"It was freezing cold, a pitch black night, very stormy with a rolling sea. I realised that our chances of rescue were not good. We could see lights glowing in the distance but no evidence of rescue vessels approaching.*

---

[1] Schilling's account reproduced courtesy of Pamela Armstrong who in turn drew on information from researcher Klaus Peter Pohland and translator Heiko Rotger to whom grateful thanks are also extended.

59

Greenock Cemetery Burial Record # 11,645 for the deceased from U-33, 16 February 1940

Initially, I found myself in a large group of boatmates. From time to time someone would plaintively ask: 'Will they come and rescue us?' to which I replied: 'They will come all right, lad. Hold on. Keep swimming. Give it everything you've got.' Some shadows appeared.

"*I did not want to go under so I kept on swimming, concentrating on those shadows ahead. I did not feel the cold and never gave up hope but our group became smaller and smaller. At the end all that remained were Johne, Weber, Keller and some others who swam right behind us.*

[Weber survived. Keller died and his body was recovered. Johne was among four deceased from U-33 whose bodies were not recovered. It will become apparent that assuming the *Scottish Daily Mail* report of 18 February 2000 is factually accurate there must have been two lookout men in U-33's conning tower who drowned when the earlier order to submerge was given.]

"*All of a sudden a searchlight stabbed out, just a short distance away. 'We've made it,' I shouted. 'Come on.'*

"*I saw a high hull and grabbed at a rope hanging from the side. Next to me I saw Obergefreiter Weber hanging on to another rope.*

"*I don't know what happened next and I must have fallen unconscious.*"

The Fleetwood motor drifter *Floradora*, skippered by John Farquhar, rescued one officer. The fishing trawler, *Bohemian Girl*, picked up two officers and seven ratings, beginning with Max Schiller, a first-rate swimmer.

Max told his son Ray that he had held on to one of his boatmates for a gruelling four hours before they were both rescued. Schiller's high level of personal fitness, owed in no small part to his training regime as a member of the Kriegsmarine's water polo team, was a major factor that contributed to his survival. Throughout this time his ordeal was exacerbated by the large quantity of seawater he was ingesting, which made him sick. He was also severely hampered by the heavy, newly issued fur-lined Wellington boots he was wearing. Finally, worn out by their weight, he had lain on his back and pulled them off. Max was very fond of his new boots and his family described how it was always a source of great irritation to him that he had had to cast them away.

Schiller described the awful circumstances to Kirsty Wark. It was a case of survival of the fittest. The water was dreadfully cold. A man had to swim for his life. The sea was very rough. A sailor in the water could not see any of those fellow boatmates who were similarly engaged in their own desperate fight for survival.

At one time Schiller said that he heard a voice not far away. He and the other fellow identified themselves. Max then said a curious thing to Wark. He said that he had told himself in those moments: "I'd better keep away from him, if he gets in any difficulty, I could'na help him." Schiller therefore resolved to keep his distance and concentrate on keeping himself alive. He told Wark that the man was among those who were saved.

Schiller's remarks sit incongruously alongside his selfless action in caring for a fellow submariner for a full four hours until help arrived. The man he referred to in his interview with Wark could not have been the sailor whom Max held onto in the water. Did this encounter therefore take place earlier, perhaps very soon after the men jumped from U-33 into the sea?

At this early juncture was there something about this particular man that discouraged Max Schiller from trying better to position himself so that he could offer assistance if called upon? Or was it simply the brutal but understandably necessary demands of survival in extremely dire conditions that shaped Max's thinking in those awful moments? It is less likely to have been the latter circumstance because by Ray Schiller's account his father selflessly spent almost all of his time in the firth's feezing waters making sure that a comrade did not slip under.

In the BBC programme Schiller answered a question from Kirsty Wark about von Dresky going down with his boat. Schiller said that if one were to go down and find bones they would belong to his captain, adding that: "he was the only pass…"

Max abruptly cut short this sentence, finishing by saying: "He went down with the boat." Was Schiller biting his tongue at this point in the interview, catching himself before saying something that might have indicated an uncomfortable fact about an undocumented passenger on U-33—one who survived?

Shortly, we shall review indisputable evidence that there were at least two unlisted persons among the dead of U-33 who, research indicates, were not regular Kriegsmarine sailors.

Presently, Schiller heard a 'putt, putt, putt' of a boat, saw a light and tried to grab a dangling rope but it came away when men on board pulled. They tried again and this time Schiller put it around his wrist. He was then pulled clear of the water. A kindly crewman gave Max chocolate and hot tea. Little did the trawlerman know how much Max, later to become a first-rate patisserie cook, adored chocolate!

Like Kumpf's escapade with the tea kettle, Robert Puchta threw himself bodily on to the galley stove and Max had to pull him off. When no one was looking Puchta did the same thing again, sustaining severe burns and lapsing into semi-consciousness.

Two of the ratings on board *Bohemian Girl* died as the little rescue convoy struggled for the shelter of Lamlash Bay on Arran's southwest coast. They were MaschOGfr Steiner and MechGfr Kampert.

The ten sailors who were picked up by *Floradora* and *Bohemian Girl* (three officers and seven ratings, including the two deceased) were transferred to *Gleaner* (British naval account ADM 199/123) during the brief call at Lamlash Bay. *Gleaner* made its way to Greenock and handed over seventeen survivors to the Military Authorities.

The "Javelin" class destroyer HMS *Kingston* also arrived in Greenock that day having picked up twenty-two men, only two being alive the others having died from exposure.

The bodies of von Dresky, Braun, Johne and Winterhoff were not recovered. The two lookout men who died when the submerge order was given must be among these names. Von Dresky went down with the boat and Johne drowned among his comrades after abandoning ship. It follows, therefore, that the ratings Braun and Winterhoff were the two men who did not make it back down through the conning tower hatch in time.

All four boats had struggled to pick up as many bodies as possible in spite of difficult weather conditions. When transferred to the *Gleaner* Max Schiller was first grouped with the officers but then put in with the ratings when the mistake about rank was realised. He must have dozed off because in the Interrogation report Schiller states that he woke up on a couch in *Gleaner*'s wardroom. He and his boatmates were given a hot bath, a massage and whisky.

He asked Commander Price why he had waited so long before coming to their rescue. Price gave several reasons. Firstly, he was wary in case the Germans had two U-boats operating in the area. Secondly, Price said that initially the sea was too high to launch boats. Lastly, the explosion and flames on U-33 had made him doubly suspicious. He feared the placement of a deadly device designed to lure *Gleaner* to her destruction.

Schiller told his captors ruefully: *"Gleaner landed us in Greenock. Nineteen of our men had been rescued but only seventeen survived their two-hour ordeal. So many more could have survived."*

Schiller's remarks highlight an extremely important factor that must be very carefully considered in one's efforts to investigate the "mystery" of U-33. One must question on what grounds Lieutenant-Commander Price delayed the immediate rescue of U-33 sailors in case, as he confirmed to Schiller, there were other U-boats in the area. Why might Price have held his suspicions about the presence of other hostile subs? His reply to Schiller's question can be reasonably interpreted in the context that Price was not just wary of the proximity of another other U-boat but that he was more or less *certain* that there was another boat in the vicinity.

Perhaps in Dönitz's own words we get an insight into the truth of the matter. The Admiral wrote in his diary on 12 February 1940: *"Radio intelligence service reports the sinking of a U-boat in the Clyde. If this is correct it can only be U-33. But the reports are not so definite that hope of the boats only having been seen need not be abandoned."*

Why did Dönitz refer to boats plural and not to boat singular?

To tarry in undertaking the rescuing of men in immediate danger of death through freezing and possible injuries caused by the explosions on U-33 is a serious matter. A responsible officer such as Price would not have held back, knowing that delay could add to fatalities, unless he was in receipt of hard intelligence that indicated a nearby secondary threat.

Another strand of consideration is the possibility that Price knew of a previous occasion when a U-boat had been seen in the Firth of Clyde and did not want the Navy to be caught out a second time. We will see that this was precisely the position, the successful incursion by a U-boat inside the defence boom in November 1939 having been a source of great official embarrassment.

It would come as no surprise if one were to learn that it was as a consequence of a U-boat's successful passage into the Clyde Anchorage in November 1939 that Navy chiefs decided to redeploy HMS *Gleaner* as a member of the 3rd Anti-Submarine Striking Force charged with the protection of the Firth of Clyde and its approaches.

The consequence of delay was, as Schiller sadly noted, to prolong the agony of men in the water. Schiller's unequivocal view was that fewer men would have died had *Gleaner* acted immediately. None can now say.

The table provides the official list of survivors and deceased (see table in Appendix for details of each man's rank):

Survivors (17)	Deceased (25)
Becker, Johannes LtzSee	Anger, Paul StOStrm
Ehrhardt, Hans-Joachim MtrGfr	Bergfeld, Hans-Georg MaschGfr
Galileia, Paul BtsMt	Braun, Friedrich MechMt
Krampe, Manfred MaschGfr	Dresky von, Hans-Wilhelm Kplt
Krink, Heinz MaschOGfr	Enders, Werner OMasch

Kumpf, Friedrich StObMasch	Gross, Karl MaschGfr
Lingscheidt, Peter MtrOGfr	Heckerodt, Adalbert MaschGfr
Marticke, Heinz MaschMt	Henneberg, Gustav BtsMt
Masanek, Ernst OMaschMt	Johne, Johannes MtrHGfr
Puchta, Robert MaschOGfr	Kampert, Heinrich MaschGfr
Rottmann, Heinz OLt (Ing)	Keller, Werner MtrOGfr
Scherer, Ernst MaschOGfr	Kunick, Walter MtrGfr
Schiller, Max Matrose	Kursiefen, Heinrich MtrOGfr
Schilling, Friedrich-Ernst Otto	Liebert, Heinrich OMaschGfr
KpltLt (Ing)	Mohr, Heinz BtsMt
Siegert, Werner MaschHGfr	Patten, Erich OFkMt
Vietor, Karl OltzSee	Peters, Karl-Heinz MaschGfr
Weber, Heinrich MtrOGfr	Pöppel, Leopold FkGfr
	Raath, Herbert OMaschMt
	Rausch, Paul OMaschMt
	Schmid, Christian OMaschMt
	Steiner, Willibald OMaschGfr
	Wagner, Ludwig MaschMt
	Wilden, Wilhelm MaschOGfr
	Winterhoff, August MtrGfr

The NHB correspondence concludes that, in total, 4 officers (1 *Gleaner*, 1 *Floradora*, 2 *Bohemian Girl*) and 17 Ratings (8 *Gleaner*, 7 *Bohemian Girl*, 2 *Kingston*) were picked up alive from the waters around U-33—a total of 21 persons. As noted, 2 of the ratings aboard *Bohemian Girl* died during the process of transfers to *Gleaner* at Lamlash Bay, reducing the total number of survivors borne by *Gleaner* to Greenock to 17 persons, *Kingston* carried 2.

The men pulled aboard *Bohemian Girl* were put into the lower deck living quarters. Neither of the two officers from U-33 was able to walk but they could speak English. One of the crew from *Bohemian Girl* came down and spoke to an officer who then turned to Schiller, saying that two of the U-33 crew who had been pulled on board had died. He asked if Schiller would go upstairs and identify them. As noted, ratings Steiner and Kampert died while on *Bohemian Girl* and so identification should have been a straightforward matter.

Schiller went on deck. He later told his captors that he was able to recognize one man straightaway because of his beard but, oddly, he could not identify the second. He told the BBC that he stood over the corpse for some time before the man's name registered with him. Let us reflect on this. The closely packed crew of U-33 had been at sea for seven days in very cramped conditions. Schiller told Wark that *"we were a good crew, we got on well...we we were more like a family."* Clearly, everyone knew each other and pulled together to make life under the waves run smoothly and amicably.

Life for a submariner was a regular four hours watch and four hours off. A sailor had hardly snatched a brief nap (because during the four hours off he had to eat something) before he was up again. In effect, he was seeing everyone around him more or less constantly.

Other factors contributed to the close-knit nature of life on U-33. Max said that due to lack of fresh water supplies and the consequent effect on regular dishwashing two to three sailors shared one cup and plate. The one just handed them over to another and thought nothing of it. Taking these factors together, it is barely credible that a submarine sailor would not immediately recognise one of his boatmates. If the person he struggled to recognise on *Bohemian Girl* was neither Steiner nor Kampert then who was he?

One obstacle to permitting instant recognition of a crewmate after enemy attack would have been severe facial injury but this circumstance was not reported. However, another barrier to recognition would have been unfamiliarity with a person who had been taking pains to avoid contact or had been forbidden from mixing with the general crew population during the voyage...or even a person who had not been a member of the U-33 crew but had died in the water nearby. May it have been the case that three men died while on the trawler, including one whose identity could not be acknowledged or recorded in the post-event official reports?

In the case of U-33 this scenario is more than a possibility when one considers the actual numbers in or associated with the boat compared with historical record and the nature of covert activities reported as undertaken by U-33 (reviewed in PART TWO—OFF RECORD).

In correspondence the NHB's Curatorial Office noted ingenuously that: "These (official) figures do not quite tally with the total of 17 survivors and 25 dead recorded in the *Interrogation of Survivors*." Just how far out are the NHB's figures? Its tally can be clearly set out on a sliding scale basis beginning with the officially listed crew complement of 42.

The reducing scale, employing the NHB figures for survivors and deceased as a benchmark position, should culminate in zero but obviously does not. Nevertheless, the NHB has been candid about the overall discrepancies (if not the detail):

ANALYSIS of U-33 SURVIVORS and DECEASED NUMBERS

U-33 personnel—the historical starting point   **42**

Less deceased as listed by NHB

Von Dresky, Braun, Johne, Winterhoff—not recovered	38
2 who died on on *Bohemian Girl* at Lamlash Bay (Steiner and Kampert)	36
20 corpses recovered by *Kingston* from the water	**16**

Less survivors as listed by NHB

1 Officer picked up by *Gleaner*	15
1 Officer from *Floradora*	14
2 Officers from *Bohemian Girl*	12
8 ratings from *Gleaner*	4
5 ratings (7 picked up less 2 who died en route) from *Bohemian Girl*	-1
2 ratings *Kingston*	**-3**

The analysis of the NHB's final tally suggests that 42 + 3 = 45 people were on U-33.

The 17 survivors recorded in the *Interrogation of Survivors*, split between officers and ratings, are as follows:

4 surviving senior officers:
o   Schilling, Friedrich-Ernst Otto KpltLt (Ing)
o   Vietor, Karl OLtzS
o   Rottmann, Heinz OLt (Ing)
o   Becker, Johannes LtzS

13 surviving junior officers / ratings:
o   Kumpf, Friedrich StObMasch
o   Masanek, Ernst OBtsMt
o   Scherer, Ernst OMaschGfr
o   Ehrhardt, Hans-Joachim MtrGfr
o   Galileia, Paul BtsMt
o   Krampe, Manfred MaschGfr
o   Krink, Heinz MaschOGfr
o   Lingscheidt, Peter MtrOGfr
o   Marticke, Heinz MaschMt

- o   Puchta, Robert MaschOGfr
- o   Schiller, Max Matrose
- o   Siegert, Werner MaschHGfr
- o   Weber, Heinrich MtrOGfr

It is evident that the NHB's statistics report a gross overall total of 45 persons for U-33: 19 survivors and 26 deceased compared with 17 survivors and 25 deceased (42 crewmen) from the *Interrogation of Survivors* records—a net error of 3 persons. By the NHB's own remarks it is aware of the discrepancy. How then does one explain it?

One could accept that the exigencies of rescue and retrieval by multiple vessels in dark choppy, wintry waters may result in some minor but net balancing variations in the recording of survivor and deceased figures within the overall number. Nevertheless, none of those mitigating factors, even taken together, should amount to credible grounds for getting the total number of persons wrong by such a wide margin of error.

One logical explanation, however contradictory to historical record or unpalatable to present day official sensitivities, is that the NHB's information about the total number is a piece of *disinformation* given out to mask details about U-33 and its true mission that, to this day, the authorities are anxious to keep out of the public domain.

When we come to a detailed review and analysis of burial records both at Greenock Cemetery and Cannock Chase Military Cemetery, Staffordshire, we will learn that there were two more persons buried among the dead of U-33 compared with the known crew population. In light of these new facts, the NHB's underlying figure of 45 persons for U-33, read against official record, begins to look not just increasingly credible but to be historical fact suppressed to this day.

The two unlisted persons buried at Greenock are documented as being among those from U-33 who died. Significant questions remain, however, about the identities of the two, the operational capacity in which they were on board U-33 and how, when and if they boarded, which could have been in Wilhelmshaven, in Helgoland during the repairs stopover (as has been speculated), or even at various locations during U-33's passage into Scottish waters and its western isles.

Perhaps it is significant that between 8-10 February,[2] by which

---

[2] Experts differ on the date. Mallmann Showell (Malman Showell, Jak P., *U-boats at War Landings on Hostile Shores*, Naval Institute Press, Maryland, 2000) refers to a landing on 9-10 February while the UBootwaffe website (http://www.ubootwaffe.net) refers to one on the 8th.

latter date U-33 was well into Scottish waters, U-37, also recently departed from Wilhelmshaven, landed Abwehr II[3] spy Ernst Weber-Drohl (also landing a second unnamed spy, according to the Ubootwaffe network) at Killala Bay in Donegal, County Sligo, northwest Ireland.

Weber-Drohl, nearing 60, boarded U-37 at Wilhelmshaven disguised as a war correspondent. He carried a number of heavy cases, which included a 'Ufa' transmitter. He also had a large amount of cash and instructions for Seamus (Jim) O'Donovan, the chief Irish Republican Army (IRA) contact for Abwehr I/II.

It was only when U-37 had reached the Atlantic that its crew were told of Weber-Drohl's real identity and ordered to sign a paper alerting them to the conditions of special secrecy and binding them to silence or suffer the death sentence.

Two days later U-33, seemingly carrying (at least) two unlisted persons, was abroad in the Firth of Clyde to undertake activities whose exact nature is unknown. Von Dresky, too, did not reveal to his crew the precise nature of U-33's mission until well into Scottish waters. The two events may not be linked but it is the kind of coincidence apt to trigger asdic signals of its own.

In an interesting sideshoot to the account of the deceased from U-33 we should note Brian Osborne's story. Osborne, co-author of *Clyde at War*,[4] undertook considerable research on U-33 having been struck by a photograph of German POWs standing by a grave for their comrades in Greenock Cemetery. The photo was taken in March 1946. The prisoners were working on a housing project in Greenock and had been given permission to conduct a memorial ceremony by the graveside. For the occasion the men painted new gravemarkers.

The *Glasgow Herald* reported: "*The men, who sang a German song of remembrance and observed a minute's silence, were addressed by a German officer in their own language. He exhorted them never to forget that they were of German blood and to look forward to the day when Germany would be freed from the heavy yoke which she now bore.*"

Subsequently, Osborne produced a magazine article on U-33 and was later contacted by a Polish woman who described herself as the

---

[3] Abwehr II was a unit of the third division of the Abwehr. Dedicated to Sabotage activities Abwehr II, headed by Generalmajor Erwin von Lahousen, was tasked with directing covert contact and exploitation of discontented minority groups in foreign countries for intelligence purposes.

[4] Armstrong A. and Osborne B. D., *Clyde at War*, Birlinn Ltd, Edinburgh, 2001

great-granddaughter of U-33's coxswain, Paul Anger, one of the deceased. She was seeking information about her great-grandfather and about the fate of the submarine. One wonders if the Polish woman's keen interest to learn more about her wartime family was connected with a visit made to Greenock Library at around the same time as the publication of Osborne's article by a man seeking similar facts. The library visit is addressed more fully in Chapter 8.

In early 1960 John Drummond persuaded Max and Jessie Schiller to visit Greenock Cemetery to pose for photographs by Max's "grave." It is likely that Drummond wanted photos for his book (*A River Runs to War*), which was published that year. Ray and Edna Schiller told me the details of the story as related to them by their father when he arrived back home that day.

Whether planned or spur of the moment Drummond suggested that it would make a good shot to photograph Max placing flowers on his 'grave' but he had brought none with him. Max told his family that to solve this problem Drummond borrowed flowers from another grave for the Kriegsmarine veteran's pose for the photo.

Max, a mild-mannered, good-natured person, was very rarely moved to anger. However, on that day he returned home hopping mad. He exclaimed angrily: "*Fertig!*" (Finished).

He brought out his old photos and memorabilia, tore them up and threw them away; he would have no more to do with the past and with U-33. Among the treasures he destroyed was a wonderful triptych of photos of U-33, which were viewed alongside each other to get a grand panoramic perspective of the submarine. Max maintained his silence for forty years, pausing only to give an interview to the Scottish *Sunday Post* in the mid-sixties before agreeing to be interviewed by the BBC in 2000 for a short television documentary. We are very fortunate that, today, even a few remnants survive in the Schiller family legacy and for posterity.

In PART TWO—OFF RECORD—we begin by moving forward forty-five years after the event. In was in 1984-1985 that stories from local Firth of Clyde residents began to come forward in a series of newspaper articles about events reported to have taken place in mid-February 1940. But their story was not a repeat of the general line about U-33 but, sensationally, was a new and startling account that challenged the notion that the epicentre of U-boat action was off the Isle of Arran.

They speak passionately about dramatic events that took place on their doorstep, more precisely in the waters of the Clyde from the Wemyss Bay-Innellan area to a point five miles north at the Tail of the

Bank gateway to the Clyde Anchorage between Gourock and Dunoon.

Scots' confident recollections must have sent a shiver through the halls of officialdom because the Establishment's continuing response to questions about the local story is all-round denial and, in effect, it has accused its narrators of collective dementia.

That is a gross injustice and it is, therefore, of no surprise that Inverclyde residents want the authorities to come clean about the events that took place in the Firth of Clyde in the early stages of WWII, to which many in their youth were witness or were direct recipients of descriptions from family and friends.

German POWs at graveside of U-33 fallen, Greenock, March 1946

Others, like Patti Duncan, overheard careless conversations, which even in the privacy of the home contravened secrecy protocols and should never have taken place.

In a diary entry dated 25 February 1940 Horace Oakes, at that time a young reporter on *The Greenock Telegraph*, wrote of: *"reports that German torpedoes from one of the U-boats sunk in the Firth, along with several magnetic mines, were sent to the R.N.T.F. (*Royal Navy Torpedo Factory*) at Greenock for inspection and examination by Admiralty* *experts*."

Why does one suppose that Oakes, a man who was seriously well informed as per the demands of his profession wrote, just as Dönitz had in his War Diary, about U-boats *plural*?

PART TWO

OFF RECORD

*What seest thou else in the
dark backward and abysm of time?*

Chapter FOUR

August 1985 — the story breaks

The hour's now come;
The very minute bids thee ope thine ear;
Obey and be attentive.

In response to my request in 2001 for information about U-33 the U-Boot-Archiv at Cuxhaven in Germany sent me a package of material. Included with the various papers, reports, photos and map reproductions were copies of two articles published by a Western Scotland provincial newspaper, the *Largs and Millport Weekly News*, in 1985 and 1986.

Both articles were printed in a section titled "*Out & About with John McCreadie*," the then editor of the newspaper. The common subject matter was U-boat sinkings in the Firth of Clyde. McCreadie makes it clear that they are follow-ups from two earlier articles.

The first of these earlier pieces, "*Drama of U-boat sunk in the Clyde*" (published Friday 2 August 1985), was an account by Mr David B. Hendry of Pinelea, Largs, about the sinking of U-33 off Pladda (the same David Hendry mentioned earlier in connection with discussions he had with Max Schiller.) Hendry led readers briskly through a short summary about the Arran sinking and did not provide any more information than was already in the public domain.

The real point of interest in the article, however, is McCreadie's opening paragraph in which the editor states that: "early in the war, there were rumours that a U-boat had been sunk in the Clyde. The story had it that the submarine was attacked while trying to go underneath the boom at the Tail of the Bank."

McCreadie then goes on to say in the following paragraph that his report in the 26 July 1985 edition about the recent visit to Clyde waters of the (new) survey vessel HMS *Gleaner* had prompted Mr Hendry to come forward with his research data on the sinking of U-33.

An objective review of the whole article leaves one in little doubt that the content of McCreadie's introductory paragraph is somewhat of a *non sequitur* when read alongside the piece's main story: the sinking of U-33 off the Isle of Arran. Evidently, however, McCreadie was keen to make an opening reference to the 'Tail of the Bank' incident, even though the article's next two columns of text make no follow-up reference to the journalist's startling claim but are wholly devoted to Hendry's rather prosaic offering about U-33 and its demise in February 1940.

A study of the back issues of the *Largs and Millport Weekly News* from 1984 onwards confirms that this was the newspaper's first mention of what would become several over the next two years about the U-boat Clyde Anchorage boom event. One distinctly gets the impression that editor McCreadie's subtle objective was to elicit readers' responses to it rather than to the details surrounding the old hat story about the sinking of U-33 off Pladda more than thirty miles to the southwest.

If that was indeed McCreadie's barely concealed ambition then he did not have to wait long before faith in his readers paid off. Just two weeks later McCreadie published an article headed "*Another U-boat drama*" (see Appendix), which recalled for another Largs man "his eyewitness experience of an attack and the believed sinking of a U-boat after it went through the 'gateway' at the Tail of the Bank boom." One may picture McCreadie at this point feeling quietly satisfied that his thinly veiled invitation for others to come forward with information to support his own evident belief in the "other" U-boat sinking was bearing fruit.

McCreadie's correspondent was Mr Gavin Crawford of Church Street, Largs. Crawford's account is probably the most important eyewitness testimony on record about the U-boat Tail of the Bank incursion. McCreadie prefaced the quoting of the full text of Crawford's remarks with a couple of introductory sentences of his own, which read:

"Mr Gavin Crawford, before being called up to the RAF served for three nights a week on a small patrol launch, which logged ships between Bowling and Port Glasgow. On a night in mid-February 1940 while on his way to Greenock he parked his car at the Cloch."

It is a critically important factor to note in our review of the U-boat boom event that in this and in ensuing articles on the topic in the *Largs and Millport Weekly News* it is McCreadie alone who associates it with the date of "mid-February 1940." This date will be shown to be incorrect. We have eyewitness accounts and, surprisingly, the phases of the moon to thank for making possible an accurate dating.

But the fact that McCreadie's dating is incorrect does not in any way lessen, dilute or otherwise detract from the power and accuracy of the first rate personal testimonies provided by readers like Gavin Crawford. The event he and others described simply took place at another time, a fact that these correspondents did not seek to conceal or confuse. From the very beginning of his series of articles McCreadie set off on the wrong foot and, for whatever reason, commingled the dates of the Tail of the Bank event and the later sinking of U-33, perpetuating the error over several months of reporting. The two incidents actually took place nearly twelve weeks apart. The times and common date of the Tail of the Bank incursion and the even less well documented Carradale Bay U-boat event are known and will be carefully investigated in the coming chapters.

Returning to Crawford, he recalled for readers: *"...the moon[1] was full, you could see everything. The gate at the boom was opened for the Royal Ulsterman,[2] inward bound from Belfast, to pass through.*

"I could see distinctly a submarine on the surface 200 yards behind.

It went through the gate. All of a sudden searchlights on both the Cowal (Argyllshire) and Cloch (Renfrewshire) sides beamed onto the submarine, which crash-dived. A Royal Navy ship closed in and dropped four of five depth charges.

"Of course, there was no publicity about the incident nor have I read anything of the matter since.

The *Royal Ulsterman* in 1943

"The story going round the next day was that a U-boat had been camouflaged to look like a British submarine and that its target was the Queen Mary lying off Greenock.

"It was said that the U-boat intended to surrender after it had attacked the liner with torpedoes.

"The only evidence I saw of the attack next day were hundreds of dead fish on the shore at Gourock, while windows were shattered at

---

[1] That Crawford was describing a date other than 12 Febuary 1940 for the appearance of a U-boat at the boomgate is made abundantly clear by his remark about the "full moon." The night of February 12th was just four days after the New Moon and hence a relatively dark sky.

[2] The *Royal Ulsterman* was a 3,000-ton passenger ship, which sailed the Glasgow-Belfast run for Burns and Laird Lines Ltd. During WWII the *Royal Ulsterman* served as a Royal Navy Reserve troop transport, taking part in nearly all of the major Allied amphibious operations of the European war.

Gourock and also on the Cowal coast."

McCreadie concluded the piece by saying that Crawford was seeking confirmation from the MoD that a sinking did take place. From my own unfruitful experience in seeking identical verification I would be surprised if the MoD gave Crawford what he was asking for.

Crawford's remarkable testimony provokes a number of questions, which shall be addressed. For now we may reflect on just one. If this and other local accounts of a U-boat seeking to gain passage through the boom into the Clyde Anchorage are patently untrue, as the MoD and British naval authorities insist then and now, how did it possibly become knowledge that "the U-boat intended to surrender after it had attacked the liner with torpedoes?"

What was the source of this remark—local rumour (unfounded and easily discountable) or naval/security forces (insider knowledge)? If the offending vessel was a German U-boat then knowledge of this detail and quality could only have come from direct interrogation of the occupants of the submarine; and/or from informed persons in the German Navy or German Intelligence; and/or from persons in the British security services who had advance notification of the U-boat's mission and objectives.

Another possibility is that it had been so obvious to civilian witnesses such as Crawford that a submarine had travelled in the light of the moon up to and through the boomgate that official blanket denial was not a credible option. Faced with this, naval authorities rapidly cooked up the story about an intended attack on the RMS *Queen Mary*. However, it is very difficult to understand why the Navy would have spun this particular tale considering that the *Queen Mary* had been in New York since September 1939 and would not arrive in the Clyde until 16 June 1940. Had the rumour been about a planned attack on the *Queen Elizabeth* it might have been more credible, seeing that the liner was undergoing fitting-out work upriver.

In accordance with McCreadie's evident plan to garner local intelligence about the Tail of the Bank incident his 30 August 1985 edition reported more first hand testimony, this time from Mr Douglas McKillop of West Kilbride in an article titled "*U-boat Dramas in the Clyde.*" In it McKillop corroborates Gavin Crawford's report:

"*I have read with great interest your two reports (*Hendry's and Crawford's*) on the U-boat dramas in the Firth of Clyde. The U-boat sunk off Pladda was confirmed after the war.*

"*With regard to the U-boat sinking at the boom, as reported by Mr Gavin Crawford, I wish to state that I was a sapper with the Fort*

Matilda Fortress Royal Engineers' Searchlight Company Territorials at the start of the war in 1939.

"One evening in 1940 while stationed at Fort Matilda, Greenock, there was a telephone call from the searchlight station emplacement at the Cloch that flares had gone off at the boom and that a U-boat had been sighted.

"The destroyer stationed at the boom had tried to ram the submarine and consequently ran aground (HMS Foxhound). Owing to censorship then in force no confirmation of this sinking was made. The Admiralty at that time denied any sinking. What Mr Crawford reported was true: a U-boat tried to force the boom at the Cloch."

Both Gavin Crawford's and Douglas McKillop's statements to the *Largs and Millport Weekly News* are unequivocal, first-hand eyewitness accounts from responsible, informed citizens of a major submarine incident that took place at the Cloch-Dunoon defence boom. Crawford did not supply a date. McKillop mentions "one evening in 1940." By these latter words McKillop was dating the event as accurately as he could recall because both Crawford and he were describing an event that took place just a few weeks after the onset of war.

McKillop went on to provide further information, which indicated that he was not the kind of man simply to accept official denials at face value. He gave evidence of similar official refutations made during the war about incidents that he knew to be true based on impeccable third party confirmation. McKillop gave the example of a radio broadcast made in the early summer of 1940 just after the Dunkirk rescue operation. The broadcast stated that the Germans had tried to invade Britain. When Mr McKillop got home to Gourock from his posting at Bordeaux friends who were serving in destroyers confirmed that the German invasion barges had been cut to ribbons by destroyers led by Lord Louis Mountbatten. All aspects of this matter were denied in Parliament just as the Cloch U-boat event was denied.

The next article to be published on the topic by the *Largs and Millport Weekly News* was fourteen months later in October 1986. The earlier stories from Crawford and McKillop had interested Joe Breuckmann (spelled incorrectly in the article as 'Beuckmann') who described himself as having served as a Chief Petty Officer on board U-532, which, Breuckmann explained, had surfaced in the Irish Sea in May 1945 after receiving a signal from the German Naval Command to all U-boats alerting them to Germany's capitulation.

U-532 was commanded by Kplt Ottoheinrich Junker who, as noted earlier, had previously commanded U-33 on two occasions. Like Max

Schiller, Joe Breuckmann had married a local girl and settled in Scotland after the war.

In the article's introductory remarks John McCreadie reiterated that in "mid-February 1940" a U-boat had passed through the 'gateway' into the Clyde Anchorage. Breuckmann was sufficiently inspired about the reports to contact the U-Boot-Archiv at Cuxhaven and seek more information on the sub that had reportedly breached the boom, enclosing copies of the articles. Cuxhaven replied that except for U-33: *"within the bounds of probability* (author's italics) no other German U-boat has been sunk in the Firth of Clyde." The Cuxhaven respondent was so interested in the accounts that he asked if the archive could keep the articles. It was these copies, I believe, which were subsequently re-xeroxed by the archive and sent to me in their package of material about U-33.

The story of U-532's surrender is fascinating. What details that can be gathered together indicate that U-532 was submerged in the Irish Sea when the signal to surrender was received. It surfaced but it was not until two days later that a fishing boat with an astonished crew came alongside and escorted the U-boat to the Kyle of Loch Alsh in northwest Scotland where it waited until a destroyer arrived (HMS *Rupert*). U-532 was then escorted to Liverpool where it was put on display to the public. Later it was taken out into the Atlantic and sunk.

It is probable that the story told by a fishing party enjoying a boating holiday in the waters off the Isle of Man refers also to U-532's surrender. On 10 May 1945 the fishing boat, sailing off the coast by the island's capital Douglas was ordered to hove to by a destroyer, which then lowered a launch. At the same time a Sunderland flying boat roared overhead and dropped flares. They were then amazed to see a rusty U-boat burst up onto the surface just in front of their small boat. The crew came out of the conning tower hoisting the white flag and a Royal Navy party went on board. Later that afternoon, destroyer and submarine came into Douglas harbour and the crew was marched off to Onchan Head prison camp. The U-boat was then taken across to the River Mersey in Liverpool to a much publicised reception.

One suspects that between the two accounts lie the true details of U-532's surrender. However, there is less certainty about the proximity of Joe Breuckmann amidst all the action. Online U-boat database records state that a Josef Breuckmann served on U-109 and U-233 but there is no mention of a posting on U-532. The periods that Breuckmann spent on each boat are not itemised nor is his rank specified. U-109 sank south of Ireland in May 1943 and U-233 sank southeast of Halifax,

Canada, in July 1944. One should treat these apparent discrepancies with caution as it was common for one man's records to commingle with another's, even to go missing entirely. (No person named Beuckmann served in the Kriegsmarine in WWII.)

McCreadie noted Breuckmann's contribution to the story and added some concluding remarks, posing the question once more: "What vessel, if any, was attacked at the Cloch boom in February 1940?" He repeated Crawford's eyewitness testimony (and what were clearly McCreadie's own convictions in the matter) that two destroyers dropped depth charges, large quantities of dead fish were found on the shore the next day and that windows in Gourock and on the Cowal side had been shattered.

Clearly, McCreadie did not want to drop the story there and then, seeing that local readers had offered their contributions based on firsthand experience and were obviously resolute in their belief that a U-boat had tried to force the boom and, moreover, according to Crawford, had actually done so and then passed through it.

Shortly after receiving the *Largs and Millport Weekly News* material I made contact with the paper's readership via a letter it printed on my behalf. I referred in summary to the articles published fifteen years previously, pointing out the apparent wide discrepancies between the official reports and the local observations. I asked for readers' recollections or details of information passed down to them from family and friends about the Cloch boom incident.

I was taken aback by the number of replies I received and, importantly, by the quality of the information provided by enthusiastic correspondents. Their accounts will be reviewed in depth in Chapter 8; however, first things first. In reading the material it appeared that McCreadie's "February 1940" account was not the first occasion, according to local citizens, that a U-boat had travelled up to the boom. People spoke also about an event dubbed the Tail of the Bank incident, which took place in the autumn of 1939.

Naturally, officials denied that this earlier event took place despite the weight of local reporting. The following four chapters are devoted to this incident and its associated activities, beginning with extraordinary events that took place off the western shore of the Kintyre Peninsula earlier on the day in question.

A detailed analysis indicates that, remarkably, the activities of U-33 during that autumn are directly related to the occurrence of the mysterious Carradale Bay and Tail of the Bank U-boat incursions, which occurred just hours apart.

It also became abundantly clear over the eight-year period of my investigations into U-33 that the event described by Gavin Crawford and Douglas McKillop in McCreadie's weekly "Out and About" column and that described by local citizens replying to my published letter in the *Largs and Millport Weekly News* are one and the same.

That event took place not in mid-February 1940 but on a night in November 1939.

Intriguingly, there is also widespread opinion among respondents that there are two enemy submarines lying at the bottom of the firth— U-33 off Arran and another, some say a "special" or midget sub, twenty to thirty miles to the north.

This is a challenging proposition because research proves that the submarine that passed through the boom in November 1939 *was* U-33, a boat that cannot have been killed on two separate occasions.

Chapter FIVE

The Carradale U-boat

Come unto these yellow sands,
And then take hands.

A little over half way down the east coast of the Kintyre Peninsula, at a point where the Kilbrannan Sound looking across to Arran is less than three miles wide, is the village of Carradale. Described as Scotland's only mainland island, Kintyre in the southwest of Argyll and Bute is on the extreme west coast of the country. It is the gateway to the Southern Hebridean islands of Arran, Gigha, Islay and Jura. The peninsula, joined to the mainland by a narrow isthmus at Tarbert, is forty miles long and blessed with a wealth of natural features—hills, lochs, rivers, forests, stunning seascapes, hidden coves, sandy beaches, renowned local produce and impressive archaeology.

The coastal areas and hinterland are rich and fertile, a characteristic which, over the centuries, has made Kintyre a magnet for settlers—from the early Scots who migrated from Ulster to western Scotland to the Vikings who conquered the area in the latter part of the first millennium. The Gulf Stream effect ensures a low average rainfall (less than forty percent of the rest of the west of Scotland) and a mean temperature warm enough to sustain the growth of palm trees.

On the afternoon of 22 November 1939 an earlier winter gale subsiding, a U-boat was observed emerging from the foamy waters south of Carradale Bay as the local service bus from Tarbert, eleven miles to the northwest, was heading to Campbeltown. Such details of the incident as can be drawn together have been collated by local Scots, most comprehensively by Donald Kelly, a Kintyre-based historian and marine enthusiast whose substantial work, *Kintyre at War*, is an invaluable chronology compiled for educational and historical research purposes.[1] (Kelly's maternal grandfather was skipper of HMS

---

[1] Kelly, D., *Kintyre at War 1939-1945*, Kintyre Antiquarian and Natural History Society, Scotland, 2005

Gleaner's predecessor, which was disposed of in 1905.) I am grateful to Mr Kelly for the opportunity to draw from his diligent researches.

Kelly's detailed investigations have led him to conclude that the Carradale U-boat and Tail of the Bank events (the latter covered in the next chapter) occurred just hours apart on Wednesday 22 November.

Shortly, it shall be seen that the only source for the hitherto reported date of 23 November for the Tail of the Bank event is Captain W.C. Tancred, present at the scene in the Clyde Anchorage but who wrote his account eight years later in *The Greenock Telegraph*. Subsequent reporters have not reviewed primary sources and have simply repeated Tancred's date with the text of his 1947 article seemingly before them. War reporter Horace Oakes wrote in his diary: *"rumours of U-boats at the Cloch on 23rd Nov. Confirmed by newspaper reports on 4th Dec,"* but this need not have referred to the date of the U-boats' arrival but to the date the rumours started or to the timing and duration of the after-events, which lasted well into the early hours.

Having studied Kelly's findings and in the absence of contemporary official documentation which can solidly prove otherwise, I am persuaded that a strong case holds for the Carradale Bay sighting taking place on Wednesday the 22nd and the Tail of the Bank incursion occurring hours later on the same day. The date of the 22nd also provides a logical (but not immutable) timeframe in terms of the feasibility of U-33 executing the post-Tail of the Bank actions attributed to it by history, namely the sinking of the German steamer *Borkum* in the Orkneys on the afternoon of the 23rd. Logic does not amount to proof but it shall be seen in later pages that in the case of the

circumstances surrounding the sinking of the *Borkum* it may well be irrelevant whether U-33 entered the Clyde Anchorage on the 22nd or the 23rd.

The Carradale U-boat, clearly identifiable as U-33 (a task requiring no effort as evidenced in the picture), is reported in *Kintyre at War* to have been spotted by a sharp-eyed pupil observing the activity from a school bus, most likely on Arran. Other reports, including the online reference source *Secret Scotland*,[2] describe the witness

[2] http://www.secretscotland.org.uk/index.php/Secrets/CampbeltownLochBoom

as the local school bus driver. What is not generally disputed among local sources is that an occupant from a school bus reported the incident by telephone to the Navy control room in Greenock at around 15:45.

Publicly available British Admiralty records do refer to a sighting of a submarine in the vicinity but that is the full extent of the official entry. If the Admiralty record is connected with the telephone alert to Greenock 'Control' why, at minimum, does it not go on to note the time and place of the reported sighting off Carradale? What was it about this event that had to be kept so quiet?

Though the Home Fleet, consequent to the sinking of the *Royal Oak* in Scapa Flow, was operating from the Clyde there was a far more prestigious target further upriver. The new Cunard liner RMS *Queen Elizabeth* was undergoing extensive work at John Brown's fitting out basin at Clydebank. News about any preparations for fuelling her for sea and a projected date for her departure from Clydebank (to join the RMS *Queen Mary* in New York before sailing to Australia) would doubtlessly have provided encouragement for the risky business of landing saboteurs.

There were several suspected German sympathisers in the Argyll area. Churchill referred to what he described as a number of Irish traitors in and around Glasgow. He was acutely worried that with telephone communications with Ireland being wholly unrestricted and with the presence of a German Ambassador in Dublin, there was a likelihood of intelligence reports being fed back to Berlin about ships' arrivals.

Churchill, First Lord of the Admiralty at the time U-33 visited Carradale Bay, had every right to be concerned about treacherous activities undertaken by Irish activists in partnership with disaffected Scots. Spy Ernst Weber-Drohl and his unknown confederate(s) were landed off Donegal in early February 1940 by U-37 bearing instructions for Jim O'Donovan, the IRA contact for Abwehr I/II. One does not need to overly exercise the imagination to conclude that O'Donovan's instructions were to harm the British war effort.

Moreover, the fact that U-33, evidently carrying unlisted personnel, came into the Clyde at the same time strongly suggests that covert activities in Scotland were designed to complement corresponding secret undertakings in Ireland masterminded by Admiral Wilhelm Canaris and his ubiquitous Abwehr network.

In executing this key military requirement, it was a relatively simple task to land and take off agents from the Argyllshire coast. The Campbeltown passenger steamer still operated to Wemyss Bay. There was also an indirect run to Glasgow going by steamer to Innellan, then a short bus ride or brisk walk to Dunoon where travellers could cross the Firth of Clyde by steamer passenger services to Craigendoran, Gourock, Greenock and, significantly, right through to the strategically vital Tail of the Bank anchorages.

U-33 left Wilhelmshaven on 29 October 1930 to embark on her second patrol—the laying of mines in the Bristol Channel.

Max Schiller told his family that he had served on U-33 during its second excursion. Crucially, he added that during this occasion the *U-boat travelled all the way up the Firth of Clyde to the mouth of the Clyde Anchorage*. The crew understood that their (suicide) mission was to pass into the Anchorage to sink the *Hood*. Schiller's remarks after his capture about U-33 going beyond The Cumbraes become clearer. In making these comments, is it more likely that Schiller was referring to U-33's second patrol rather than to its third?

During her second patrol, after lying on the seabed for three days while one of her diesels was repaired, U-33 made its way northwest of Ireland, sinking five ships and arrived in the Orkneys on the 23 November where she is recorded as attacking the *Borkum*.

It was noted in Chapter 1 that over the 48-hour period of 20-21 November 1939 U-33 sank five vessels in Irish and Scottish waters, going on to sink the *Borkum* on the 23rd in the Orkneys while heading home to Wilhelmshaven. Why did it take U-33 two days to run from a point southeast of the Inner Hebrides Isle of Tiree where it sank the *Sulby* and the *William Humphries* to the Orkneys?

Donald Kelly contends that U-33 used the forty-eight hours to run into the Firth of Clyde, most likely to pick up an agent. However, there is anecdotal evidence that during the early part of this period U-33 had firstly to carry out other covert undertakings.

One time resident of Carradale, Ken McCoy, has passed on a local story that a U-boat landed a man on the Isle of Islay, a position roughly 60 miles southeast of the site near the Isle of Tiree where U-33 sank the two boats on the morning of 21 November. The story adds that a U-boat also landed men near McArthur's Head on the southeastern corner of Islay to collect fresh water before going on to steal a sheep for good measure!

This would not have been the first occasion when a German submarine was observed at the island of Islay. During the 1914-1918 Great War a U-boat visited Glas Uig on the island's southeast coast. In 1921 the U-boat captain turned up at the White Hart Hotel in Port Ellen before going on to Glas Uig. Many years later Sir John MacTaggart wrote to Islay resident Charles Batchelor and related the curious story told to him by his father. One of the shepherds employed on the family's Ardtalla Estate in 1921 encountered the former U-boat captain walking in the grounds. When challenged, the German told the shepherd that he had made the return visit to Islay to have a look at "his sanctuary."

If, twenty years later, U-33 was the guilty party in undertaking the water collection and sheep stealing activities on Islay (and it is an absolutely fruitless task attempting to identify alternative suspect U-boats within the time period in question), it had more than enough time to carry them out.

U-boat carrying sheep carcasses in WWI

From Islay to Carradale via the southern tip of the Mull of Kintyre is also a journey of approximately 60 miles, no more than 4-5 hours travelling time. This timeframe suggests that between leaving the waters by Isle of Tiree and arriving at Carradale 30 hours later not only did U-33 have time to land spies, collect water and rustle sheep on Islay (maybe 2-3 hours of work at most) but roughly 20 hours spare to have either remained submerged and/or to have pulled into a sheltered bay on Islay or Kintyre to wait things out; even to engage in other unspecified clandestine activities.

In this latter category one must seriously consider the involvement of U-33 in events on the Isle of Bute. It is likely that during this 20-hour timegap a handful of U-33 crewmembers reportedly rowed to the south shore of Bute by rubber dinghy to collect fresh water just as the U-boat had done on the Isle of Islay.

An account of this activity was imparted by a German submariner, by his own statement a former crewmember on U-33, to the cousin of J. Malcolm McMillan, resident of Port Ballantyne, Isle of Bute. McMillan's relative had been commissioned by the Clyde Coastguard during 1950-1952 to recover U-boat wrecks in the British Zone of Germany. He was based in Bad Salzuflen in North Rhine-Westphalia.

In 1950 the (regretfully unnamed) U-33 sailor told the Scot that he had been a member of the Isle of Bute shore detail and described the area where the dinghy had pulled ashore. During a period of subsequent shore leave back home in Scotland the cousin checked the man's description of the area and found it to be accurate in every detail.

J. Malcolm McMillan recounts, too, that at around the time mentioned (November 1939) he was on Home Guard duty at Ettrick Bay on the west side of the Isle of Bute. During his night watch a submarine came in close to the shore. McMillan's guard leader telephoned HQ to make enquiries and was told that there were no Allied subs in that area. Immediately, the guard leader had his men spread out in three locations around the bay with instructions to await the anticipated arrival of the U-boat crewmen coming ashore. His orders were to open fire as soon as the first man stepped from the dinghy onto the sand. However, before daylight the U-boat departed without having made any landing that the Home Guard men could observe. McMillan's verdict is that the U-boat lookouts saw the guards in hiding and decided against a landing at that position on the island.

In an interview with *The Greenock Telegraph* in July 1946 Admiral Sir James S.G. Fraser, Naval-Officer-in-Chief Bagatelle, rebutted a persistent local rumour that a patrol ship had spotted a U-boat somewhere off Bute. He claimed that what had actually been observed was a "shadow caused by a river searchlight." Fraser's denial did not dampen public speculation, which expanded to include a story that prisoners from the U-boat had been seen in Rothesay, the island's principal town.

The position of the alleged sighting off Bute was not confirmed. Bute is approximately fifteen miles long and its southeastern coastline runs parallel with the The Cumbraes. Max Schiller said that U-33 got at least as far as this point. As we shall see, a significant number of local firth citizens believed, too, that a U-boat reached The Cumbraes and beyond.

If there is any truth to the rumour about captured prisoners on the Isle of Bute it throws a different complexion upon the circumstances of the arrival of a U-boat on the west side of the island and its separate fresh water collection task to the south as described to J. Malcolm McMillan's cousin.

It seems barely conceivable that the descriptions of the west shore and south shore events on the Isle of Bute refer to visits by U-33 during two separate patrols. A logical sequence of events would have seen U-33 making its water detail visit to the south side of the island on the morning of the 22 November after departing from its nightlong stop at Ettrick Bay. The approximate 140-mile trip to the Isle of Bute from the Isle of Tiree where U-33 sank the *William Humphries* at 08:30 on the

21st would have taken roughly 12 hours. By that time night had fallen and Ettrick Bay beckoned.

This timetable—a visit to Isle of Bute's west shore followed by another to its south shore—concurs with Max Schiller's comment about U-33 "lying off Largs all day." McMillan makes it clear that the U-boat was not observed landing men prior to setting off from Ettrick Bay before sunrise. Similarly, the ex-U-33 submariner telling the story to McMillan's cousin made no mention of any members of the southern Bute fresh water detail having been apprehended.

Neither account precludes the possibility that during the November 1939 visit to the Isle of Bute U-33 landed operatives, an act not witnessed by the Home Guard. This would have been a calculated enterprise with an ever-present risk of capture, which may have been precisely the outcome judging by the buzz of subsequent rumour and Fraser's denials.

Taking all the facts together, the capturing of enemy sailors and/or spies could clearly have taken place. The colourful cocktail of activities described by observers—landing men, collecting water, rustling sheep—begins to resemble more and more U-33's standard practice, certainly during the latter stages of its second excursion.

Why von Dresky then chose to park U-33 by Largs for several hours is not known but bearing in mind the remarkable train of events about to unfold one cannot rule out that he was awaiting radio instructions—either from German Naval High Command and/or from British sources.

Donald Kelly suggests that considering the relative ease by which people could get to and from places even in these early days of the war, it may be imagined that a person to be picked up by U-33 at Carradale would have firstly travelled freely and easily from a key population centre such as Glasgow.

In this scenario the agent would have taken the train to Wemyss Bay, hopped onto the passenger steamer *Dalradia* to Carradale where on Tuesday 21 November he obtained easily available overnight accommodation. The following afternoon U-33 would have picked up the agent in an unobtrusive spot.

The only difficulty in this conjecture is that David Hendry's researches (including those he undertook in personal interviews with Max Schiller before his death in 2002) have revealed that local Kintyre fishermen reported seeing U-33 *landing* men at Carradale, not picking them up. No matter, the corollary train of events equally holds true.

In line with the fishermen's observations, a person or persons would have disembarked from U-33. They would have secured a berth in a Carradale guesthouse, boarded the *Dalradia* for Wemyss Bay the next available crossing day and then made their way to the place on the mainland where they were to carry out their covert duties.

The "Carradale" U-boat seems to have gone about its business with impunity. On Sunday 19 November the clocks had changed back to Greenwich Mean Time. This ensured that there was at least a good hour of daylight left for the U-boat to launch a dinghy and land people into Torrisdale Bay, a mile south of Carradale.

Equally, the U-boat, having dropped off its agents (and unseen by the fishermen) would have had ample time to pick up a person or persons from the shore for the return trip back to the sub before darkness fell.

The U-boat then headed north up Kilbrannon Sound off the west coast of Arran and then travelled east and then north to Garroch Head, Isle of Bute, where it lay in waiting for the inward-bound Irish boat, the *Royal Ulsterman*.

It then followed her upriver towards the A/S boom at the mouth of the Clyde Anchorage between Dunoon and the Cloch Lighthouse.

In this chapter we have seen a clearly emerging picture in which U-33 makes full use of a two-day period while making its recorded attacks on enemy ships. During these 48 hours U-33 is reported to have landed men in separate, remote locations on western Scottish soil before going on to undertake what could so easily have turned out to be a suicidally foolhardy operation inside the heavily defended Clyde Anchorage.

The following pages track U-33's course through the Firth of Clyde upon that moonlit night in November 1939 as it prepared to enact that bold mission.

Aerial photo of Greenock taken 2 October 1939 by a German spy
plane at 18,500 feet. Outlined at **A** are the Torpedo factory at top end
of Gourock Bay and the Harland and Wolff shipyards at **B** by Albert
Harbour (the latter having closed many years previously anyway).
Neither of the two sites were bombed during the war. Also
highlighted is the Flak battery station at Larkfield east of Gourock.

Chapter SIX

The Tail of the Bank Event

I find my zenith doth depend upon
A most auspicious star.

In the July 1946 interview with *The Greenock Telegraph* Admiral Fraser took the opportunity to scotch the persistent rumours that "flooded the district on several occasions during the war." He stated unequivocally that, irrespective of the reasons why heavy depth charging had been heard on the river late in 1939, it was *not* because of the presence of a U-boat inside the boom. It is noteworthy that Fraser did not deny that heavy depth charging had taken place nor did he explain why it had been necessary.

Horace Oakes wrote in his diary: "*strong rumours of submarine (U-boat) sunk at Cloch.*" (Mr Oakes' invaluable diary testimony about the secret burial ceremony on 16 February 1940 for the deceased from U-33 will be reviewed in depth in later pages.)

While Fraser was an arch debunker of the Tail of the Bank event, Captain W.C. Tancred, OBE RN, Extended Defence Officer at Greenock during the war, writing in *The Greenock Telegraph* on 3 July 1947, gave what he described as an "accurate and first-hand account of what really happened." Tancred wanted to "put the record straight," dating the event as 23 November. As discussed earlier, this date should be treated with healthy scepticism.

Captain Tancred wanted to "cut a long story short" about the account of a U-boat that was seen to pass upstream through the Dunoon gap in the Greenock defence boom. He confirmed the truth of reports that exploding depth charges had rattled the town windows and that the water had been churned up by the passage of naval vessels speeding about the anchorage. That much, at least, was fact.

Tancred recalled, too, the following morning's windfall when local residents were able to pick up basketfuls of dead fish along the shore at Ashton near Gourock. He then went into detail.

On the night in question the inhabitants of Dunoon, Greenock and the upper reaches of the firth were physically shaken by a series of heavy explosions near the boom, which had been laid across the firth a month or so before. Rumours gathered apace that a German U-boat had penetrated the anchorage defences and, moreover, had been sunk.

As Extended Defence Officer for the Clyde, Tancred was responsible to the Flag Officer for the safety of the waters from Gourock to The Cumbraes. His official quarters had not been prepared and so, in the interim, Tancred was undertaking his duties from Greenock with frequent visits to the Cloch where his watchkeepers kept vigil with the gunners.

The battleship HMS *Royal Oak* had recently been torpedoed by a U-boat that had penetrated the boom in Scapa Bay. Consequently, the Home Fleet battleships, cruisers and destroyers sought safe anchorage at the Tail of the Bank. It was considered likely that the Germans would attempt to make a foray into the Clyde and all possible precautions were in place to avoid a repeat of the Scapa Flow disaster.

Darkness fell quickly and completely. The moon was almost full.[1] Tancred visited the Cloch at sunset to see his patrols stationed. These consisted of two A/S trawlers, three small armed yachts and two motor A/S boats. He ordered one of the latter to remain in the gap near Dunoon Pier. Presently, Tancred's private telephone rang with the message he dreaded—an enemy submarine had entered the boom.

The Dunoon A/S boat signalled that she had seen the submarine pass through the gap. Amplifying reports stated that a man had been seen on the conning tower and, later, that the U-boat had dived.

Five depth charges (three at first, then two more) were dropped and the Commanding Officer of the A/S boat reported that a long, black object had surfaced. In the meantime, Tancred had ordered other boats into the vicinity of the submarine contact and signalled a report to the Commander-in-Chief Home Fleet on HMS *Nelson* and to the Flag Officer, Clyde, in Glasgow.

The C-in-C ordered four destroyers standing by to proceed into the area and these were followed by ships' motorboats, each carrying two depth charges.

The relatively narrow Cloch-Gourock-Dunoon stretch of water was no place for destroyers to manoeuvre at high speed, especially at night without navigation lights and with the extra complication of numerous ships anchored in that part of the river. To add to the difficulties, a convoy of 6-8 merchant ships was gathering just inside the boom

---

[1] The moon was three-quarters full (waxing gibbous) with the full moon taking place on Sunday 26 November.

waiting for Tancred to open the gate and let them out. Everyone was getting in each other's way and the hunting ships, fitted with asdic, were continually obtaining false contacts on each other and on other ships and submerged parts of the boom.

Depth charges were dropped in profusion in the boom area and nearby parts of the firth, shaking houses in the towns on both sides of the river.

Gradually, the turmoil subsided with relatively few accidents reported. An A/S trawler, *Stonehaven*, managed to ram a ship in the convoy and two other merchant ships had a slight collision. An "F" Class destroyer, *Foxhound*, ran aground on the beach near the Cloch Ferry, her bow almost blocking the main road.

Tancred interviewed the Commanding Officer of the motor launch that had started the "picnic." He and his crew were adamant that they had seen a submarine and had sunk or badly damaged it.

Opinion among local people was that the sub was depth charged but had not been found and had *passed by unscathed.*

An oil slick was seen on the surface about one mile north of Cloch Lighthouse (well inside the Tail of the Bank) and when investigated by divers they found only the wreck of an old sugar boat.

Tancred declared that he was sceptical and passed off the incident as having been the sighting of a whale or a shoal of large fish, to which the local response was to remind officialdom that whales are rarely seen in the Clyde and, in any case, only swim in the firth's upper reaches in the summer months. (It also ignores that fact that whales do not sport conning towers from which Kriegsmarine boatmen scanning their "quarter" of the sea may be observed by shore-based onlookers.)

However, the overall tenor of Tancred's account suggests that he had more sympathy with the locals' description of events than he was allowed to acknowledge in his public statements.

Thirty-two years later *The Greenock Telegraph* returned once more to the story. In its 26 May 1979 edition Lieutenant Alan D. Roche RN, having contacted the NHB for help in gathering information, contributed an article about the Tail of the Bank event and the sinking of U-33. The *Telegraph* thanked Roche for "*this first official account of the U-boat which, as far as is known, managed to get nearer the Clyde Anchorage than any other.*"

Obviously the account was not the first go into detail about the incident. That honour had fallen to Captain Tancred writing in the same journal in 1947. Roche's text was simply a regurgitation of Tancred's earlier report; nothing new was added and it perpetuated the notion that the event took place on 23 November. In fact, either Roche or the NHB must have been in possession of the earlier article whose text was repeated virtually verbatim throughout the "new" account. Roche concluded, as before, that the sighting had been a whale or some other big fish.

Similarly, the second half of the article, about U-33, added no more to the story than was already on official record.

In 2002 the *Telegraph* returned for a fourth outing on the topic. This time the trigger was their publication of an article of mine about U-33. Part of the article had addressed the rumour that Otto Rahn, German language specialist and Grail explorer for Himmler's SS, had been on U-33. A subsequent item of correspondence, submitted shortly afterwards to the *Telegraph* by local history group, Magic Torch, lent keen support to the possibility of a Rahn connection with U-33 by drawing upon the remarkable historical links in Renfrewshire with the Holy Grail, the Arthurian legends and the Knights Templar.

On 3 October *The Greenock Telegraph* reported the story of former Port Glasgow Provost (Chief Magistrate) Andrew Wilson. Wilson had popped into the *Telegraph*'s offices to show reporters his diary for the start of the war and the night of the supposed U-boat incident in November 1939. Wilson's visit had been prompted by the publication of the U-33 / Rahn article.

Wilson was a member of the Royal Engineers team manning a searchlight at the Cloch boom at the time of the Tail of the Bank incident. In his account Wilson merely says the event took place in November (no date specified, which seems odd if he had his diary with him). Wilson and his fellow soldiers were billeted in huts on the gunsite manned by the Port Glasgow coastal battery. Their night duties were to 'expose' the lights when ordered, usually two or three times nightly.

The lights at the Cloch were a sentry beam, which lit up the area alongside the shipping boom on the downriver side of the anchorage and the No 2 emplacement beam, which carried out a wide search downriver from the sentry beam. Wilson and another sapper, Joe Reid, were on duty at the No 1 emplacement, the sentry beam.

They received the alarm to expose the light and a message that this was the real thing. A cargo ship (Irish transport ship *Royal Ulsterman*) going through the boom gate had reported that a U-boat was following in her wake heading towards the Tail of the Bank.

As the boom gate closed several torpedo boats and corvettes raced to the boom and then, turning themselves upriver, spread a pattern of depth charges around the suspect area. This went on for some time with no sign of a U-boat.

In the manoeuvres one of the corvettes ran bow first onto a slipway at a point where Western Ferries now operates.

Wilson told *The Greenock Telegraph* that while a U-boat may have followed the cargo ship part of the way up the firth there was nothing to suggest one had actually penetrated the boom. He served at the Cloch for some time after the alert but, to his knowledge, no debris from a German submarine ever came ashore.

In 2001 the NHB sought to add provenance to its continuing U-boat-up-to-and-through-the-boom denial by referring to entries made by Dönitz in 1939 in his War Diary.

Dönitz refers to radio intelligence reports, which had provided information on the whereabouts of the British battlefleet. The reports stated that the fast battleships, battle cruisers and several anti-aircraft carriers were not in home waters but were on special operations (chasing pocket battleships or escorting particularly valuable convoys from Canada) and that the major part of the remaining battleships used, in the main, the Firth of Clyde as anchorage.

Admiral Dönitz wrote that the question of U-boat action in the Clyde against the English fleet had been considered. In Chapter 2 we noted the Admiral's Diary remarks that U-boats could not attack the anchorages themselves, seeing that the ships were lying in a long, fairly narrow strip of water, the only access to which was closed by a boom. The assessment went on to conclude that it would be quite possible for U-boats to penetrate into the wider part of the firth, as far as the boom, to a shallow position exactly on the main route where mines could be laid.

The NHB used this diary entry to indicate that Dönitz had no intention of sending a U-boat through the Cloch-Dunoon boom and that this intention was unlikely to have changed between November 1939 and February 1940.

Borrowing Dönitz's diary themes so ardently to underpin its rebuttal of the reported Tail of the Bank U-boat incursion is a disingenuous move for the NHB. Dönitz makes his diary entries in the understandable context of why U-boats could not realistically make a direct *attack* on the Clyde Anchorage. However, one could not reasonably use the Admiral's Diary remarks as reason to rule out the deployment of a U-boat in the upper reaches of the Clyde for intelligence purposes should the need have been sufficiently compelling.

The presence of cutting gear mounted on U-33's bow illustrates, too, the German Navy's pragmatic attitude towards deploying derring-do measures when stakes were sufficiently high. Moreover, Dönitz's Diary records would have had little currency in the event that U-33 was ordered to enter the Clyde Anchorage by a superior, Hitler being the prime suspect considering Schiller's remarks about the Führer's overruling of the Rear Admiral's wishes in February 1940.

Any U-boat intelligence activities masterminded by the Abwehr could count, too, on Bureau chief Admiral Wilhelm Canaris' sympathetic hand on the tiller. Canaris was a submarine commander in WWI and in 1918 was Admiral-Staff-Officer in the Staff of the Leader of Submarines Mediterranean (the German Mediterranean Submarine Flotilla) at Pula.

We have already noted U-37's disembarking of Abwehr II spy Ernst Weber-Drohl in Donegal two or three days before U-33 entered the Clyde in February 1940. By the time we reach the last page of this present work we will no longer be asking ourselves if U-33 was similarly engaged in covert activity but, taking that as certain fact, asking what was its purpose, for whom and the nature of its outcome.

In August 2001 Donald Kelly wrote to me enclosing a copy of an article titled "*U-boats about Kintyre*" that he had written for the *Campbeltown Courier & Advertiser* (21 January 2000). His carefully researched piece gives details of a number of U-boat events in the waters around the Kintyre Peninsula in both World Wars. Subsequently, Kelly returned to the incident in his excellent *Kintyre at War* omnibus. His account of events at the Tail of the Bank, drawn from a careful analysis of local sources, begins where the Carradale U-boat story leaves off.

Kelly describes how at 20:55 on 22 November the HM A/S *Boat 4* was lying alongside Dunoon Pier watching the gap at the end of the boom. The wind had died off and the firth was bathed in the light of a three-quarter moon. He then draws on Gavin Crawford's story. Crawford, a volunteer on a log recovery launch working between Bowling and Glasgow, had stopped to light a cigarette on his way to work. Casually, he watched the inward-bound *Royal Ulsterman* make her way through the boom. To Crawford's astonishment he saw in the moonlight the shadow of a submarine conning tower travelling in the wake of the Irish transporter.

When sappers Wilson and Reid responded to the order "Expose light" Crawford immediately saw in the glare of the searchlight the submarine, by now well into the boom. On the other side of the river the crew of *A/S Boat 4* also saw a dark cylindrical shape about a half-mile north inside the boom. They set off to investigate, certain that they were looking at a vanishing submarine conning tower. Rapidly closing, they began dropping two groups of three depth charges. After the fifth depth charge had exploded a long black cigar-shaped object broke to the surface and, momentarily rolling, submerged.

Depth charge explosion

Two more depth charges were dropped and then a ninth into the centre of a large oil slick, which had appeared on the surface. None of the nine depth charges succeeded in forcing the submarine to the surface. The enemy boat appeared to have got away. At 21:45, joined by another launch, *A/S Boat 4* began a search northwards and into Holy Loch. Nothing was found.

At 22:07 the C-in-C put out a signal: "Send all available ships to search." *Firedrake, Forester,* and *Foxhound* (the latter, together with *Faulknor*, being responsible for sinking the first U-boat of the war, U-39, off St. Kilda on 14 September 1939), two trawlers (the *Lunar* and one other) and a number of small picket-boats quickly responded.

At the same time, the *Kingfisher* and *Widgeon* searched the firth below the A/S boom and south of the Toward Lighthouse minefield.

By now the boom gate had been closed, the net's flotation buoys having fouled earlier in the winter gale.

Inside the boom eight more depth charges were dropped on mystery contacts without result. The *Foxhound* managed to run herself aground in the darkness at McInroy's Point, today a ferry terminal.

Quickly tipped-off about 'the U-boat,' John McLaughlan, Greenock correspondent of *The Glasgow Evening News*, telephoned his Glasgow Office which, in turn, phoned photographer Jimmy Morrison and reporter Angus Shaw. Together they tried to get corroboration of the U-boat story but without success. When dawn broke they were arrested as "spies" at the Cloch Lighthouse and frogmarched down the road until interrogation had established their credentials.

Taking these various reports together, there is no consensus for the time when the U-boat passed through the boom. Kelly's in-depth researches indicate that the U-boat entered the boom at 20:55. Roche and Tancred refer to events taking place at approximately 22:00, which could refer either to the sighting of the U-boat at the boom or, equally, to the prolonged series of events that unfolded afterwards. Crawford mentions a time of 22:30 while Wilson simply speaks about night activities.

Commander Bill Jones, Staff of Flag Officer Scotland, Northern England and Northern Ireland, replied to an email enquiry of mine in June 2002. He made a point about how personal memories can be misleading, evidencing his remark by referring to an "eyewitness who said he interrupted a football match to watch the action," pointing out that as the first attack on U-33 began at 03:40 on a February morning this was difficult to believe!

One may readily agree that such a claim would be sheer nonsense. But if the eyewitness was referring to a soccer game that he interrupted at 15:45 on the afternoon of Wednesday 22 November (sunset occurring that day at around 16:35) to observe a U-boat landing men at Carradale Bay then our local football fan's claim becomes highly plausible. It also suggests that other players and spectators would have paused to watch extraordinary events unfold offshore and yet, bafflingly, there is no record of Greenock Control visibly responding to public alerts.

In contrast to the Carradale Bay U-boat event there are no independent eyewitness accounts that identify U-33 as the submarine that passed through the boom later that evening. Up to this point in our investigations we have identified U-33 as the transgressor by a process of logic that places the submarine, observed by Kintyre fishermen landing men at Carradale on the afternoon of the 22 November, in exactly the right place and time to be the only realistic contender for the U-boat which, hours later, entered the boom and gained passage into the Clyde Anchorage.

Our deductive reasoning is corroborated, too, by Max Schiller's confirmation to his family that U-33 travelled up to the Clyde Anchorage during its second patrol.

But can this initial, tentative identification of U-33 be supported by a detailed analysis of its known operational programme of activities? Does Kelly's revised dating of the Tail of the Bank event assist the task of bringing forward compelling documented evidence to confirm that U-33 was in the right place at the right time?

Not only does Kelly's research, supported by numerous corroborative accounts from citizens on Arran, Kintyre, Bute and elsewhere, help us move our efforts forward, but it leads to the unarguable conclusion that U-33 was the *only* submarine that could have passed and returned through the boom that bright November night.

Chapter SEVEN

In the wake of U-33

Ye elves of hills, brooks, standing lakes and groves,
And ye that on the sands with printless foot
Do chase the ebbing Neptune and do fly him
When he comes back.

According to the UBootwaffe online database the only other German submarine in addition to U-33 sailing in Scottish waters in late November was U-35, which left Wilhelmshaven on 18 November for operations against British naval forces near the Orkneys.

It was around 23 November that U-35 moved north from the Pentland Firth to Fair Isle Passage. While on patrol on 28 November, sixty miles east of the Shetland Islands, U-35 was attacked by British Destroyers HMS *Icarus*, HMS *Kingston* and HMS *Kashmir*. U-35's entire crew of 43 survived. We noted in Chapter 1 the story of the arrival in Greenock on 1 December of U-35's captured crewmen. It follows, therefore, that U-35 could not have been the submarine that entered the Firth of Clyde on the 22nd and was observed landing men off Carradale Bay.

However, based on Kelly's carefully researched date of Wednesday 22 November for the Tail of the Bank event we have seen that there is another, unarguable contender, as evidenced by German war records, for the suspect submarine—U-33.

By this date U-33 had concluded its operations in the Bristol Channel and was en route for the Orkneys where on the 23rd U-33 sank the steam freighter SS *Borkum* at 14:30.

What is the possibility, based on a detailed evaluation of the known and documented trail of its operational activities, that U-33 could have been the Tail of the Bank culprit? Where was U-33 on the 22nd?

It is a remarkably simple task to track U-33's movements between 20th and 23rd November based on its schedule of activities officially recorded as undertaken during this period.

U-33 timeline—the known:

1. 20 November 1939—U-33 was ranging back and forth between northwest and northeast of Tory Island, a few miles off the Donegal coast of Northern Ireland, where in a short burst of hyper-aggressive activity it sank the steam trawlers *Thomas Hankins* at 13:30, *Delphine* at 15:00 and *Sea Sweeper* at 16:05.

   Glasgow man Alistair Alexander who helped me with the early research into U-33 made contact with an Icelandic researcher with expertise in WWII marine chart positions. Alexander passed to me the expert's comment that on 20 November 1939 U-33 was at coordinates 55:05N 07:45W, a position reported by the Icelander as being in the Orkneys. This information was given as an opportunity to help clarify my deepening suspicions that it had been U-33, which had been responsible for the Tail of the Bank incident.

   I was ready to agree with expert authority but before doing so I naturally checked the coordinates for myself. I quickly saw that they corresponded with a position by Tory Island, the exact same place off the coast of Northern Ireland where all the official U-boat records confirm the whereabouts of U-33 on the 20th when it sank the three boats. I have no idea why the position associated with the expert's coordinates was wide of the mark by 300 miles.

2. 21 November—U-33 sank two more fishing trawlers 75 miles northwest of Rathlin Island: the *Sulby* at around 07:30 and the *William Humphries* at 08:20. Rathlin Island is just off the northeast coast of Northern Ireland. The area 75 miles northwest of Rathlin Island approximately coincides with a position a few miles southeast of the Island of Tiree in the Inner Hebrides;

3. 2 days later on the 23rd U-33 attacked the German freighter *Borkum* in the Orkneys.

U-33 timeline—a scenario based on careful analysis of the facts:

1. The zig-zag distance from the area of the sinking of the two boats by the Island of Tiree to the Clyde Anchorage via the Isle of Islay, the Isle of Bute, Carradale Bay and then to the boom via Garroch Head is approximately 200 miles. A type VII U-boat could attain a top speed on the surface of 17.9 knots. Underwater its maximum speed was 8 knots, average of 4 knots. As Max Schiller remarked to David Hendry, wherever possible a boat would travel on the surface in waters considered relatively 'safe.' Erring on the side of conservatism, a trip of 200 miles would have taken U-33 no more than 14-16 hours.

2. If U-33 had departed the position where it sank the *William Humphries* more or less immediately (by 08:30 on the 21st) it could have reached Ettrick Bay on the west of Isle of Bute by 23:00 that evening, 22 hours before the Tail of the Bank U-boat breach.

It is evident by this calculation that in this scenario U-33 had ample *opportunity* to: i) land a man upon the Isle of Islay later on the 21st; ii) park up in Ettrick Bay during the night of 21st-22nd (observed by the local Home Guard); iii) fetch fresh water from the southern end of the Isle of Bute and then "rest off Largs all day" on the 22nd; iv) land men at Carradale Bay during the mid-afternoon; and v) travel to the Cloch-Dunoon boom via Garroch Head, Isle of Bute, by 20:55 that evening.

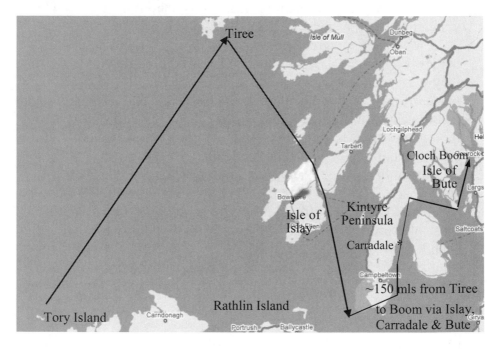

3. While U-33 lay off Largs it was observed by local residents. The wife of a local chemist thought she saw a periscope in the firth. She telephoned the police but no action was taken, an absence of official response identical to Greenock Control ignoring the school bus passenger's telephone warning about U-33 landing men at Carradale Bay later that afternoon.

Why were these critical alerts not acted upon? Who in high authority may have had compelling reasons to allow U-33 to carry out its business unhindered by British counter activity? And what might have been the nature of those remarkable (and seemingly treasonous) imperatives?

4. The approximate distance from the upper reaches of the Firth of Clyde to the position in the Orkneys where the *Borkum* was sunk (59.33N 03.57W) is approximately 310 miles. Donald Kelly plots the distance from Carradale, via "the Minches" (the Inner Scottish Sea), to the northwest Orkneys attack position as 270 miles. The distance from the boom to Carradale is approximately 40 miles.

Is it feasible that U-33 could have set out from the Firth of Clyde at around 21:00 on the night of 22 November to arrive in time the following day to torpedo and shell the *Borkum* at 14:30? To succeed, U-33 would have had to travel at an average speed of around 16 knots over a 17-hour period (1 nautical mile is 1.15 times a statute mile). I asked the experts.

The renowned Sharkhunters U-boat global network confirmed that provided sea conditions were fairly calm (and we have heard that the earlier gale had died down), a Type VII would have had no difficulty sustaining a speed in this higher range of its capabilities, mainly on the surface, for a voyage of that duration.

In the opinion of expert members of the online ubootwaffe forum the outcome would have depended upon a combination of prevailing weather conditions, wind speed and direction, seas, currents and, last but not least, the endurance of the two MAN Diesel engines running at that relatively high speed. Increased fuel consumption over that distance would have been of no concern but perhaps would have become an issue over a greater distance. Their advice indicates that the 16 knots speed could have been comfortably maintained provided that conditions, in the round, were reasonably fair.

Taking these points of expert opinion together, it is clear that the trip was operationally feasible within the appropriate timeframe.

5. Ergo, U-33 had the opportunity within its recorded itinerary of activities to make a detour to pass through the Cloch-Dunoon boom on the night of the 22 November 1939, via Carradale Bay and other stops earlier that day, and then go on to sink the *Borkum* in the Orkneys on the afternoon of the 23rd.

Did U-33 pass through the boom in November 1939? Max Schiller said it did but no one in official circles can or will say. However, in these pages it has been demonstrated that U-33 had the opportunity to do so. Moreover, the case for opportunity advances to one of certainty due to the swell of local reports, including the identification of U-33 by

Kintyre fishermen as the sub that landed men off Carradale Bay on the afternoon of the 22nd.

Up to now the counter-argument against a U-boat travelling up the Firth of Clyde at this time was that there were no German submarines within the vicinity. That is simply not the case. U-33 had made its way from its operations in the Bristol Channel and still had work to do. Despatching the *Thomas Hankins, Delphine, Sea Sweeper, Sulby* and *William Humphries* was a part of that. Nevertheless, those kills took place in relatively close proximity to the entrance of the Firth of Clyde. Von Dresky and his team could have made the trip up to the boom and have been back in the open sea for its passage to the Orkneys in time to fire upon its sixth victim, the *Borkum*, on the 23rd. The scenario fits precisely.

It is interesting that Donald Kelly has offered an alternative date of 24 November for the sinking of the *Borkum*. He arrives at this date from a reading of Kenneth Wynn's U-boat histories in which Wynn records the content of the F.d.U./BdU's War Log for 16-30 November 1939, PG30252. It has this entry for 24 November: *"U-33 reported that she had sunk a Q-ship.*[1] *Radio Intelligence reports received late this afternoon indicate that an enemy unit may have been sunk in connection with the operation of our surface forces, begun on the 22nd, north of the line Shetlands-Norway..."*

The overall weight of opinion, as put forward in all of the principle U-boat records and databases, is that U-33's sinking of the *Borkum* took place on the 23rd and so it is more likely (but not absolutely certain) that the War Log, although dated the 24th, is referring to an incident that occurred the day before. If, indeed, U-33 did sink the *Borkum* on the 24th then, of course, any remaining doubt as to whether it had the time to get to the Orkneys to make its attack at 14:30 falls away; it would have had more than enough time.

We read in Chapter 6 that west of Scotland history group Magic Torch threw its weight of support behind the supposition that U-33 had been carrying German language specialist Otto Rahn, a remarkable assertion seeing that Rahn is reported as having died by his own hand in March 1939. In my book I challenged the suicide story, arguing that Rahn cheated his SS protagonists and made his way to a place of safety.

Over the years there have been whispers that Rahn's destiny and the fate of U-33 were linked. While that theory continues to resonate,

---

[1] A Q-ship was a ruse dating from WWI where merchant steamers, trading schooners etc had deckhouses with 'drop-down walls' concealing weapons and bits of artillery. The disguise was dropped when the enemy was in range and an attack could be made.

seeking resolution in some shape or form, there remains the cubic centimetre of suspicion that Otto Rahn was a passenger on U-33.

In his August 2002 letter Donald Kelly describes, tongue in cheek, "a nice little film plot" in which a German agent, Rahn, is landed by U-boat at Carradale in November 1939. He carries out his orders and the sub, returning in February 1940, picks him up. All things considered, perhaps there is a germ of intuitive truth in Kelly's "fictional" scenario.

Before moving on let us reflect upon a tantalising question. We have noted the record from history that U-33 was the destroyer of SS *Borkum*. In all certainty it is entirely coincidental that U-35 appears to have been in the immediate neighbourhood of U-33's assault on the freighter. Perhaps it even witnessed U-33 despatch the *Borkum*.

At some time during these events on the 23rd might U-33 and U-35 have rendezvoused for a particular reason, other than to exchange pleasantries, before U-35 moved 60 miles northeast to Fair Isle Passage later that day? If they did link up might one have passed to the other cargo of some kind—a person or persons even?

Moreover, there is an altogether more sinister strand to this story that should be considered. According to Max Schiller, Hitler personally ordered U-33 to make its mission to Scotland for undisclosed reasons. Add to this remarkable statement the details of new facts about U-33— the revelation that it made two excursions to the Firth of Clyde within a twelve week period; its landing of men on Scottish soil; the appearance of high-ranking Nazi officials among the deceased—and we see an emerging picture in which U-33 undertakes above-top-secret missions under the Führer's personal directions, the circumstances and knowledge of which have to be safeguarded at all costs.

There is no official evidence on either the British or German side to confirm or deny these conjectures about German agents being in the area at the time but, if true, might one assume that the agent(s) returned safely to Germany and put to good use what had been learned? The facts about immaculately dressed men lying among the deceased from U-33 militate against making such an assumption but it was the case that the German authorities were given to re-writing patrol records as it suited them politically. We have studied compelling evidence including eyewitness accounts, which indicate that U-33 did come inside the Clyde to land and/or pick up agents.

This circumstance demanded that every effort be made to shroud U-33's secret agenda. Consequently, one of the elements of disinformation could have included a concocted story that U-33 was responsible for the attack upon the *Borkum* in the Orkneys on 23 November, thereby firmly disassociating U-33 from involvement in murky events in and around the Firth of Clyde in the same time period.

The attack could also have been a fortuitous coincidence subsequently seized upon by the Nazi leadership to shield U-33 from a connection with the Carradale and Tail of the Bank events. It may even have been planned in advance. Either way, in these alternative versions of events, U-33 would not in fact unleash the torpedoes and shells upon the *Borkum* but would nevertheless go down in history as its destroyer.

If the Tail of the Bank incursion did actually take place on Thursday 23 November (although Donald Kelly's case for the 22nd is sound) another attack that same day attributed to U-33 three hundred and twenty miles away in the Orkneys would have provided a perfect alibi.

The fact stands that U-35 was in the vicinity of the attack upon the *Borkum*. If serendipity put U-35 in the right place and time to make the assault then what a gift for Hitler. It would have been the simplest task to ascribe the action to U-33 with history none the wiser. After all, if the records of 5,000 German naval personnel could go missing (as we shall read in Chapter 11) then the laws of statistics would have inevitably resulted in the misreporting of attacks by U-boats. In later pages we shall return to the disinformation theme.

The BdU war log for 26 November 1939, the date that U-33 returned to her home port of Wilhelmshaven, records that: "*U-33 entered port; she laid mines according to plan and encountered little patrol. There was no traffic in her operations area off the North Channel and in the end she attacked fishing trawlers before she left in order not to come home empty-handed. The C.O.'s report shows that this was a well-conducted patrol and it is not the fault of the boat that she had so little success.*"

The war log's downbeat tone reflects U-33's failure to sink a high profile ship such as the *Hood*. Nothing in it, of course, gives any hint about the subterfuge and high excitement that had characterised U-33's covert activities in between sinking the "small fry" fishing boats, an obvious omission in keeping with the clear necessity to conceal the true nature of the submarine's operational programme during its 2nd patrol.

Up to this point we have reviewed the remarkable events of 22 November 1939 largely from the official perspective, not an information channel through which one can generally expect to build an unvarnished picture in areas of political or military sensitivity. That task falls to the citizens of the Firth of Clyde and it is to them we must now turn. These men and women know and remember far too much to be dismissed wanly by the Establishment as misty-headed pensioners.

Max Schiller in 2000 remarking that
U-33's was a "suicide mission."

Chapter EIGHT

"We, the people..."

How many goodly creatures are there here!
How beauteous mankind is! O brave new world,
That has such people in't!

Senior citizens of the firth with healthy memories want to fire a broadside across the bows of the "brass bounders at the Admiralty." They are indignant that even today British naval authorities throw cold water upon their ardent belief that a U-boat came and went through the boom in late 1939. As we shall see, there are those who believe that the sub did not get away scot-free and that its remains lie on the bottom of the Firth of Clyde. Beginning in 2001 men and women told me their stories.

After seeing my letter in the *Largs and Millport Weekly News* Mr Robert Brown contacted his older brother who had a story to tell. He recalled that the Captain of one of the passenger ships (the *Royal Ulsterman*), which sailed daily between Belfast and Glasgow suspected that his ship was being shadowed to get through the boom. He alerted the naval authorities using an Aldis lamp and they took the relevant action. Mr Brown's brother did not describe the "relevant action" but certainly it refers to the night-long period of heavy depth charging that took place immediately after the sighting of the enemy vessel.

Iain Crosbie told me of the knowledge possessed by his friend Sandy Young, a Scottish submarine researcher who was given a story about U-33. It was Young's account which revealed for the first time that when the crew was being picked up from the water by HMS *Gleaner* on 12 February 1940 Lieutenant-Commander Price was anxious to leave the scene as quickly as possible in case another U-boat was nearby. In fact, Price was so desperately keen to move off that at first he was willing to leave a man in the water.

The story as told to Young was that a British crewman, seeing the man in difficulty, jumped over the side and rescued the German sailor (the eighteen-year old Max Schiller) who in gratitude gave him his dog tag as a keepsake. Subsequently, because of the missing dog tag Schiller's name was added to the list of lost crew members on the gravestone in Greenock cemetery. This was only discovered when Schiller visited the site years later and saw his name on the headstone. Bemused, Schiller wondered how the mistake could have come about and then he remembered the incident with his identification disc.

The man who had rescued Schiller from the water was an unidentified fisherman from *Bohemian Girl*. When he was pulled aboard the trawler Schiller was handed a mug of tea but because his fingers were icy cold he dropped it, the mug shattering into pieces. Schiller expected an angry response, even a blow but instead was kindly offered a fresh cup. In gratitude, Schiller gave his rescuer his dog tag as a memento of the occasion.

Afraid that he would be caught in possession of the dog tag and accused by the Navy of looting from the deceased, the trawlerman handed in the identity disc when *Bohemian Girl* arrived in Greenock. Subsequently, Schiller's dog tag was placed on a table in a pile, along with other identification tags taken from genuinely deceased U-33 crewmen.

And so it was that the name of Max Schiller, the eighteen-year old from the village of Holleben near Halle in eastern Germany, was inadvertantly included in the overall list of deceased and "buried" in Greenock Cemetery, his name added to a gravemarker along with boatmates Kunick, Kampert and Steiner.

Having established that the Greenock Cemetery records confused Schiller's name with that of Karl-Heinz Peters (a mistake corrected by the Commonwealth War Graves Commission at the time of the re-interment of the bodies in Cannock in 1962), one can picture a scenario in which Peters' dog tag was not found on his body and in the confusion Schiller's tag, dumped in a heap with others, was carelessly associated with Peters' body.

By Young's account, not only did Price dally in beginning the U-33 rescue operation in case there was another U-boat in the vicinity but that once he had got on with it he evidently became so nervous about a neighbouring threat that he was prepared to curtail the operation and leave freezing cold men to their fate. By all accounts, Price was privy to intelligence that made him very anxious. As we have noted, one can reasonably surmise that Price was aware of a U-boat's successful breach of the defence boom at the Cloch the previous November and was worried that the Germans were up to their same tricks.

Former Royal Naval operative Mr M.S. of Greenock (name

withheld by request) gave me a number of interesting facts by letter and by phone, including texts of emails exchanged with an equally knowledgeable ex-Royal Navy pal after the publication in 2002 of a feature on my U-33 project in *The Greenock Telegraph*. One of the emails to M.S. from his associate notes that: "you should also be aware that there were at (at least) two U-boats...I understand one is on the bottom near Millport and the other (U-33) off Arran."

M.S. revealed that another friend had told him a remarkable story. A woman who had served in the W.R.V.S.[1] in the war confided to her niece that in 1940 she had observed the bodies from U-33 laid out in Greenock Town Hall. She added the startling revelation that some were decked out in "immaculate" uniforms and wore swastika (Nazi Party membership) gold rings. All this seemed very peculiar for normal Kriegsmarine submariners and those examining the bodies at the time thought that this group might have been "*some kind of special unit.*"

M.S. also hinted that he was in the intelligence services in WWII and if there is truth to his claim then his ex-minesweeper pal may have been similarly associated. This would help explain their remarks' intimate sense of "knowing," which could admittedly be Walter Mitty fantasy but equally may be an indication of prior insight about the presence of "at least" two U-boats in the Clyde, one of which carried members of a "special unit." We will read in the next few pages of the belief held by some Dunoon locals that a German midget submarine was trapped and sunk in Holy Loch.

"Immaculate" is a curious adjective to apply to uniforms worn by men pulled from the sea. One hesitates to doubt the sincerity of eye witness descriptions. If, indeed, the men attired in such fashion did look as if they had just been dressed by their valets had they been pulled from the water at all? Bearing in mind the activities described in the Carradale U-boat incident, might these men have been killed on shore during the process of being landed, after being landed or while being picked up from the shore by U-33?

M.S. also referred to "boom defences at The Cumbraes." One might have dismissed his remarks as inaccurate recall unless one was to find subsequently information that corroborates reports of defence installations in the region other than the boom at Cloch-Dunoon. This supporting information has now been brought to light.

Mr Thomas Moody has recalled life in Wemyss Bay in WWII. He describes a row of four houses in the village that residents called 'The Parsonage.' During the war one of the houses opposite the village social

---

[1] Women's Royal Voluntary Service

club was made into a listening post to detect any U-boats trying to sneak up the Clyde under a ship bringing in supplies. There was a device of some kind that stretched across the Clyde under the sea to a site near Innellan on Argyll and Bute. The sailors that manned the station used to sit wearing headphones, listening. It would be of little surprise if one were to discover that the listening device was installed after the November 1939 U-boat event—the Royal Navy was not going to be caught out a second time.

Mr Robert Brown also told of going down to the Cloch lighthouse as a nine-year old and finding dead herring strewn on the beach. He also found German sailors' hats at the same place. In answer to my questions about his find, Mr Brown said he had assumed they were German hats because of the circumstance in which he found them: that is, he saw them immediately after the rumpus at the boom when all hell broke loose and he put two and two together. Brown said that the hats had trailing ribbons at the back. He also confirmed that for "unknown reasons no one would admit (even off-the-record) that a U-boat had been sunk at the Defence Boom at this time."

An anonymous correspondent told how he and his pals used to gather whelks on the shore at Portencross village in West Kilbride. He described the occasion when they came upon Kriegsmarine ribboned hats and other personal items washed up in tidal pools among the rocks. They took some of the items to the police station and told them where to find more. Two weeks later the finders went back to Portencross to find it barricaded and guarded by armed naval sentries—strictly off-limits.

Experts have confirmed that Kriegsmarine submariners *did* wear caps with trailing ribbons. By 1940 it would have been unusual for crewmembers to wear them on the cramped and uncomfortable boats in action, reserving them more for time on shore. But the event that is being depicted so vividly by these local reports refers to the Tail of the Bank incursion of November 1939, an earlier period in the war when it was evidently more customary for boatmen to wear their hats while on duty (such as depicted in the top photo reproduced on page 34).

The finding of the hats poses challenging questions. By all accounts the U-boat that came and went though the boom during that first autumn of the war was not captured, the presumption being that it got away. But did it get clean away? A surprising number of Scots believe that the upper reaches of the Firth of Clyde, far from Arran, are home to a sunken U-boat. Were there casualties?

A body was washed up in Gourock open air swimming pool after the November event. Had someone died as a consequence of the Tail of the Bank explosions? Were they German? Were there other enemy decedents whose recovery was not reported? If any of the hats belonged to submariners who were killed by the heavy and prolonged depth charging (local citizens said the sounds of explosions carried on through the night) then how did they get into the Clyde? They could only have fallen there if crewmembers standing outside of the boat during the attacks had either sustained injuries, lost their hats while losing their footing or for reasons hard to fathom dumped their hats from the fleeing sub.

Or did they belong to occupants of one or more additional enemy vessels?

How does one go about reconciling a scenario in which a U-boat, having crash-dived inside the boom after being spotted and fleeing for its life from a small armada of hostile British vessels climbs to the surface with men swarming up into the conning tower? U-boats travelled faster on the surface than when submerged. Possibly, but unlikely, having been spotted and with destroyers giving chase the only strategy for the U-boat to get away with any chance of success was to flee upon the waves while four lookout men manned their quadrants in the conning tower and gave moment-by-moment reports to the Captain.

Patti Duncan was a small girl in 1940. Her parents had many friends in the navy, from the higher ranks down to lieutenants. Many of those high-ranking friends regularly visited their house and talked freely, paying no heed to the little girl and believing, wrongly, that she would not understand or listen to their conversations. But Patti was attentive. In these candid (and careless) discussions between her parents and senior naval officers she definitely heard that a German submarine *did* breach the boom.

Greenock resident Mrs Elizabeth Redwanz told of her brother, Alex Munro, who worked in WWII for the Greenock Central Co-operative Undertaking Department. Mr Munro was sent down to the defence boom across the Clyde to perform undertaking duties. He returned upset about the young German sailors who had drowned there.

By this account we learn for the first time from eyewitness testimony that there *were* German personnel killed near the boom. These deaths can only have taken place in November 1939 during the Tail of the Bank event. Seeing that Greenock Cemetery records do not list burial details for any German deceased between the boom event and 16 February 1940, one must ask what became of these bodies. This question assumes a far greater urgency when one reflects upon Mr

McDougall's remarks below that decedents from a U-boat sunk near the boom *were* buried at Greenock.

There is a strong argument that one of the bodies seen by Munro was one "Sikh Hidtalla," buried unceremoniously at Greenock on 3 January 1940. The suspicious circumstances surrounding this person are explored fully in later chapters.

Seeking to make contact with ex-sapper, Douglas McKillop, who had posted his story in the *Largs and Milport Weekly News* in August 1985, I wrote to more than twenty persons named McKillop in Ayrshire and Renfrewshire. I received a reply from Mrs T. Edwards McKillop who confirmed that when a little girl her father talked to her "about the U-boat that came up to the Cloch Lighthouse."

Mr McDougall of Dunoon told me that he wrote to Scottish author Peter Moir in April 1991, explaining that during WWII a German U-boat was sunk either inside the defence boom between Dunoon and the Cloch Lighthouse or in the Inverkip-Lunderston Bay area. McDougall was a schoolboy in the early forties and remembers the night the U-boat came up the Clyde. He believes it was sunk somewhere between the Gantocks Hotel (at Dunoon) and the Cloch Lighthouse on the Renfrewshire side. He said that some of the crew were buried in Greenock cemetery. When McDougall wrote his letter he believed that the wreck was still where it was sunk. In Chapter 9 we will make a thorough review of the many stories about wrecks in the Clyde.

McDougall told me that a few days before writing to Moir he had spoken to an old schoolfriend who also remembered the night and had agreed with McDougall that the sub was sunk inside the boom.

Yet another old pal, formerly of Innellan on Argyll, said the sub was sunk over by Lunderston Bay a little south of the Gantocks Hotel and he, too, mentioned the German sailors' caps, which were washed ashore around Innellan the following day.

In his letter to me McDougall posed the question as to whether there had been *two* U-boats that came up the Clyde (U-33 and a second sub) or whether, in fact, the two subs were actually one and the same vessel, the "official" account of U-33's sinking at Arran having been fabricated to hide the embarrassment of the Government being forced to admit that a U-boat had penetrated the boom defences.

McDougall's latter theory is in line with Alistair Alexander's thinking back in 2002. Alexander advanced the notion that if U-33 did get further up the firth than Arran in February 1940 (in the early days of our research there was no evidence of a prior Tail of the Bank event) the Royal Navy had it lifted and brought to its eventual resting place off

Pladda to preserve for propaganda purposes the Clyde's aura of impregnability.

McDougall concluded by saying that despite the passing of time and the tricks the mind can play with advancing years he remembered the night it happened quite clearly. He said he could distinctly remember seeing the searchlights on the water over by the Cloch and hearing the explosions (the depth charges attacking the U-boat) out on the firth. Everybody thought it was an air raid at first but the sirens never sounded. Next day the story was all over Dunoon—that a U-boat had got through the boom and had been sunk inside. McDougall wrote to Moir because the author was seeking details on whether the U-boat had been sunk inside or outside the boom and if that boat and U-33 were one and the same or separate vessels.

We now know that what McDougall and his fellow Scots heard that night was the sustained, frantic activity in the night hours of 22-23 November 1939 after a moonlit U-boat had been seen passing through the boom .

Without a doubt, retired Enginering Draughtsman Mr William McGee, one-time resident of Gourock, is the most determined among his Inverclyde neighbours to set the record straight. In his first letter to me he proclaimed: *"If some brass-bounder at the Admiralty Historical Branch gives their official view of U-33's position as being off Pladda, then he is talking bunkum!"* Hear, hear!

In February 1940 McGee lived with his parents and younger sister in Shore Street, Gourock, paralleling the L.M.S. railway lines. He was just under ten years of age at the time but his memories are still vivid because he has a retentive memory and, in his own words, they were stirring times. He recalls the night of the event. Residents were awakened by the sound of rumbling explosions, which went on for about ten minutes before fading out. Accompanying the rumblings were faint but palpable vibrations and tremours.

During those early months of the war the family had not experienced bomb explosions. Excited, they sat up discussing them until their father told them to go back to sleep.

The following morning McGee and his sister were leaving for school. They had barely cleared the first flight of stairs descending from their bedroom when they noticed a change in the partition wall separating the upper and lower flights. The large stone blocks of the wall had been visibly moved out of alignment. This was a wall that their father kept regularly whitewashed and the successive coats of paint had built up to a considerable depth. The displacement of the stones had caused a great profusion of whitewash flakes from between the blocks to litter the steps.

Seeing that the McGee's Shore Street house was a shade further than two miles from the Cloch Lighthouse as the crow flies, tremours strong enough to cause the damage in their stairwell had to have come from a very powerful source.

Gourock, being a steamer railhead, had become a highly essential seaport for war supplies and personnel. Naturally in such an environment rumours abounded. After this incident at the Cloch Boom, the McGees heard that a U-boat had come up the Clyde on the surface flying the White Ensign. She was challenged by the defence boat inside the boom and answered the challenge successfully. But the second part of the challenge was not properly answered whereupon the U-boat hauled down the ensign, went about quickly and steamed at full speed down the Clyde, remarkably escaping without sustaining attack damage.

By this time the guardboat, unable to desert her station, had radioed for assistance to Albert Harbour in Greenock. Several A/S vessels including HMS *Gleaner* went after the U-boat, which had presumably dived thus slowing her escape. She was then depth charged and sunk.

McGee's family heard later that a U-boat was sunk to the west of the Gantocks, a reef off Dunoon. A week or so later they learned that a body was washed up into the Gourock lido, a swimming pool open to the sea that floods with the rising tides.

The Greenock Cemetery Register does record the interment of people with foreign names in addition to those from U-33 in the early months of the war. The first is the forementioned Sikh Hidtalla, buried in January 1940, whom I consider for compelling reasons to be a fatal casualty of the tumultuous attack on U-33 in November 1939. Additionally, in July 1940 two unnamed Italians and two unnamed Germans were buried in lair (grave) 3C with those from U-33. It is possible that the body from Gourock pool was any one of these five. However, if it was one of the Germans or Italians how does one account for an interval of eight months between the Tail of the Bank event (which McGee is clearly describing) and the July 1940 burials?

One must also question why these latter persons were unnamed. It stretches credulity that four foreigners found dead in the vicinity during wartime should be anonymous as if none between them had been carrying even the least item that would have helped identify them. Is it not more likely that the authorities took the decision not to publish the names of the deceased because of precisely who they were and/or because of the singular circumstances in which they were found? Might they have been enemy agents carrying no papers? If that was the case then the time required to undertake secret investigations and perhaps carry out post-mortems would account for a delay in committing them to burial.

McGee's father was a passenger guard with the L.M.S. railway and came in daily contact with the pier staff and the Caledonian Steam Packet Co. staff, all of whom he knew well. They heard things that became common knowledge and then shared them with McGee senior. Also, the Royal Navy had taken over the pier clocktower and had converted it into a signalling station for the warport. Naval staff let things slip out that they should have kept to themselves

The wife of Mr McGee corroborated her husband's account. She told her husband about an uncle who owned a small boarding house and shop in Dunoon at the northern end of the Cloch-Gantocks defence boom. She was visiting with her family and remembers that night. Her uncle had a dairy business in the building and she recalls hearing milk bottles crashing to the floor during the night and feeling the earth tremours. The location of this house was closer to the north end of the boom defence than her husband's parents' house at the south end.

McGee is absolutely adamant that a U-boat pulled off a spectacular ruse and passed briefly through the boom before the deception was recognised. The mighty ground-shocks that subsequently rent the freezing cold night air and shook houses were not a figment of the imaginations of hundreds of citizens living on both sides of the water. He is convinced that "we are still having the truth kept from us by the authorities" and that "for a long time 'they' have treated us like mushrooms."

The account of the U-boat flying the White Ensign is a critical factor in our analysis of events. We examine it in more detail in Chapter 19. For now we may note that it was clumsily handled, to a degree of ineptitude that it poses the question as to whether the submarine was acting more to draw attention and, thus, allow another enemy action to proceed unobserved than to make a clean passage into the Clyde Anchorage.

At the time of the sinking everyone in Gourock was party to the same rumours—that the U-boat was sunk to to the west of the Gantocks where, McGee insists, it lies today north of Great Cumbrae close to Skelmorlie-Wemyss Bay, the same wreck area indicated by Max Schiller in his report to the Scottish press reproduced below.

Archie McKenzie, an old pal of Mr McGee, provided me with his own account of the event. Fifteen-year old McKenzie was at the local Picture House at the time of the incident. Details were flashed on the cinema screen—all Navy personnel were to return to their ships. Destroyers and frigates were tied up at action stations alongside Gourock Pier about five minutes from the boom at the Cloch Lighthouse. That night there was gunfire until the early hours and the booming sounds of depth charges. In the morning dead fish were all over the beach.

IN a graveyard at Carrick Cross, in Staffordshire, there are several memorials to German sailors who died in the last war. One of them is to the men of U-33, who perished in the Firth of Clyde in 1940.

The name Max Schiller is on that memorial.

Yet Max Schiller is alive and well, living in Cummertrees, near Annan, Dumfries-shire!

On February 11, 1940, U-33 nosed its way silently into the Clyde on a mine-laying expedition.

A chemist's wife was sure she saw a periscope out in the river.

She telephoned Greenock police, but no action seems to have been taken.

The U-boat lay off Largs all that day. At night she surfaced and moved slowly upstream.

Max Schiller, only 18, was one of the look-outs.

A British destroyer passed close to the U-boat but didn't spot them.

LATER that night the alarm bells shrilled.

Another destroyer had finally spotted them.

Up went the flares as the British ship attacked. Depth charges straddled the sub as she plunged to the bottom of the Clyde, bounced and settled in the mud.

A second set of charges exploded around them.

An attempt to blow the sub's tanks and get her to the surface failed.

When a third pattern of charges blasted the U-boat, Capt. Von. Tresky ordered scuttle charges to be fixed.

A last desperate attempt to raise the sub seemed to work.

The crew breathed a sigh of relief as she broke the surface. But the worst was still to come.

The scuttle charges exploded. The order came to abandon ship. The sub's crew plunged into the freezing rough waters of the Clyde.

It was 3½ hours before Max was picked up by a trawler. Others weren't so fortunate. From a crew of 43 officers and men, only 28 survived.

Astonished

MAX spent the war as a P.O.W. in Canada. Then he came back to Scotland after the war and worked on a farm in Dumfries-shire.

He met and married Jessie, the farmer's daughter.

When he heard about a memorial to the U-33 at Greenock, he went to see it and was astonished to see his name carved in deep letters in the granite.

When the memorial was transferred to Carrick Cross, Max's name was still there.

Max was the only survivor of U-33 to stay in Britain.

He believes now the mistake is being put right, and that his name will be removed from the memorial.

U-33? It seems the sub is still at the bottom of the Clyde. Its last known position was somewhere between Wemyss Bay and Skelmorlie.

Max Schiller's 1960s interview with the Scottish *Sunday Post* in which he says that the wreck of U-33 lies "between Wemyss Bay and Skelmorlie"

Mr McKenzie believes the U-boat wreck to be off Skelmorlie, precisely the location which Max Schiller named as the resting place of U-33 in his newspaper interview. In a subsequent letter McKenzie referred to the local story that a U-boat had tried to enter the Clyde at the rear of a ship when the boom was opened to allow in a vessel.

A local man wrote to me in August 2008, declining to give his name because he did not want *The Greenock Telegraph* to "pester" him. During the war he had a small boat licence to fish in the Clyde outside the boom for a distance of four hundred yards from the shore. The rowing boat was in use by him at the time. He also used it after school and on Saturdays. While out on the river a patrol boat from the boom steamed at full speed downriver. When about three-quarters of a mile off Innellan Pier the boat dropped several depth charges into the deep channel. The explosives caused shockwaves, which struck his wooden boat like a hammer blow. Many times afterwards over a period of two years there was activity by naval divers at that same spot.

In a telephone conversation with M.S. in January 2008 he added to his previous accounts, stating not for the first time that I was "right on track" and "very near the mark." He said that the U-boat came through the boom underneath a tanker. Speaking once again as if with insider knowledge M.S. claimed that U-33 was a decoy—that there were two U-boats abroad on that night. One was U-33. Another was a specialised U-boat whose wreck is said to be in the Cloch-Dunoon-Cumbraes triangle.

M.S.' decoy remark gives substance to William McGee's about the U-boat flying the White Ensign, a clumsy deception which was highly unlikely to succeed—perhaps precisely the outcome sought.

His remark also helps to clarify the paradoxical comment from the old plumber about fatalities occurring during the Tail of the Bank event when all indications confirm that the culprit, U-33, got away. If there was a specialised U-boat in the locality that night then it is possible that it was destroyed and its occupants killed. Might these have been Sikh Hidtalla and/or the four unnamed Germans and Italians?

Perhaps light is shed on this scenario from the account by Mrs Leslie Couperwhite, former librarian at Greenock. She tells of the occasion in June 2001 when a German submarine naval officer came into the library.

He told Mrs Couperwhite that he was seeking details of his uncle who had died in a U-boat sinking in the Firth of Clyde in WWII. He emphasised that he was *not* referring to the U-boat that had sunk off Arran but to one, he claimed, that was sunk by the British in the upper reaches of the Firth of Clyde.

In support of the German's remarkable statement Mrs Couperwhite quotes her mother-in-law's recollections that when living in Millport on the Isle of Cumbrae during the war she saw a U-boat travelling along the Firth of Clyde. Its existence was "one of the war's worst kept secrets."

In 2003-2004 U-boat message boards were abuzz with fellow Scots swapping stories about the U-boat Cloch-Dunoon boom story from the early 1940s. Each remembered being told by a parent, relative or neighbour a little bit about it and they were seeking through the message boards to get a fuller picture.

Mr Terry McGonagle posted a story in June 2003 about the "U-boat Lost in Holy Loch." He had worked in Dunoon near the old U.S. Navy Base. Locals told him that a U-boat entered the Loch in WWII, became trapped and was sunk. Some said that the boat was actually a *two-man midget submarine*.

Stan Lockhart wrote about how pupils at Dunoon Grammar School in the early 1940s were alert to rumours circulating about sounds of explosions connected with an attempt by a German submarine to penetrate the A/S boom defence.

"JP" logged his story, *U-boat Captured in Scotland*, in April 2004. His source was a local man who had died four years earlier. The story went that the British Navy deliberately left the boom open for a U-boat while luring it in with the RMS *Queen Mary*. It remained a secret because the U.S.A. would not appreciate their men being used as bait. The submarine was seen on the surface by use of searchlights between the Cloch and Dunoon.

An old friend of JP's father provided supporting information. As a boy he worked in his father's butcher's shop. He remembered the whole town talking about the incident from the night before. The U-boat had been seen on the surface being chased by the Navy. People in the shop said they had seen it.

In 2002 Forrest Angeron confirmed that his father, a trawler skipper prior to joining the Royal Navy in February 1940, was asked to take the trawler *Foss* from Fleetwood to Glasgow where she was wanted for war work. This was around "December 1939." En route to Naismith in Glasgow carrying the trawler's papers, Angeron's father and his crewmates reached Dunoon where they put up the 'G-flag' for the Pilot. Immediately, they were surprised to be approached by two Royal Navy destroyers and challenged about why they were there. Angeron Sr. explained and was then told that on no account was he to leave his anchorage. They were there for two days and only then allowed into port because they had no food on board. In 1978 his father was working the trawler standby for the North Sea Rigs when he came across a newspaper article, possibly *The Glasgow Herald*, referring to this incident. This story also stated that the *Queen Mary* had been used as a decoy and that a German submarine had been trapped in the Clyde.

Graham Turner, too, posted the story of how his father, resident of Dunoon, often used to tell of the day a U-boat was captured in the Clyde near to the boom. Like many other residents he remembered vividly picking up German sailors' hats and other debris from the shoreline. Specifically, the hats were found along the three-mile stretch on the west bay between the Dunoon Castle rocks and the lido at Innellan. Turner Sr. also recalled seeing the *Queen Mary* in the area.

However, neither J.P.'s source, Angeron Sr. nor Turner Sr. could have seen the RMS *Queen Mary* in the Clyde area during the periods they specified. As noted in earlier pages she was berthed in U.S. waters at this time. The decoy theory cannot, therefore, be linked with the *Queen Mary*.

Another champion of the decoy story was a man named Ferguson who was employed in a reserved occupation by the Royal Navy in WWII to drag telegraph poles across the peat bogs above and around the installations opposite Greenock-Gourock. His son Alan picks up the story in his forum post. One night there arose what Alan's father described as "an unholy commotion." Not unusually, convoy vessels were assembling in the pool by the Tail of the Bank along with other (non-convoy related) elements of the Royal Navy. There had been a number of repeated scares that U-boats had attempted to breach the defences and enter the Tail of the Bank. Although these occasions had prompted activity on the river it was "as nothing" compared with the evening about which Ferguson Sr. spoke. The searching and occasional depth charging went on most of the night.

The newspapers made no reference to the event the next day or on any other day. This may not have appeared unusual given the wartime need to safeguard security but apparently it was quite common for there to be reports of successful repulsions of German naval attacks—real or otherwise—and Mr Ferguson was always puzzled that news of such an event should have simply disappeared in this way.

Alan Ferguson commented that if a U-boat had got loose inside the boom in a position and condition to attack it would have been a duck shoot with so many targets hoved to. But subsequent escape would have seemed almost impossible. The only possibility would be to run into and lie low in one of the deepwater lochs that spur out of the Clyde, making a reverse attempt to sail out under a ship once the peril was assumed to have dissipated. (Another possibility for a clean escape, of course, would have been with assistance from the authorities.)

If the decoy theory holds water then what large vessel could have been used to lure a U-boat into the Clyde? Among locals the conclusion drawn and passed down was that an attacker had managed to penetrate under the hull of a large merchantman ship while the boom was dropped to allow it entry. No one appears to have suggested that the lure was one of the great ocean going liners of the day, either the *Queen Mary* or the *Queen Elizabeth*, under which the U-boat sneaked into the boom. We now know that the vessel in question was the *Royal Ulsterman*.

Coming full circle in reviewing our digest of citizens' reports, Isle of Bute man J. Malcolm McMillan wrote to me of his recollection of events in November 1939. He tells of the time an "Irish Ferry" was coming up the Firth of Clyde and noticed a submarine following dead astern. The ferry contacted HQ ashore and was told to continue on up to the gate on the Dunoon side of the boom. McMillan went on to say that somewhere between Innellan and the Cloch Lighthouse destroyers dropped depth charges. He thought that an old fisherman friend might remember where the wreckage of the U-boat is located but, on asking him, was told that he had no knowledge of what had happened to the U-boat. This is not surprising as it is evident from the collected reports that the submarine was able (permitted?) to make its escape.

In fact, the *Queen Elizabeth* was in port at the time the U-boat passed in and out of the boom. The twin-funnelled liner had been stationed in the Clyde shipyards since September 1938. When war broke out she was immediately painted grey. The liner did not leave the river until the end of February 1940.

The Germans, like everyone else, had expected the *Queen Elizabeth* to go to Southampton, the usual peacetime port. On the night that she had been expected to arrive from the Clyde the Germans subjected Southampton Docks to heavy bombing.

To fool everyone about her destination, the *Queen Elizabeth* sailed from the Clyde with a Southampton pilot on board and an official docking plan for berthing there. To further evidence her apparent intentions, cases of furnishings and fittings were openly delivered to Southampton Docks.

To add more weight to the deception, some 500 civilian workers were also signed on to the bogus run to Southampton for which each received a £30 bonus. Those who decided to disembark before the *Queen Elizabeth* left the Clyde were sailed into the middle of the Gareloch and kept there on a tender to wait until the liner was well clear of the Clyde. They were then allowed ashore.

The *Queen Elizabeth* sailed down-river from Clydebank and after a brief stop at the Tail of the Bank set off on 2 March, direct to New York. A fortnight later she left New York and then via Trinidad and Cape Town made her way to Sydney to complete fitting out as a troop carrier.

Theoretically, it is plain that the *Queen Elizabeth* was ready and available in late November 1939 for the ruse to draw a U-boat into the Clyde Anchorage and so one wonders why there were occasional and clearly erroneous reports that the *Queen Mary* was involved.

What have we learned from the mass of reports from local citizens past and present?

We hear very distinctly that there is a belief among these Scots that the authorities then and now are hiding the truth. This duplicity is made all the more condescending by the Establishment's continuing practice of offering versions of history that are clearly fatuous when set alongside the mass of contrary (and inconvenient) reporting from those who saw or heard about the events that took place.

Others have declared their conviction that there is a U-boat (possibly a "special" or midget submarine) lying on the bottom of the Firth of Clyde thirty miles north of the reported resting place of U-33 off the southeast corner of Arran by Pladda. If the British Navy and the MoD are to be believed, and there is no convincing reason to doubt the existence of a wreck (of *something*) off Arran, then the sole conclusion one reaches is that there is more than one U-boat rusting in the firth.

We will examine these local reports, which sit uncomfortably but defiantly alongside historical record in the next chapter.

We have heard, too, about both evidence and indications of German submariners who lost their lives in these incidents—a body washed up in the Gourock open pool, sailors' hats with trailing ribbons seen in diverse locations, a nephew enquiring at Greenock library about a deceased uncle from the U-boat that came up to the boom, and mysterious burials of unnamed foreign nationals after the Cloch boom event.

Many have spoken about other physical signs of engagement with the enemy—the dead fish strewn over the beaches following a night of ferocious depth charging activity, falling whitewash flakes caused by internal walls shaken by depth charge tremours, beach barricades set up by naval security personnel to prohibit local scrutiny, testimony from several sources about a U-boat entering the Clyde Anchorage underneath another vessel and, hard to contradict, the statements from the undertaker, the plumber and the blacksmith, each painting a graphic picture about detailed aspects of the U-boat, including bodies found at the boom, which was in a place that history denies.

Correspondents referred to "repeated scares" that U-boats had attempted to breach the boom defences. Had there been a U-boat excursion into the upper reaches of the Firth of Clyde even earlier than November 1939, perhaps even by U-33 during its first patrol in September en route to or returning home from the Scilly Isles?

Startlingly, we have also learned about another deception—the brazen attempt by a U-boat to pass itself off as a British submarine by hoisting the White Ensign.

The U-boat incursion in November 1939 was not the last occasion on which the Clyde Anchorage was witness to dramatic events. Five months later on 30 April the French vessel *Maillé Brézé* (which can translate as the 'armoured fist') met a terrible fate. I am indebted to Mr William McGee for his account.

The *Maillé Brézé* was a 4-funnelled Vauquelin Class Contre-Torpilleur (anti-torpedo) vessel. It was very "rakish" looking and appeared more fit-for-purpose than the American four-stackers, which came along later in the war. The American ships were poor sea-boats, which were said to roll in wet grass!

Mr McGee was at school in Gourock High School on the afternoon of the massive explosion and his classmates wondered what was happening. Later that day he learned all about it. Evidently, a torpedo was swinging in its strops preparatory to stowage in the magazine. Owing to the wash from a passing vessel, the torpedo swung and before those on *Maillé Brézé* could control the swing it struck a bulkhead and exploded. Retired employees of *The Greenock Telegraph* speak today about hearing the explosion from their infant school classroom.

What McGee could never fathom was that in order for the torpedo to explode, the contact firing pistol must have been in the 'live' position when the torpedo was being moved. This certainly was not the procedure in the Royal Navy but it would seem to have been accepted practice in the F.N.F.L. (Forces Navales Françaises Libres—Free French Naval Forces) during WWII. It could be said that the French armourers, like the rest of the ship's company, were not at their best. After all, they had just been kicked out of their homeland by the 'Boche' and were demoralised by their defeat.

When the *Maillé Brézé* anchored offshore from Gourock pier McGee was actually standing on the pier and so he can be certain of his impressions at the time. He saw that the crew were in "shite order" and when they came ashore in their ship's boats they appeared somewhat wild-eyed and excitable. Having been in a period of relative calm and order aboard ship they wanted to unwind.

And unwind they did. Within hours, in every pub in Gourock from 'Cleat's Bar' to the 'Bungalow' every bottle of wine was sold out, even tonic wines. This did not affect the men of Gourock; they did not drink wine—that was for 'Jessies' (wimps)!

The *Maillé Brézé* before the disaster at Greenock

The *Maillé Brézé* on fire

The matelots came ashore, some of them with sidearms. Later some boys of school-age were spoken to by local police (all two of them) because the boys had been given clips of five bullets for French rifles. The boys played a form of Russian roulette by prising the bullets from their cases, then pouring the propellant powder out of it to form a cone, then lighting the cone with a match. What larks!

When the sailors' shore-leave expired they all straggled back to the Pilot-cutters wharf at the west end of the pier. In the water were five or six large lifeboats and into these tumbled the drunken men. One or two fell from the pier.

The lifeboats were all roped in a line, bows to sterns, and a motor pinnace towed this line of boats out to the transport. The matelots were so very happy singing all the way, which changed when they drew alongside the transport up whose starboard side they had to climb via cargo-nets. This was hilarious as many of them, still singing, fell back into boats accompanied by many "*Sacre Bleus!*"

After the explosion the nursing and surgical staff-members of the Greenock Royal Infirmary were overwhelmed by the large number of French casualties and the dreadful extent of their injuries. McGee was told that help from the Greenock Telephone Exchange was sought. Switchboards were closed down and the female operators streamed down in a body to the Infirmary to help with bandages and bedsheets. No sooner had a casualty been placed in a bed and tucked in than the bedsheets became re-saturated with blood and had to be changed again. These telephonists never received any form of counselling for the trauma they suffered and for which they were so completely unequipped to handle.

Royal Navy and other services personnel were sent to patrol the Clyde shoreline to secure any limbs washed up. These were still being found here and there many hours after the catastrophe.

In 1946 McGee's family had moved upriver to Glasgow where the young man began employment with a Marine Air Conditioning company on a 5-year apprenticeship as an Engineering Draughtsman. The company's programme mandated that the first six weeks of training were spent in Central Stores. One day, working with two ex-Merchant seamen in the stores, McGee and his workmates got to talking about the *Maillé Brézé*.

At that time in 1940 the two men were crewmates aboard a merchant ship anchored '3 cables off the Frenchie'—600 yards. The two of them were off-watch and leaning on the bulwark having a 'smoke-o' when one of the men, Tim, was surprised by a bright flash.

Looking towards the shore, Tim actually *saw* the blast-wave heading towards their ship. He had time to shout to his mate "get down" and they both hit the deck, sheltered by the bulwark, as the next thing was the roar of the explosion. Tim's mate started to get to his feet but Tim pulled him down as "things were falling from the sky." When they got up they saw many launches and pulling-boats on the water making for the *Maillé Brézé* to assist.

McGee was told about the French sailors being given merciful lethal injections. A British naval sailor explained to McGee's father why this was done. Evidently, the blast-wave from the exploding torpedo buckled the fore and aft walls of the alleyways and bulkheads. Hatch-coamings distorted and jammed the escape-hatches, trapping terribly burned sailors below.

On French warships the scuttles (portholes) are of smaller diameter than on British ships. Nine times out of ten if a man can get his head and one arm through a British ship's scuttle he will make it out of the ship. The smaller dimensions on the *Maillé Brézé* almost certainly accounted for the stories heard at the time about the French sailors thrusting their arms through the scuttles to receive a lethal injection of morphine. Other reports state that men beyond saving were also killed by shooting.

The ship was taken to Sandbank for scuttling to save Greenock. The accident killed twenty-seven and wounded forty-seven. The bodies of those buried in Greenock Cemetery (21 bodies went down with the boat) were exhumed in 1949 and transported to France.

In September 1954 the vessel was raised, the largest tidal lift undertaken at that time. The wreck was moved to the Ardmore Bank where the 21 bodies were taken ashore with full naval honours before being returned to France for burial. The remaining munitions were removed from the wreck, which was then taken to Smith and Houston's shipbreaking yard at Port Glasgow for scrapping.

Records indicate that sabotage was suspected but there are no evident reasons why this action might have been taken.

It is little wonder that the Clyde Anchorage, a strategically vital naval centre, which at times held the biggest collection of ships ever assembled anywhere, was witness to dramatic events from the earliest days of the war. Beginning with the Tail of the Bank event, then the sinking of U-33 off Arran and, weeks later, the *Maillé Brézé* disaster we get a clear picture of action, drama and mystery in a location distinguished by its immense naval presence and by its strategic intelligence function as evidenced by the work of Bagatelle HQ in

Greenock masterminding the planning of all wartime Atlantic convoys.

Only twenty-four hours before the Tail of the Bank U-boat breach HMS *Hood* and HMS *Rodney*, together with eight destroyers, had called into the Clyde Anchorage, remaining in harbour for a fortnight until departing on Sunday 3 December.

In addition two German cargo vessels, the *Rheingold* and the *Isar*, were in Greenock on 21 November having been captured in the North Sea. Considering the facts about U-33 accommodating unlisted personnel and its landing of men at Islay and Carradale during this period, can one confidently dismiss the possibility that one or both of the cargo boats were complicit in a Nazi programme of subterfuge and the carrying of agents?

What distinguishes the Firth of Clyde events, the Tail of the Bank incident and the February 1940 U-33 sinking especially, is a strong sense of "things are never what they seem." The incidents are riddled with questions, none of which has been satisfactorily answered at any time in the seventy years that have elapsed. More than this the Establishment's denial policy appears as entrenched today as at any time in the intervening years. Nevertheless, it does not take a blinding flash of inspiration to formulate a connection between the occurrence of incidents of mystery and drama in the Firth of Clyde and the region's importance as a WWII naval intelligence hub.

Without exception all of the individual descriptions in this chapter have been made by Scots in connection with a submarine that, incredibly, passed freely through the boom defences between Dunoon and Gourock. None of them refer to witnessed events in connection with the sinking of U-33 by Arran.

We have reviewed evidence, which argues that the Tail of the Bank incursion took place on 22 November 1939 and not the following day as commonly accepted. Narrators' vivid recollections and dramatic stories passed down to families and friends all focus on an extraordinary occurrence taking place that autumn day in the waters around the Kintrye Peninsula and, hours later, in the Clyde Anchorage.

No citizen has proferred any corroborative evidence to support the opinion mistakenly disseminated to his readership by *Largs and Millport Weekly News* editor John McCreadie that a U-boat passed through the Boom at or around the time that U-33 was attacked by HMS *Gleaner*. News and rumours of the autumn 1939 event were evidently in local circulation quickly and, as we have seen, journalist Horace Oakes wasted no time in recording the details in his diary. The November U-boat sensation had been a momentous event that could not be kept quiet despite officials' best efforts.

Today I am far from certain that U-33 was sunk off the southeast coast of Arran. Stories about the use of heavy lifting gear, Max Schiller's remarks which place the sub in the Wemyss Bay-Skelmorlie area and a whole raft of other conflicting comments from Clyde citizens plant a growing seed of doubt about the true circumstances and whereabouts of U-33's sinking.

Add to this confusion the presence of the "mystery men," a circumstance suggestive of a plan by von Dresky to travel upriver either to land them (just as he had had done off Carradale twelve weeks before) or to pick them up, and the last shreds of certainty simply fall away.

Where one can be more confident is in the fact that the genesis of the mystery of U-33 began in November 1939, a few weeks after commencement of hostilities. At this stage, all the evidence suggests that U-33's clandestine mission and its actions to undertake it—landing of men by Carradale Bay and passing into and out of the Clyde Anchorage boom defences—were connected with a secret agenda ordered by Hitler under a Führer directive, which Admiral Dönitz deplored but was powerless to countermand.

Nevertheless, it is also evident that U-33's February 1940 mission was to be an extension, a progressive next step in a top-secret process, which had little to do with minelaying, sinking the *Hood* or with any other kind of operational activity routinely undertaken by U-boats (although success in these supplementary actions would undoubtedly have been welcomed).

In later chapters we will explore the possibilities of what was at the heart of these extraordinary activities. But firstly we shall examine the diverse reports of wrecks in the Clyde. Which of them might be the hulk of a U-boat, U-33 or other, whose existence for undivulged reasons cannot be acknowledged by officialdom in the twenty-first century, the age that favours public interest, full disclosure and freedom of information?

The *Maillé Brézé* after the explosion

Chapter NINE

Wrecks

Now would I give a thousand furlongs of sea for an
acre of barren ground

The official historical record states that the wreck of U-33 lies at Map Reference 55:21:48.3N 05:01:75.2W, 5 miles South of Pladda, off Arran, in the Firth of Clyde at depth 57 metres.

Subsequent contradictory reports from Firth of Clyde citizens have placed the wreck of a U-boat purportedly sunk in the upper reaches of the Firth of Clyde in varying positions of relative proximity within the area described as the Cloch-Dunoon-Cumbraes triangle.

Four correspondents place it specifically in the area between Inverkip-Lunderston Bay on the Renfrewshire side and the stretch of coast between Dunoon and Innellan Pier, Argyll and Bute; while another four, including Max Schiller, place it in the environs of Skelmorlie-Wemyss Bay. One correspondent alone places the wreck on the bottom near Millport on Great Cumbrae.

Dunoon-Lunderston Bay is 35 miles northeast of Pladda. The Wemyss Bay-Skelmorlie position to the south is 29 miles from that point while Millport, farther south still, is 22 miles distant.

It is obvious that all three positions, although individually separated amongst their grouping by a north-to-south length of 13 miles, are strikingly distant from the southeastern tip of Arran. Either each of the nine correspondents is woefully wrong about their respective beliefs or one can only conclude that there is more than one U-boat sunk in the Firth of Clyde, the majority view holding that the wreck is situated just a few miles south of Dunoon-Greenock.

Official statements about the position of U-33 should be considered in due perspective. In the matter of pinpointing wrecks it is evident from numerous case studies that no one body has a monopoly on accuracy and that positionings can be badly out of true. Take the example of the given position for HMS *Hood*, sunk in the Denmark

Strait in May 1941. The Navy initially pinpointed the wreck of the *Hood* 15 miles from its actual position.

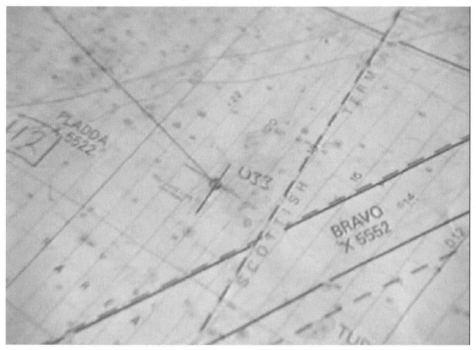

A Royal Naval chart pinpointing the official position of U-33 by Pladda

In a similar case the wreck of U-12, sunk in 1915, was believed for more than ninety years to be resting 15 miles from where it was eventually found by Jim MacLeod and Martin Sinclair in January 2008. The wreckage of the 60m boat, the first ever submarine to have an aeroplane carried on its deck, was found 25 miles from the Berwickshire port of Eyemouth. The site of discovery came as little surprise to the finders because the two divers had homed in on the correct position after tracking down the relevant naval documents.

That being the case, it suggests strongly that the Royal Navy, possessing the necessary tables, charts and maps and the professional skills to use them should be more than capable of matching the efforts of amateurs in pinpointing wrecks accurately. The question therefore arises as to why the Navy gets it wrong and by such a wide margin.

William Magee told of the memoir of a Master Mariner who had suffered the sinking of two ships by torpedo and a third sunk by a German 'oyster' (pressure mine). In his memoir the the master seaman was very dismissive of the Royal Navy's ability to pinpoint an accurate position for any ship as he had absolutely no faith in the "Grey Funnel's" ability to navigate outside a harbour! (The Grey Funnel Line dates back to a time when Britain held the largest mercantile fleet in the world. Each shipping company registered their colours and emblem, which were to be displayed on the funnel so that the owners could be recognised at a distance. The Cunard colours were red, for example. Around the turn of the last century the colour of the ships of the Royal Navy tended increasingly to be all grey, along with the funnel, and so gradually the merchant mariners came to refer to the Navy as the Grey Funnel Line.)

Nevertheless, it is barely credible that the Admiralty would make a mistake of between 22 to 35 miles in the positioning of U-33. If we are to accept the Admiralty's confirmation of U-33's position by Pladda are we to believe, too, that the explosive effect of British depth charges in seawater could cause structural damage 35 miles north-northeast in the Gourock-Cowal areas? No, the notion cannot be seriously entertained. U-33 (or at least a wreck said to be U-33) lies off Arran; if there is another U-boat in the firth its identity is a mystery.

Having established the facts of one remarkable event denied by history—a U-boat, most certainly U-33, passing through the boom in November 1939 then seemingly making a clean escape—there are no logical grounds for denying the possibility that other clandestine submarine activities took place in the Clyde in WWII, which culminated in a vessel, a midget or special sub, being sent to the bottom.

What of other wrecks in Scottish waters? Interestingly, while most of New Zealand and Australia's waters have been surveyed, for example, Scotland's are largely unsurveyed and could therefore be the repository for any number of wartime vessels.

The Scotsman published a story "*Mystery of submarines' watery grave*" on 9 November 2006. Wrecks of two submarines had been discovered off the coast of Orkney in an area where there were no reports of wartime sinkings. A survey team examining the sea floor around the islands discovered the wrecks lying in about 70 metres of water to the east of Sanday Sound. Grainy images of the submarines were captured using the latest three-dimensional sonar device but their identity and nationalities were unknown.

An Orkney diver speculated that the vessels might have been German U-boats sunk during the Second World War. There were reports that the Royal Navy had successfully depth charged U-boats but these activities had taken place several miles away.

The survey team also produced new images of captured German ships that were scuttled by their crews at the end of the First World War.

Rob Spillard, hydrography manager of the Maritime and Coastguard Agency, was reported as saying that the sunken submarines were something of a mystery. The Agency passed the details on to various divers. There was some interest but the 70m depth presented particular challenges.

It is possible that one of the wrecks is that of U-53, which was sunk by depth charges from Destroyer HMS *Gurkha* on 23 February west of the Orkneys. All hands were lost. German records referenced in 2008 confirm that the exact location and depth of the wreck of U-53 were not known.

In a telephone conversation wth M.S. in 2001 he claimed that for many years there was a rusting, skeletal hulk of a submarine lying against the sea wall at Princes Pier about three miles or so from the Dunoon-Cloch area. He also spoke of his conversations with divers in the Greenock area who are of the belief that there is submarine wreckage in the Cloch waters and that it is not British. M.S. added the intriguing comment that there are maps classified for navy use only and that these could show wrecks not marked on maps for public access.

A diving group webforum[1] posted messages about suggestions that an unidentified U-boat lies at depth of approximately 64m to the west

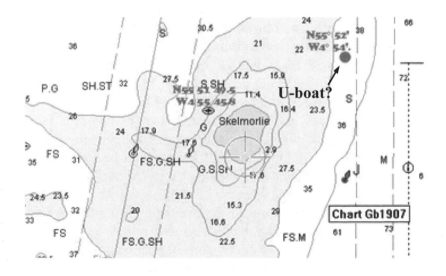

[1] http://www.congeralley.com/forum/showthread.php?t=715&highlight=U-boat

of Skelmorlie, the same location named by Max Schiller for the wreck of U-33. The precise coordinates named by the divers are NS1967, 55 52N 04 54W. Very close to this position are the remains of a paddle steamer, which leads some divers to believe that the supposed wreck of a U-boat and that of the paddle steamer is one and the same object, the submarine story being no more than myth. But there are others who believe otherwise.

Other members of the divers' community advance the beguiling theory that the signal picked up by the Royal Navy when chasing the U-boat fleeing from the Tail of the Bank in November 1939 merged unbeknowingly to the pursuers with the signal reflected by the wreck of the *Princess of Wales*, which sank in 1888. Depth charging was commenced with great vigour but, as we have seen, there is no indication that a fleeing U-boat was captured nor is there any evidence that it was sunk.

The asdic equipment used in 1939 was far less sophisticated than that in use today and may well have indicated to listeners that the submerged object was a submarine. This part of the Clyde is very silty and a sunken object would merge with the seabed very easily. The *Princess of Wales* is inverted, lying hull upwards. Its length is 216 feet, compared with U-33's 210 feet. It is likely that to accurately identify the sixty-year old hull as something other than a submarine would have required levels of technological competence and interpretative skills unavailable in 1939. It is interesting to speculate on whether the high volume of depth charging was undertaken, at least in part, because the sonar evidence identified an object whose length appeared to be exactly the same as the quarry they were chasing, which would indicate that the Royal Navy knew that the sub that had breached the boom was U-33 or, at least, that it was a Type VII U-boat.

Kevin McDonald, keen diver and a former Fleet Street editor posted a message in November 2005.[2] He asked fellow enthusiasts if any of them had dived onto the U-33 and had managed to get exact coordination numbers. McDonald had tried at what he believed was a reliable position but had had no luck. Iain McArthur replied to McDonald's post, saying that there was a rumour that the whole U-boat was lifted soon after her loss to recover her Enigma machine, a statement that echoes Donald Kelly's remark that a heavy lifting operation was mounted to move U-33 from its seabed position.

This raises a number of questions. If the lifting did take place then what is the complete inventory of any items that were retrieved by

---

[2] http://divernet.com/cgi-bin/articles.pl?ac=d&an=&id=4096&sc

investigators and, equally importantly, was the submarine put back in the same place from where it was raised?

Other forum respondents stated that authors Moir and Crawford confirmed that when diving U-33 they had always found it at 55 21.494N 05 01.759W, adding that it is still largely intact despite the depth charging and scuttling charges with its gun still in place. The hull is heavily encrusted with growths, which harbour fine silt that drastically reduces visibility when disturbed.

In January 2003 I sought contact with the Chippenham divers group. Their website stated that the wreck of U-33 rises 5 metres from the seabed and posed the question among its members if the wreck had been Club Dived. I asked if they would confirm that the wreck's position and its elevation above the seabed had been physically verified by its members. I stressed that I was anxious to receive clear indications on these points because U-33 survivor Max Schiller had said that the remains of U-33 lay in fairly shallow water between Wemyss Bay and Skelmorlie, roughly 25 miles northeast of the Pladda position. The Chippenham divers group did not reply, a pity because their expert information would have provided valuable supplementary data in building the wider picture of U-33's final hours and resting place.

Another online forum[3] reports the existence of an old A/S boom at Loch Fyne on the west coast of Argyll and Bute. The respondent had studied Admiralty charts and had noticed a surface-broaching wreck in the area of the boom. He wondered somewhat tongue in cheek if it was a U-boat.

Nevertheless, bearing in mind the story about a two-man midget submarine, which local legend has it was lost and sunk in Holy Loch in WWII after becoming trapped, one should keep an open mind on wreck reports, especially considering that so little of Scotland's waters has been surveyed.

No one can point definitively to the wreck of an enemy WWII submarine in the Firth of Clyde, other than that of U-33. And even the supposed position of the latter has expert divers scratching their heads, positive that they have dived upon the official chart position following the plunge pattern of authorities like Moir and Crawford but finding nothing.

This should not be surprising. Tides and currents are capable of shifting seabed objects a considerable distance from where they descended. Notwithstanding the power of the sea to toss things around, it stretches credibility several fathoms too far to posit that the ebb and

---

[3] http://www.users.zetnet.co.uk:80/mbriscoe/PAGES/Otter.htm

flow of the Clyde has moved U-33 a distance of between 22 and 35 miles (somewhere between Millport and Lunderston Bay) since 1940.

The steadfast opinions of local Scots must be considered respectfully. The belief in the presence of another U-boat in the Clyde is widespread and merely because one has not yet been discovered (or the fruits of secret discovery have not yet been made public) that does not mean the day will not arrive.

From consigning U-boats to the salty bed of the Firth of Clyde let us move to the sorry task of consigning brave submariners to the cold bed of the earth.

A reflective Max Schiller on HMS *Cromer*

Chapter TEN

The Greenock Lairs

There's nothing ill can dwell in such a temple:
If the ill spirit have so fair a house,
Good things will strive to dwell with't.

On Friday 16 February 1940 *Greenock Telegraph* reporter Horace Oakes arose earlier than usual and shortly after dawn walked three miles to Greenock Cemetery. It was a bitterly cold day with ice and snow on the ground. On reaching the cemetery he hid behond some gravestones. Oakes would not have made the freezing cold trip without good cause and it is to be assumed that he had received advance intelligence, not unusual for a local newshound with his ear to the ground that something extraordinary was to take place well away from public gaze.

In an earlier brief diary entry Oakes describes "piquant scenes" on 12 February at James Watt dock when the bodies of "22 German sailors" were landed from "destroyers." (One is curious as to why Oakes specified the number as 22 bodies when it is on record that 23 were buried at Greenock Cemetery. If there were 22 bodies on board the ship where was the 23rd and whose was it?)

Forty-four years later Oakes wrote to Liz Neeson, Producer of Documentaries at Thames Television, London. He had read that Neeson was researching for a documentary about Britain in the Second World War, which would possibly include something about Clydeside. Oakes was keen to persuade Neeson to draw on his detailed local knowledge for the production.

What Oakes said in his letter about U-33 is extremely challenging to the official story. Writing in more detail than in his diary notes, he said that a chance call in February 1940 brought him to a local pier where he saw a British warship at berth. This was a common enough occurrence, he said, but this time he noticed a Nazi flag spread out on deck covering not all but "some" of the bodies.

Local reports state that the bodies from U-33 were subsequently laid out in Greenock Town Hall. Sensationally, some were observed wearing "immaculate" high-ranking uniforms and chunky gold rings adorned with the swastika, denoting Nazi Party membership. It was extremely unusual for Kriegsmarine sailors to be members of the Nazi Party let alone wear smart, pressed uniforms while at sea. Interpreting Oakes' account logically, one may deduce that the deceased so smartly attired were those that had been hidden under the German flag.

Four days later, unseen, the reporter watched as officials turned up at the cemetery in three cars. Their arrival was followed by the enactment of a short ceremony for a mass burial. A swastika flag was partly draped over the coffins of the dead from U-33.

Although the Greenock Cemetery burial ledger lists 23 bodies buried that day, its separate INTERMENTS register lists 7 names for the 15 February and 16 for the 16th. It is therefore unclear how many bodies Horace Oakes saw committed to the earth on that icy Friday morning. Whether it was 16 or 23 decedents for burial the bodies were commemorated with full military honours and then lowered into a communal grave to the volley of rifle fire. The service was conducted on a hill. Staff members with knowledge of the geography in 1940 have confirmed that the hill position is area 3C in the present day cemetery site plan (see Appendix). Since WWII, Greenock Cemetery has been considerably extended.

After the ceremony the officials got into their cars and moved off. Owing to the treacherous conditions, one of the vehicles skidded on the ice and careered off the narrow road leading down from the hill. It came to rest awkwardly in the rough, trapping a man inside. The trapped man noticed the War Reporter watching and shouted for assistance.

Oakes helped the man out of his fix. Because it turned out that the two men knew each other, the official repaid Oakes' selfless action by keeping quiet about the reporter's unauthorised presence and his witnessing of the mass burial.

The journalist tried to get the official Censor (all copy related to the war had to be passed by the Censor) to authorise his story for publication. Two months later the Censor agreed to pass it but insisted that the story should simply tell of the burial of U-boat men "in a west of Scotland cemetery."

In June 2003 the *Scots Magazine* published an article by Brian D. Osborne titled "Mission Impossible." The piece quoted in full the text of the April 1940 story published in *The Times*. It read: *"Early one morning a few weeks ago the bodies of 23 German sailors, which had been recovered from the sea after the destruction of an enemy submarine, were buried with full military honours at a port on the west coast of Scotland. The bodies, which had lain for several days in a local mortuary, were taken in black coffins to the cemetery where a large grave had been prepared. The coffins were covered with a Nazi flag."*

Osborne's article goes on to say that two bodies, including von Dresky, were not recovered. Presumably, he provided this figure from the perspective of one who buys into the official line that of the 42 persons officially listed on U-33, 17 survived and 25 perished. Therefore, if 23 were buried (and few would doubt an account in *The Times*) there cannot have been more than 2 bodies not recovered.

However, we know from numerous sources, including the Naval Historical Branch, that 4 bodies were not recovered- -Braun, von Dresky, Johne and Winterhoff—by which fact the *Scots Magazine*'s number of 23 bodies recovered from the sea plus the 4 not recovered demonstrates by omission that 27 persons died which, added to the 17 survivors, gives a total of 44 persons on U-33, not 42.

It is a fact of no little irony, therefore, that as early as eight weeks after the event the censor and the press, doubtless unwittingly, were confirming that there were two more people buried among the dead from U-33 than recorded. The genie was out of the bottle and all ensuing efforts of officialdom to push it back in and play down the numbers were doomed to fail.

The bodies were buried in "lairs" 931 through 935 two days after the burial plots had been purchased by the Crown on behalf of Rear Admiral B.C. Watson, Flag Officer in Charge Greenock. The Greenock Cemetery burial ledger, recording the purchase dated 14 February 1940, is headed: No. 11,645 H.M. King George VI per Rear Admiral B.C. Watson. Strictly speaking, a lair refers either to a plot of ground purchased for burial or to a grave. Usually, a lair is dug out for burial but occasionally they remain unused.

In 2002 Greenock Cemetery personnel were kind enough to make a copy of the relevant burial ledger, which in a remarks column states that the bodies were exhumed in October 1962 at the request of the Commonwealth War Graves Commission (CWGC). The comments refer to a letter of 30 October from the CWGC and an accompanying list. The CWGC letter, signed on behalf of its Regional Director, confirms that the German War Grave Commission had exhumed the burials annotated on the list and that the corresponding 7 graves (lairs) should be deleted from the "Agreement signed in December 1947 by the (Greenock) Deputy Town Clerk."

Why would it have been deemed necessary for an agreement to be

The gravemarkers at Greenock Cemetery for the deceased from U-33

drawn up between Greenock and the CWGC nearly eight years after the dead from U-33 had been buried? What is its form and content? What might have taken place that warranted the drawing up of an agreement? Did the agreement give authority for activity of some description to proceed or did it "sign off" an action that had already taken place?

The 1962 exhumation list (reproduced in the Appendix) comprises 27 entries and their respective grave locations: lairs CCC-931A through 935C. Five of the exhumed are listed as "Unknown" under column titled Name. The date of death for 23 entries, including 1 unknown, is 12 February 1940.

From this, one can conclude with certainty that this latter unknown is, in fact, a person named as "Klinger" in the records. The dates of death for the other 4 unknowns (lair CCC-931A) are not given and therefore it is likely that these are the 2 unnamed Italians and 2 unnamed Germans who were buried in Greenock Cemetery in lair 931 on 5 July 1940.

One can only speculate as to why officials robbed Klinger of his name in the exhumation list. It cannot have been because he did not exist. Klinger's name is unequivocally stated in two separate Greenock

Gravemarker showing incorrectly Schiller's name

interment records as being among the 23 buried decedents from U-33 on 16 February 1940. One might ask what top level confidences had to be maintained such that when the CWGC reported the exhumation of Klinger's body in October 1962 it was considered essential to assign it anonymity.

Or maybe the body was exhumed on an earlier date. Could Klinger simply be *commemorated* at Cannock, having been disinterred many years previously? This would provide an explanation for the seeming dichotomy between a Sharkhunters spokesman's baffling remark that Klinger and another unlisted U-33 occupant named "Albrecht" were exhumed "shortly after burial" and the written record that they are counted among the dead at Cannock.

After all, if one did not know any better a first reading of the Cannock records indicates that Braun, von Dresky, Johne and Winterhoff are buried at the German Cemetery. It is only because historical record makes plain that the four men were not recovered from the sea does one arrive at the only logical explanation, which is that these deceased are merely commemorated. This fact was confirmed by the NHB.

In the same way, just because the exhumation transfer records between Greenock and Cannock in 1962 list both Klinger and Albrecht this does not necessarily mean that their bodies *were* among those disinterred in the October of that year.

The actual date of exhumation of the pair may tie in with the circumstances that were the foundation for the Agreement signed in December 1947 by the Greenock Deputy Town Clerk and deleted in October 1962. This would explain how the CWGC staff can reply to my letter stating that they are unaware of any exhumations (from Cannock) before October 1962 because it is entirely feasible that the Staffordshire cemetery never received these two bodies in the first instance. In this scenario the bodies were exhumed in Greenock in or before 1947 and then shipped to Germany or wherever.

Or maybe there is another explanation. Greenock Cemetery records show that Messieurs Charles Haryog, Modiste Handy, Gaston Bolard, Marcel Albrand, Jean Coucherat and Falicien Alleon were buried 3 May 1940 and exhumed 12 October 1949. Surprisingly, the General Register Office (GRO) for Scotland is only able to produce death certification entries for the latter four (see Appendix for burial and death certification records). The usual residence of each is noted as the *Maillé Brézé*. The record of deaths (in the West District of Greenock, Renfrew) goes on to state that Bolard and Alleon died in Greenock Royal Infirmary on 30 April, Albrand died in the hospital the following day and Coucherat died there on the 2nd.

Haryog and Handy evoke special interest. Haryog does not appear to be a name in any language. In the 2009 records of French surnames listed by Départements there is not one person with this name living in France. (There are 171 named Handy.)

Curiously, like 'Sikh Hidtalla,' Haryog does have an Asian connection, HarYog being the 7th of 11 handsigns in Indian palmistry (the 11th being the Swastika). Ironically, it is the sign of Neptune's trident, indicating a person of a kindly, often religious disposition.

Was the same idiosyncratic, tongue-in-cheek personality that one suspects manufactured the name "Hidtalla" once again at play, wedding a palmistry sign for the god of the sea to a Hand(y), indicating that the real story should be read between the 'lines'?

The absence of official death records for the pair is unexplained. It is to be assumed (perhaps unwisely) that they were fellow boatmates from the *Maillé Brézé*, buried and exhumed together on the same dates, but if the GRO can provide death registrations for four men recovered from the French anti-torpedo boat why not for all six?

Can it truly be no more than coincidence that the reported dates of interment for the elusive Haryog and Handy occur "shortly after burial" of the deceased from U-33, a boat among whose dead were two unlisted people about whom there is a profound mystery? May there be a direct connection between Haryog and Handy and Albrecht and Klinger?

Commemoration to the Free French at Greenock

For readers moved to investigate further, the lack of death particulars for French decedents does not end here. Eight bodies also categorized in Greenock Cemetery records as 'French' were disinterred between August and November 1948. Extracts from the records list the exhumed as:

Name	Interred	Exhumed	Description
Lucien Vengues	3/9/1940	17/10/1948	French Admiralty
Jean Parsmoguer	31/1/1941	2/11/1948	French Admiralty
Raymond Ouffule	19/1/1942	12/8/1948	French Naval
Jean Ichivonga	11/2/1943	12/10/1948	Free French
André Pira	31/8/1943	" "	Free French
Raymond Gusvard	28/8/1944	" "	Free French
Roger le Trol	24/10/1944	" "	Free French
Jean Marie Allane	28/10/1944	" "	Free French

Some of the names are unusual, too, bizarre even. In fact, a search reveals no references whatsoever to the names Parsmoguer, Ouffule, Ichivonga, Gusvard or le Trol (the latter meaning a troll as in English). Interestingly, the Extract Services Section of the GRO said that because they found some of the names so unusual their curiosity prompted them to run a free check on them all, waiving the customary fee.

The Clyde was swarming with vessels night and day during the war and statistical certainty had it that from time to time fatal accidents would occur, including amongst the communities of friendly forces such as the Free French Navy. Nevertheless, the striking fact that unites the eight French naval sailors exhumed in 1948 is that just as with Haryog and Handy the GRO for Scotland cannot locate a single entry in its records relating to them. Under British law a death has to be registered in the area where death takes place.

Perhaps, too, there is a story of intrigue to be found among these eight men, one entirely unconnected with U-33. However, by reason of their reported dates of burial it is Haryog and Handy who represent the persons of especial interest in the Albrecht and Klinger affair. We return to them in the final pages.

The following are the persons buried in Greenock from U-33 in order of ledger entry, listed alongside the official roll of deceased from German records:

Greenock Cemetery ledger entries (with spellings as in the handwritten ledger entries)	Official list of deceased (from German archive records)
Klinger	(not in official crew list)
Bergfeld	Bergfeld, Hans-Georg
Werner Enders	Enders, Werner
Rausch	Rausch, Paul
Kursiefen	Kursiefen, Heinrich
Albrecht	(not in official crew list)
Anger	Anger, Paul
Hickerodt	Heckerodt, Adalbert
Gross	Gross, Karl
Leopold Pöppel	Pöppel, Leopold
Ludwig Wagner	Wagner, Ludwig
Christian Schmid	Schmid, Christian
Keller	Keller, Werner
Wilhelm Wilden	Wilden, Wilhelm
Patten	Patten, Erich
Schiller (listed in error due to the dog tag mix-up. The correct name for the deceased is Karl Heinz Peters)	Peters, Karl-Heinz
Walter Kunick	Kunick, Walter
Kampert	Kampert, Heinrich
Steiner	Steiner, Willibald
Herbert Ruath	Raath, Herbert
Heinz Mohr	Mohr, Heinz
Heinrich Liebert	Liebert, Heinrich

Henneberg **(23 bodies buried)**	Henneberg, Gustav **(21 bodies recovered for burial)**
	Braun, Friedrich von Dresky, Hans-Wilhelm Johne, Johannes Winterhoff, August **(4 bodies not recovered)**
TOTAL DECEASED = 27 (23 buried in Greenock Cemetery plus 4 not recovered)	**OFFICIAL TOTAL OF DECEASED FROM U-33 = 25**

One cannot reasonably argue with a cemetery's burial records. They are written at the time of interment and list only those laid to rest. Greenock Cemetery's burial ledger lists 23 bodies buried on 16 February 1940. There is no argument about the number of bodies from U-33 not recovered fom the scene—there were 4 in total (von Dresky, Johne, Braun and Winterhoff). The total number of deceased, adding the cemetery's tally to the known number of unrecovered bodies, is 27. This is 2 more than the official German count.

Let us pause to remind ourselves that the total number of persons recorded as being on U-33 during its third and final cruise was 42. The official breakdown of this figure is 17 survivors and 25 deceased. The breakdown based on Greenock Cemetery's ledger records including unrecovered bodies is 17 survivors and 27 deceased, a total of 44 persons on board U-33. How do both sets of figures compare with the NHB's statistics?

Based on careful analysis we saw in Chapter 3 that the Royal Navy's tally is 19 survivors and 26 deceased, making 45 persons on U-33 in total. In summary:

- ➢ History says 42 persons—17 survivors and 25 deceased
- ➢ Greenock Cemetery records say 44—17 survivors plus 27 deceased
- ➢ The Royal Naval Historical Branch says 45—19 survivors and 26 deceased.

What may one deduce from these figures? A cemetery's first duty is to honour the dead under its turf. It follows that in documenting the persons committed for burial cemeteries have a prima facie responsibility to maintain formal, accurate records. It would be extraordinary if this age-old duty of care was to be compromised, even in time of war.

The Greenock Cemetery records list 23 Germans buried on 16 February 1940. This is 2 more than the officially accepted figure. The German U-Boot-Archiv papers reproduced in the appendix, for example, report 25 deceased as does a whole slew of authoritative U-boat networks, forums and websites.

The following table lists the names of those buried at Greenock, alongside the corresponding entries in the CWGC records when the bodies were disinterred in October 1962 on behalf of the German War Graves Commission and re-buried at the German Cemetery section of the Cannock Chase Military Cemetery in Staffordshire, England.

The Greenock list incorrectly names Schiller as among the deceased (due to the consequent mix up when Max Schiller gave his dog tag as a keepsake to a fisherman from the rescue trawler *Bohemian Girl*), while the CWGC list correctly names the deceased as MaschGfr Karl-Heinz Peters. As we shall see, the NHB tried to argue that Klinger was, in fact, Peters, thereby seeking to rationalise (read "reduce") the death list accordingly.

The problem with the NHB's position, as we saw in detail in Chapter 3, is that its starting point on U-33 crew numbers is considerably wide of the mark to begin with. Analysis of its numbers indicates that there were 45 people on board U-33, of whom 26 died.

If the NHB seeks to find error in the Greenock or CWGC burial numbers it must first, logically, look to its own and seek to understand why its information sources conclude that there were 3 more people on board than generally acknowledged. Ironically, the Greenock/CWGC records partially vindicate the NHB's position, a corroboration it could probably do without because it strengthens the key contention that there were at least two mystery persons among the dead from U-33.

Greenock burials in lairs 931 through 935 in section 3C	Corresponding CWGC entry in its letter to Greenock Cemetery of 30 October 1962 (all deceased buried in Block 3, Row 11)
Klinger	listed but classed as "Unknown"
Bergfeld	Hans Bergfeld (serial/entry N.2700/38.T Grave 345)
Werner Enders	Werner Paul Enders (serial/entry N.32/31.T Grave 346)

Rausch	Paul Rausch (serial/entry N.467/33.T Grave 343)
Kursiefen	Heinrich Kursiefen, Grave 342
Albrecht	Albrecht (serial/entry N.28336/38.S. Grave 341)
Anger	Paul Anger (serial/entry N.52/27.S Grave 340)
Hickerodt	Adalbert Heckerodt (serial/entry N.1091/39.T Grave 339)
Gross	Karl Gross (serial/entry N.1009/38.T Grave 338)
Leopold Pöppel	Leopold Pöppel (scrial/entry N.461/38.T Grave 337)
Ludwig Wagner	Ludwig Wagner (serial/entry N.1590/35.T Grave 336)
Christian Schmid	Christian Schmid (serial/entry N.384/33.J Grave 33)
Keller	Werner Keller (serial/entry N.390/36.K Grave 334)
Wilhelm Wilden	Wilhelm Wilden (serial/entry N.2937/37.T Grave 333)
Patten	Erich Patten, Grave 332
Schiller	Karl-Heinz Peters (serial/entry N.1175/39.T Grave 344)
Walter Kunick	Walter Kunick (serial/entry N.3266/38.S Grave 330)
Kampert	Heinrich Kampert (serial/entry N.4005/38.S Grave 329)
Steiner	Willibald Steiner, Grave 328
Herbert Ruath	Herbert Raath (serial/entry N.1018/34.T Grave 327)
Heinz Mohr	Heinz Karl Mohr (serial/entry N.1921/35.S Grave 326)
Heinrich Liebert	Heinrich E. Liebert (serial/entry N.2298/37.T Grave 325)
Henneberg	Gustav Henneberg (serial/entry N.834/33, Grave 369)
23 buried	**23 buried**

The CGWC records also state that:

> ➢ Wilhelm von Dresky rests in Grave 340
> ➢ August Winterhoff rests in Grave 344
> ➢ Friedrich Braun rests in Grave 331
> ➢ Johannes Johne rests in Grave 342

As we have observed, these latter entries refer to commemorations for the 4 deceased and not, of course, to actual burials. This will be a very important point to consider when we return for a closer look at the facts surrounding the exhumation of bodies from Greenock Cemetery—for two men in particular.

One sees readily in the preceding tables that the two extra persons among the bodies buried in Greenock Cemetery are "Klinger" and "Albrecht."

Considering Greenock Cemetery's obligation to keep accurate records, there is no reason to question the reported timing of interment of these two individuals. The cemetery register says that they were buried on 16 February 1940. This indicates that Klinger and Albrecht were among the fatalities from U-33's encounter with HMS *Gleaner* four days earlier. It is an intriguing thought that their bodies were those concealed under the Nazi flag on board the destroyer that brought the deceased from U-33 into Greenock.

In the absence of further corroborative proof one cannot nevertheless be absolutely sure that the pair was on U-33 on this date. Consequently, it would be premature to conclude beyond all doubt that they either came from this submarine on this occasion or were buried in Greenock Cemetery at the same time as the 21 boatmates from U-33. Were they even buried at all?

What is certain is that the two deceased bear surnames—German surnames—and so one can accept that the two bodies carried sufficient identification to provide names to burial personnel, or that identities / cover names were attributed to the pair by someone who knew them (such as surviving crewmen from U-33 but recall Max Schiller's evident difficulty in identifying the body of a shipmate on *Bohemian Girl*) or by British naval personnel, for example.

If Klinger and Albrecht were not among the fatalities from the sinking of U-33 on 12 February might they have been casualties from the ferocious and prolonged depth charging at the Tail of the Bank in November 1939? We have already established that the only plausible suspect for the identity of the audacious U-boat in the Firth of Clyde that autumn night is U-33.

Although the submarine on that occasion was apparently not sunk nor, if it was apprehended, was it detained (we saw in Chapter 5 that U-33 reportedly had to make a 17-hour dash to the Orkneys to be in position to sink the *Borkum* on the 23rd), this does not necessarily mean there were no casualties. Perhaps the presence of sailors' hats on local beaches told a sorry tale after all.

If Albrecht and Klinger were fatalities during that operation, or even at a time afterwards, they could have been buried in Greenock at any time between November 1939 and February 1940. The dead from U-33 would thereafter simply have been buried with them. However, if the two men were buried prior to the 16 February then someone in authority had to take responsibility to falsify the burial records. There is no evidence that such an action was undertaken and all indications appear to support the record of Albrecht and Klinger's date of death as 12 February 1940, along with the other deceased from U-33.

In earlier pages, though, at least two other occasions have been referenced when a body, or bodies, came to light in the Dunoon-Greenock area, which could feasibly have been linked with the activities of U-33 in either November 1939 or in February 1940. However, Greenock Cemetery records for the period November through February list no persons with "foreign" names, other than the deceased from U-33.

The exceptions are an Italian from a family of local residents and Sikh Hidtalla who was buried in a pauper's grave in an anonymous grassed area of Common Ground (lair 315) on 3 January 1940, which suggests that the deceased had either insufficient funds to buy a grave or no known family.

A corpse, for example, which turned up in a local swimming pool carrying neither identification nor money and unknown to local residents would be classified in such manner.

Hidtalla's is a most enigmatic entry in the INTERMENTS records. Alone among nearly 500 entries (see Appendix) in the Greenock Cemetery Interments Day Book for the 12-week period between November 1939 and February 1940, it is the only one written in pencil. Other parts of Hidtalla's entry—age (given as "adult"), lair, class, section and so on—are entered in ink. Evidently, it was intended by the writer that the name would in the first instance be entered into the records temporarily, either pending resolution of the deceased's particulars or deciding on the preferred *nom de guerre*.

There is a degree of doubt about the actual spelling of the name. The Day Book spelling appears to be 'Hiddtalla' but cemetery officials, when questioned, have confirmed that to their knowledge the correct spelling is 'Hidtalla.' It is likely that in making this clarification officials had other records before them because in correspondence they also confirmed that Hidtalla is buried in a pauper's grave, a fact not present in the Day Book entry.

Enquiries undertaken with the Registrar of Deaths in Greenock have proved as fruitless in locating a death certificate for Hidtalla as for the French sailors. The certificate can usually provide valuable information such as who registered the death, their relationship to the deceased and also the deceased's age and date of birth.

There is no firm evidence that Hidtalla was connected with the Gourock lido corpse or with enemy fatalities. But who can refute the possibility that the body washed up in the swimming pool after the November event was from or connected with U-33?

Who can also state without question that none of the four bodies buried in Greenock Cemetery in lair 931 in July 1940, described as 2 Italians and 2 Germans, were unconnected with U-33?

Despite these questions the Greenock Cemetery records still reflect an overall certainty of detail in terms of who was buried in which lair.

Let us return to the NHB's figures—45 persons on board U-33—of which the analysis indicates that 26 died and 19 survived. Taking the Greenock Cemetery numbers as the definitive record of burials, we know that there were 27 fatalities (23 buried and 4 not recovered): 2 more than the history books and German records indicate.

If one substitutes this correct number of fatalities into the NHB tally (accepting for argument that in the NHB figures there is a solid core of truth about the overall number of persons on board U-33), their figure for the deceased increases by 1 to 27 while that for the survivors therefore reduces by 1 to 18 (1 more than the official survivors number of 17) in order to keep to its overall total of 45.

The startling conclusion that one may draw from this amended position is that there was an additional 18th person on or intimately connected with U-33, unidentifiable from a reading of the official crew list, who survived its sinking. If this remarkable scenario has substance then who was the 18th survivor and, critically, what became of this person?

On 5 November 1962 the Corporation of Greenock's Town Clerk Depute wrote to the Superintendent of Parks enclosing a copy of a letter dated 30 October 1962 from the CWGC regarding the exhumation of deceased, details of which were appended to the letter. The Town Clerk asked the Superintendent to amend his (Greenock Cemetery) records accordingly.

The 30 October letter, headed *Greenock Cemetery, Renfrew, Exhumation of German War Dead*, was a confirmation notice from the CWGC Regional Director to the Town Clerk that the German War Graves Commission[1] (on whose behalf the CWGC maintains the German Cemetery at Cannock Chase) had exhumed the deceased per an attached list.

The list makes for interesting reading. The number of "German War Dead" exhumed was 27, not 23. The list is columnised under: Name, Christian Name, Born, Date of Death and Grave Location. 22 of the 27 were named on the list, while 5 were dubbed "unknown." The grave locations (Greenock Cemetery lairs) were: CCC-931A (4 bodies), CCC-932 A through D (4 bodies), CCC-933 A through D (8 bodies), CCC-934 A through D (8 bodies) and CCC-935 A through C (3 bodies).

It is clear from this list that the exhumed bodies came from 5 grave locations, not 7 as stated by the CWGC's letter to the Town Clerk. A detailed review of the corresponding Greenock Cemetery burial record, dated 14 February 1940, confirms that 4 of the 5 'unknowns' were the bodies of 2 Italians and 2 Germans buried in lair 931A on 5 July 1940, while the 5th unknown is Klinger, one of our two mysterious ghost 'crewmen' recovered from the firth.

The record concerns itself with: Lairs, Class 7, Section 3C. Lairs 931 through 935 were used for the burials of 27 bodies, per the breakdown above. The Remarks column states that i) Lair 930 was not used; and ii) "all Bodies exhumed. See attached letter dated 30 Oct 1962." Under "Name of Deceased" are:

- ➤ Unknown (Klinger)
- ➤ Unknown ⎞
- ➤ Unknown ⎟ 2 Italians and 2 Germans
- ➤ Unknown ⎟
- ➤ Unknown ⎠
- ➤ Bergfeld
- ➤ Enders
- ➤ Rausch
- ➤ Kursiefen
- ➤ Albrecht
- ➤ Anger
- ➤ Hickerodt
- ➤ Gross

---

[1] Volksbund Deutsche Kriegsgraberfursorge e.v.

- Pöppel
- Wagner
- Schmid
- Keller
- Kunick
- Kampert
- Steiner
- Raath
- Mohr
- Liebert
- Henneberg
- Patten
- Wilden
- Peters

Notably, out of the 27 handwritten entries there are just 2 which are suffixed by a distinct hyphen—Klinger and Albrecht—as if to indicate that these two individuals stood out for reasons not specified in the ledger and/or that there was supplementary information concerning them listed elsewhere.

Who were the 2 Germans and 2 Italians buried in July 1940? Where had they been on Scottish soil (or in water) when they were killed? If they had been in military service then to which of their respective armed forces had they belonged? Had they been sailors? How did they die? What had they been doing at the time they died?

Why did the CWGC letter in 1962 include the Italians under the heading "German War Dead?"

In fact, why exhume the Italian pair at all as part of a disinterment exercise carried out by CWGC ostensibly for the *German* dead from U-33? Could the authorities have made it any plainer that these two persons were connected with enemy activities undertaken in Scottish waters and/or on Scottish soil?

In addressing these questions, the NHB observed that the bodies may have been washed ashore following an action that had taken place weeks before and it was merely expedient to dispose of the bodies in a plot previously purchased for this purpose. Perhaps the NHB did not make this remark so seemingly off the cuff as first appears.

Taking all the circumstances together, the most obvious recent actions during which the four individuals (and Hidtalla) could have died were the Isle of Islay, Isle of Bute, Carradale Bay and Tail of the Bank U-boat events of 21-22 November 1939—actions that can accurately be described as taking place "weeks before," eleven and a half to be precise.

In a separate record provided to me by Greenock Cemetery, headed INTERMENTS, 23 entries are listed (a copy of the interment sheet for the 2 Germans and 2 Italians was not supplied) alongside each deceased's unique interment number (128 through 150) and the dates of interment.

It might have been due to lazy penmanship (all the Greenock records are handwritten) but the burials of Raath, Mohr, Liebert, Henneberg, "Schiller" (i.e. Peters), Kunick and Kampert are listed as taking place on 15 February 1940, the day before what has been regarded as the sole and complete mass burial, which Horace Oakes witnessed in secret.

Were two ceremonies held—one on the 15th and one on the 16th? If so, why?

The CWGC correspondence in October 1962 requests that "7 graves should be deleted." Greenock records explain the actual deployment of just 5 (excluding lair 930, which was not used). If indeed there was a sixth and a seventh lair involving the "German War Dead" which were not listed in Greenock Cemetery record No. 11,465 then why were they not recorded and, crucially, if one or more persons had been buried in them what was their identity?

Let us turn to the vexed issue of death certificates for the deceased. The Greenock Cemetery records for the 23 deceased from U-33 are available for inspection (although by 2008 researchers were no longer able to visit in person to examine and copy documents because of their increasing fragility). In what is now becoming a depressingly familiar pattern, just as there are no Death Registration records in Scotland at either local or national level for the French decedents from the *Maillé Brézé*, the Free French Navy and Sikh Hidtalla there are none for the 23 deceased from U-33.

As noted earlier, British law demands that a death has to be registered in the area where it takes place. In common with the other undocumented decedents, men from U-33 died in Scotland and were buried in Greenock. Evidently, the law was contravened. Officials with whom I spoke and corresponded are at a complete loss as to how this extraordinary circumstance can have arisen. In the words of one, the matter is "very strange."

The GRO officials firstly suggested that I contact the General Register Office for England and Wales in the belief that records of WWII enemy personnel killed in the United Kingdom may be held there. Once more, I drew a blank. As far as the English officials are concerned records of people who die in Scotland, friend and foe alike, should be held in Scotland.

Subsequently, the Scottish GRO's Extract Services Section sent me a letter in which it sought to ascribe to the U-33 deceased a status of "special circumstance," adding that it is to be assumed (though unable to back up its assumption with corroborative documentation) that the relevant records are held in Germany.

Written death registration details for the 23 men from U-33 have been expunged from British official public record. Give thanks for small mercies that the cemetery details have remained intact. It is only by virtue of the public availability of these burial records that one may learn at all about the joint presence of Albrecht and Klinger on U-33.

Having stated that it could find no trace in its records of any of the names that I had forwarded for investigation (I had supplied copies of the Greenock Cemetery burials and CWGC exhumation list) claiming "special circumstance," the GRO adds that it similarly cannot find any trace of a Sikh Hidtalla buried in 1940.

One cannot imagine that the death of a local Greenock resident dying in poverty would have necessitated the flouting of the law surrounding registration. Records would still have to have been made and put on file. From a reading of the facts (and by inference from their absence), one draws the inevitable conclusion that Hidtalla was not of local stock and, instead, was a party to the "special circumstance" associated with the decedents from U-33.

The name or word Hidtalla cannot be found under any search category. It appears to be pure concoction. The only close resemblance that has both Indian (Sikh being Hindi for disciple) and Scottish connotations is the literary character Hidalla. In the 1760s Scottish poet James Macpherson published to great acclaim the Ossian cycle of poems in which Hidalla is a servant of a powerful Irish chieftain. If this is a possible source of the name for the deceased why would the concocter in 1939-1940 go on to complete his fabrication by choosing the given name Sikh to go with Hidtalla?

Interestingly, Dorothea Chaplain[2] researched a number of Celto-Vedic connections in Scotland. Near to Oban on Argyll and Bute is Loch Nell, derived from Loch-a-Neala—the Lake of Swans. Close by, there is a serpentine mound where half-cremated bones were discovered. Legends associate the bones with the burial-place of Ossian (a name whose etymology is related to bones or stones). Chaplain

---

[2] Chaplain D., *Matter, Myth, and Spirit, or Keltic and Hindu Links*, Rider & Co, 1935

associated Neala with Nala, the King of Nishada in Indian mythology who is associated with Swans.

Readers of my book about 1930s German medievalist and treasure hunter Otto Rahn will have noted the importance of the Swan motif in his work and personal relationships. In the mid-1930s, for example, Rahn became good friends with Russian author Grigol Robakidse who was a member of the Schwannen, a group linked with the 11th Century Order of the Black Swan also known as the Guardian Order of the Holy Grail.

In my book I investigated the connections between the Order of the Black Swan and the efforts of a mysterious anti-Nazi faction headed by scientist Dr. Karl Obermayer to prevent Adolf Hitler ordering the carrying out of potentially catastrophic space-time experiments.

Rahn had both Italian and British associates. His friend Joachim Kohlhaas recalled visiting Rahn during the mid-1930s in the Italian Tyrolean town of Merano where he saw his pal in the company of a German-speaking Italian officer and an Englishman named Thomas Lambert.

On 23 February 2009 *The Greenock Telegraph* published a follow-up piece to its 2002 article, which linked the Holy Grail with a local story about a U-boat that managed to enter the Clyde. The earlier story had speculated that the submarine might have carried Nazi language specialist Otto Rahn, a man routinely and intimately associated with the Third Reich's search for biblical artefacts.

The new article (*U-33 and the real Indiana Jones*) reported for the first time publicly that U-33 had breached the Tail of the Bank in November 1939. Once again, the *Telegraph* reflected on the claim endorsed a few years earlier by the Magic Torch Inverclyde history group that the activities of U-33 may have been linked, at least in part, to the area's longstanding Knights Templar associations and to rumours that the Grail treasures are concealed hereabouts. For readers who are interested in the topic I refer them to Chapter 27 (*Arthur's Bosom*) in my book on Rahn.

Legends abound. In 1997, for example, the *Scottish Sun* magazine published a story about recent research, which indicated that the Knights Templar brought to Scotland the biblical Ark of the Covenant and a host of other material and spiritual treasures.

Three years later researcher Andrew Sinclair was describing in the *Daily Mail* his discovery in a Masonic Lodge in Kirkwall, Orkney, of a massive 15th Century wall hanging. It is filled with mystic Templar imagery, including seaborne angels and the Ark of the Covenant floating above the waves. These were emblems of the Ancient Ark Mariners Guild, a Masonic brotherhood of shipwrights who constructed the Scottish St. Clair family shipping fleet.

The images tell of the Knights Templars' two hundred year history from its early days in Jerusalem as protectors of pilgrims to its final flight to Scotland where survivors from the French king's bloody pogrom subsequently revealed their secrets to the Guildmen.

Against the background of these exciting tales of treasure might there be more to the rumours, after all, about a Rahn-Scotland scenario other than Donald Kelly's lighthearted movie script remarks?

May there be a link, too, between Rahn and the unnamed Italians buried in Greenock in the summer of 1940?

Just *who* was the person whose body fetched up in Gourock swimming pool a few weeks after the Tail of the Bank event? Had this individual been on U-33 in November 1939, either having boarded when the submarine left port or been taken aboard at Helgoland or during one of its clandestine calls at Islay, Bute or Carradale?

Or were they an occupant of a special submarine shielded by U-33 as it attempted and failed to gain passage through the boom into the Clyde Anchorage?

Hidtalla was consigned to a pauper's grave on 3 January 1940, precisely six weeks after the event. The timing fits.

In the next chapter efforts will be made to identify the hyphenated mystery men—Messrs. Albrecht and Klinger.

The Greenock Telegraph article of 23 February 2009 (reproduced by courtesy of *The Greenock Telegraph*)

Chapter ELEVEN

The Mystery Men

Misery acquaints a man with strange bedfellows.

The German practice was to take 'operatives' on board U-boats disguised as 'officers in training' as there was absolutely no way that a non-seaman could fake their rank, duties, social background and so on. The ruse would have quickly been discovered by regular sailors, angry that the faker was unable to pull his weight with duties. U-boat crews were a very tight knit bunch and usually took an intense dislike to spies and 'political' types, including propaganda officers and photographers.

U-boats also occasionally carried 'party officers' on board. Nevertheless, in the case of a sinking they merited no preferential treatment and had to take their chances for survival together with the regular crewmen.

There is no reason why Kriegsmarine personnel should not among themselves have been a rich source of expertise and experience from which agents could be recruited. Submariners came from highly diverse backgrounds. For example, some U-boat crews and commanders transferred into the Luftwaffe in the early part of WWII, only to return to U-boats later. Such versatility and adaptability would have been prized by Intelligence chiefs who may have had little hesitation in selecting agents from U-boat crews.

Overall, though, landing men ashore from U-boats was, for the most part, an unsuccessful practice by the Germans. Most, if not all, agents landed were captured or killed within hours or days. One man who had been spying on shipping was even pursued by a destroyer, having fled from Britain in a rowing boat and was heading for Ireland. He was captured, completely exhausted by his effort, with a copy of *Mein Kampf* in his gear!

Such incidents can present conflicting facts. Earlier we noted U-37's landing of Abwehr II spy Ernst Weber-Drohl at Killala Bay in February 1940. (The Abwehr would use small yachts to ferry people to and from Ireland and aircraft were used for parachute drops.) U-33 was deep into Scotland's Atlantic waters by this time. Author Jak P. Mallman Showell [1] refers to the landing of just one man, Weber-Drohl, on 9-10 Feb 1940 at Sligo Bay. However, the UBootwaffe website records that on 8 February U-37 landed two Abwehr agents at Donegal Bay in Ireland.

Here we have a discrepancy between Malmann Showell and the UBootwaffe network about three points—date of landing, the location of landing and the number of agents landed.

In his description of another event Mallmann Showell reports that U-38 landed two agents, Willy Preetz and Walter Simon, on 12 June 1940, exact location unknown but somewhere in the Brandon Bay-Ventry Bay-Dingle Bay area of County Kerry in southwest Ireland. The UBootwaffe network says that U-38 landed one agent.

One should not read too much into these and other such discrepancies (and it is certainly not my intention to criticise the first rate research work of acknowledged experts such as Mallman Showell). After all, these are examples of acts of espionage, secret and hazy by nature. It would be surprising if the details of covert operations undertaken nearly seventy years ago could today be read like an open book.

Nevertheless, Mallmann Showell records the telling fact that in researching for his book it should have been relatively straightforward to reconstruct the details for boats that were lost after special missions. To his surprise, he found that in at least two cases the records for the periods in question had been defaced by the removal of key pages. To Mallmann Showell's thinking this could only mean that something significant took place during these operations, something of such importance that even today's researchers are denied the opportunity to piece together these mission records. Seeing that it would not make sense for U-boat Commanders to enter information in logs only to tear it out later, one can only conclude that tampering was carried out after the war by those who captured the documents.

The "Albrecht and Klinger" case surely falls into this category of official denial and disinformation. Can our pair of mystery men from U-33 be identified?

A search in the Ubootwaffe crew records confirms that there were 11 persons named Klinger and 69 persons named Albrecht who served on U-boats either in WWI or in WWII. Of the 69 Albrechts, 4 of them appear to have died during WWI or between the wars. None of the 11

[1] Ibid

Klingers is reported as dying prior to WWII. None of the 65 "WWII" Albrechts or the 11 Klingers is reported to have died between the outbreak of WWII and the 12 February 1940 date of U-33's sinking in the Firth of Clyde. This leaves a pool of 76 individuals from which efforts to make identifications can be made. How does one proceed to narrow it down?

In seeking an authoritative answer as to identity, I went back to Herr Horst Bredow at the U-Boot-Archiv in Cuxhaven. I described what I was looking for, explaining that I was investigating the circumstances of the sinking of U-33 and, among other tasks, seeking to address emerging questions about the number and identities of the deceased, in particular the riddle of Albrecht and Klinger.

Herr Bredow subsequently undertook a tremendous job of work in combing the records, putting forward three particular individuals for consideration. One or more of them was either connected previously with U-33, had been serving in U-boats in Scottish waters in February 1940 or fulfilled both criteria.

It should be stressed that there is no cast iron certainty that any of the three men were on U-33 on 12 February 1940. In fact, although these three represent the best "near misses" among the seventy-six men in the Albrecht and Klinger Kriegsmarine pool there is no obvious way in which one, let alone two of them (both an Albrecht and a Klinger), can be confirmed as having been among the deceased from U-33.

But let us review Herr Bredow's investigations. It is a notable fact that there were three U-boats, which having departed from Wilhelmshaven at various dates between January and early February 1940 were all at sea simultaneously between 6–12 February and each were carrying (or, in the case of U-33, subsequently reported to have been carrying) a crewmember named either Albrecht, Klinger or both: U-25, U-53 and U-33.

U-25 left Wilhelmshaven on 13 January 1940 under the command of Viktor Schütze for operations in the North Atlantic, arriving back at base on 19 February. Among the crew was MtrGfr Edmund Albrecht (13.12.1908 to 01.08.1940). The UBoot forum lists this Albrecht as lost at sea on U-25 on 3 August 1940.

According to Herr Bredow, Edmund had previously served on U-33. This statement is not verifiable from a search of the UBootwaffe database in which names of Kriegsmarine personnel can be searched by surname or by U-boat. The database records only that U-25 was the serving boat for the Edmund Albrecht in Bredow's list. In compiling his response to me, Herr Bredow must have looked at documents that had not been fully referenced or made available for public review by forum database administrators.

U-53 is the only U-boat on which both a Klinger and an Albrecht were serving simultaneously. StOMasch (Chief Petty Officer) Josef Albrecht (04.04.1907 to 21.02.1940) was aboard U-53 when it departed under Harald Grosse from Wilhelmshaven on 2 February 1940. OMaschMt (Petty Officer 2nd Class) Walter Klinger (29.03.1914 to 21.2.1940) was Albrecht's crewmate. U-53 hit 6 ships during this voyage including the Swedish 3,927-ton *Dalarö* on 12 February, the day that U-33 was sunk off Arran. As noted in Chapter 9, U-53 was sunk 23 February 1940 west of the Orkneys and current records cannot confirm the exact location and depth of the wreck.

For completeness, Gefreiter Walter Klinger, born 20 December 1920, died along with his boatmates from U-122 whose exact date and cause of loss remains unknown, although the online U-Boot forum lists this Klinger as lost at sea on 1 July 1940. U-122 did not make an operational patrol until 16 May 1940, three months after U-33 was sunk. U-122 was declared missing between the North Sea and the Bay of Biscay from 22 June 1940.

Consulting U-boat experts did little to shine light on the Albrecht-Klinger puzzle, except to raise a few points of general interest. It was remarked, for instance, that the Klinger on U-122, being six years older than the one who served on U-53, is a more likely candidate for operations on foreign shores. This is a vague observation, which does little to progress the enquiries.

Mention was made, too, of the work of researcher Timothy Mulligan who has estimated that as many as 5,000 Kriegsmarine personnel records are missing. One of the reasons for inaccuracies is that many records were destroyed in the last days of the war, especially before imminent capture as in the case of the U-boat bases in France.

Often records went missing because crews were shuffled about as needed. Men might be seconded to a different boat with pressing personnel requirements if their own sub was not yet ready to leave port. Under this circumstance it would have been more common for men based in the same location and/or attached to the same Flotilla to have been subject to these kinds of last-minute movements.

One should also note the NHB's comment that it is aware of at least two cases where U-boat ratings were pulled from the crew at the eleventh hour (both for having a tubercular shadow on the lung highlighted by a routine X-ray), replaced by another sailor from their U-Flotille but never deleted from the crew list and, consequently, recorded as lost in the sinking of their U-boat. This is a helpful comment but, as we shall see, one that has little practical value to our study of U-33.

U-25, U-33 and U-122 were a part of 2.U-Flotille, based in Wilhelmshaven. U-53 belonged to 7.U-Flotille Kiel and St. Nazaire but did set off from Wilhelmshaven for its patrol in the North Atlantic.

In this hypothetical scenario Able Seaman 2nd Class Edmond Albrecht, attached to U-25 but with prior experience serving on U-33 (according to Herr Bredow's research), could have been made available to the latter submarine, which was to depart Wilhelmshaven 23 days after U-25's sailing date because it was short of a junior seaman who, fortuitously, had prior experience of serving on U-33.

Equally, there is a degree of possibility about machinists Josef Albrecht and Walter Klinger from U-53 being candidates for secondment to sister boat U-33. U-53 set off from Wilhelmshaven on 2 February, three days before U-33 left its pen. Neither man had had previous experience of sailing on U-33, a fact that does not rule out a loan from U-53 *if* they had possessed certain skills necessary for the operational efficiency of the later departing boat. One should bear in mind that the pair was recorded as lost when U-53 was sunk west of the Orkneys on 23 February 1940, although the records could simply be incorrect.

What about transfers of these two men at sea? Here there is more scope for identifying possible opportunities. However, on the day U-33 was sunk in the lower reaches of the Firth of Clyde U-53 was in the North Atlantic where it sank the *Dalarö*. That position (56.44N 11.44W) is roughly 140 miles northwest of Londonderry and 200 miles west by northwest of the Firth of Clyde, much too far away to have enabled the men to transfer to U-33 on the same day (12 February).

Could the two submarines have rendezvoused earlier than the 12th? The date of the first operational activity carried out by U-53, subsequent to its departure from Wilhelmshaven on 2 February, is listed in the UBootwaffe database as 11 February. It records U-53's sinking that day of the 4,114-ton Norwegian vessel *Snested*. Norwegian ship records go further and provide coordinates of 58.40N 13.40W, placing the scene about 100 miles west of the Hebrides. In Chapter 1 we saw that on the 11th von Dresky surfaced to take a star-sighting to correct U-33's position and was pleased to see that he was ten miles closer to the Isle of Mull than expected, a point approximately 300 miles southeast of the sinking of the *Snested*. This fact rules out the 11th as a possibility for a transfer.

What about before the 11th? Could U-33 and U-53 have met at a point between Helgoland and northern Scottish waters between the 7th and the 10th? There is little doubt that they had the opportunity. We know, for instance, that U-33 passed through Fair Isle Channel between Orkney and Shetland during the night of 9-10 February. A rendezvous in this general area would have allowed both U-boats to transfer personnel and then gone on to do what history records they did—U-53 sinking the *Snested* on the 11th, for example, and U-33 continuing with its voyage to the Firth of Clyde.

But in this scenario, irrespective of this or that date for possible transfers of sailors from U-53 to U-33, we are talking about two men, albeit of senior rank who, although necessary for the overall operational efficiency of a U-boat at sea, were unlikely to have had such impressive technical abilities that they had to be taken aboard U-33 during a mid-ocean exercise.

Staying with the subject of skills, it has been speculated that because it was to be the first time that the Firth of Clyde was to be mined (U-32 having previously shied away from the task) Albrecht and Klinger may have been technicians on hand to resolve any mechanical issues with the new mines. However, Kriegsmarine naval titles were sometimes very lengthy because they accurately described, usually in just one long word, a sailor's specific appointment.

Neither Able Seaman Edmund Albrecht from U-25 nor the more experienced pair from U-53, Josef Albrecht and Walter Klinger, had the telltale "Mech" description within their job titles to indicate that they had expertise in torpedo or artillery mechanics. Moreover, the "Masch" suffix for the pair from U-53 denotes expertise in electrics and/or diesels, which means that they were adept at fixing a U-boat's diesel engine problems but far less competent, if at all, to resolve complex munitions issues.

On balance, the latter pair could *feasibly* have been the Albrecht and Klinger associated with U-33 but in light of the facts it is unlikely. Moreover, if one associates the bodies attired in immaculate uniforms (which were suggestive to onlookers in Greenock Town Hall as being members of a "special unit") with Albrecht and Klinger (and there is every reason for doing so), then this weakens any theory that connects the pair with consumptive sailors replaced at very short notice, the handy able seaman from U-25 or with the two diesel mechanics from U-53.

It has been remarked that when it came to choice of dress on board U-boats crews generally wore all kinds of mufti, including in some cases British uniforms captured after Dunkirk. There is no reason why Albrecht and Klinger on U-53, for example, would have chosen to dress any differently. Crews valued highly the British cloth, regarding it as far superior to the homespun variety. Officers and leaders turned a blind eye to what was worn on patrol; the conditions, danger and discomfort of submarine life meant that "whatever suits you" was the order of the day. The eyewitness descriptions in Greenock, however, paint a picture of well dressed men, suggestive of high rank, their overall appearance made sinister by the wearing of the Nazi party membership swastika ring.

This is mindful of senior Nazi figures on a high level mission. It seems very far removed from the traditional image of U-boat crewmen, including officers (the excellent and realistic portrayals in *Das Boot* spring to mind), who were comfortable wearing any old garb and who was generally suspicious of politicos and disdainful of formal Nazi Party membership.

When Max Schiller was interviewed by BBC Scotland Kirsty Wark asked pointedly if U-33's Captain had been a Nazi:

Schiller: "No. No way. No way!"

Wark: "Were any of the crew Nazis?"

Schiller: "No, no really, no. It's just…we were sailors, that's it."

Max was emphatic that his commanding officer was Kriegsmarine through and through but he equivocated about his crewmates and Nazi loyalties. He said: "no really…it's just that…," leaving something hanging in the air, unsaid and unsayable even after 60 years.

David Hendry told me that Schiller was nervous of speaking out. The U-33 survivor was mindful of the vandalism to the memorial stone erected at Rudolf Hess' landing site on Eaglesham Moor, a few miles from the Duke of Hamilton's former family home at Dungavel. He was concerned that speaking about U-33 would encourage the same kind of emotional responses.

But was this really the basis for Max's reticence to speak about his experiences? Might he have been using this explanation as a way of saying something indirectly about U-33's true agenda in November 1939 and February 1940 in the Firth of Clyde? Was he saying in a roundabout way that the clandestine aspects of U-33's activities were the first part of a contiguous text of German-British political intrigue in whose later pages we find other sensational and wholly related events, including Hess' subsequent peace flight to Scotland in May 1941? We will examine this and related questions in Part 4.

Our mystery men remain a mystery. They resist definitive

identification. The burial and exhumation records refer to an Albrecht and to a Klinger, suggesting either that the bodies bore at least some cursory means of identification or that they were identified by survivors or other persons brought to view the bodies. Our detailed review of the known Albrechts and Klingers has produced no firm answers, suggesting that these were more likely to have been cover or code names or passwords, which were used to conceal the identities of the individuals involved.

The etymologies of Albrecht and Klinger provide no clear insights or clues that may help with identification. Albrecht is a surname of Austrian origin deriving from *adal* and *berht* (noble and bright). It is also common in Slovenia where it is usually spelt as Albrcht. Adalbert is a Christian name associated with greater usage in the middle ages when it was popular both in France and in Germany. Eventually, the name was supplanted by the shortened Albert. (Coincidentally, Adalbert was the first name of 1st Class Seaman Heckenrodt, one of the 25 genuine Kriegsmarine fatalities from U-33. One might say, therefore, with no hint of flippancy that two Albrechts were among the deceased associated with the U-boat.)

Klinger has both German and Czech origins. Specifically, it originates in Germany from Swabia and derives from the Middle German 'Klinge' meaning "murmuring brook." No clues here but one fascinating point of consideration is the name's near match with "Klingsor," the evil magician in Wagner's opera Parsifal (based on the medieval Grail epic poem by Wolfram von Eschenbach), which was a great favourite of Hitler's.

According to Trevor Ravenscroft,[2] Grail scholar Walter Johannes Stein learned in meetings with the young Adolf Hitler in the 1920s that the latter personally identified with Klingsor whom he equated with the notorious 9th century 'Führer' Landulf II, Bishop and Count of Capua in Southern Italy. Landulf's thirst for power led him to practise the black arts for which he was excommunicated in 875 CE. Another fact about Landulf with which Hitler may have identified was Eschenbach's description of the Count as "the man who was smooth between the legs"; that is, either partly or wholly castrated.

In this context someone inventing a cover name would not, of course, have chosen Klingsor because it was not a name in current German usage (as is the case with Albrecht); a near match in 'Klinger' to denote the intended sense (and to provide a clue?) would have fitted the bill. If the 'Klingsor' supposition has weight it suggests that the

---

[2] Ravenscroft T., *The Spear of Destiny*, Sphere Books Ltd, 1983

educated name-maker was German; not just any German but one who had knowledge of the exclusive and rarefied circle around Hitler which believed that occultism was a valuable weapon in the war to establish the Third Reich.

Moreover, when one factors in the key part played by diplomat Albrecht Haushofer (Chapter 20) in the unofficial peace discussions between Germany and Britain both for Hitler and, at great personal risk, against him we may appreciate with keen insight that in the names Albrecht and Klinger we are not just given food for thought to assess the objectives of U-33's clandestine agenda but a seven-course banquet.

The cover names need not have been assigned to the men in Germany. One can picture a dramatic but entirely plausible scenario in which these men were so obviously high profile, travelling to Britain for top-secret political purposes (possibly expected, invited even), that their deaths demanded immediate measures by British security officials to ensure a blanket cover-up. Unfortunately, though, bodies have to be buried, no matter their background and someone has to come up with names for the gravemarkers and for burial and exhumation records. This scenario need not seem as farfetched as it might first appear. The brief descriptions of Albrecht and Klinger that have come down to us depict men who were clearly far removed from the day to day life of a Kriegsmarine officer or rating. They smack of high authority and the pursuit of extraordinary actions. The absence of identifiable men does not dilute the mystery; on the contrary it deepens it.

If the matter had turned out to be no more than an administrative mixup then an essential element of the "mystery of U-33" would have stopped right here, case closed. But not one among the 76 Albrechts and Klingers attached to various U-boats in WWII and, in particular, none of the possibilities proferred by Herr Bredow can be confidently matched to U-33. The evidence strongly suggests that these names either belonged or were assigned to individuals of high rank to conceal covert operations.

Furthermore, the analysis of survivors and deceased indicates that hidden among the NHB's figures there was a possible third unrecorded passenger who, not featuring in the various burial records, lived to tell the extraordinary tale of U-33. This only consolidates the overall scope and depth of this puzzling affair.

In the early days of my researches I put the main points of my U-33 investigations to experts in the MoD, including the emerging facts about Albrecht and Klinger. It is time to examine the subsequent criss-cross of correspondence for the official line about the history of U-33.

Chapter TWELVE

"Brass bounders at the Admiralty"

Your tale, sir, would cure deafness.

In June 2002 I wrote to a number of British naval enquiry centres, explaining that I was keen to clear up apparent contradictions in the official reporting of the circumstances surrounding the sinking of U-33. To evidence the background to my enquiry, I made reference to articles from the *Largs and Millport Weekly News* and to the wealth of detailed information subsequently passed to me by Scots who wanted to amplify the newspaper's reports based upon their personal eyewitness experiences or stories narrated to them by family and friends. Additionally, my plea to the Establishment was to come forward with any previously undisclosed material that might provide an explanation for the U-boat sightings at the Cloch Point-Dunoon boom that defended the strategically vital Clyde Anchorage in WWII.

At the time I embarked upon this correspondence (and for many years afterwards) I had no reason to doubt the accuracy of John McCreadie's dating of the Tail of the Bank U-boat event as taking place in mid-February 1940, synchronous with the sinking of U-33 by Arran. Because of the tone of certainty expressed in McCreadie's articles and the equally compelling facts surrounding the known history about HMS *Gleaner*'s fateful attack on U-33 it appeared that there were two separate and distinct U-boat events, which took place in the Firth of Clyde on or around 12 February. It was this basis of an apparent dual event scenario that characterised my chain of correspondence with British naval authorities.

It followed that my line of enquiry and principal contention was that at the same time as U-33 was being attacked off the coast of Arran by HMS *Gleaner* another U-boat was observed passing through the boom into the Clyde Anchorage. It was this latter event about which I sought details from British naval archivists and historians to complement the volume of sincere recollections from time witnesses and those in receipt of stories from families and friends.

Obviously, those with whom I corresponded in the Security

Services replied in kind, fielding my questions from the perspective of the known facts surrounding the drama in the Firth of Clyde on 12 February 1940. As far as history is concerned the only contemporary event that took place was the sinking of U-33. Officials in the NHB used Dönitz's remarks in his memoirs about the "bold and hazardous enterprise" of operating in the "very jaws" of the enemy to illustrate the unlikelihood of his sending a second U-boat into the restricted waters of the Clyde. The NHB reasoned that had two U-boats been in the Clyde together the possibility of interception would have made it difficult for the submarines to maintain joint communications.

Moreover, the NHB commented that seeing that U-33 had been charged with laying mines *somewhere* in the Firth of Clyde, a second U-boat might have very easily ploughed into the freshly laid minefield. One can have few arguments with these remarks.

It was therefore the case that because of my early insouciance in accepting the *Largs and Millport Weekly News'* date of February 1940 for the Tail of the Bank event I would receive no direct insights about the earlier, sensational occurrence no matter how many letters I wrote to the Navy. Indeed, the NHB referred to its contribution to Lt. Roche's article published in *The Greenock Telegraph* on 26 May 1979, which passed off the locals' sightings of a U-boat in the Clyde in November 1939 as a whale, a big fish, even a shoal of fish. Without possession of the raft of new facts subsequently gathered about the event there were no means available by which to challenge the Navy's position in 2002. Nevertheless, despite the prolonged error in assigning the same date to the two events, the exchange of correspondence with the MoD in these early years of investigative research was not without reward.

In our in-depth scrutiny of U-33's survivors and deceased we have already concluded that within the seeming confusion of figures provided by the NHB the startling fact emerges that not only were there two more people among the dead of U-33 than previously acknowledged (corroborating the Greenock Cemetery records) but that statistical circumstance suggests that there was an additional, unnamed survivor associated with the U-boat.

Tellingly, the NHB appeared to hedge its bets about the existence of agents on U-33 when it stated coyly in correspondence that it did not know enough about German Intelligence missions to confirm whether or not a submarine was, in fact, sent to the Clyde to perform a covert operation or to drop off German Intelligence officers. The tone of these remarks indicates that the Royal Navy was suspicious that U-33's objectives in the Firth of Clyde *did* include clandestine activities involving intelligence personnel.

NHB officials stated that the record of Anti-Submarine Attacks September 1939 through September 1940 lists four such A/S attacks made in the Firth of Clyde between February and March 1940. One was the *Gleaner*'s successful attack on U-33; one was an attack by HM Trawler *Lord Essenden*, which was so inconclusive that no details were submitted; a third was an attack by HMS *Folkestone* on 11 March, which also failed to produce any visible results. The fourth and final attack, by HMS *Forester* and HM Tug *Buccaneer* on 22 February, appeared to be on a firm submarine contact but was brought to a stop after it was realised that the target was stationary and that the ships were probably attacking a wreck, perhaps even that of U-33.

The NHB offered the suggestion that if the wreck of U-33 had been the subject of the attack and if depth charges had pierced the boat's pressure hull then this might conceivably have caused wreckage such as the German sailors' hats to float to the surface and wash ashore.

At the same time, in an obvious effort to discourage me from placing too much credence in Mr Robert Brown's comments about the hats (he was the first of a number of firth residents to mention them to me), officials added a note of caution, remarking that one would not expect to see hats without the presence of other telltale items, particularly fragments of wood which would have been an indication that the casing on the pressure hull had been breached. It was not entirely unknown for German vessels, U-boats or otherwise, to jettison material over the side in an attempt to confuse the British about precisely where they had been operating.

The key argument against both the MoD's suggestion and its note of caution is that Brown and other time-witnesses saw the German sailors' hats on the shore immediately following the *only* recorded instance of prolonged depth charging that took place in the upper reaches of the Firth of Clyde, namely the Tail of the Bank event in late November 1939. They did not observe them three months later when the *Forester* and *Buccaneer* were possibly engaged in operations off the coast of Arran.

I pressed hard on the issue of the survivor and deceased disparities, especially on the "Albrecht and Klinger" paradox. I emphasised the glaring fact that both the Greenock and CWGC lists contain references to two persons buried 16 February 1940, (seemingly) exhumed in October 1962, who do not appear on the official U-33 personnel list for her last patrol. I put to them the logical assumption that one might reasonably expect the cemetery (Greenock) that commits persons to the earth a mere four days after death to have access to the most accurately available records in the form of personal belongings, clothing, papers and survivors' statements. Greenock Cemetery officials clearly included Albrecht and Klinger in its interment and burial records and so, I asked, who were these people and why were they not listed in the official U-33 crew complement?

The NHB confirmed that it has access to two lists of casualties. One is the list published in the *Interrogation of Survivors* (ref: BR1907 [103]), also available at the British Public Records Office under document reference ADM 186/805. The other is a list received by the *Oberkommando der Kriegsmarine (OKM)* from the British Admiralty within 6 months of U-33's sinking. This latter document was captured by an Anglo-American force at the end of WWII, along with most of the rest of the German Navy's archive at Tambach. The records were microfilmed in London before being returned to Germany.

NHB officials remarked upon the discrepancies between the two lists, pointing out that they are easily explained both by the difference in purpose between them and by the difficulties of identifying bodies that have been in the water for some length of time. In the case of U-33 none of the men who died either in the water or in transit to Greenock had been in the sea for more than an hour or so, a period sufficient to bring about death from complications caused by the freezing conditions but not nearly long enough to begin the decomposition process. The NHB explained that the crew lists given in the *Interrogations of Survivors* are almost always incomplete, remarking for example that it was often the case that traumatized survivors struggled to remember the full names of the dead, given that boatmates often used surnames or nicknames to address each other, thereby making the recollection of first names difficult.

The list recorded by the *OKM* is accompanied by notes giving some further explanation. The names of the surviving officers were received 28 March 1940 and those of the surviving ratings were received 1 April 1940. The names of the casualties from U-33 buried in Greenock were not received by the *OKM* until 16 August 1940. The list in the *Interrogation of Survivors* appeared in March 1940:

List of casualties in the Report of Interrogation of Survivors of U-33, Public Record Office Ref.erence ADM 186/805 (Col. A)	List of casualties in Greenock Cemetery sent in August 1940 to *Oberkommando der Kriegsmarine* by the Admiralty, Reference PG33325a (Col. B)
no corresponding name	Albrecht

Anger, Paul	Anger, Paul
Bergfeld	Bergfeld
Braun	*(body not recovered)*
Enders, Werner	Enders, Werner
Gross	Gross
Heckenrodt, Adalbert	Heckerodt
Henneberg, Gustav	Henneberg
Johne Hans	*(body not recovered)*
Kampert	Kampert
Keller, Werner	Keller
Kunick, Walter	Kunik, Walter
Kursiefen, Heinrich (Koch)	Kursiefen
Liebert	Liebert, Heinrich
Mohr	Mohr, Heinz
Patten, Erich	Patten
Peters, Karl Heinz	Klinger or Peters
Poeppel, Leopold	Pöppel, Leopold
Raath, Herbert	Raath, Herbert
Rausch, Paul	
	Schiller
Schmidt, Christian	Schmid, Christian
Steiner, Willibald	Sterner
Von Dresky, Hans (known to have gone down with his ship)	*(body not recovered)*
Wagner, Ludwig	Wagner, Ludwig
Wilden, Wilhelm	Wilden, Wilhelm
Winterhof	*(body not recovered)*
Total: 25	**Total: 21 (excluding Schiller)**

The notes subsequently appended by the *OKM* to the list state that Albrecht was not on board U-33 and that confirmation would be sought.

The NHB stated that the series of casualty lists in PG3325a were disrupted soon after the compilation of this list, skipping from 16 August 1940 to the autumn of 1941 before ceasing altogether, so there was no place to record the results of the investigation carried out by the *OKM* and the Second U-Flotille into the particulars of this person.

The list of casualties based on the Interrogation of Survivors provides names for 25 dead, the number one would expect the surviving sailors from U-33 to itemise (so much for the NHB's remark that interrogation numbers are almost always incomplete). The figure of 25, less 4 bodies not recovered, is matched by the burials in Greenock Cemetery for the deaths among U-33's *known* crew population. One would not expect survivors to offer readily details of those who had come on board, prior to or during a voyage, in an intelligence capacity.

It is known that U-33 survivors worked to a code of silence in exchanges with their captors. Schiller told David Hendry that during their time in the Kensington detention centre (the "London Cage") U-33's surviving officers passed between themselves a Morse code message through the pipes: "Give name and rank only."

The names in Column A are therefore one hundred percent correct in terms of the members of the official crew complement on U-33 who died. In contrast, the details in Column B prepared by the British authorities for the *OKM* contain numerous errors. Comparing like with like (Column A with B), it inexplicably omits Paul Rausch from those buried in Greenock. It includes Max Schiller when a quick cross-check with the Interrgogation of Survivors records would have confirmed he was among the living. It then muddles Peters and Klinger. If these errors are corrected the total among the Column B names for those buried at Greenock becomes 20 in accordance with the names provided by Interrogation of Survivors.

To complete the reconciliation for Column B against the survivors' list in Column A one must: add back Rausch and the 4 bodies not recovered, retain Peters and delete Schiller, bringing the total to 25 matching the Interrogation of Survivors Report. Column B's references to Albrecht and Klinger reveal that the Admiralty officials who drew up the list for *OKM* were probably unaware of the significance that would emerge about the pair and, hence, of the necessity to exercise caution before including their names in documentation for external circulation. Finally, when one does add Albrecht and Klinger into the equation the total deceased becomes, correctly, 27. The following table compares the Greenock Cemetery, CWGC and Admiralty lists, itemising discrepancies and highlighting comments and questions:

Greenock Cemetery (in order of ledger entry)	Corresponding CWGC entries in its letter and attachments to Greenock of 30 October 1962 for the exhumation and re-burial of 27 bodies	List of casualties buried in Greenock Cemetery—sent to *OKM* by British Authorities, Admiralty ref PG33325a	Comments
Klinger	Unknown		
Bergfeld	Hans Bergfeld	Bergfeld	
Werner Enders	Werner Paul Enders	Enders, Werner	
Rausch	Paul Rausch		Why did Admiralty list to *OKM* omit Rausch?
Kursiefen	Heinrich Kursiefen	Kursiefen	
Albrecht	Albrecht	Albrecht	
Anger	Paul Anger	Paul Anger	
Hickerodt	Adalbert Heckerodt	Heckerodt	
Gross	Karl Gross	Gross	
Leopold Pöppel	Leopold Pöppel	Pöppel, Leopold	
Ludwig Wagner	Ludwig Wagner	Wagner, Ludwig	
Christian Schmid	Christian Schmid	Schmid, Christian	
Keller	Werner Keller	Keller	
Wilhelm Wilden	Wilhelm Wilden	Wilden, Wilhelm	
Patten	Erich Patten	Patten	
Schiller (*should be Peters*)	Karl-Heinz Peters	Klinger or Peters	CWGC correcting Schiller error in Greenock ledger adding Peter's name
Walter Kunick	Walter Kunick	Kunik, Walter	
Kampert	Heinrich Kampert	Kampert	
Steiner	Willibald Steiner	Steiner	
Herbert Ruath	Herbert Raath	Raath, Herbert	
Heinz Mohr	Heinz Karl Mohr	Mohr, Heinz	
		Schiller	NHB's letter confirms this was a mistake
Heinrich Liebert	Heinrich E. Liebert	Liebert, Heinrich	
Henneberg	Gustav Henneberg	Henneberg	
23	**23 (plus the 4 unnamed Italians and Germans)**	21 (excl. Schiller)	

The NHB sought to explain away "Klinger" by making a direct comparison of the Interrogation of Survivors and the Admiralty's *OKM* lists. It suggested that Admiralty authorities were not clear at the time whether the decedent's name was Klinger or Peters and offered the German authorities both. The Admiralty's doubtful position on the degree of trustworthiness of records drawn up from the Interrogation of Survivors ensured that it sought other corroborative points of reference before preparing its *OKM* list.

The obvious unimpeachable reference source was Greenock Cemetery's burial records for 16 February 1940. These contained the names of both Klinger and Albrecht whom, one suspects, were regarded by junior grade Admiralty officials in those early months of 1940 as just names in a ledger flagging no necessity for extra care and scrutiny.

At the heart of the Admiralty's decision to offer *OKM* the names of both Klinger and Peters was the Schiller dog tag mix-up.

In the case of Albrecht the issue of identification becomes much more equivocal. This was not a situation where two names had been confused, eventually allowing one (Peters) to be chosen and the other (Klinger) discarded. In the words of a senior official in the NHB *"the identity of Sailor Albrecht is problematic."*

The NHB owns to the fact that the *OKM*, in reviewing the list of deceased sent to it by the Admiralty, did not recognize Albrecht as a member of the crew of U-33, adding somewhat surprisingly that *OKM* did not have direct access to the records of U-boat personnel of 2. U-Flotille. In conclusion, the NHB sought to explain the presence of Albrecht as "administrative error."

Here we have a genuine puzzle. Neither the German nor British authorities offered a satisfactory explanation for 'Sailor Albrecht' (at least none that is in the public domain). This suggests that Albrecht was not a genuine Kriegsmarine sailor.

And when the NHB is confronted with the evidence that there was both a Klinger *and* a Peters on board U-33 it cannot offer even the weakest explanation for the former. At the very least the Klinger and Albrecht issues and the very obvious gaps in knowledge must be an uncomfortable and embarrassing position for Admiralty officials and certainly not one on which they care to be pressed.

Their reluctance to be drawn further became increasingly evident as I continued to challenge the NHB's unforthcoming comments about the mystery men, emphasising that both Greenock Cemetery and the CWGC refer to 23 bodies buried from U-33, not 21.

Ultimately, my line of questioning was clearly regarded as an increasing source of exasperation. One day in May 2003 I received a letter from a senior officer in the NHB stating that: *"our views on the matter of U-33 are now very similar. I have nothing else to add to my last letter, which was based on all the relevant documents we hold."*

In fact, our respective views were wholly dissimilar. Nevertheless, twelve months of written exchanges had resulted in disclosure of highly informative U-33 crew details and statistics. When studied alongside other key information sources such as the Greenock Cemetery and CWGC records, these reveal significant inconsistencies permitting continuing challenge to the official line and encouraging deeper investigation.

U-Boat officers at Gravenshurst camp, Canada. Commander Werner Lott (U-35) is 5th from left. Chief Engineer Friedrich-Ernst Schilling (U-33) is 7th from left

Chapter THIRTEEN

Captain's Log

How many goodly creatures are there here!
I have great comfort from this fellow: methinks he
hath no drowning mark upon him

In twelve chapters we have charted the course of U-33's excursions into Scottish waters. To the uninformed the story of U-33 is not the stuff of headlines. It did its job with deadly efficiency, despatching eleven vessels in the course of its first two patrols, embarked on a third just weeks later and was sunk by HMS *Gleaner* before it could reach its attack destination in the upper reaches of the Clyde. Had it not been for Kumpf's reported inattentiveness and the consequent discovery of Enigma rotor parts, U-33 would not have merited more than passing mention in the history books.

But by the date of U-33's destruction it had forged a secret history, one whose sensational components can only now be laid before a patient public. Citizens of the Clyde will especially welcome a full disclosure of all of the facts pertinent to U-33, particularly those elements of the story that have been kept from public scrutiny for seventy years. In striving to see beyond the obvious, we have taken an uncompromising look at the:

➤ unusual circumstances of U-33's departure from Wilhelmshaven, including Hitler's role and influence in setting U-33's mission objectives;

➤ unseaworthy condition of U-33 and the hasty, botched repairs that did little to ameliorate the problems but did help to ensure that U-33 could make it to the Clyde to carry out its Führer-driven agenda of activities, irrespective of the crew's safety;

➤ consequent shared sentiment among the crew that U-33, in setting out on its 3rd mission, was embarking on a suicide mission;

➤ emerging suggestion in the contents of former *Greenock Telegraph* reporter Horace Oakes' correspondence that HMS *Gleaner* was not

U-33's nemesis;

➤ non-compliance with rigid operational rules that ultimately led to the seizure of Enigma parts, an unresolved mystery compounded by new revelations from U-33 survivor Max Schiller's family about the role of Friedrich Kumpf in the matter. If the Enigma parts were not found on Kumpf then how did the Royal Navy retrieve them? Were they from U-33 at all? What was the Navy really searching for in the prolonged diving operation undertaken after U-33's sinking?

➤ other remarks made over the years by Schiller, in particular statements that added to the known facts and/or contradicted the official line, including stating that U-33 went up to the Clyde Anchorage during its 2nd patrol, thereby providing new lines of research enquiry and fresh avenues for argument and analysis;

➤ questions about the true number of people on or associated with U-33 and the survivor / deceased statistics;

➤ riddle of the mystery men—Albrecht and Klinger—and the drawing of a blank, even with Herr Bredow's first-rate help, in isolating their specific identities from a study of all possible Kriegsmarine personnel who bore these surnames. Were the cover-up names concocted by an exceptionally well connected German present in Britain in the early months of the war?

➤ stories that began to emerge in 1985 in the pages of the *Largs and Millport Weekly News*, which referred to not one but to two U-boat excursions deep into the Firth of Clyde in the early months of WWII;

➤ subsequent elaboration of these accounts that positively identify U-33 as the submarine that landed men off Carradale Bay in November 1939 before going on later that autumn day to enter the Clyde Anchorage in the shadow of the Irish transporter the *Royal Ulsterman*;

➤ time-witness and family and friend descriptions that identify U-33 as the enemy submarine that landed men and performed tasks such as sheep rustling and water collection on the Isles of Islay and Bute around the time of the Carradale and Tail of the Bank events;

➤ seemingly impossible task (considering the armada of action-ready British vessels on hand) of U-33 passing into and out of the Cloch-Dunoon defence boom on the night of 22 November 1939, unscathed (or relatively unscathed), to keep its deadly appointment with the *Borkum* in the Orkneys on the following day. Did it, in fact, keep it at all?

➢ strange circumstance of the body washed up in Gourock open air swimming pool in early December 1939. Was it a fatality from a German U-boat, perhaps a special submarine, which entered the Clyde Anchorage just days before?

➢ bulging postbag of Scots' stories about these incidents, often told from first-hand knowledge, that confirm without a shadow of doubt the accounts of two separate and distinct U-boat incursions into the Firth of Clyde in November 1939 and February 1940, U-33 identified by the evidence as the culprit on both occasions;

➢ numerous accounts of enemy submarine wrecks in the Clyde, including stories about special and midget subs;

➢ secret dawn burials of the dead from U-33 in Greenock Cemetery on 16 February 1940, fortunately witnessed and diarised by newshound Horace Oakes. Were Albrecht and Klinger among them?

➢ questions surrounding the exhumation of the deceased in October 1962 for re-interment in the German Section at the Commonwealth War Graves Cemetery at Cannock in Staffordshire, including the emerging possibility that Albrecht and Klinger were exhumed in the early 1940s and are simply *commemorated* at Cannock;

➢ inconsistencies about the burials and exhumations of Messieurs Charles Haryog and Modiste Handy, allegedly sailors from the stricken *Maillé Brézé*. Do the curious circumstances surrounding the pair support the Albrecht and Klinger "shortly after burial" exhumation hypothesis?

➢ questions, too, about a number of other French deceased exhumed from Greenock Cemetery in 1948;

➢ enigma of "Sikh Hidtalla" buried in a pauper's grave in Greenock Cemetery 6 weeks after the Tail of the Bank event;

➢ absence of legally required death registration papers and certification for the deceased from U-33, Hidtalla and a number of French sailors;

➢ exchanges with the British Ministry of Defence's Naval Historical Branch, which provided the raw data to get to grips seriously with the vexed issues surrounding U-33's personnel numbers and indentities, and which finally provoked the revealing remark from the NHB that: "Sailor Albrecht is problematic."

In Part 4—Endgame—we will seek to identify what U-33 was *really* doing when it passed through the Cloch-Dunoon boom defences in November 1939. Without doubt it was engaged upon a special mission, perhaps one of the most remarkable of WWII in terms of its role in the frantic (and wholly unofficial) efforts on both sides to seek an early solution to the growing conflict.

That purpose alone would have been remarkable enough but to do justice to the full breadth of Scottish opinion one must seriously consider the subject of a parallel search for much sought after documents and/or items of great value, including legendary artefacts such as the Treasures of the Temple of Solomon and the Ark of the Covenant.

Was U-33 also an Ark whose Covenant was forged with men of high influence in the shadows of the Reich to secure for Germany ancient talismans of power?

While dwelling on these questions let us pause before returning to U-33 in Part 4 to look at other extraordinary stories of U-boat special missions undertaken around the globe in WWII.

After *Max Schiller through the Lens* we will begin Part 3 with the puzzle of what became of all the missing U-boats at the end of the war and conclude it with a fascinating look at how U-Boats in Scotland have featured in books and films over the years.

Max Schiller through the lens

Scanned from a poor quality original, this is the only known photo of
Max with his German family: mother Bertha, father Max, sister Irene,
brothers Otto and Fritz

Max (front centre) with fellow POWs in Canada (one side of a Prisoner of War postcard)

The two sides of a Prisoner of War postcard sent by Max (front centre) from
Bowmanville Camp, Ottawa, to his family at Angersdorf-über-Halle near Leipzig

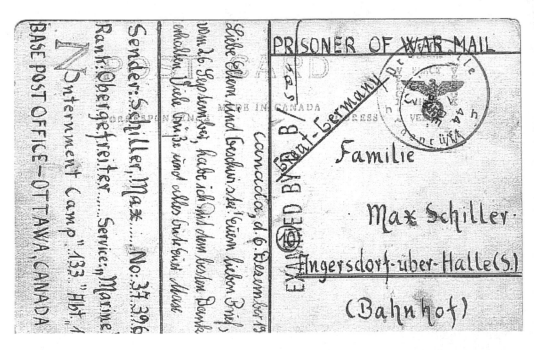

Another Prisoner of War postcard sent from Max (back row 1st left)

...and another (max 2nd from left)

Max in foreground, 2nd from left, with fellow POWs

Football was Max Schiller's great passion (front 2nd from left)

Max with workmates and farm boys, Barrasgait Farm, August 1947

Max and Jessie with dairy cattle at Barrasgait Farm

Jessie, Max and son Ray circa 1951

Max and Jessie at a wedding

Three pictures…..

…of a happy

…reunion of U-33 boatmates

Reunion at Restaurant-Hotel Lindenhof, Groß Ellershausen, Göttingen, 8 August 1990

Max with U-33 pals Peter Lingscheidt and Manfred (Fred) Krampe

Max with Ernst Masanek (U-33) and Siegfried Meltzer (not Kriegsmarine)

Max at home in Annan

Max photographed just before his death in 2002 aged 81

Absorbed in private memories after tossing the wreath into the Firth
of Clyde over the resting place of U-33 in February 2000

PART THREE

U-BOAT SPECIAL MISSIONS

The rarer action is
In virtue than in vengeance

Chapter FOURTEEN

Neu-Schwabenland and Station 211

Hell is empty
And all the devils are here.

Far from diminishing, the size of the U-boat fleet in the early months of 1945 was increasing, reaching its peak strength of 463 submarines in March of that year. After Germany surrendered in May 159 U-boats gave themselves up to the Allies but a further 203 were scuttled by their crews. By 10 June 1945 when an unmarked German U-boat surrendered to the Argentine Navy the whereabouts of the other 100 U-boats was still a mystery. Gradually, a number began to appear here and there but, ultimately, there were still more than 40 unaccounted for. By and large historians tend to gloss over the question of the missing U-boats. But where were they?

A suspicion grew that the missing U-boats were part of an Antarctic puzzle that Britain had been piecing together since Marshall Hermann Göring sent Captain Alfred Ritscher on a polar mission in 1938. With Britain's Intelligence network providing virtually all the information to its allies via the Enigma machine and its immense European spy network, a picture slowly began to emerge.

When U-boats were captured off the southern coast of South America, minus their commanding officers, it was assumed at first that they had dropped off the officers in Argentina then gone off in another direction to hide the location where they had been disembarked. But the U-boat crews said something different. Bizarrely, many reported that they had landed their officers in an underground base in Antarctica, which they had entered from beneath the ice-shelf.

A strong contender for the location of the Antarctic base was a part of Queen Maud Land, "Neu-Schwabenland," claimed by Germany between 1938 and 1945. The Reich had had a prior interest in Antarctica for many years but in 1938 this intensified with the mounting of an air and sea expedition whose purpose was to claim possession of a huge portion of the subcontinent in the name of the

Fatherland. Captain Ritscher's flagship was the *Schwabenland*. To prepare them for their mission, the project planners invited the great American polar explorer Richard E. Byrd to lecture them on what to expect. A second expedition followed in 1939.

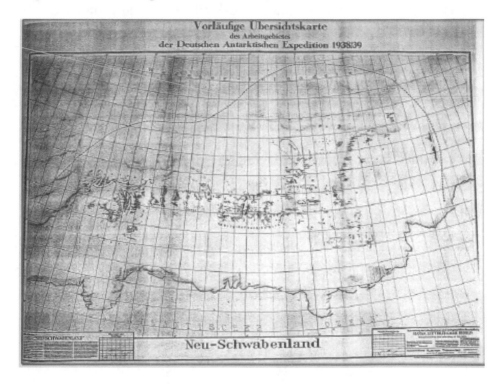

The region was named after Swabia, one of the original duchies of the German Kingdom. Swabia was home to the powerful Hohenstaufen Dynasty, which ruled the Holy Roman Empire in the 12th and 13th centuries. Frederick Barbarossa was the greatest of the Hohenstaufen kings and a wielder of the Holy Lance (Chapter 16). It is claimed that Hitler believed he was a reincarnation of Barbarossa. He named one of his houses after him and dubbed the invasion of Russia Operation Barbarossa.

Bizarrely, Adolf Hitler was fascinated by a belief that had gained considerable currency among the 'New Age' faddists of the day (including influential members of the Thule Society) that the earth was hollow. The theory held that the entrances into inner earth were at the North and South Poles (the much vaunted "holes at the poles") from which one could travel to the mythical land in the earth's centre called Agarthi, whose residents were survivors from the legendary antediluvian land of Hyperborea—the realm of the original Aryans.

On 18 July 1945 newspapers around the world were bearing

headlines about Antarctica. The *New York Times* stated "Antarctic Haven Reported," whilst others proclaimed that "Hitler had been at the South Pole." It is claimed that these sensational headlines were based, in part, on fact.

While Britain still possesed strategically based territories in the Falklands and Antarctica and one of the world's largest navies, it was ideally positioned among the Allies to investigate claims of a polar Nazi stronghold. With 16 German U-boats sunk in the South Atlantic area between October 1942 and September 1944 and most of those sunk engaged in covert activities, Britain had long been aware of Neu-Schwabenland being a possible base. It was not until after the war in Europe had ended in May 1945 that the world awoke to the possibility. Interrogations of the captains of both the U-977 and U-530 served to deepen the Allies' suspicions.

The German Antarctica Expedition of 1938-39 overflew nearly one-fifth of the continent, taking some 11,000 photographs. The expedition's aircraft also dropped several thousand small Nazi flags as well as special metal poles with the expedition's insignia and the swastika, claiming the territory for Germany.

Airmen from the German Antarctica Expedition of 1938-39

Ostensibly, the expeditions were undertaken to investigate the feasibility of whaling operations in the region but in reality they were carried out to assess if Antarctica could suitably accommodate a military base for planes, submarines and long-range missiles.

During the expedition several ice-free regions with lakes and signs of vegetation (mostly lichen and moss) were found in the territory's interior. The expedition's geologists said that this phenomenon was due to hot springs or to other geothermal sources. This discovery, it is claimed, led Reichsführer-SS Heinrich Himmler to draw up a plan to build a permanent base in Antarctica.

Under the command of Captain Heinrich Brodda U-209 is said to have made a trip to Antarctica in 1942 to explore various ice caverns discovered during Admiral Ritscher's 1939 excursion. One of the caverns investigated was found to to contain an immense hole spanned by a bridge of emerald green ice, which appeared to be bottomless. A number of tunnels were seen to lead into the depths of the mountain from which emanated strange whispering sounds resembling human voices.

Colonel Howard A. Buechner, the first American physician to enter Dachau in May 1945, wrote[1] that in 1943 U-629, commanded by OLt.z.S Hans-Helmuth Bugs, travelled to Antarctica to build a permanent entrance to the Emerald Cave with special cold-resistant metal. Perhaps a successful outcome to this mission prompted Dönitz to state in 1943: "The German submarine fleet is proud of having built for the Führer, in another part of the world, a Shangri-La on land, an impregnable fortress." Buechner also mentions unsubstantiated stories of several follow up submarine missions in 1942-1945 during which a second Berchtesgaden was constructed somewhere on Antarctica. He makes reference, too, of a U-boat excursion to Tierra del Fuego where a replica of Hitler's Berghof was built.

For more than sixty years rumours about an Antarctic base codenamed "Station 211" have excited historians and researchers. Some researchers claim that Hitler's deputy, Rudolf Hess, was entrusted with coordinating the effort to build Station 211. Most of the rumours agree that Station 211, if it really existed, was located inside a prominent ice-free mountain in the Muhlig-Hofmann Mountains of Neu-Schwabenland.

In 1946-47 Admiral Byrd may have searched for Station 211. The prospect of post-war Germany establishing a secret underground base in Antarctica was of such concern that in 1947 Admiral Byrd launched "Operation High Jump." Ostensibly, this was a massive training exercise to familiarise U.S. forces with cold-weather warfare. Byrd had at his disposal 4,700 men, 13 ships (including an aircraft carrier, a

---

[1] Beuchner Colonel Howard A., Bernhart Captain W., *Adolf Hitler and the Secrets of the Holy Lance,* Thunderbird Press Inc, Metairie, Louisiana, 1989

submarine and two destroyers) and two-dozen aircraft.

Beginning 30 December 1946, Byrd's ships variously arrived at three different rendezvous points inside the Antarctic Circle. What, if anything, did Admiral Byrd encounter? An early "casualty" of "Byrd's War" was the submarine USS *Sennet*. The official story is that the ice proved to be too dangerous for the vessel, which was towed back to Scott Island but there has been considerable speculation that she hit German anti-submarine defences.

On another occasion a PBM flying boat, George One, struck the top of a mountain and went down killing three. Scores of aerial mapping flights were made deep into the heart of the frozen continent, including several overflights of the South Pole. In total over 73,000 photographs were taken but, surprisingly, only a few thousand were said to be of any value. The problem was blamed on a lack of adequate ground control points, which resulted in a vast number of meaningless pictures of ice…or so it was claimed.

Admiral Richard E. Byrd

The following year a much smaller expedition, Operation Windmill, was launched to get these needed coordinates. Some researchers have suggested that Windmill's real purpose was to see if Station 211 was still occupied; that the need to establish ground control points was a cover story.

One of the most remarkable expedition discoveries was that of "Bunger's Oasis." During an exploratory flight PBM pilot Lieutenant Commander David E. Bunger and his flight crew saw a dark spot rising up over the barren white horizon before them. To their complete disbelief as they drew closer they saw a "land of blue and green lakes and brown hills in an otherwise limitless expanse of ice." Several days later Bunger and his crew returned for another look, finding one of the lakes big enough to land on. Bunger carefully landed the plane and slowly came to a stop. The water was actually quite warm for Antarctica, about 30°C, as the men dipped their hands in up to the elbow. The lake's distinctive colour was an effect of a great profusion of red, blue and green algae. Byrd later wrote that the airmen "seemed to have dropped out of the twentieth century into a landscape of thousands of years ago when land was just starting to emerge from one of the great ice ages." He described the discovery as "by far the most important so far as the public interest was concerned of the expedition." There are elements here mindful of Edgar Rice Burroughs' classic story "*The Land that Time Forgot*," in which a Jurassic nightmare confronts the crew of First World War U-boat 33 when it surfaces in a lagoon on the uncharted island of Caprona.

The official record of the Byrd missions appears innocuous yet there have been persistent rumours of violent battles, large-scale casualties, planes shot down and more. Byrd's log entry for a flight made on 19 February 1947 reportedly contains sensational remarks, among them : "Ahead we spot what seems to be a city" and "my God, off our port and starboard wings are a strange type of aircraft...they are closing rapidly...they're disc-shaped...with Swastika markings."

According to investigator Alan DeWalton Admiral Byrd stated in a press conference that the Antarctic continent should be surrounded by a "wall of defence installations since it represented the last line of defence for America." Another claim made by investigators is that on his return to the U.S.A. Admiral Byrd flew into a rage in front of the President and Joint Chiefs of Staff, urging that Antarctica be turned into a thermonuclear test range.

The question has been posed that if the Antarctic accounts are little more than wild tales then why did Captain Richard H. Cruzen, the operational commander of the expedition, order its abrupt end after just eight weeks when they had enough provisions for six to eight months in the polar region? In Admiral Byrd's own words (press release of 12 November 1946) "the mission was 'primarily of a military nature.' " Byrd also spoke of "flying objects that could fly from pole to pole at incredible speeds" (*El Mercurio*, 5 March 1947—Admiral Byrd interviewed by Lee van Atta).

During the period between 1956 and 1960 a Norwegian expedition mapped most of Queen Maud Land from land surveys and air photos. Remarkably, they did find an ice-free mountain that matched the description of the one in the Station 211 rumours. They called it Svarthamaren (the black hammer). The site has been designated an Antarctic Specially Protected Area and Site of Special Scientific Interest under the Antarctic Conservation Act of 1978. It was listed as an "exceptional natural research laboratory for ornithological research on the Antarctic petrel, snow petrel and south polar skua and their adaptation to breeding in the inland / interior of Antarctica." Access is limited to a handful of specially selected scientists.

James Robert, WWII historian and writer, interviewed an

(unnamed) British wartime SAS officer described by Robert as the last survivor of the Neu-Schwabenland campaign. According to Robert, during his four week pre-mission training on the island of South Georgia the officer was told that he would be one of a party investigating anomalous activities around the Mühlig-Hoffmann Mountains from the British base in Maudheim, Antarctica. Antarctica, he was told, was "Britain's secret war."[2] Maudheim was within 200 miles of where the Nazis had supposedly built their Antarctic base.

In the summer of 1944 British scientists and commandos had found an "ancient tunnel." Under orders the thirty-strong force went through the tunnel but only two returned before the Antarctic winter set in. During the winter months the two survivors made absurd claims over the radio about Polar Men, ancient tunnels and Nazis. Radio contact was finally lost in July 1945. The last broadcast concluded abruptly with an anguished scream: "...*the Polar Men have found us!*"

Against this macabre backdrop the mission took place. The SAS team found one survivor who said that in Bunker One would be found the other survivor. The bunker door was opened and an unrecognisable figure dashed out. Inside was the soldier's comrade. His throat had been ripped open and, gruesomely, he had been stripped to the bone.

Under questioning the surviving soldier described finding a tunnel, which led to a vast abnormally warm underground cavern filled with lakes. Startlingly, the cavern was lit artificially. Investigation showed that the Nazis had constructed a huge base inside the caverns and had even built docks for U-boats. The survivor reported that "hangars for strange planes and excavations galore" had been documented. The British exploration team had been spotted and all executed except for the two soldiers.

The survivor said that the "Polar Men" were a product of Nazi science although the SAS veteran's account does not elaborate on how he arrived at this conclusion. The team captured and killed one of the Polar Men and the mission scientist declared that he was human but it seemed he had been able to produce more hair and withstand the cold far more effectively. The survivor went on to say that the Nazis' power source was volcanic, which gave them heat for steam and also helped to produce electricity.

The scientist in the SAS man's party dismissed most of what was divulged and rebuked the survivor for his lack of scientific education, implying that his revelations could not possibly be true.

---

[2] Robert J., *Britain's Secret War in Antarctica*, NEXUS Magazine, volume 12, number 5, 2005

Nine SAS commandos entered the tunnel, eventually reaching the vast, lit cavern. From their place of concealment they were astounded to see a great number of people scurrying antlike around the cavern. They were also confronted by a staggering scale of construction activity.

After two days of reconnaissance mines were placed. At the same time a hostage was taken as well as physical proof of the base (including the slain "Polar Man") and photographs of advanced Nazi technology. The mines destroyed much of the cavern's infrastructure and closed the tunnel but seven of the team were killed in heavy fighting during the retreat from the scene. On their return to South Georgia the mission team was ordered never to reveal what it had seen, heard or encountered. The tunnel was explained away as glacial erosion. The Polar Men were merely "unkempt soldiers that had gone crazy."

Stories about U-boat activity in the area continued for many years after the war. A French newsagency reported in September 1946 that: "the continuous rumors about German U-boat activity in the region of Tierra del Fuego between the southernmost tip of Latin America and the continent of Antarctica are based on true happenings."

France Soir then published an account describing the Icelandic whaler *Juliana*'s purported encounter eighteen months after the cessation of hostilities. The *Juliana* was in the Antarctic region around the Malvinas Islands (today the Falklands) when a large German submarine surfaced and raised the German official Flag of Mourning— red with a black edge. The submarine commander sent out a boarding party, which approached the *Juliana* in a rubber dinghy. The boarding party demanded of the whaler's Captain Hekla part of his fresh food stocks. The German officer spoke correct English and paid for his provisions in U.S. dollars, giving Hekla a bonus of $10 for each member of the *Juliana* crew.

Whilst the foodstuffs were being transferred the U-boat commander informed Captain Hekla of the exact location of a large school of whales, which were subsequently found in precisely that region. Critics of this account have claimed that Icelandic whalers have never operated in the South Atlantic and, moreover, that there has never been a whaler named the *Juliana*. They also point out that Hekla is an active volcano in Iceland, not a name, and that 99 percent of all Icelandic last names for males end in "-son."

Author Wilhelm Landig claimed that it was not just in Antarctica that Nazi strongholds were established. During WWII Landig held a senior position in the central Nazi archive in Berlin where information from all around the world came in for analysis and filing. In 1971 Landig published *Kampf gegen Thule*—Battle against Thule, (later republished as *Götzen gegen Thule*—Godlets against Thule), claiming that his book was not a work of fiction but one based on facts that his higher-ups had given him leave to publish.

Styling himself, thus, as a "man in the know," Landig writes extensively in *Götzen gegen Thule* about the Nazis' polar bases, which included the Canadian Arctic, the "Alps" on the Argentine/Chilean border (reportedly named Colonia Dignidad) and a base in Eastern Greenland called by the Germans Biber Damm (Beaver Dam), which Landig said was accessed via U-boat through underwater tunnels. This method of U-boat access was also described for the base at Neu-Schwabenland.

In fact, this type of entrance was actually built and an example can be seen at the German base on the island of Fuerteventura in the Canary Islands. Steven Spielberg is said to have got the idea for the submarine base scene in *Raiders of the Lost Ark* from the Beaver Dam facility, which some researchers claim was a secret joint Nazi-NATO base until well after the war.

Landig also provides a dramatic description of the Ark of the Covenant as an ancient day 'Weapon of Mass Destruction' wielded by Israeli sorcerers against the first (pre-flood) Aryans, sensational images brought to cinematic life in the final island scene of *Raiders of the Lost Ark* when archaeologist René Belloq (an ill-deserved synonym for Grail historian Otto Rahn) and his Nazi cohorts are incendiarised by the Light of God released from the Ark. In another of his works Landig claimed that Neu-Schwabenland was abandoned around 1959-1960 because its inhabitants, having no natural immunity due to the absence of germs in the pure air of Antarctica, suffered sickness epidemics when new arrivals arrived with so much as a cold.

Tales also circulated from time to time about U-boats destined for Antarctica bearing strange cargoes. One such story focused on submarines carrying large quantities of mercury. WWII mythology offers the proposition that cargoes of this toxic metal were transported to Neu-Schwabenland for use in futuristic Nazi technologies, including advanced fuel systems.

The case of U-864, examined in the next chapter, is probably the most well known example of a U-boat apprehended while ferrying mercury. In this instance, however, its quicksilver cargo was bound, not for Station 211, but for Germany's Axis ally, Japan.

Chapter FIFTEEN

Mercury Rising

...for which foul deed
The powers, delaying, not forgetting, have
Incensed the seas and shores...

On 9 February 9 1944 U-864 was intercepted by the Royal Navy submarine HMS *Venturer* near the Norwegian island of Fedje, north of Bergen. The U-boat was carrying 1,857 canisters of mercury weighing a total of 65 tons. At the time of its sinking, U-864 was beginning a long journey from Nazi Germany to Jakarta, Indonesia, then under the control of Imperial Japan.

As part of Operation Caesar the U-boat was delivering materials, parts and plans to Germany's Axis ally. Approximately 1,500 tons of mercury was purchased by the Japanese from Italy between 1942 and Italy's surrender in September 1943. This had the highest priority for submarine shipment to Japan and was used in the manufacture of explosives, most especially primers.

In addition to the on-board mercury U-864 also reportedly carried Me-262 jet engine parts, detailed plans for manufacturing the combat jets as well as German and Japanese scientists and engineers.

Commanded throughout its entire career by Korvettenkapitän Ralf-Reimar Wolfram, U-864 served with the 4th Submarine Flotilla undergoing crew training from her commissioning until 31 October 1944. She was then re-assigned to the 33rd Submarine Flotilla.

HMS *Venturer*, commanded by Lieutenant James "Jimmy" S. Launders, was sent on her eleventh patrol from the British submarine base at Lerwick in the Shetland Islands to Fedje. After German radio transmissions concerning U-864 were decrypted she was rerouted to intercept the U-boat.

On 6 February she passed the Fedje area without being detected but one of her engines began to misfire and was ordered to return to Bergen. A signal stated that a new escort would be provided to her at Hellisøy on 10 February. She made for there but on 9 February

Venturer heard U-864's engine noise (Launders had decided not to use asdic since it would betray his position) and spotted the U-boat's periscope.

In an unusually long engagement for a submarine, in a situation for which neither of the submarines' crews had been trained, Launders waited 45 minutes after first contact before going into action stations, waiting in vain for U-864 to surface to present an easier target.

Upon realizing they were being followed by the British submarine and that their escort had still not arrived, U-864 zig-zagged in evasive manoeuvres while each submarine took the risk of raising its periscope.

Venturer had only 8 torpedoes (4 tubes and 4 reloads) as opposed to U-864's total of 22. After 3 hours Launders decided to make a prediction of his opponent's course and released a spread of torpedoes into its predicted path. The first torpedo was released at 12:12 and thereafter at 17-second intervals (taking 4 minutes to reach their target). Launders then dived suddenly to evade any retaliation.

U-864 heard the torpedoes coming and also dived deeper and turned away. It managed to avoid the first three but unwittingly steered into the path of the fourth. Imploding, she split in two sinking with all hands, coming to rest more than 500 feet below the surface on the seafloor 2.3 miles west of the island of Fedje. Even in death the U-boat still posed a threat to its surroundings.

U-864 has gone down in history as the only submarine to be sunk by another submarine while underwater. The two parts of the wreck were discovered in 2003, 2.2 miles from Fedje in the North Sea at 500 feet. In 2006 it was found that the canisters holding the mercury were corroding.

It is noteworthy that in the intervening 59-year period U-864 had shifted only one-tenth of a mile from its original wreck position. This fact only serves to emphasise the extreme unlikelihood that U-33 could have drifted between 22-35 miles northwards up the firth between the Millport and Lunderston Bay area in a similar time period, thus supporting Scots' claims that there is a second U-boat wreck in this vicinity.

There was some speculation as to whether U-864 was carrying uranium oxide but the Det Norske Veritas Foundation concluded that there was no evidence that uranium oxide was on board U-864 when she departed Bergen. During the Norwegian Coastal Administration's investigation of the wreck of U-864 in 2005 radiation was measured but no traces of uranium oxide were found.

Since 2005 locals and fishermen have pleaded for the wreck to be raised but the authorities' first response was to refuse to undertake the operation, citing the very high risks involved.

So far, 4 kilograms per year of mercury are leaking out into the surrounding environment, resulting in high levels of contamination in cod, torsk and edible crab around the wreck. Boating and fishing near the wreck have been prohibited. Although attempts using robotic vehicles to dig into the half-buried keel were abandoned after the unstable wreck shifted, one of the steel bottles was recovered. Its original 5-mm thick wall was found to have corroded badly, leaving in places only a 1-mm thickness of steel.

Mercury jars from U-864 retrieved in 2005

The delicate condition of the 2,400-ton wreck, the rusting mercury bottles and the live torpedoes on board make a lifting operation extremely dangerous, with significant potential for an environmental catastrophe.

A three-year study by the Norwegian Coastal Administration recommended entombing the wreck in a 12-metre thickness of sand with a reinforcing layer of gravel or concrete to prevent erosion. This was proposed as a permanent solution to the problem, noting that similar techniques had been successfully used around thirty times to contain mercury-contaminated sites over the past twenty years. However, the proposal of entombing the wreck rather than removing it was criticised by locals concerned about possible future leakage.

Plans then changed. In November 2008 the Norwegian Coastal Administration awarded the contract for the possible salvage of U-864 and its cargo of mercury to salvage company Mammoet Salvage BV.

Mammoet, which recovered the salvage of Russian nuclear submarine Kursk in 2001, had proposed a method of raising U-864 using innovative lifting techniques, which would satisfy the environmental requirements. It was described as "a safe and innovative salvage solution."

What makes the salvage particularly tricky are the 22 unexploded torpedoes at the wreck site, some in the bow section, some in the stern. Because of the danger from these still potent weapons the salvage will be directed from the surface by remote control. No divers will be used.

In January 2009 the Norwegian government approved Mammoet's proposed method of raising the wreck in an operation costed at more than one billion kroner.

Chapter SIXTEEN

The Holy Lance

Some kinds of baseness are nobly undergone.

One of the more sensational stories in Nazi mythology is Adolf Hitler's purported possession of the Holy Lance (the "Spear of Destiny"), which the Roman centurion Gaius Cassius Longinus used to pierce the side of Christ on the Cross in order to hasten Jesus' death. Over the centuries it is claimed that the Lance passed through the hands of some of Europe's foremost leaders including Constantine, Justinian, Charlemagne, Otto the Great and the Habsburg Emperors.

In the course of time the legend grew that "whosoever possesses this Holy Lance and understands the powers it serves, holds in his hand the destiny of the world for good or evil." Trevor Ravenscroft[1] claimed that in the twentieth century Adolf Hitler seized the Lance to wield as an almighty talisman of power against Germany's enemies.

According to author Dale Pollock,[2] Philip Kaufman, one of the principal writers for *Raiders of the Lost Ark*, was inspired to develop the storyline for this first *Indiana Jones* escapade having learned of Hitler's obsession to seize the Spear of Longinus.

Colonel Howard Buechner believed that Hitler had the Lance sent to Kiel in mid-April 1945 in the custody of one of his most trusted officers. Dr. Buechner based his claims[3] on the sworn statements of his co-author, U-boat sailor 'Captain Wilhelm Bernhart,' a pseudonym chosen to protect the man who even in 1989 "knew too much." Bernhart claimed that he could prove that the famous Spear of Destiny on display in the Schatzkammer Museum in Vienna is a fake. What follows is Buechner's account.

He claimed that on 2 May 1945 the Holy Lance was transported on

---

[1] ibid

[2] Pollock D., Photographic Illustrations *Skywalking - The Life and Films of George Lucas*, Harmony Books, 1983.

[3] Beuchner Colonel Howard A., Bernhart Captain W., *Adolf Hitler and the Secrets of the Holy Lance,* Thunderbird Press Inc, Metairie, Louisiana, 1989

U-530 to Antarctica where it was cached in an ice cave in the Mühlig Hoffman Mountains.

On the same day as U-530's departure Buechner records the sailing of a second boat, U-977, bound for the same destination.

In late March 1945 when it was evident to Hitler that the war was lost he activated special project "Valkure Zwei" (Valkyrie Two), whose objectives were to transport certain items of the Reich's treasures to

German Antarctica. Some believe that Hitler chose to call the mission Valkyrie Two (Valkyrie One having been the Von Stauffenberg assassination attempt that Hitler survived) to signify that it was his plan to live on after the war's end.

Buechner says that Dönitz was charged with the responsibility for making all the necessary preparations for despatch but that a 'Colonel Maximilian Hartmann' (also a pseudonym) was placed in absolute command of the mission on Hitler's orders. Hartmann was the man whom SS-Obergruppenführer Reinhard Heydrich (the Black Prince of the Third Reich) had named as his successor.

While Heydrich was slowly dying from wounds he sustained in the British-backed assassination attempt in Prague on 27 May 1942, he set about writing quickly and extensively. No one dared ask what he was doing but it was assumed Heydrich was compiling his memoirs.

On 2 June he sent for an SS-Lieutenant-General named Karl Müller and three other SS officers. According to Buechner, Heydrich entrusted the men with several tasks.

Müller was given a large, sealed package to be delivered to Professor

Karl Haushofer in Munich and to wait for further instructions. Heydrich died from septicaemia on 4 June, a direct result of the assassination attack eight days before.

In Munich Haushofer gave Müller a large bronze, lead-lined box and was instructed to take it to a place in Bavaria and bury it. He was also asked to prepare an addendum to the documented coded location of the box and deliver it to a Swiss bank as instructed by Heydrich. Subsequent to carrying out these tasks Müller was killed in a car accident.

Notes found in Haushofer's possession after his suicide in March 1946 revealed that the bronze box was to be found at the foot of the Schleigeiss Glacier near the Zillertal Mountain Pass. Only Müller, deceased, knew the exact whereabouts of the box. Haushofer had known the identity of the contents of the box: rune-coded papers describing the power of the Holy Lance and the secret of how its power may be utilised. The box had been intended for Heydrich's successor.

Buechner claims that U-530 and U-977 respectively brought the Holy Lance and the ashes of Adolf Hitler and Eva Braun to the Emerald Cave. Also said to have been cached on U-530 was a metre-high hollow black basalt obelisk in which was hidden a parchment providing a detailed description and hiding place of the Grail Cup. The obelisk had belonged to Karl Haushofer who had had inscribed on its base in gold lettering the legend: "There are truly more things in heaven and 'in earth' than man has dreamt (Beyond this point is AGHARTA)."

Captain Bernhart, an officer on U-530 (he has been described as a junior torpedo officer), claimed that under Operation Valkure Zwei his U-boat set off from its German port in February 1945, operating in Norwegian waters for four weeks before departing for the Antarctic on 13 March.

The story goes that the Reich treasures were carefully packed into six bronze lead-lined boxes, each adorned with a special mark. The boxes were transported to Kiel where they were loaded onto U-530 and became the responsibility of Oberleutnant sur Zee Otto Wermuth. Hartmann handed Wermuth his preliminary orders and another sealed package containing his final instructions, this latter envelope not to be opened until one hundred miles out to sea. Until its departure U-530 was protected and concealed in a massive concrete slip.

From Kiel U-530 made its way to Christiansand, Norway, departing 2 May 1945, eventually arriving in Antarctica without incident at approximate position 71:30S 14:51W. The story goes that a party of sixteen men (including Bernhart) brought the six bronze boxes ashore, together with sleds and special survival gear. The plan was for the landing party to fulfil its mission in 16 days, 18 maximum. After 18 days it had not returned and scouts were unable to trace it. On day 19 the party re-appeared. Their map had been incorrectly drawn and several days had been lost. Nevertheless, the mission had been successful—the Emerald Cave had been located and the boxes stowed inside, Haushofer's obelisk placed beside them. Bernhart told Beuchman that U-530's log was destroyed and a substitute one put in its place.

On 10 July 1945 U-530 entered the harbour of Mar del Plata, Argentina, 250 miles south of Buenos Aires, and surrendered to the authorities nine weeks after the end of the war in Europe. Wermuth had jettisoned the submarine's guns. Owing to the late surrender of the U-boat a special Allied intelligence team was despatched to Argentina to assess the situation.

U-530's physical condition raised eyebrows. According to eyewitnesses its hull was rusting, its conning tower was splitting apart and the corroded casing bore traces of a recent serious fire. A determined attempt had been made to sabotage the diesels.

Wermuth reported that U-530 had sailed from Horten, Norway, on 3 March 1945 and had observed radio silence from the time they entered U.S. coastal waters on 24 April. He said that U-530 had been very close to New York City and described seeing trains and automobiles through the periscope. Allegedly, the boat had no further radio contact with anybody until 12 May when the crew finally learned that Germany had surrendered the previous week.

The submarine was carrying 54 men, a seemingly abnormally high number although Wermuth insisted it was the boat's normal crew complement. The cargo consisted of 540 barrels of cigarettes and, unusually, large stocks of food. Wermuth was 25 years old, the second officer was 22 and the crew's average age was 25. This unusually young crew professed, to a man, that they had no living relatives. None of the crew was a cigarette smoker. Almost none carried identity documents and so it was impossible to work out just who was who.

The fake ship's log indicated that the U-boat's mission had been to disrupt Allied shipping in the South Atlantic and that it had remained at sea for two months after Germany's capitulation because of uncertainty over a time and a place for its surrender. The investigators concluded that if, as Wermuth had stated, U-530 had been at sea for five months she must have been obtaining supplies from somewhere or had been lying in a concealed harbour for part of the time.

Investigators formed the opinion that there had been a mutiny aboard U-530 and that Wermuth had not always been in command of the boat.

It was even speculated by the investigators that the short and dark-haired person calling himself Otto Wermuth was an imposter who had taken the place of the legitimate tall blond Oberleutnant at some place on the Argentine coast. To support this theory, investigators pointed to the captain's vagueness as to details of the voyage and his statement that "the deck gun was unshipped in Germany and left on the quayside" while the crew all remember having manhandled it overboard into the Atlantic. He was unable to explain the absence of one of the U-boat's six inflatable dinghies and admitted to destroying all the books, diaries, charts, code books and other documents of "a secret character."

Not long afterwards the crew was released from custody and the men went their separate ways.

Bernhart and Buechner's claims appear to be very farfetched but, curiously, Pravda reported on 16 January 2003 that in 1983 Special Services seized a confidential letter that Captain Heinz Scheffer, commander of U-977, wrote to Bernhart. In the letter Scheffer pleads with Bernhart not to publish his memoirs in too much detail, stressing that: "we all made an oath to keep the secret; we did nothing wrong: we just obeyed orders and fought for our loved Germany and its survival. Please think again; isn't it better to picture everything as a fable? What results do you plan to achieve with your revelations? Think about it, please."

The clock then moves forward thirty-four years with Buechner going on to describe the activities of an alleged German expedition in 1979, which sailed to Antarctica under the leadership of "Hartmann" and retrieved four of the bronze boxes. Buechner states that the obelisk was ignored because the members of the retrieval team had no knowledge of its contents. The other four boxes could not be taken away because of transportation problems. Buechner claims that Hartmann entrusted to him the log of this expedition.

Buechner and his mysterious co-author went into detail about how the 1979 Hartmann expedition came about. They claimed that several days after Rudolf Hess was taken in 1969 to a British hospital for the treatment of ulcers, a former crewmember of U-530 received the key to a bank box in Switzerland. This box led to another in which was a number of sealed envelopes, including one containing a large sum of money. A message in the box was signed "H."

The ex-submariner opened the envelopes and found instructions to deliver the contents of the box to the man whom Hitler had personally entrusted with sending some of his most prized possessions, including the Holy Lance, to Antarctica. Buechner and Bernhart refer to this trustee as "Colonel Maximilian Hartmann." The claim is made that Hartmann did not leave Germany at the end of the war and instead stayed to ensure that senior Reich figures such as Martin Bormann and the Reich treasure were given passage out of Germany in the closing days of the war. The submarines chosen to perform these tasks have been referred to as the "Führer Convoy."

In the first envelope Hartmann found a coded message from Professor Karl Haushofer, the éminence grise and chief architect of Nazi occult and esoteric philosophy. Once decoded, the message revealed the exact location of the bronze boxes Hartmann had sent to Antarctica in the care of Captain Otto Wermuth on U-530 twenty-four years earlier.

The second envelope instructed Hartmann to recreate Himmler's Knight's Grand Council with the express proviso that it was to use the power of the Holy Lance to bring about world peace. The third envelope contained the funds to finance the establishment of the revamped Council (the Knights of the Holy Lance), whose first objective was to recover the Lance from its Antarctica hiding place.

Hartmann and three other Knights of the Holy Lance arrived in the region by helicopter. They located the cache of bronze boxes, four of which were left behind due to the helicopter's weight restrictions.

The team made their way back to Brazil, the starting point for their journey, and successfully obtained export papers for the Lance by declaring it an art object. Hartmann's colleagues returned to Germany but he went on to the United States and met with an unidentified former crewman from one of the Führer Convoy submarines. Buechner-Bernhart claim that Hartmann left certain items with this seaman, including a copy of the log of the Hartmann Expedition and a signed, handwritten letter of authenticity. Hartmann then departed, taking the Lance back to Germany.

In his conclusion Buechner stated (in 1988) that the Holy Lance was located in Germany, probably in Westphalia, not far from Paderborn.

And what became of U-530? After its surrender at Mar del Plata U-530 was transferred to the U.S.A. and used for tests. In November 1947 it was scuttled during one of these tests by a torpedo northeast of Cape Cod.

Chapter SEVENTEEN

U-boats in Scotland
Fact in Fiction

I think he will carry this island home in his pocket
and give it his son for an apple.

Scotland is well served in fiction, in print and on celluloid for stories in which U-boats feature either as lead or bit player.

In Book 4 of their feted *Adept* series of novels co-writers Katherine Kurtz and Deborah Turner Harris describe in *Dagger Magic*[1] how a U-boat was hidden by Tibetan sorcerers at the end of WWII in a cave off the coast of Donegal. The U-boat would remain in its place of concealment until an auspicious time when its dreadful cargo could be recovered to create a new and invincible Reich.

The authors used U-636 as the model for their sensational piece of fiction, an opportunistic act of poetic licence drawing on the known and convenient history of the U-boat, which was depth charged by Royal Navy frigates in April 1945 ninety miles northeast of Donegal.

In correspondence with Katherine Kurtz she told me she had first got hooked on the subject in the early 1980s. Subsequently, Turner Harris and Kurtz undertook research from a number of sources (the 'occult' Reich, Tibetan priests brought to pre-WWII Germany *et al*) and together wove it into the appealing story of *Dagger Magic*.

Kurtz added that she had also had a keen interest in the Knights Templar connections with Scotland, beginning with the enforced dissolution of the warrior monks in 1307 and the purported subsequent arrival to the country of a contingent of survivors bearing untold riches.

Survivors from Pope Boniface VIII and French King Philippe IV's bloody pogrom dispersed to regions in Europe sympathetic to the plight of the Templars. Legend has it that one group of Knights made for

---

[1] Kurtz K. and Turner Harris D., *The Adept 4: Dagger Magic*, Ace, 1996.

Scotland on a number of ships loaded to the gunnels with treasure (including, allegedly, the Treasures of the Temple of Solomon, hence the ensuing stories about the Grail at Rosslyn Chapel and other Scottish locations).

The authors locate the sanctuary of a Tibetan sage on Holy Island situated off Arran's east coast. The centenarian lama agrees to assist the Scottish adepts in the battle against the black monks. He resides in St. Molaise's cave, named after the Celtic Christian saint who lived on the island at the end of the 6th century. Considering the authors' favoured research topics it is also likely that in choosing to locate the Tibetan sage in St Molaise's cave they were making a vigorous nod to the reported historical associations between the Knights Templar and Scotland. The 23rd Grand Master of the Knights Templar at the time of its violent undoing was Jacques de Molay who was roasted over an open fire in 1314.

St.Molaise's Cave, Holy Island, Arran

Dagger Magic begins fifty years after war's end when Irish coastal fisheries officials disturb the efforts of two Tibetan sorcerers (*ngagspas)* to locate the corroding hulk of U-636 in a cave at the base of Horn Head cliffs near Sheephaven on the Donegal coast. Inside the submarine are four wooden crates and a larger chest of brass-bound teakwood containing sacred pre-Buddhist texts—the *Black Termas*.

Using their magical daggers (*phurbas*) the *ngagspas* murder the officials, one of whose bodies is washed up on the Mull of Kintyre. News of its discovery soon reaches Argyll and Bute police. A senior officer, unbeknown to his colleagues a member of a powerful Scottish Lodge of white magicians, contacts his fellow adepts who take action to thwart the Tibetans' demonic plans.

The head of the Tibetans' monastery in Switzerland is a German who as a young boy in the final months of WWII was identified as the legitimate new reincarnation of the "Man with the Green Gloves," the all-powerful *Rinpoche* who had been the spiritual leader of the community of Tibetan lamas resident in Germany since the 1920s.

The Man with the Green Gloves was an actual historical figure on whom Hitler placed considerable reliance for guidance in esoteric matters. On one particularly memorable occasion the eminent Buddhist impressed the Führer by correctly forecasting the number of seats that the Nationalsozialistische Deutsche Arbeiterpartei would win in the Reichstag in its accession to power in 1933.

Researchers, notably Pauwels and Bergier,[2] have written of the bizarre discovery by Russian troops in Berlin in early May 1940 of hundreds of suicided Tibetan monks, many of whom were laid out in a ritual star formation.

Kurtz and Turner Harris depict a scenario where the Man with the Green Gloves, prior to his death, made detailed preparations to conceal and safeguard the *Termas*.

At a date in the future the Patrons of Shadows would retrieve the *Termas* and use them to call forth the dread god Shinjed, Lord of the Dead and Devourer of the Living, to allow access to the Keys to Agartha and to unleash the forces of Hell.

The novel culminates in the inevitable battle between the forces of Good and Evil. It is touch and go. The *ngagspas* are defeated and the *Termas* destroyed but not before the Tibetans re-animate the decayed corpses of the submarine's captain and crew to refloat U-636 into open water. All the while, the world remains wholly ignorant of the peril before it.

There are clear correspondences in *Dagger Magic* with the story of U-33. Horn Head, the epicentre of the confrontation, is just a few miles from Tory Island, a focal point round which U-33 made attacks in November 1939 and a location easily viewable from either of the

---

[2] Pauwels L. and Bergier J., *The Dawn of Magic,* Anthony Gibb and Phillips, London, 1963

headland's two lookout towers, one built in Napoleonic times, the other in WWII.

In earlier pages it was demonstrated that in November 1939 U-33 undertook a circuitous route from Tory Island (known historical fact) to Carradale Bay where it landed men (historical fact uncovered). From there U-33 travelled northeast to the Cloch-Dunoon defence boom and passed briefly and audaciously into the heavily populated Clyde Anchorage in the light of a three-quarter moon.

Twelve weeks later between the 8th and 10th of February, U-37 landed Abwehr spy Ernst Weber-Drohl and an unknown accomplice at Killala Bay in Donegal. On the 10th U-33 was in Scottish waters approaching the Mull of Kintyre. Recalling the covert aspects of U-33's activities identified in this present work and the relative proximity of the two submarines, the likelihood that the operational objectives of U-37 and U-33 shared common purpose must be seriously addressed.

Buddhist monks first established a retreat in Scotland in late 1961. The Venerable Kyabje Namgyal Rinpoche Anandabodhi (Canadian Leslie George Dawson 1931-2003) founded at Eskdalemuir in Dumfriesshire the Johnstone House Contemplative Community of the Theravadin branch of Buddhism (literally, the "Ancient Teaching," the oldest surviving Buddhist school).

Interestingly, before embracing Buddhism Dawson, a friend of Anna Freud, Julian Huxley and R.D. Laing, envisaged a life in socialist politics. Disillusioned after addressing an international youth conference in Moscow, Dawson moved from the U.S.A. to London in 1956 and embraced the esoteric teachings of Rosicrucianism and, later, the works of renowned Russian mystic and founder of Theosophy Helena Petrovna Blavatsky.

It was not long before Anandabodhi's Theravada community dwindled. In 1965 he transferred ownership of the Eskdalemuir site to two Tibetan refugees (Dr. Akong Tulku Rinpoche and Chogyam Trungpa Rinpoche) who renamed it Samye Ling. Anandabodhi returned to Canada where with the help of his senior students he established the Centennial Lodge of the Theosophical Society.

Today Samye Ling is a monastery and international centre of Buddhist training, renowned for the authenticity of its teachings and tradition. It offers instruction in Buddhist philosophy and meditation within the Karma Kagyu lineage of Tibetan Buddhism.

It is evident that the excellent reputation of Samye Ling went before it because in 1990 the then owners of Holy Island, James and Catherine Morris, offered it to Lame Yeshe because they believed its future would be best taken care of by "the Buddhists from Samye Ling." The £1 million asking price was eventually dropped to £350,000, which Lama Yeshe managed to raise by April 1992. The Holy Island project was then established, broadening Tibetan Buddhism's community of faith in Scotland. Interestingly, the ownership of Arran resided with the ducal Hamilton family for about five hundred years up into the twentieth century.

In past times Arran was called Emain Ablach, which translates literally as "the place of apples." Another translation of Arran is "the sleeping lord." Many readers will recognise in these two descriptions unmistakeable references to the legend of Arthur who today resides in timeless slumber upon the Enchanted Isle of Avalon (Isle of Apples), awaiting re-awakenment in Britain's darkest hour.

Medieval language scholar and Grailseeker Otto Rahn, visitor to Scotland (Arthur's Seat in Edinburgh) both in 1936 and, it is speculated, in late 1939-early 1940 in U-33 (months after Rahn's reported suicide), wrote extensively about Arthurian imagery, drawing on Rosicrucian and other skeins of philosophical symbolism in support of his brilliant insights into European history and its metaphysical traditions. (Rahn also used to practise Tibetan exercises in telepathy in Berlin's busy streets with his friend Gabriele Dechend. Standartenführer-SS Dr. Ernest Schafer, leader of SS expeditions to Tibet made on behalf of Reichsführer-SS Heinrich Himmler in the 1930s, imparted to Rahn the details of these ancient practices.)

It is a little known fact that one of the consequences of the harsh treatment to which Templar captives were subjected by Philip IV's torturers was that information came to light about the legend of Camelot. In their extreme pain the Knights appeared to indicate that Camelot was not a physical place that one could simply find on a map and travel to by foot or by horse but was rather a 'dimensional' area, the pathway to which could only be found by those who had a sense of "inner" sight and perception. Once in Arthur's Court the visitor would undertake an initiatory experience in the form of a Quest Adventure. Subsequently, the fully formed Knight of the Round Table would return to the "real" world, swearing never to divulge details of his experiences.

This otherworldly description of Camelot meshes closely with the story of Arthur's resting place in a place of enchantment. It is therefore fascinating that Arran Island in Scotland, rather than a location more traditionally associated with Camelot such as Glastonbury and Tintagel, is most evidently associated with the key theme of the Sleeping Lord who resides in the unfindable Isle of Apples.

The Arran-Isle of Apples link is not the only facet of a supposed connection between Scotland and the seat of Camelot. Tantallon Castle in North Berwick, for example, has long been mooted as the true castle of Arthur. Just south of Melrose on the Scottish Borders lie the Eildon Hills within which, according to legend, resides a sleeping army of ancient ghostly warriors led by King Arthur.

Some claim that Merlin's resting place is at the root of a thorn tree in a field beside the village of Drumelzier near the River Tweed in the south of Scotland. These are just a handful of the many stories that associate Arthurian lore and its locations with Scotland.

The enchantment theme elaborates further. The Gaelic name for Horn Head is Corran Binne, meaning "Hollow in the Hills." As any reader of Mary Stewart's excellent Arthurian Saga series will know the Hollow Hills refer to Merlin's magical nature places from where he kept watch over the young Arthur Pendragon until he could claim Caliburn and embark on his destiny.

Holy Island is separated from the main island of Arran by Lamlash Bay, the inlet where the U-33 rescue convoy made a brief stop on the night of 12 February 1940 to allow ship-to-ship transfers of survivors before making for Greenock.

The island was chosen for a Centre because it was offered at a knock-down price by owners who were keen that it should accommodate a Tibetan Buddhist community. However, it is more difficult to understand why Eskdalemuir should have been selected in the 1960s by Anandabodhi. Having chosen the location, why then might it have been named the Johnstone House Community?

The Renfrewshire village of Johnstone near Paisley is approximately fifty miles northwest of Eskdalemuir. Despite its modest size Johnstone is not without importance in Scottish history and folklore. During the twelfth and thirteenth centuries the Templars owned considerable land holdings around the Clyde, including the site of Houston village, two miles northwest of Johnstone, which derives its name from one Hugo de Pavinan who built his castle there. Members of the Clyde based Magic Torch history group have suggested that Hugo de Pavinan was, in fact, Hugh de Payens, founder of the Poor Fellow-Soldiers of Christ and of the Temple of Solomon (more popularly known as the Knights Templar or Order of the Temple) in 1118. It is recorded fact that Hugh de Payens did visit Scotland around the time of Houston's foundation.

They also point out that Houston, together with Kilbarchan and Kilmacolm villages, forms a "Golden Triangle," an equilateral triangle with the River Gryffe at the apex. The Golden Triangle is typical of the ancient geometry utilised by the Templars and encompasses an area associated with pagan worship.

Johnstone is the home of Saint John's Parish Church. Saint John is an important saint for both Freemasons and the Knights Templar. Johnstone lies on almost exactly the same latitude of Roslin, home of Rosslyn Chapel. Roslin lies at *55 51.15* and Johnstone, significantly, is located at the sacred number *55 50*. The line between these two latitudes was known as the "serpent rouge" or Roseline, an ancient meridian once used for telling the time.

Paisley Abbey also lies on this sacred latitude and Hugo de Pavinan appears as a witness in the abbey's foundation charter. Notably, Tibetan Tantric Buddhists today declare that Rosslyn Chapel, a Christian edifice known as the Grail in Stone and an important node in a powerful pan-global earth energy grid system, is a centre for world peace.

In *Hellboy* the choice of location in Scotland for the Nazis' occult activities is determined largely by the confluence of a network of powerful ley lines. *Hellboy* is the creation of writer-artist Mike Mignola. The comics started appearing in 1993 and it was not until 2004 that Director Guillermo del Toro's first highly successful film adaption appeared.

The story begins in the final months of World War II. A party of fanatical Nazis come to the ruins of fictional 'Trondhem Abbey' on the equally fictional Tarmagant Island.

The U-boat that surely brought the party of Nazi occultists to the island is neither seen nor referred to but, then again, neither did the official eyeglass of history observe U-33 landing men at the Isle of Islay and at Carradale.

The Nazi personnel have come to Trondhem Abbey to conduct a black magic ceremony to wake the Gods of Chaos and win the war. A U.S. army contingent raids the proceedings but not before a demon, subsequently nicknamed *Hellboy* by paranormal expert Trevor "Broom" Bruttenholm (Dr. Broom), comes into this world through an open portal to Hell.

Dr. Broom recognises amongst the sorcerers the fearsome figure of arch-Nazi, Karl Rupert Kronen, SS officer, fictional head of the Thule occult society and Hitler's number one assassin. Kronen is directing operations. The date is 9 October 1944, time 01:00 hours.

It is evident that those who developed the film's storyline had a detailed knowledge of astrological symbology because at this precise hour and date there had just been a partial eclipse of the moon. The Sun, Mercury and Mars were all in the sign of Libra, an auspicious time for rituals, particularly those involving time manipulation. The moon is in its exalted position in Cancer, corresponding to the 16th degree. The imagery in the astrological Sabian Symbols[3] for the sixteenth degree is a man studying a mandala with the help of a very ancient book, which is precisely the sight that greets the army team when they burst into the Abbey grounds.

There before them is the terrifying figure of Grigori Rasputin, dead since 1916 but impossibly alive, clutching the *Des Vermis Mysteriis*, a Black Magic Grimoire. He is uttering powerful incantations, which are keeping open a gateway to Hell for access to the sleeping Seven Gods of Chaos (strong echoes of *Dagger Magic* in this imagery). The portal is represented as a mandala-like swirling pattern of electrical energy.

A pitched battle ensues in which Rasputin is propelled headlong into the portal and the Nazis are overcome. Kronen makes his escape (to make his next appearance in *Hellboy III*).

While making his way to the Abbey Dr. Broom had told the American soldiers that the location was an intersection of a number of ley lines. It is evident that this explicit mention of the island's powerful geomantic properties is designed to indicate to film viewers that Rasputin's magical ceremony is at least being partly assisted by the violent flux of earth energies active in and around the Abbey ruins.

In our review of *Dagger Magic* we acknowledged the importance of Scotland's earth energy topology. Students of geomancy point, for example, to the array of ley lines that constitute the so-called Edinburgh Matrix, which combines with corresponding energy centres in the Orkneys and south of Thurso. The Matrix is also said to be the anchor point for a far wider pan-European energy grid (an example of which is the "Tavhara Line," which runs from Thurso to San Sebastian in Spain). The leyline from the Midlothian village of Balantrodoch, now known as Temple, which passes through Rosslyn is the Magnetic Grid axis for Edinburgh.

The grid's generating system or "Glory Pole" is Holyrood Sanctuary, within which in former times debtors were immune from arrest. The Sanctuary's area was extensive with the main node located at Arthur's Seat. It generates a large energy grid around Edinburgh about forty miles in diameter, with Rosslyn Chapel occupying its control point position.

---

[3] The Sabian Symbols were formulated in the 1920s and are a set of 360 phrases that correspond with each of the 360 degrees of the wheel of the zodiac.

It is claimed that the Scottish energy grids and key structures also act as a means to "encode" key elements of esoteric and Grail symbology, an example being the representation of the mystical Sinclair Shield within the dimensions and measurements of Rosslyn Chapel Crypt.

The film *Rocket Post* highlights a poignant chapter in Scotland's wartime cultural history. Shot on Taransay in 2001 but not released (with extra footage) until 2006, the film is loosely based on the real life story of German engineer Gerhard Zucker who travelled to Scotland in 1934 to help the British Post Office develop rockets for delivering the mail.

Aided by a German colleague, Zucker's task is to design and commission a rocket that will safely propel mail from the Hebridean island of Scarp to its neighbouring communities. When Zucher arrived in this remote corner of Scotland he had to deal with pronounced local hostility, not only to new technology but also to Germans as during the Great War the Highlands and Islands had lost, per capita, the greatest number of soldiers in the British Isles.

The first attempt at building a working rocket failed. Undeterred, Zucher ploughed on. At the heart of the film is the endearing story of how local support for the project grew over time into a strong sense of collective enthusiasm that, together with his love affair with a beautiful local school teacher, spurs Zucher's efforts and gradually forges a unique bond with the Scarp community.

One day a U-boat surfaces off-shore and Nazi representatives seek to persuade Zucher into returning with them to Germany to aid the war effort. He refuses and is murdered for his principled stand. The island's inhabitants are devastated at the loss of the dashing, brave German who had become one of their own.

In Robert Harris' *Enigma*,[4] turned into a successful film in 2001, suspicion grows that Polish cryptanalyst, Jozef "Puck" Pukowski, is prepared to betray Bletchley's code-breaking secrets to the Nazis in order to take revenge on Stalin for the mass murder of around 22,000 Polish officers during the infamous Katyn Massacre in April 1943.

Not long after this date analyst Tom Jericho (a character loosely modelled upon mathematical genius Alan Turin) embarks on a quest to discover the truth surrounding the disappearance of his dear friend, clerk-typist Claire Romilly, and to confirm the identity of the traitor.

---

[4] Harris R., *Enigma*, Random House, 1995

Eventually, Jericho realises there is an important clue in a postcard that Claire had sent to him earlier in their relationship.

The card depicts a pretty cottage built on the banks of Loch Feochan, a four by one mile sealoch of the Lorn district of Argyll and Bute located 4 miles south of Oban and 39 miles northwest of Greenock. Jericho races up to Scotland and arrives breathlessly at the Loch in time to do physical battle with Pukowski. Out of sight, a team of British intelligence personnel and armed soldiers is ready to pounce but sit back when they see that Jericho, uninvited, is effectively doing their job for them.

While Pukowski and Jericho are exchanging furious blows a U-boat surfaces to spirit away the Pole but submerges and makes off quickly when those on board see what is going on. The U-boat rising from Loch Feochan to pick up an agent has striking resonance with the undocumented activities of U-33, involving the landing or collection of men on remote locations in the west of Scotland. Moreover, the picture postcard scene is highly suggestive.

On 4 May 1942 Reinhard Heydrich sent to the German Ambassador in London, Joachim von Ribbentrop, a report from one of his agents in Britain, which stated that Rudolf Hess was being held in a villa in Scotland. He added that there were other stories circulating about Hess being kept in a house near Fort William, a location less than thirty miles northeast of Loch Feochan. This report reached von Ribbentrop at the time that a mentally unstable Hess was supposed to be holed up in

Maindiff Court Military Hospital in Abergavenny in South Wales. To all appearances Heydrich's report was flawed but Scots' testimony supports his findings.

Alec Kennedy was brought up in the war in Fort William. He remembers his parents, newsagents, talking about Hess. They said he was kept at an isolated address, Inverlair House near the town, where he was interrogated by Intelligence Officers who lived opposite their shop in a building known as Granite House. Kennedy's account is also taking place during Hess' "Maindiff Court" period.

Fast-forward fifty years later when in May 1993 Lord Thurso made the statement that as a wartime teenager he remembered Hess being kept in a hunting lodge belonging to Sir Archibald Sinclair. This was Braemore Lodge, Caithness, in the valley of Berriedale Water to the southwest of Dunbeath on the adjoining estate of the Duke of Portland.

Tellingly, Lord Thurso also remembered his mother telling him that in 1942 Hess had been kept at Lochmore Cottage on his father's estate on the shore of Loch More near Thurso.

Rudolf Hess flew to Scotland on 10 May 1941 to seek a peace solution to hostilities between German and Britain. There are compelling indications that Hitler was not only aware of the flight (despite subsequently professing to the contrary and labelling his Deputy as mentally unbalanced) but actually sanctioned it.

We will return to this and associated topics in the final chapters when we seek to arrive at a more complete understanding of the "mystery" of U-33.

PART FOUR

ENDGAME

Now my charms are all o'erthrown,
And what strength I have's mine own,
Which is most faint.

Chapter EIGHTEEN

What happened…?

This is as strange a maze as e'er men trod…some oracle
must rectify our knowledge.

The principal events undertaken by U-33 as described in these pages occurred over an eighty-one day period. In this chapter, working backwards from February 1940 to November 1939, these will be captured, noting particularly the successive tipping points that transform seemingly run of the mill operational activities into something distinctly more sinister and duplicitous.

Our exposé will establish an inquisitive position in direct positive empathy with that highlighted by researchers such as Hugh Sebag-Montefiore who have cogently described the unusual nature of U-33's WWII Clyde activities.

By Max Schiller's account U-33 set off from Wilhelmshaven on 5 February 1940 under Hitler's personal orders bound for the Firth of Clyde. It embarked on this mission in an unseaworthy condition and carrying an Enigma machine contrary to operational custom.

A careful analysis of burial and exhumation records proves that there were at least two more persons (Albrecht and Klinger) among the dead from U-33 than officially recorded. Moreover, based on a careful reading of the NHB's statistics it is possible that there was a third unidentified individual who survived the February attack.

Confronted about decedents Albrecht and Klinger, the NHB appears to confirm by deliberate omission that it is wholly familiar with the pair in stating that it knows little about German Intelligence WWII activities involving submarines and agents in Scottish waters. Can one really be expected to swallow this official line when the Admiralty has had seventy years to put all the pieces together? The strength of the Establishment's declared ignorance about the clandestine dimension of U-33's Firth of Clyde patrols surely reveals the depth of its certain knowledge.

With this in mind we should consider two important facts from Max

Schiller. He told the BBC that when in the water after abandoning ship he heard cries for help from a boatmate but decided he would keep away from him if he got into any difficulty. We have also learned that Max did not recognise one of his rescued crewmates on *Bohemian Girl*, a remarkable occurrence considering the close-knit nature of Kriegsmarine life on board a U-boat.

Does the former event really reflect the natural tendency toward self-preservation in a desperate life and death situation and the latter Max's subsequent and understandable confusion brought about by his fight for survival in the freezing water?

Or do they point to a turbulent emotional response provoked by the unwelcome presence of men on U-33 or in its vicinity (members of a waiting shore party?) who were not submariners in the general crew population but were, in fact, high level intelligence or political operatives travelling to Scotland under Hitler's express orders?

And while one dwells on these questions it is intellectual energy well spent in reflecting on the stretch-too-far coincidence that while U-33 was traversing Scottish waters en route to the firth gateway, U-37 was a relatively short distance away landing two Abwehr II spies off the coast of Donegal. The disembarkation point was a brief hop from Tory Island where U-33 conspicuously sank three trawlers in November 1939 a period when, hours later, local reports speak of it landing men at various remote locations in the west of Scotland. One sees emerging here an unmistakeable, strategically directed joint pattern of subterfuge.

The Commanding Officers of both U-33 and U-37 did not share with their crews the covert aspects of their respective missions until the submarines were well into enemy waters. In the case of U-37 the men were sworn to secrecy on pain of death. Seeing that with the exception of Max Schiller's candid exchanges with David Hendry there is no recorded instance of a survivor from U-33 braking silence, one may confidently suppose that its officers and ratings were similarly constrained both by the insistence of their own superiors and, one suspects, by the Royal Navy after U-33's sinking.

Seven days after U-33's departure from Wilhelmshaven in the early hours of Monday the 12th the minesweeper HMS *Gleaner* made three rounds of depth charge attacks upon U-33, eventually forcing the crew to abandon ship while Kplt Hans-Wilhelm von Dresky, having issued orders to scuttle the boat, chose to go down with it.

Subsequent local stories that tell of a heavy lifting operation to move U-33 from its seabed position may refer to the speedy recovery of Engima parts. However, it would be unwise to discount the undertaking of such an operation in a circumstance where U-33 travelled at least as far as The Cumbraes or even further up the firth to the Wemyss Bay-Skelmorlie area. We know from Max Schiller's statements to his family that U-33 travelled up to the Clyde Anchorage in November 1939. From a careful review of the facts it is eminently feasible that twelve weeks later U-33 did indeed advance further north than Arran to a spot beyond The Cumbraes, which became its actual place of destruction.

My former U-33 research colleague, Alistair Alexander, has advanced the theory (also proposed by Mr McDougall of Dunoon) that the hull of U-33 was raised from the Clyde's 40m depths by Skelmorlie and then sunk again off Pladda to prevent German Intelligence from discovering how close to success U-33's mission had been. The re-sinking would have been carried out to support the notion of the unassailability of the Clyde Estuary so that no German submarine would ever again attempt such a dangerous mission. Alexander's conclusions are entirely plausible.

The McDougall / Alexander theory of events is also supported by the contents of an email message sent a few years ago by a wartime friend to M.S. in Greenock. His pal revealed that during the war when he was returning to Glasgow in the Clyde Division RNR minesweeper his staff officer told him about a U-boat that had been found off Wemyss Bay. The find had been a source of surprise to the Navy and, apparently, to the Germans. The Kriegsmarine knew that it had not returned from patrol but nothing more. It had obviously got through the boom defences at The Cumbraes (between Wemyss Bay by the 'Parsonage' listening station and Innellan) but no one knew how. The wreck position was known but by all accounts difficult to dive on because of tidal movements.

The Wemyss Bay wreck theory is given weight by the story of the German sailors' hats found by children on Portencross shore after the 1939 event. No sooner had they reported the finds and location to West Kilbride police than the area was barricaded, manned by sentries and was the centre of a prolonged period of busy off-limits naval diving upon an undisclosed target.

Why would the military have stirred up such a fuss? One obvious reason would have been the close proximity of a sunken enemy vessel known to be carrying cargo of such value that search after search had to be carried out until the thing was wholly retrieved or its presence ruled out.

The minesweeper sailor's story strengthens considerably Max Schiller's confident assertion that U-33 went beyond The Cumbraes, after which it encountered hostile forces and was sent to the bottom in the Wemyss Bay-Skelmorlie area.

The three signals Dönitz picked up via B-dienst from HMS *Gleaner* simply appear to have confirmed that U-33 was in trouble and that, twenty minutes later, the crew were surrendering. The transmissions do not appear to have pinpointed the submarine's coordinates. As far as Dönitz was concerned, U-33 could have been at a position on the compass many miles distant from the location last logged or advised by von Dresky to Command. In such a situation the Royal Navy was in a prime position to feed such disinformation to the enemy as it deemed necessary.

The disinformation scenario is roundly supported by the doughty Horace Oakes. In his 1984 letter to Thames Television producer Liz Neeson the newspaperman said that he had been tipped off that there was something worth seeing at James Watt Dock. At berth was a British destroyer with bodies on deck covered by a Nazi flag. He told Neeson that discreet enquiries had revealed that a German U-boat—the U-33— had been discovered just off the island of Arran. It had been forced to the surface by the minesweeper HMS *Gleaner* and damaged by depth charges.

Oakes added that a nearby destroyer on the scene sank the U-boat. Her survivors were taken prisoner and the dead taken aboard the *Gleaner* for burial. In this contemporary account we learn that Oakes' intelligence sources had revealed to him that U-33 was *not* sunk as a result of the damage inflicted by minesweeper HMS *Gleaner* but was sunk by an "*attendant British destroyer.*"

> But the stories flood on. A chance call one day in February 1940 let me see a British warship berth at a local pier. A common enough occurrence, but this time I noticed a German (Nazi) flag spread out on deck, evidently covering some bodies. Discreet inquiries revealed that a German U-Boat - the U33 -had been discovered just off the island of ARRan, an forced to the surface by the minesweeper HMS Gleaner. She had been damaged by depth charges. An attendant destroyer sank the U-Boat, her survivors were taken prisoner, and the dead taken aboard the Gleaner for burial.

Extract from Horace Oakes's 1984 letter to Thames Television.
Who was concealed under the flag? Note Oakes' comment that an
"attendant destroyer" sank the U-boat.

If Oakes' comment is accurate what was the identity of this vessel and why have details of its role in sinking U-33 not been made public at any time since 1940? Could it have been the Javelin class destroyer HMS *Kingston*, which bore twenty corpses and two survivors to Greenock after the sinking? Oakes undoubtedly knew. He topped off his letter to Neeson by saying that he had more stories to tell but would wait to see if Thames were interested in his offer (presumably in exchange for a reasonable fee) to provide material for the Clydeside bit of the planned documentary.

If U-33 was sunk in entirely diffferent circumstances than those set out in official accounts, with British ships involved whose identity had to be preserved, it would come of no surprise that steps such as a major lifting operation were taken to mask the true location and sequence of events. Is there any formal indication that things were not what they seemed with regard to U-33's wreck location in the war years?

On 3 March 1945 British submarine HMS *Sea Lion* was sunk as an asdic target 2½ miles southwest of Pladda in a depth of 62 metres, 55 23.380N 05 08.233W, rising 7 to 8 metres from the seabed at an angle of 140 / 320 degrees. This is in very close proximity to the official reported resting place of U-33. In which case, why would the Royal Navy in 1945 require an asdic target to be created using HMS *Sea Lion* when by all accounts they had the hull of a real U-boat to serve the purpose a relatively short distance away?

One may reasonably deduce from these facts that in 1945 U-33 was *not* lying off Arran. In fact, it was probably lying elsewhere at least as late as 1965. According to Max Schiller's family he gave his interview to *The Sunday Post* and made his "lying off Largs all day" remark when he was in his forties, dating it roughly to the mid-sixties. By that time U-33 had been at the bottom for twenty-five years, time enough for local divers to have tried getting down to it; also time enough for the Navy to have become increasingly twitchy about the mounting (and embarrassing) level of diving activity and had decided to put U-33 where it was supposed to have been all along.

On which note we arrive at an inevitable point for consideration. In reflecting upon a disinformation theory, one must ultimately reach a dramatic possibility—that the remains of U-33 may *never* have been off Arran at all. In this startling scenario U-33, having been lifted, was simply put back by the Royal Navy where it had lain after concluding its search for Enigma parts and other valuable finds.

We said in Chapter 9 that the overwhelming facts of history dictate a single absolute truth: that U-33 must lie off Arran and that if there is another U-boat in the firth its identity is a mystery. Within the context of a disinformation scenario the statement is reversed—U-33 *cannot* lie off Arran and if there is another U-boat nearby its identity is unknown.

The wreck is certainly not easy to find by all accounts. Diving enthusiast Kevin McDonald had tried and failed to locate U-33 off Pladda, despite Moir and Crawford's confident claim that they had always found it at 55 21.494N 05 01.759W. Subsequently, McDonald's request to fellow forum members asking for U-33's specific coordinates drew a blank.

In fact, member Ian McArthur suggested that one reason why McDonald and others could not find it was to be found in the rumours that U-33 was lifted to retrieve its Enigma parts. Once more, we come back to a heavy lifting scenario, which may have shrouded so much more of the actual purpose and circumstances behind the clandestine naval operation than it seems.

Where there is distinctly more unanimity among the Scottish divers community is in its shared belief in the presence of a U-boat wreck off Skelmorlie. The Congeralley forum members place the wreck at 64 metres in position 55:52N 04:54W. It would appear that there is at least as great a common acceptance of a Skelmorlie U-boat as there is of an Arran wreck. In fact, the location of the former seems to be the more accurately recorded of the two as far as some divers are concerned.

Is it conceivable that the reason why HMS *Cromer* would not send down for Max Schiller's benefit a midget sub and camera to the sea-bottom in February 2000 was to avoid revealing that what lay below was not actually the wreck of U-33?

Schiller told his BBC television interviewer that (at least part of) U-33's mission was to enter the Clyde Anchorage to sink HMS *Hood*. It is known that prior to official commencement of the war German military planners ordered a number of aerial reconnaissance surveys of the Firth of Clyde and surrounding areas. The efficient and comprehensive undertaking of these activities typified the Germans' customary disciplined style of approach in intelligence operations and so one struggles to understand how, on the occasion of U-33's entry into the Clyde in February 1940, they were not in receipt of the vital information that the *Hood* had departed its mooring in the Clyde Anchorage four days before the 12th.

We now know that Schiller was referring to the nature of U-33's mission (the one von Dresky is likely to have imparted to the crew as a cover story) in the Clyde Anchorage in late November 1939.

By a little after 05:30 on 12 February U-33 was on the seabed

(officially off Pladda but we have made a strong case for Wemyss Bay - Skelmorlie) and British officials needed to tend to the dead. Eyewitnesses observed the bodies from U-33 laid out in Greenock Town Hall where, extraordinarily, some were seen dressed in "immaculate" uniforms and adorned with chunky gold rings with swastika emblems denoting Nazi Party membership.

This latter fact effectively rules out the possibility of identifying these men as everyday U-boat matelots who had little or no time for Nazi higher-ups, spies and politicos. Those at the scene in Greenock Town Hall believed that the men in this well-dressed group might have comprised a 'special unit.'

The bodies must then have been stored in an appropriate place pending burial. History states that 23 deceased were buried at Greenock Cemetery on Friday 16 February but interment records suggest something different. They speak of the burial of 7 men on the previous day and 16 on the 16th.

Evidently both ceremonies were secret affairs, the first especially so because there has never been any suggestion that it was held at all while the second was conducted a little after dawn and officiated by "men from the Ministry." Thankfully, the latter proceedings were witnessed by the concealed *Greenock Telegraph* War Reporter Horace Oakes.

Nine days later Oakes was writing in his diary about "torpedoes from one of the U-boats sunk in the firth," a startling reference to enemy submarines in the plural.

Such was the ultimate fate of U-33. But the seeds of its inevitable destruction were sewed eighty-one days before, a fact that helps considerably to explain Lieutenant-Commander Price's remark to Chief Engineer Schilling that he delayed the immediate task of rescuing men in the water in case there were other U-boats in the area.

We noted in Chapter 4 Admiral Dönitz's puzzling diary entry made on the day of U-33's sinking, which refers to his hope that "the boats [*plural*] only having been seen need not be abandoned." We also noted in the same pages that Oakes and Price held suspicions about the presence of more than one hostile sub at that time.

Why might this have been the case? Was it purely because it was the day-to-day business of the newshound and the officer to know that U-boats had been active in the Firth of Clyde in the recent past or was there something more?

Oakes wrote about the November 1939 event in his diary, not naming the enemy sub, which is not to say the journalist was unaware it was U-33. Furthermore, Price, a senior naval commander deeply involved in defending local waters, will surely have known that it was U-33 that had breached the Tail of the Bank several weeks earlier and, moreover, that she had not been acting alone.

Did he have cause to suspect that U-33 might have similarly been in cahoots with a sister boat on its subsequent patrol in February?

It is a fair question but one not currently capable of resolution one way or the other. There is no available evidence to refute or confirm that any such partnering took place. Records do show that there were four U-boats which were on operations in Scottish or British waters on the 12th. In terms of time and opportunity (not in terms of evidence) one of the four, U-22, *could* have been in the same waters as U-33 between 6-12 February, viz:

➢ U-29 left Wilhelmshaven on 6 February under the command of Otto Schuhart, putting in at Helgoland and setting off from there on the 11th for operations in the Bristol Channel. She returned to

Wilhelmshaven on 12 March. This timing rules out U-29 as a contender;

> U-23 left Wilhemshaven on 9 February under the command of Otto Kretschmer for operations east of the Orkneys and arrived back at base on the 28th. Three days would not have been anywhere near enough time for U-23 to get from its German base to the Firth of Clyde;

> U-9 departed under Wolfgang Lüth from Wilhelmshaven on 5th February, U-33's departure date, for operations off Scotland. It was engaged in an operation in Cromarty Firth on the night of 9-10 Feb and sank a vessel at Utsire off Norway on the 11th. This timing clearly rules her out, too;

> On the 6th under Karl-Heinrich Jenisch U-22 departed Wilhelmshaven for operations east of the Orkneys, returning to base on 25 February. In investigating the theory that just as U-33 was undoubtedly accompanying other German submarines in the firth in November 1939 it was doing the same the following February, U-22 did have time to join its partner boat and, therefore, has to be a contender. There is no record of U-22 sinking any ships while on patrol and so it could have been roaming anywhere in Scottish waters. It cannot be overly stressed, however, that there is no recorded sighting of U-22 at any position in or near the Firth of Clyde on 12 February. U-22 survived to make a 7th and final sailing mission in March 1940. (Coincidentally, U-33's Chief Engineer Friedrich-Ernst Schilling was a crewman on U-22 in November 1939.)

What was the earlier train of events on 21-22 November 1939 that Lieutenant-Commander Price was so nervous about? The day after U-33 sank three Fleetwood trawlers some 75 miles northwest of Rathlin Island on Tuesday 21 November 1939 she headed east into the Clyde for reasons of secrecy about her mission and, therefore, the details of this detour are unrecorded in official German records.

The weight of accumulated evidence suggests that U-33's passage into the lower reaches of the Firth of Clyde was not made until it had made the most of an approximate 30-hour time-gap between leaving the waters to the southeast of the Isle of Tiree on the 21st and arriving off Carradale Bay on the afternoon of Wednesday the 22nd to engage in clandestine activity. In this period U-33 made firstly a 60-mile journey southeast to the Isle of Islay where it landed at least one person, collected fresh water and rustled sheep.

The next most likely act was for U-33 to make its way to the Isle of Bute where a submarine was observed by British Home Guard personnel arriving off the shore of Ettrick Bay on the west coast of the island. At dawn on the 22nd it moved away. Considering this report alongside the testimony from the ex-U-33 submariner to J. Malcolm McMillan's cousin that it was U-33 which made a morning call for fresh water collection at the southern end of the Isle of Bute, the logical inference to be drawn is that the identity of the west shore and south shore U-boat was in both cases U-33.

All indications point to U-33 making its trip to the Isle of Bute within the rapid series of island stop-offs it made between 21st and 22nd November 1939.

However, there must remain a niggling doubt about the date. In recent pages we reviewed evidence that U-33 may have travelled considerably further up the firth in February 1940, in which case the Isle of Bute trip could have taken place at that time seeing that the west coast of the smaller Little Cumbrae island runs parallel to its larger cousin a mile westward. It is also possible, of course, that U-33, having got the taste for island hopping during its second patrol visited the Isle of Bute during its third. The Isle of Bute sighting also helps to provide a plausible background to the rumours, denied by naval officials such as Admiral Fraser, that a British patrol ship had spotted a U-boat off Bute and that, subsequently, prisoners captured from the enemy sub were seen at Rothesay.

After collecting water the next step in the submarine's travels, reflecting the remarks made by Max Schiller and the pharmacist's wife, was for U-33 to "lie off Largs all day" in a channel close by The Cumbraes before moving 35 miles southwest to the Kintyre Peninsular.

At 15:45, according to Donald Kelly's investigations, U-33 was seen emerging off Carradale Bay. U-33 enthusiast David Hendry goes further and offers the startling insight derived from his discussions with Max Schiller and from local knowledge that fishermen observed U-33 landing men here, too.

Taking these facts together, we see a clear pattern of activity in which U-33, just 12 weeks after commencement of hostilities between Germany and Britain, is hard at work landing agents in various remote West of Scotland locations while at the same time undertaking more mundane chores like water collection and stealing sheep for the galley cook.

Five hours after U-33 departed Carradale Gavin Crawford observed in bright moonlight a submarine trailing 200 yards behind the Irish transporter *Royal Ulsterman* before passing through the Clock-Dunoon boom gateway into the heavily packed Clyde Anchorage. The following day Crawford heard the story doing the rounds locally that a U-boat had been camouflaged to look like a British submarine. Donald Kelly tells, too, of Clydeside resident Angus Shaw who witnessed a "silhouette astern" behind the inward-bound Irish boat *Royal Ulsterman* and watched as chaos ensued.

There is no unequivocal eyewitness testimony, apart from Max Schiller's statements, that names U-33 as the Cloch boom marauder but the mass of corroborative evidence does not provide an alternative candidate. The boom incursion drew a furious naval response. Depth charges were dropped in such profusion over a period of many hours that houses were shaken to their foundations. As a measure of the attacks' sustained ferocity we have William McGee's testimony that the walls of his family house, sited a good two miles from the Cloch Lighthouse, were twisted out of alignment.

The day afterwards a multitude of dead fish was seen strewn over the beaches in such quantity that residents carried them away by the basketload and German sailors' hats were picked up here and there, in particular at Portencross, West Kilbride and along the three-mile stretch on the west bay (the shore closer to the boom gateway) between the Dunoon Castle rocks and the lido at Innellan.

The Tail of the Bank event generated a busy flow of citizens' commentary, the quality of which swung between truth and near-fiction depending on the legitimacy and standing of the source. We have seen that some firth residents were especially well informed, including bystanders like young Patti Duncan who overheard indiscreet remarks passed between garrulous high-ranking Royal Naval officers and her parents.

Variously, stories were told about a U-boat sunk inside the defence boom on a reef between the Gantocks Hotel and the Cloch Lighthouse, in Lunderston Bay a little further south, in Holy Loch (the story of the presence of a two-man midget submarine), locations both north and south of Great Cumbrae, and inside the Cloch-Dunoon-Cumbraes triangle whose epicentre is roughly the line between Innellan and Skelmorlie. It would come as no surprise to learn that it was as a consequence of the Tail of the Bank security disaster that the underwater listening device between Wemyss Bay and Innellan was installed shortly thereafter.

A week or so later an unidentified body was washed up in the Gourock lido, which indicates that there was at least one fatality during the Tail of the Bank fracas. It is my contention that Sikh Hidtalla, laid in a pauper's grave on 3 January 1940, was the body from the pool but buried anonymously because to reveal in Greenock Cemetery's records the decedent's real identity would have constituted a grave embarrassment to Britain's naval and security forces.

Sixty years later a former Kriegsmarine naval officer came to Greenock Library asking for information about an uncle who had died in a U-boat sinking in the Firth of Clyde in WWII. The visitor specified that he was not talking about a casualty from U-33 but about another submarine sunk by the British in the upper reaches of the firth. Were Sikh Hidtalla and the enquirer's uncle fellow occupants in a special sub that passed through the boom—one and the same man even?

It is plain from correspondents' stories that the Firth of Clyde U-boat(s) activities prompted lengthy and extensive Royal Navy search operations. In the sea by West Kilbride, quickly fortified by barbed wire barricades, navel investigators were hard at work in a quest to find something of apparent exceptional value. Twelve miles north in the vicinity of Innellan Pier, another location where Kriegsmarine hats were found, the boat lad with the fishing licence observed similar actions undertaken over a two-year period. What were the naval authorities looking for so assiduously? Were their trips to the seabed simply concerned with finding Enigma components (having learned, perhaps, that Chief Engineer Schilling had ditched his parts by Innellan-Skelmorlie) or was there an altogether more exotic prize sought?

The story that U-33 in November 1939 was lured into the Clyde Anchorage by the prospect of netting a great catch—the Capital liner RMS *Queen Mary*—makes no sense. On that date the *Queen Mary* had been in New York for nearly three months. The new Cunard liner RMS *Queen Elizabeth* was in the area, however, undergoing extensive fitting out work at John Brown's works at Clydebank. But there is no evidence of its involvement in an intelligence ruse directed towards drawing an enemy submarine into the Clyde Anchorage. In recognition, though, of the weight of local rumour the Cunard ship's alleged complicity in such an exercise remains on the cold case file.

In this chapter we have summarised the story of U-33 along a backward pathway in time, beginning with its consignment to the depths *somewhere* in the Firth of Clyde in February 1940 and ending with its bravura performance at the Cloch-Dunoon defence boom in November 1939. Our description of the latter sensational episode has stopped at the boom's open gateway.

Now we follow it inside…

Chapter NINETEEN

...when U-33 went through?

*Shortly shall all my labours end, and thou
shalt have the air at freedom.*

At around the time of the *Largs and Millport Weekly News* articles in the mid-1980s an unnamed elderly man came forward with a graphic story. He had been a plumber in the Clyde shipyards during the war working in Garvel Dock next to the larger James Watt Dock.

There was a frigate in Garvel Dock having a fit-out. Suddenly the alarm was sounded that a U-boat had got up as far as the Dunoon-Cloch defence boom. As illustrated earlier the Tail of the Bank at Greenock was packed with all types of tankers and convoy ships. Every available loch and mooring space was given over to ships. One could practically step from one to another, the ships were so close. When the alarm went up the dock was immediately cleared and flooded within minutes. The frigate raced out of the dock dragging with it welding plants, burning cables, bottles, generators and gangplanks. People were chopping away furiously with axes to try to cut them free of the racing frigate.

The old plumber said that the mêlée concluded with the hunting down and sinking of the U-boat and that its sailors were buried in Greenock cemetery and re-buried in Germany. If the plumber's story is accurate then to which U-boat and crewmembers was he referring? What was sunk in or near the Clyde Anchorage in November 1939?

As the night of 22-23 November progressed, the hubbub gradually died down. When the smoke of battle cleared there were no visible signs of a mortally wounded U-boat despite the *Foxhound* skipper's adamant belief that his crew had seen a submarine and had sunk or badly damaged it (a belief shared by the plumber and many others on the scene that night).

We know that U-33, the boat that had passed through the gate on the surface, lived to return to the Clyde twelve weeks later. Had the vessel that had forcibly entered the Clyde Anchorage underwater been so fortunate?

The densely populated Clyde Anchorage during WWII

In face of the large number of Royal Navy attack vessels abroad in the Clyde that night how could enemy success like that have taken place or, shockingly, have been permitted? Nine depth charges were dropped by *Anti-Submarine Boat 4* alone without success and she was just one among many that unleashed a furious rally of explosive charges on the enemy visitors.

In Gavin Crawford's account of the Tail of the Bank event we are presented with the clear understanding that a submarine passed *through* the open gateway. Consider this witness fact against the testimony of former West Kilbride sapper Douglas McKillop, also present at the scene on that night in November 1939, in which he told the *Largs and Millport Weekly News* readership in the mid-1980s that: "…a U-boat tried to *force the boom* at the Cloch."

Here we see a sharp distinction between the two accounts—one describing a submarine passing through the Dunoon side open gateway in the guise of a vessel with legitimate business among the dense Clyde Anchorage traffic; the other of a submarine that attempted to gain passage below the waves by ramming or otherwise cutting the boom's netting structure.

We know from the testimony of George "Dodsy" Barratt, a blacksmith serving in the Royal Navy Boom Defence team that he was one among a team ordered to repair the netting after a submarine tried to force its way through. The two descriptions are suggestive of a simultaneous pair of actions where two enemy submarines are intent on passing through into the Anchorage, one suicidally bold and open in execution while the other seeks to get through unseen under the cover of its on-surface partner bringing tumult upon itself as its (deliberately clumsy?) ruse is discovered.

That there was some substance to this story is evidenced by the subsequent weight of local opinion. Quickly, the rumour mill went into full swing with subsequent talk about the presence of a mini or special sub in the vicinity of the boom.

How did U-33 manage to get through the open gateway? Commentators have pointed out that, in reality, it would have been easy enough in most weathers for an intruder to get through the boom defences at the Cloch behind any inward-bound tonnage at periscope depth, rather than running on the surface, as there is plenty of water depth in the channelway. But if the object of the deception was to raise a mighty hue and cry to divert attention from a second vessel a surface passage was by far the most effective option.

But timing was all important. If, as the weight of evidence indicates, U-33 was to provide cover while another submarine made its way into the Anchorage below the surface the operation had to be executed with stopwatch precision. The ploy was being played out for very high stakes. There was no room for failure.

William McGee provided details of the story that did the rounds locally about how the U-boat entered the gateway. The original source of the account has not been named but we have seen how loose lips among Royal Navy personnel let slip classified information and it is likely that similar indiscreet practice was at work here also.

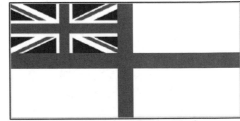
The Royal Navy White Ensign

U-33 arrived at the boom gate. It was flying the White Ensign—a Royal Navy flag. It could not have been flying its own ensign at the same time. Lawrence Paterson, Ministry of Defence WWII submarine consultant, confirmed to me that raising a White Ensign above a Kriegsmarine ensign indicated that a U-boat wished to surrender. That was not the case here, at least initially. In Paterson's view, the flying of the single White Ensign smacks of a deliberate attempt by U-33 to pass itself off as a Royal Navy sub and enter the inner harbour. Paterson remarked on the discovery of this startling information: *"You have definitely unearthed something quite special there."*

It was not unheard of for ships to use this subterfuge, which was perfectly within the rules of war as long as the White Ensign was replaced with the Kriegsmarine ensign should firing break out between the two sides.

In compliance with operational procedure the boom guard began to carry out a two-part challenge to determine if the sub was friendly. The challenge codes would have been known to legitimate Royal Navy vessels. U-33 provided the correct code for the first part of the challenge. It failed to do so for the second part. Mayhem ensued.

It has been speculated that U-33 failed the challenge due to a number of possible reasons, namely: i) Von Dresky was in receipt of the correct part-two response but delivered it incorrectly; ii) German intelligence planners had supplied the Commander with incorrect information (innocently or knowingly); iii) information that had been correct on departing from Wilhelmshaven was changed by the Royal Navy while U-33 was en route for Scotland.

There is a fourth possibility—that von Dresky, working to a precise plan, carried the ruse forward to a certain point making time for another activity to take place underwater. He then deliberately provided the wrong response to provoke an almighty fracas under the cover of which its companion submarine(s) could attempt to make for a landing point somewhere in the inner harbour.

Mr Magee goes on to say that the U-boat then raised its own ensign. This would fit with a scenario where von Dresky, having provoked the necessary responses, raised its flag above the White Ensign to signal its intention to surrender. This would have bought U-33 more valuable time in which to mount the final part of its plan, which was to turnabout and make a run for freedom, precisely the astonishing outcome described in Bill McGee's locally sourced account of events. Theirs might have been a suicide mission but none aboard U-33 wanted the Last Wills and Testaments lying in tin boxes back at Wilhelmshaven to be prematurely read by grieving loved ones.

And what of the vessel that tricked its way into the inner harbour? *Anti-Submarine Boat 4*, observing a "dark cylindrical shape" on the surface a full half a mile inside the boom, dropped six depth charges and then saw a "long black cigar-shaped object" brake onto the surface, roll and submerge. Three more charges were then dropped upon a target that already appeared to be badly wounded, drastically increasing the probability of scoring a fatal hit.

In the aftermath of the release of depth charges *A/S Boat 4* and a sister launch mounted a search in nearby Holy Loch, the incident referenced in Terry McGonagle's 2003 forum posting about the sinking of a 2-man midget sub.

By all accounts blood was drawn. We have the evidence of the body washed up in Gourock lido a few days later; the strange interment record of pauper 'Sikh Hidtalla' buried at Greenock on 3 January 1940, a timing that broadly fits with the appearance of the body in the pool; the visit to Greenock library by the German submariner asking about the uncle who had died in the firth on a boat that was *not* U-33; the avowed testimony from *Foxhound*'s skipper that he had sunk *something*; and undertaker Alex Munro's sadness that German sailors he committed to burial in Greenock cemetery had drowned by the boom.

Add to these points of evidence Gavin Crawford's impressively informed comment that the U-boat which penetrated the boom intended to surrender after carrying out its business and one can only conclude that the secret sub was chased, trapped and forcibly apprehended.

There is no indication that any member of the crew from U-33 was killed. One may only conclude that one or more occupants from another enemy boat were killed and that at least one other survived to face interrogation.

We saw earlier that in 1943 there was a successful penetration of the boom by a top secret British midget submarine, which was making practice raids in preparation for subsequent attacks on ships like the *Tirpitz*. How the British midget sub passed through the boom is unrecorded. It is possible that it used cutting equipment, the likely method used by an enemy vessel at the Anchorage in November 1939. Its successful passage must have caused considerable embarrassment among boom defence guard personnel. If it could be carried out to plan in 1943 who is to say that it did not succeed in 1939?

The problem with placing credence in this outcome is that all the available evidence points to the contrary, that the sub was apprehended and mortally damaged. Blood was spilt. More than one person was killed. This is evident from the comments made by both Alex Munro and the old plumber.

But is this another case of "things are never what they seem" in the U-33 story? Returning to Horace Oakes' diary, he notes on 7 December 1939 "strong rumours of submarine (U-boat) sunk at Cloch." This was the man with his finger on every newsworthy pulse in and around Greenock. If he wrote it the chances were there was something to it.

Which U-boat had been sunk? It was not U-33. We noted in Chapter 7 that U-35 was in the vicinity of U-33's attack on the German steamer SS *Borkum* in the Orkneys in the early afternoon of 23 November 1939. We then briefly considered the next logical possibility in this argument that U-35 *could* have sunk the *Borkum* with history none the wiser. This would have allowed the Germans to ascribe the act to U-33, so providing an alibi for its role as a decoy for a second Nazi submarine in the Firth of Clyde on that night (until Donald Kelly's review the commonly agreed date for the Tail of the Bank incursion was 23 November).

An X-Class Royal Navy Midget Submarine circa 1943

But what if U-33's role in the Clyde Anchorage was far more than that of a bit player in a grander scheme of Anglo-German deception? What if it was *the* major player and really did require at least several hours to act out its part in the affair, rather than the minutes needed to shield a sister sub's passage below the waves into the Tail of the Bank? In this bigger picture there is no need for U-33 to heap strain on its two MAN Diesel engines in making a frantic 17-hour 320-mile dash to sink the grain boat because its attention was fully occupied in performing vital and time-consuming tasks in the Anchorage. By a process of elimination U-35 then becomes the sole candidate for the attacker of the *Borkum*.

This alternative visualisation of events at the boom declares that the vessel seen travelling in the wake of the *Royal Ulsterman* was *either* U-

33 *or* a midget or special submarine (German made or even a British precursor of the later 4-man X-Class used in the sinking of the *Tirpitz*). The three-quarter moon merely allowed shore-based onlookers such as Gavin Crawford and Archie Shaw to see that there was *something* resembling a submarine behind the transporter, which could not be positively identified (no time-witnesses are able to say that it was U-33 specifically that they saw that night in the firth).

(Bearing in mind Crawford's 1985 testimony in the *Largs and Millport Weekly News*, there is a third possible scenario—that the observed vessel was actually a U-boat camouflaged as a British submarine or even a real British submarine that was part of a deception being played for exceedingly high stakes.)

If it was a midget sub observed in its wake then U-33 was therefore beneath it, out of sight and awaiting the rumpus to begin from the boom challenge failure before using its bow-mounted serrated equipment to cut the netting. If it was, indeed, U-33 seen behind the *Royal Ulsterman* then, in carefully rehearsed synchronized actions, it ducked beneath the surface to cut the net while its partner broke the waves to undertake the challenge process with the boom defence guard that was planned to fail.

Either way, in this hypothesis it was U-33 that passed unnoticed and unscathed into the Tail of the Bank while the decoy, by all accounts, fared much worse. Descriptions of a cigar-shaped object rising and rolling on the surface, a subsequently observed oil slick suggesting disaster and Greenock undertaker Alex Munro's morose account of the drowned young German fatalities tell a sobering story.

Nazi Party membership ring

Once inside, U-33 could have undertaken any number of activities in the Clyde Anchorage or thereabouts (such as in Holy Loch) for up to 20 hours or so and still have sufficient time to make the approximate 1,000 mile trip back to Wilhelmshaven for its return on the 26th.

This lengthy period would have allowed on-board emissaries (Otto Rahn even) to come ashore to engage in meetings with Britons seeking an early end to hostilities with Germany or, indeed, to undertake anything else with which they were tasked (including, for example, making a quick round trip to Rosslyn Chapel to search for Templar artefacts).

Even if Kelly is incorrect about the Tail of the Bank date and the Boom event took place on the 23rd, in this scenario U-33 would still have had a few hours available to fulfil a secret agenda before quietly slipping away for its 65 to70-hour trip home.

This alternative description also provides a new "wild card" scenario for the train of events leading to the discovery of Sikh Hidtalla. We considered in Chapter 7 the hypothesis that U-35 and U-33 might have rendezvoused in the Orkneys on 23 November around the time that the latter sank the Borkum in the early afternoon, a meeting that could have been used to transfer personnel. Such a meeting could still have taken place if U-33 had remained in the Firth of Clyde for up to 20 hours longer to undertake secret business. It follows that the two submarines would then have met in the Orkneys on the 24th, leaving U-33 with sufficient time to resume its journey to Wilhelmshaven for its arrival on the 26th.

On 29 December U-35 was attacked in the North Sea by three British destroyers approximately 80 miles from the Norwegian coast near Bergen. Its crew of 43 was rescued and landed at Greenock on 1 December, an occasion described in the Admiralty communiqué reproduced in Chapter 1.

Might there have been a 44th person on board U-35, someone transferred by U-33 either in life or in death consequent to operations at the Tail of the Bank, one who did not survive the encounter with the destroyers?

If after the destroyers' attack naval personnel found on U-35 a decedent of "special interest," steps would have been taken to put secure burial procedures in place at Greenock.

Nevertheless, it is far from clear why U-33 would have transferred either a body or a living person to U-35 while en route back to base. Of the two boats U-33 would be arriving first in Wilhelmshaven. U-35 was still in the North Sea three days after U-33's return. If there had been a person, alive or dead, who needed to be landed it would have made more sense for U-33 to have done so unless the plan all along was to bring the person or body onto Norwegian soil. In November 1939 Norway was free from German occupation (the Nazi invasion did not commence until the second week of the following April), a circumstance that may have been attractive for a disembarkation.

All of this, however, is little more than inspired speculation and the probable position remains that Hidtalla was found locally, the most likely place being the Gourock swimming pool open to the sea from which a body was recovered a few days after the Tail of the Bank activities.

Hitherto, we have described a situation that demanded of U-33 extemely bold and lightning fast wholly surface-based operational manouevres to act as decoy to protect another vessel beneath the waves. In this reshaped train of events the decoy is an expendable midget or special submarine whose likely destruction and casualties were an acceptable part of an extraordinary plan of deception necessary to ensure that U-33 achieved its secret agenda.

Was the November 1939 subterfuge a success or failure? Were there high level Britons, civil and military, wringing their hands in the three-quarter moonlight somewhere along the shore, horrified that treasonable plans had failed so conspicuously and noisily? Or did events unfold in line with an increasingly credible model of thinking in which U-33 secured safe passage into the Anchorage at the expense of its decoy partner and achieved its secret objectives, thereby giving succour to those outside official British Government circles who sought an early peace with Germany?

Did U-33 then return to the Firth of Clyde on Hitler's orders eighty-one days later in February 1940 carrying Albrecht, Klinger and a possible third emissary to resurrect, even to build upon previously instigated unofficial peace overtures with top level British sympathisers?

There is no doubt that two people 'christened' Albrecht and Klinger in the Greenock Cemetery records were on the list of those buried among the dead from U-33. Having interviewed Ray and Edna Schiller, I am convinced that the pair never boarded U-33, which is not the same as saying that they did not try. It is possible that they were killed in an attempt to do so.

Ray and Edna recalled that the name Klinger had been put to their father by earlier enquirers. Max professed to have no knowledge of anyone of that name who had been on U-33 during either of the two excursions during which he had served. Ray and Edna accept their father's response completely. They were a very close knit family and trusted their father's word implicitly. If there had been a mystery person or persons on U-33 they are confident that their father would have been open and frank with them about their presence.

Albrecht and Klinger could only have come from one of two times and places—i) the occasion of the Tail of the Bank event in November 1939 (we have heard evidence of fatal casualties arising from this incident); or ii) a time during U-33's 3rd patrol at a location somewhere along the Firth of Clyde, between Arran and Skelmorlie, where it attempted to pick up Nazi agents or politicos landed by the U-boat on Islay, Carradale or other remote locations for undisclosed purposes twelve weeks before.

Max Schiller's curious remarks to Kirsty Wark about the man in the water on the night of 12 February and then later not recognising one of the two men who had died on *Bohemian Girl* suggest that the latter scenario may be closer to the truth. Nevertheless, there is insufficient firm evidence to rule out the possibility that Albrecht and Klinger died during the rounds of ferocious depth charging at the boom on the night in November 1939 and that their bodies were preserved in a local mortuary for the next twelve weeks.

The only occasion when the corpse of an apparent foreign national was buried at Greenock prior to 16 February 1940 was Sikh Hidtalla on 3 January. One is therefore encouraged to believe that Albrecht and Klinger were buried at the same time as the U-33 deceased. What is not in question is the fact that their deaths must have disrupted carefully laid plans.

And what of the captured U-boat that Oakes reported in his diary was brought to the Gareloch on 17 October 1941. "Crew landed at Greenock," he wrote. Did U-boat 'X' come into the Clyde at that time in a doomed attempt to contribute to a continuing but ultimately unfruitful peace process?

There has never been an official record or statement that refers to such an incident. The southern end of Gareloch opens into the Firth of Clyde. Today its northeastern shore is dominated by Faslane Naval Base, the home of the United Kingdom's Trident nuclear submarines. Which U-boat was captured in Gareloch in 1941? What had it been doing? Which crew was landed and what became of it?

The Firth of Clyde retained its allure for the enactment of remarkable events. In April 1943 the Allies hatched 'Operation Mincemeat,' an audacious plan soon dubbed "The Man Who Never Was," to fool the Nazis into the belief that the Allies were poised to invade Greece and Sardinia when, in fact, their goal was Sicily. This was accomplished by persuading the Germans that they had, by accident, intercepted top-secret documents giving details of Allied war plans. The documents were attached to the corpse of "Major William Martin," which was deliberately left to wash up on a beach off Huelva in Spain on 30 April 1943 where it was found by fishermen.

The story goes that the coroner of St. Pancras District in London obtained the body of 34-year old Welsh vagrant Glyndwr Michael who had died of chemically-induced pneumonia as a result of ingesting rat poison, a mode of death which fills the lungs with water as if by drowning. The coroner is said to have gone along with the proposal provided that Michael's real identity was never revealed.

Subsequently, "Major Martin" was placed in a steel canister filled with dry ice and taken on board the British submarine HMS *Seraph,* which left for Spain on 19 April. *Seraph*'s commander (Lieutenant Norman "Bill" Jewell) and crew had previous special operations experience. Jewell told his men that the canister contained a top-secret meteorological device to be deployed near Spain.

The steel canister was brought to Holy Loch, adjoining the Clyde Anchorage and just a mile or so west of the Cloch-Dunoon defence boom. Bringing the body to this *western* location for a subsequent voyage to Spain does not appear to have made operational sense when it was to be collected by a submarine berthed a 750-mile sea journey away on England's northeast coast at Blyth in Northumberland. If the body had lain in a London mortuary it would have been far more expedient to have transported it 270 miles by road to HMS *Seraph* in Blyth from where the submarine would have journeyed directly south and then southwest to Spain.

It has been speculated that despite careful preparations the St. Pancras body suffered early decomposition, which called for an urgent substitution.

On 27 March 1943 there was an accidental explosion on U.S.-built escort carrier HMS *Dasher* as it passed Horse Island near Ardrossan in the Firth of Clyde. *Dasher* sank and 379 men were killed. The British authorities tried to keep the story quiet, rather than provoke public anger over alleged defective American shipbuilding. One of the deceased from *Dasher*, Harry Marston, wrote to his wife Hilda after the ship's passage from the U.S.A. He confided that *Dasher*, which started life as banana boat SS *Rio de Janeiro* before being converted in July 1942 into an Archer Class Escort Carrier in Brooklyn Naval Yard under the Lend-Lease programme, was a "death trap" and that there had been trouble with its boilers all the way across the Atlantic. These escort carriers had a very poor safety and quality reputation and were nicknamed "Woolworth's carriers."

"Major William Martin"

The dead were originally buried in an unmarked mass grave. The claim is made that the 'Mincemeat' body was *Dasher* casualty John "Jack" Melville, 37, a man for whom a service was held on the present day patrol boat HMS *Dasher* in October 2004 to commemorate him as the "Man Who Never Was."

Despite the Melville scenario the story of the "Man Who Never Was" has never been satisfactorily explained. While uncertainty exists about the true identity of "Major Martin"—the poison victim from St. Pancras or the *Dasher* casualty in Holy Loch—there remains the intriguing notion that events surrounding U-33's clandestine activities in the Firth of Clyde in 1939-1940 and the later successful "practice" passage through the boom into the loch by a Royal Navy midget submarine were entwined with the Allies' subsequent bold enterprise to deceive Hitler over invasion plans.

Were HMS *Seraph* and the British midget sub present in Holy Loch at the same time? Records indicate that this is likely. In September 1943 Royal Navy S-class submarine HMS *Sceptre* departed from Loch Cairnbawn in the Highland of Scotland with midget sub *X-10* in tow. Its aim was to attack the German battleship *Tirpitz* at Kaa Fjord in the Finnmark region of Norway. It is a fact of record that a British midget submarine successfully breached the boom defences in 1943 in preparation for the subsequent assault against the *Tirpitz*.

These facts suggest that the midget sub that made the practice pass into Holy Loch and the one that was towed by *Sceptre* to Norway a few months later in the autumn of 1943 were one and the same—the *X-10*.

Sceptre earned the title of "bring them back alive" as she was the only towing submarine which lost none of the X-craft in her care. This indicates that it was Royal Navy practice to make pairings between regular and midget submarines, the larger vessel tasked with looking after the smaller. In this instance, it would suggest that the *Sceptre* was officially paired with the *X-10*. Were *Sceptre* and the *X-10* therefore in Holy Loch at the same time as HMS *Seraph* in the early spring of 1943?

HMS *Sceptre*, built in Greenock, joined the 3rd Submarine Flotilla in April 1943 and was berthed at Holy Loch. It is probable, therefore, that when HMS *Seraph* arrived at Holy Loch both HMS *Sceptre* and the midget sub in its care, *X-10*, were there, too.

It is evidently a fact of marked coincidence that in April 1943, the inaugural month of *Sceptre*'s berth in Holy Loch, the Royal Navy "found" in the Firth of Clyde an appropriate corpse ("Major Martin") from *Dasher* for Operation Mincemeat, a discovery that demanded of

HMS *Seraph* an urgent trip requiring roughly 35 hours of travel compared with the 5 hours or so that a vehicle would have needed to transport the Welshman's corpse by road from London to *Seraph*'s berth at Blyth. Was this trip required to play out another game with equally high stakes?

In the "Man Who Never Was" story there is no mention of the deployment of a Royal Navy midget or special submarine. Nevertheless, examining these events together one may reasonably deduce that the navy executed a clear operational and/or intelligence imperative that demanded the bringing together of HMS *Seraph*, HMS *Sceptre* and the latter's *X-10* midget submarine in one specfic time and place for a task neither obviously connected with Operation Mincemeat nor with the raid on the *Tirpitz* several months later.

We will learn in the following chapter of some of the remarkable efforts made during WWII by Hitler and high-level peaceniks resident in or deeply connected with Scotland to bring an end to hostilities. We will learn also of the skilful ways in which the British security services manipulated these activities to bring about circumstances of their choosing.

Seen in this context it is entirely feasible that a rendezvous between submarines *Seraph*, *Sceptre* and *X-10* in April 1943 was, at least in part, a link in a chain of events initiated more than three years before by U-33, its mysterious occupants and highly placed Britons in furtherance of these mutual objectives.

Chapter TWENTY

...and why?

All torment, trouble, wonder and amazement
Inhabits here: some heavenly power guide us
Out of this fearful country!

What were U-33's true objectives in visiting Scottish waters during two excursions in the twelve-week period between 22 November 1939 and 12 February 1940? Did it achieve them despite its defeat by HMS *Gleaner* (or the "attendant destroyer") or were its efforts in vain?

Whether in consequence of either U-33's success or failure is there a legacy to its actions that, despite having never been acknowledged or publicised, has nevertheless reverberated down through the ensuing decades in ways one could not dream of discovering in any number of passing years?

My researches have led me to the opinion that the untold story of U-33 has both a rational and an irrational basis in fact. By rational this refers to a political dimension; by irrational to an esoteric or "unworldly" dimension, which is addressed in the last two chapters.

Hitler's personal interventions in directing U-33's operational affairs; the landing of men at Islay and by Carradale; the special submarine(s) involved during U-33's brazen actions; the presence of Albrecht and Klinger on or in the vicinity of U-33's 3rd patrol; the absence of death registration papers for U-33's deceased, 'Sikh Hidtalla' and the *Maillé Brézé* victims Haryog and Handy; the furtive burial ceremonies attended by 'Men from the Ministry'—these are the surefire signs of a political agenda.

The single most extraordinary political event that took place in Scotland during WWII was Deputy Führer Rudolf Hess' unexpected arrival on 10 May 1941. In this infamous act of history Hess force-landed by parachute on Eaglesham Moor in Lanarkshire. Farmer David McLean, having watched a figure parachute into his field, was standing over the man wielding a pitchfork before the flyer had disentangled himself from the folds of his parachute. McLean asked: "Are ye a Nazi enemy, or are ye one o' ours?" The man replied: "Not Nazi enemy, British friend."

Helped into the farmer's kitchen, the flyer said that his name was Alfred Horn and that he had come to see the Duke of Hamilton, laird of the Dungavel estate ten miles away.

Deputy Führer Rudolf Hess

To put the geographical position of Dungavel House (today a United Kingdom Immigration Removal Centre) into the context of U-33's route along the Firth of Clyde in 1939 and 1940, the estate is approximately 38 miles northeast of Pladda, 25 miles east of Largs and 25 miles southeast of Greenock.

The Glasgow Herald of 16 May 1941 published a story stating that Hess and the Duke of Hamilton met on the night of the former's arrival, saying that "the meeting between the Duke and Hess took place at a point on the road to the hospital to which Hess was removed (between Giffnock and Maryhill Barracks), and it is understood that representatives of the Intelligence Service and the Foreign Office were present." This explosive story obviously got past the censor.

Hess had taken off from an airfield at Augsburg in a Messerschmitt Bf110 (Me-110), a 5-hour 1,200-mile flight ahead of him. News broke about the flight on 12 May.

According to a letter[1] sent from Edinburgh to A.S. MacIver in Oxford on the 12th by R. Watt on behalf of Major P.C. Perfect, Scottish Regional Security Officer, the plane appeared to be new and the guns had not been used.

The letter says that the craft had been piloted by one man who stated he had a message for the Duke of Hamilton. The pilot, not named in the letter, had been detained by R.A.F. Intelligence in Maryhill Barracks, Glasgow. Watt goes on to say that he had tried to obtain further information about the incident and the pilot but had only been able to receive a confirmation that the brief facts in his possession were substantially correct. The matter, R.A.F. Intelligence Scottish Command confirmed, had been "passed to a higher authority." Watt concluded his letter to MacIver (evidently a representative of British Intelligence by the nature and tone of the letter) in stating that he was only passing on this information as the Duke of Hamilton "is on the Suspect list." The letter bears a footnote "Original in PF HAUSHOFER 68x Y Box 487 Held R.3.6."

A second document[2] dated 13 May and written by Sd. T.A. Robertson as a file note filled in a lot more detail on the incident. Robertson had the previous day visited the Air Ministry to meet with Air-Vice Marshall Medhurst A.C.A.S.I. The latter had quizzed Robertson for any information about the "case of Haushofer." Robertson gave Medhurst a brief outline on the matter. Medhurst then asked if Robertson had heard of the recent developments (Hess' flight) and then, presumably getting a shake of the head, filled in some details.

The airman who had landed in the Me-110 had been injured on landing and had been taken to hospital. On arriving the airman had asked if he could see the Duke of Hamilton as he had a message for him from Haushofer. Medhurst did not know the name of the airman. He tried to contact a Wing Commander Felkin to learn more details but bad communications prevented it. In addition to this, Medhurst confirmed to Robertson that Sir Archibald Sinclair (1st Viscount Thurso, Secretary of State for Air and owner and custodian of Rosslyn Chapel) had been

---

[1] http://www.geocities.com/CapitolHill/Congress/2106/hess/Hesspics/2_34b.gif
[2] http://www.geocities.com/CapitolHill/Congress/2106/hess/Hesspics/2_34a.gif

spending the weekend with Churchill and that they had sent for the Duke of Hamilton on Sunday. It was as a result of Sinclair's enquiries that Medhurst now wished to know more about Haushofer and was asking Robertson to do some digging. Robertson promised to push through an enquiry via their Regional Officer in Edinburgh to glean more information about the case and, in particular, the name of the pilot. Medhurst remarked that Anthony Eden, Foreign Secretary, was also interested in the case. Robertson concluded his note by stating that on the 9 o'clock evening news the day before a German Communiqué reported that Rudolf Hess had mysteriously disappeared in an aeroplane. The daily newspapers on the 13th confirmed that the pilot was none other than Rudolf Hess. Roberston spoke with one "Mair of Edinburgh" who later rang Robertson to confirm that Hess was in the custody of the Military at Maryhill Barracks and that the Duke of Hamilton had seen him for one hour on Sunday morning, after which he left to meet the Prime Minister.

In these two documents we learn that the Duke of Hamilton was on a suspect list, had met Hess briefly after his arrival and that the head of the Sinclair family was visiting the British Prime Minister at precisely the time of Hess' flight to Scotland.

Who was the 'Haushofer' referred to and what was his connection with the Duke of Hamilton and the Sinclair family?

The 6 January 2003 edition of *The Scotsman* published an article "*MSP* (Member of Scottish Parliament) *at Celebration of Life of Nazi Adviser.*"

The piece described an event, which had taken place that day in the Berlin Wall Haus am Checkpoint Charlie Museum to celebrate the life of Albrecht Haushofer, son of Professor Karl Haushofer. Haushofer Jr. was an adviser to the Nazi leadership and warned Hitler against war. He was later executed after joining the Resistance against the Third Reich.

The 2003 ceremony commemorating Albrecht Haushofer's centenary was addressed by Lothians Member of the Scottish Parliament and former Scotland Office minister James Douglas-Hamilton (Lord Selkirk), younger son of Douglas Douglas-Hamilton 14th Duke of Hamilton and 11th Duke of Brandon whom Hess had asked to see on his arrival in Scotland.

The occasion also marked the publication of a new edition of *We Are the Last* by Rainer Hildebrandt (1916-2004), a former university pupil and friend of Albrecht, who established the museum in 1963.

Lord Douglas-Hamilton described Albrecht Haushofer, one of Germany's leading experts on Britain during the 1930s, as an "unquestionably brilliant academic" who as a patriotic German realised that any course of action he adopted might have unacceptable consequences. In his address the Conservative parliamentarian noted Haushofer's written advice to Hitler and Ribbentrop in 1936 that if Germany launched a war of invasion into Eastern Europe the British would fight, a move which, in turn, would draw the full support of the United States of America. The end result would be that the Russians would come into the heart of Europe. These actions had, of course, come about just as Haushofer had predicted.

For Lord James to have made the trip to Berlin and participated so warmly in the commemoration ceremony there had evidently been a long held and cherished bond between the Douglas-Hamiltons and Albrecht Haushofer. What is the basis for the Hamilton family's enduring loyalty to the Resistance hero?

Albrecht Haushofer, one-quarter Jewish on the side of his mother Martha Mayer-Doss, was one of Deputy Führer Rudolf Hess' closest friends. He was president of the prestigious Society for Geography and Nazi Germany's top expert on Britain and the British.

By training a musician, Albrecht travelled extensively in the 1930s for the German diplomatic service under Hess' direction, making trips to Japan and China and, more frequently, to Britain and to the U.S.A. On these trips he built valuable contacts and reported back to Hess on political developments. In this period Albrecht was regarded by Britain as a man of importance and influence. He received an invitation to George VI's Coronation in 1937.

Karl and Albrecht Haushofer worked hand in glove with Hess in planning the latter's sensational flight to Scotland. On his arrival Hess was carrying the visiting cards from both father and son.

Haushofer Sr. confided to Hess that he had had dreams on three separate nights in which he saw the Deputy Führer piloting a plane and, later, walking in a great castle with tartan wall tapestries.

In my 2008 book on Otto Rahn I made the case that the true-life persona behind the movie character of *Indiana Jones* was, indeed, Rahn. I set out the key linkages between the development of the larger-than-life action hero and the known historical interests of the films' creators, especially those of producer George Lucas. In the third outing of the series, *Indiana Jones and the Last Crusade*, Jones and his beautiful heroine bluff their way into a German Schloss to retrieve his father's Grail Diary from the Nazis. They make out to the castle's occupants that Jones is a Scottish laird who has a castle of his own back home: a pointed reference to Dungavel and to Rosslyn?

Surprisingly, it is known too that in creating the famous father-son relationship of Darth Vader and Luke Skywalker in *Star Wars* Lucas drew on the parallel pairing between Karl and Albrecht Haushofer. In naming the evil-hearted father who sells his soul to the opponents of the Force, Lucas made a play on the title of the poem *Der Vater* (the Father), one of the 79 poems comprising the Moabite Sonnets, which Albrecht wrote in Moabit Prison prior to his beheading by the SS on 23 April 1945. Here is the poem in full.

Der Vater

The deepest folktale from the eastern lands
Tells us that some spirits of the foulest force
Rest imprisoned in the midnight seas,
Sealed up by the Lord God's worried hands,
Until once in a thousand years, there comes
A fisherman who's granted this decision:
Release the awful powers from their prison,
Or cast away at once those fettered demons.
For my father there was this to choose:
Push the demon back into its cell,
By strength of will confine it to its hell.
My father broke the seal and let it loose.
He did not see the breath of evil's flight.
He let the demon drift into the night.

In these lines Albrecht refers to the thousand year Reich in the rise of which his father, Karl, had had a plain choice: fight to keep it under lock and key or to set it loose. Despite the evident sincerity with which Haushofer Snr. worked with Hess and his son to find means to end the war in its early stages, Albrecht clearly arrived at the view that, ultimately, his father had made a willing pact with Hitler and his cohorts. The poem is a shocking indictment of his father's complicity with the Reich leaders.

According to Lord James Douglas-Hamilton, Hess was the instigator of a letter sent by Albrecht Haushofer to his father in September 1940 suggesting a secret meeting in Lisbon, Portugal. The letter was lodged with the British censor and a reply was never sent but eight months later Hess flew to Scotland to meet the Duke in an ill-fated bid to achieve a peace settlement.

At around the same time Albrecht Haushofer was arrested and brought to Hitler's Berghof mountain retreat at Berchtesgaden where he was required to write a report for the Führer. In doing so he "was writing for his life," according to Lord Douglas-Hamilton. After a lengthy interrogation Haushofer was released under strict surveillance. Even so, he continued to draw up peace plans in resistance to Hitler.

Eventually, after going into hiding following Colonel Claus Count von Stauffenberg's unsuccessful assassination attempt on Hitler in July 1944 (Operation Valkyrie), Albrecht Haushofer was captured by the Gestapo, imprisoned and later executed, most certainly by the SS.

In his 2003 Berlin speech Lord James Douglas-Hamilton described Haushofer's execution as a "tragic" loss to those seeking to rebuild Germany in peacetime. "In different circumstances Albrecht would have excelled and he would probably have ended up as the head of the German foreign office or as the Principal of a German university," the MSP said. "But in the days of the Third Reich Albrecht was a man who wanted to do what he believed to be right, but he could not because he found absolutely all the circumstances against him and that is why the story of Albrecht and his friends is one of tragedy." He added: "While the 1,000 year Reich did not last more than 12 years the work of the German Resistance to Hitler, the Sonnets of Moabit…cannot and will not ever be erased from the memory of mankind."

Described as the "Wizard of Germany" by controversial author Colonel Howard Buechner,[3] Albrecht's father Karl was a professor of Geopolitics at the University of Munich and Rudolf Hess' mentor and father figure. From 1907 to 1911 Haushofer Snr. lived mostly in Japan where he held the post of German Military Attaché to Tokyo. While in Japan Haushofer was initiated into the Green Dragon Buddhist society. After the Great War he became Professor of Geography at the University of Munich.

Haushofer was a leading figure behind the formation of Tibetan and Hindu colonies in Berlin and Munich from 1926 onwards. He also played a key role in the establishment of both the Thulegesellschaft (Thule Society) and the mysterious occult Luminous Lodge. Officially the Thule Society was a study group for German antiquity, mythology and folklore but, in essence, it was a heavily politicised body obsessed with matters of intrigue.

Albrecht Haushofer's son attended Gordonstoun, a school in Scotland favoured by the British Royal Family. Gordonstoun was founded by Dr. Kurt Hahn (1886-1974), a German Jew and educationalist. Hahn was co-author with the Duke of Hamilton of a

---

[3] Buechner Colonel H., *Emerald Cup-Ark of Gold*, Thunderbird Press, Inc., Metairie, LA., 1991

letter written to *The Times* in October 1939 about the escalating conflict with Germany. The letter sends a signal to Germany that it is looking forward to making peace with "honourable men." Hahn also wrote a report for Churchill about Hess' arrival in Scotland. A copy of the report was given by Hamilton to the King.

At the end of April 1938 Albrecht was a guest at Dungavel, the Hamilton family home, for one week. During the visit he drew the outlines of the Greater Germany on an atlas.

In the summer of 1940 a secret body of Britons was gathered together to work for SO1, the political warfare arm of the SOE (Special Operations Executive). The group opened a covert line of communication to Albrecht Haushofer through his father. In its correspondence with Albrecht the SO1 team pretended to be old British friends with his father and offered to pass on any correspondence should the Haushofers be in a position to bargain for peace between Germany and Britain.

Unaware of the deception, this was exactly the kind of opportunity Hitler had been seeking since the British declaration of war in September 1939. Appalled that Britain had taken this step, Hitler had made numerous secret peace offers to the British Government through the Vatican, the King of Sweden and even through his own personal lawyer whom he despatched secretly to negotiate with the British Ambassador in Stockholm at the height of the Battle of Britain. Hitler ordered Albrecht Haushofer to begin negotiations with a faction of British politicians who he understood were plotting to usurp power from Churchill and from those around him.

The joint efforts between Germany and influential brokers in Britain to reach a peace accord could be expected to achieve a greater level of success with the placement of emissaries on the ground, each side having their men based locally in the opposite camp. Germany had to have spies and intermediaries in place as did Britain. U-boats such as U-33 were ideally placed to facilitate the transportation into Britain, Scotland specifically, of personnel who had the political authority and remit to conduct and expedite ideas, proposals and exchanges between the two sides.

Albrecht, Klinger, the possible third unlisted survivor on board U-33 in February 1940 and, finally, Sikh Hidtalla were, I believe, associated with this community of German peace ambassadors.

As discussed in Chapter 11 it is notably coincidental that the cover name "Albrecht" is identical to that of the man who was so intimately connected with influential figures in Scotland and their joint efforts to bring an early end to hostilities between Germany and the United Kingdom.

We will see, too, in the penultimate chapter that the political aspects of the "stowaways' " mission, Hidtalla's in particular, may have been the lesser component of a far more exotic menu of ulterior activities.

Nevertheless, if one measures the likely success of the political imperative by the degree of luck enjoyed by U-33 in its two Firth of Clyde excursions there is little to suggest that her efforts bore fruit.

In November 1939 it entered the boom and seemingly had to turn tail very sharply to make a clean getaway. In February 1940 it reportedly got no further than the sea bottom off Pladda and twenty-seven men died.

By all appearances, U-33 achieved little or nothing on either occasion in its efforts to execute its secret agenda. But what of the persons landed by U-33 at Carradale and Islay during its first excursion into Scottish waters and possibly, considering the lifting theory, during its second? Were Albrecht, Klinger and Hidtalla among them? The reports of immaculate uniforms rule out these men as run of the mill spies like the Weber-Drohl duo tasked with making low grade mischief.

Moving up a notch in Nazi central office circles, they may have been junior party bureaucrats serving as advance scouts or support personnel for the later arrrival of top-flight German peace envoys.

Or maybe they *were* those top envoys, men with proven negotiating skills despatched to Scotland by Hitler for discussions with like-minded British personalities to secure a quick end to war in the recognition that the real common enemy was Russia.

And what of the submarine that entered the Clyde Anchorage, shielded by the pandemonium created by the decoy's suicidal actions on that night in November 1939, just weeks after Hitler commenced his peace approaches with Britain? Is it possible that Hitler's top ambassadors preferred to arrive by this means rather than be dropped in a remote island cove followed by a high risk cross-country excursion, confident in their presumed knowledge that their British hosts were taking every precaution to ensure safe passage?

The evidence reviewed in these pages suggests that in November 1939 a decoy submarine was apprehended or even destroyed by sustained depth charge attacks. However, we have also addressed the highly plausible consideration that on this occasion a second submarine, shielded by its confederate vessel, entered the Tail of the Bank and passed into the Clyde Anchorage unscathed. Standing back and reviewing the evidence with an intuitive as well as an analytical eye one has little difficulty in identifying this incursor as U-33, a boat charged by Hitler with serious business to undertake with as much as twenty hours in which to execute it.

We will see that these ambassadors were not the only Scottish-based German emissaries and go-betweens who were busy in these early months in the war to bring about the peace accord Hitler sought so badly. How might those other shadowy peacebrokers have arrived on British soil?

Hitler was not alone among the Nazi leadership in seeking strenuously to reach an accommodation with men of power and influence in Britain. Himmler was similarly preoccupied, taking care to appear seemingly detached from efforts to forge a rapprochement with the enemy while reaching out vigorously through a wide array of intermediaries. Among them were well-connected bankers such as Baron Knut Bonde and other powerful Swedes like the Bofors armaments family.

John Foster Dulles, U.S. Secretary of State, urged President Roosevelt to consider seriously Nazi peace proposals because they originated from Himmler and from factions within the most senior ranks of the Wehrmacht and not from German resistance groups.

Negotiations between Germany and Britain were channelled through SOE agent Peter Tennant who, in turn, established a liaison link with Dr. Walter Jacobson, a friend of Carl Goerdeler, former Mayor of Leipzig and a member of General Ludwig Beck's anti-Hitler private intelligence network. Goerdeler represented Himmler's financial interests in Sweden. Helmut von Moltke, leader of the Kreisau Circle resistance group, was also brought into the picture. The British understood from Swedish Intelligence sources that the Moltke-Goerdeler axis of influence was backed by Himmler. By appearances, this made Himmler anti-Hitler, too, a fact of little surprise when he knew from his contacts' despatches that there were those among the Allies who favoured him as an alternative German leader.

On 9 October 1940 Rudolf Hess wrote to Karl Haushofer saying: "...possibly a mutual acquaintance who had some business to attend to over there anyway (Scotland) might look him up (Duke of Hamilton) and make some communication to him using you or Albrecht as reference." The Duke of Hamilton always denied having met Hess before the war but this was not the case. Churchill's first draft of his book *The Second World War* said that Hamilton met Hess at the Berlin Olympics in 1936. At that time Douglas-Hamilton was the Marquess of Douglas and Clydesdale, the courtesy title of the incumbent duke's eldest son and heir (Douglas succeeded his father Alfred as the 14th Duke of Hamilton and Keeper of Holyroodhouse in 1940).

During the Olympics Clydesdale met Hess at a private dinner given by Hitler in Berlin. The Marquess denied this but it was confirmed by his younger brother, Lord Malcolm Douglas-Hamilton. A British Member of Parliament (MP) on the trip, Henry 'Chips' Channon, said that Clydesdale and he had been invited to lunch by Hess. Channon declined the invitation but confirmed that the Marquess accepted. Another MP, Kenneth Lindsay, said that he was at the lunch and that Clydesdale was present. In fact, in the Duke's own personal handwritten papers his first attempt at describing the occasion went: "During this time and at no time thereafter was I introduced to Hess," which was a clumsy way of saying that he did meet Hess on this one occasion.

By the beginning of 1941 additional operational imperatives were becoming of increasing importance for Hitler, especially his objective to strike at the Russians. His plan to fell the Western democracies before turning to the East had failed. Hitler's solution was to reach an accommodation with the British, which would leave Germany free to concentrate on the Russian invasion. However, Hitler's fifteen-month effort to secure an understanding with Britain had made no measurable progress and so he made fresh efforts to gain an insight into its attitude towards possible direct negotiations. Having been rebuffed in his earlier approaches, Hitler bypassed a direct line into Churchill's administration.

In *The Hitler-Hess Deception*[4] Martin Allen describes how Hitler had ordered Albrecht Haushofer to start new negotiations with a faction of British politicians and key influencers outside of the Churchill clique. These men included Prince George Duke of Kent (King George VI's younger brother), the Duke of Buccleuch and the Duke of Hamilton, both of the latter belonging to the Anglo-German Fellowship Association.

Subsequently, a reply arrived in Berlin expressing interest in Hitler's new approach but asking for more information. Cautiously, a plan was developed. According to Allen, British-born Ernst Wilhelm Bohle, leader of the Auslands-Organisation with party rank of Gauleiter, State Secretary in the Foreign Office and a confidant of Hess in the Deputy Führer's personal office, was chosen to go to England as Germany's emissary.

Hitler then suddenly changed his mind about Bohle, arguing that he

---

[4] Allen M., *The Hitler-Hess Deception,* Harper Collins, London, 2003

did not have sufficient national stature to impress the British. A big name among the Nazi elite would have to fill the role, one who was inseparably linked with Hitler and whose presence would command attention. Hess was the man!

After Hitler had proposed his own Deputy there was a long wait before Britain replied. Finally, an acceptance of the proposal came through, details were arranged and on May 10 Hess made his flight.

The one thing the Germans did not know was that they were negotiating the whole time with agents of the British Secret Service using the names and the handwriting of the Duke of Hamilton and other luminaries of the Anglo-German Fellowship Association.

The initial communication in January was intercepted by the Secret Service. It never reached its intended destination. From then forward the correspondence was handled entirely by British agents.

In the 1940s the *American Mercury* published an article titled "*The inside story of the Hess flight.*" The source for the article was U.S. Intelligence Agent Jack Clements. The piece includes the revelation that Hess went with Hitler's approval as a 'winged messenger of peace' and, dramatically, as a 'shining Parsifal.' The trip had been made after months of communications between Hess and the peace faction. These exchanges had been intercepted by the British Secret Service, which sent the replies to lure Hess to Scotland. At the same time as Hess was being handled by the Home Guard, the *American Mercury* continued, a "kind of official reception committee composed of Military Intelligence officers and Secret Service agents was waiting at the private aerodrome of the Hamilton Estate."

In *Otto Rahn and the Quest for the Holy Grail* I wrote of the activities undertaken by MI6 World War II operative Cecil H. Williamson (1909-1999). In two interviews in 1997 and 1998 (one by telephone, one face to face) Williamson described to me the part played by his team to trick Hitler into substituting Hess for Bohle. Williamson's story provides credible substance to the oft repeated theory that it was MI6 which was responsible for luring Hess to Scotland and that in doing so was trying, independently of the policies and decisions of the elected British Government of the day, to end the war with Germany. There is certainly strong circumstantial evidence that Sir Stewart Menzies, head of MI6, was the driving force behind the deception plan.

Cecil Williamson was born into a well-to-do family in Paignton, Devon. His father had a long and distinguished career in the Fleet Air Arm of the Royal Navy. In January 1938 Colonel Maltby of Foreign

Office Section MI6, a friend of Williamson's father, met with the twenty-eight year old. Maltby asked the young man if he would be interested in helping the Section on occult matters in Britain and Europe from time to time because war with Germany was inevitable. Williamson explained to me that at that time the German middle and upper classes were being swept up in a mass wave of interest in all occult subjects, chiefly astrology, horoscopes, graphology and prediction, together with an extraordinary interest in the prophetic works of sixteenth century seer Michel de Nostradame.

Cecil H. Williamson, WWII MI6 "occult department" operative and a leading member of the team that lured Rudolf Hess to Scotland in 1941

Part of the reason for this, Williamson ventured, was the shockingly hard terms of the Versailles Treaty. The Foreign Office felt it would be useful to have someone on the staff with contacts in these esoteric areas to keep an eye on the phenomenon and see how it might be exploited to Britain's benefit. They wanted an early indication of which Nazis, especially in the upper flights of the regime, might be addicted to and influenced by this kind of "nonsense." Williamson, a keen enthusiast of occult and witchcraft topics, readily agreed to help and straightaway he formed the Witchcraft Research Centre.

When war started Williamson was promptly sent for by Colonel Maltby and reported for duty to Brigadier Gambier-Parry at Whaddon Hall, the requisitioned home of the Selby-Lowndes family, adjacent to

Bletchley. Later the unit also occupied Wavendon Towers, another large house close to Bletchley, which Williamson and his team converted into sound recording studios and related facilities.

It is clear from what Williamson said during our interviews that he was an unrepentant supporter of Nazism. He emphasised disarmingly that this viewpoint was commonly shared by the British upper classes and had been prevalent in the wartime security services. He said Himmler was a decent chap and that an awful lot of bad press had unfairly been thrown at Hitler. Williamson told me it was a tragedy that the Hess mission went the way it did because he was a very brave man who deserved better than he got.

Williamson was also frank about his advocacy of a policy of eugenics to "cleanse" Europe of "riff-raff," whom he also defined as the "dullards of society" and, shockingly, as "semen." He said that he was also not alone in MI6 in supporting a eugenics programme. Williamson's startling accusation that the sharing of Nazi ideals in the wartime security services, including concentration camp-style cleansing programmes, was widespread is supported by the findings of author Jean-Michel Angebert.[5] Angebert (a pseudonym for writers Jean-Michel Bertrand and Jean Angelini) claims that Karl Haushofer supplied Rudolf Hess with names and addresses in England of members of the occult Order of the Golden Dawn in an effort to unite Germany with her Aryan cousin, the British, and to encourage them also to purify her race.

In light of this account it is not surprising that Albrecht was moved to write *Der Vater* about his father's complicity in supporting the very worst of Nazi policies.

Author Steve Coogan[6] states that many British conservatives believed that Hitler threatened Russia not England. Equally, Williamson sympathised with the Vatican in the face of the criticism directed towards it for providing Nazi escape routes.

For the Bohle-Hess deception a wide range of expertise was called upon by Williamson's MI6 group. With the aid of representatives from the world-renowned Bodleian Museum in Oxford, master forgers and expert paper makers his team re-wrote a page from Nostradamus' predictions, *Les Propheties,* and had it inserted into the prophecies so that it appeared as if it really was an original lost quatrain written by the French apothecary in his own hand three hundred and eighty five years

[5] Angebert J., *The Occult and the Third Reich*, Macmillan N.Y., 1971
[6] Coogan S., *Dreamer of the Day: Francis Parker Yockey and the Postwar Fascist International*, Autonomedia, NY, 1999

earlier. It would fool everyone on the German side.

Williamson did not elaborate on the content of the "new" page but it was clearly intended to convey a powerfully prophetic message of hope for Hitler's peace initiatives, plans whose successful execution could only be guaranteed if Rudolf Hess undertook the role of personal emissary. (Today there is considerable speculation as to whether Hess was actually Hitler's principal personal astrologer.)

The fake copy of Nostradamus' quatrains was deposited in a location in France where it was subsequently "discovered" and removed to Germany. It was then fed to Hess and others via Williamson's group's connections with Nazi astrologers including Dr. Ernst Schulte-Strathaus, a member of Hess' staff under British employ. German astrologers in the pay of the allies also set to work on influencing Hess' gullible wife who, too, was hooked on the subject.

Cecil Williamson was involved in other acts of intelligence, one of which concerned U-boat crews. These duties included broadcasting radio messages to submarine crews, which were designed to make the young sailors feel homesick and bring about a pervading sense of demoralisation. It is an interesting notion that Williamson may have been in direct radio contact with U-33. In light of the known facts about MI6's desire to see an early conclusion to the war with Germany and its subsequent lead in luring Hess to Scotland, it would be remarkable if the security service had not been active in shore-to-ship communications with a U-boat carrying envoys invited in secret to Britain for unofficial peace discussions.

Hitler was not in the loop at first about the explosive Nostradamus work doing the rounds among Hess and his confederates. When eventually the Hitler circle was tipped off about the discovery the Reich leader quickly recognised that the man whom the French seer identified centuries earlier as Germany's 20th century ambassador *sina pari* was none other than his faithful Deputy, his "shining Parsifal" Deputy Führer Rudolf Hess.

This was Hitler's big name, the man who had the right stuff to impress the British. Most importantly, Hess had been shown to posssess impeccable astrological credentials and, moreover, the nomination of no less than the prophetic genius Nostradamus. Hess was indeed the man.

Hess' defection followed quickly, the clear implication being that the Deputy Führer's flight was a direct consequence of the MI6 deception. (The date of 10 May 1941 was highly significant in astrological terms because of a rare conjunction of six planets in the sign of Taurus.)

A few years ago the late Stuart Russell, a British writer and historian who made Germany his home, interviewed Herbert Döhring, the administrator of the Führer's mountain retreat in Bavaria and one of a tiny circle in Nazi Germany whose members were privy to Hitler's secrets. Russell told me that Döhring had confirmed that in early 1941 he had overheard Hitler talking in his study to a senior Luftwaffe officer, asking what needed to be done to ensure that a person could fly *out of* Germany undetected. Two weeks later Hess made his flight and the Führer's servant was in no doubt that the flight and the discussion he had overheard a fortnight before were mutually connected.

Himmler's right-hand man and for all practical purposes Otto Rahn's "line manager," General Karl Wolff, said, too, that not only did Hitler agree to Hess' flight but pressed for it so that a consequent peace agreement with Britain would allow him the freedom to attack the Soviet Union.

Certainly this chimes with Stalin's belief that Britain, at least initially, was in league with Germany to destroy the Soviet Union and that the Hess mission was engineered by British Intelligence with the Duke of Hamilton as a middleman.

Moreover the Russians had some difficulty in understanding why Hess was not immediately prosecuted as a war criminal and detained instead in comfortable quarters to await a postwar trial. In October 1942 the party newspaper Pravda declared: "It is no coincidence that Hess' wife has asked certain British representatives if she could join her husband. This could mean that she does not see her husband as a prisoner. It is high time we knew whether Hess is either a criminal or a plenipotentiary who represents the Nazi government in England."

Stalin never gave up his suspicions that Hess' flight was assisted at the highest level. On 6 November 1944 Churchill made a visit to Moscow. At a supper in the Kremlin Stalin raised his glass and proposed a toast to the British Intelligence Services saying provocatively that they had "inveigled Hess into coming to England." Churchill immediately protested that he and British Intelligence had known nothing about the proposed visit. Stalin smiled and said maybe the Intelligence Services had failed to tell him about the operation.

The Russian leader was undoubtedly correct in making his remarks. The arrival of Hess' Me-110 at Dungavel was definitely expected by members of both the British Government and the military. The day after the flight, the 11th, Hamilton phoned the Foreign Office demanding to speak with the permanent Under-Secretary Sir Alexander Cadogan.

John Colville, Churchill's private secretary, took the phone instead. His first, flagrantly indiscreet words to Hamilton were: "Has somebody arrived?" Churchill must have known about the plan.

Nancy Moore, the daughter of the deputy commander of the Scottish Command of the Royal Observer Corps, Squadron Leader W. Geoffrey Moore, was told by her father when she arrived home on the night of the 10th that "he was going to breach confidence and if she absolutely promised not to tell anyone he would tell her that the pilot was Rudolf Hess."

Mrs Elizabeth Adams' father Robert was a recalled reservist of the Argyll and Sutherland Highlanders, becoming personal assistant to Major-General Douglas McConnel, Commander-in-Chief of southwest Scotland. Elizabeth said that her father was called to Dungavel in advance of Hess' arrival, specifically because there was some uncertainty about when exactly Hess was due to arrive (there is evidence that the flight had firstly been scheduled for 5 May). Her father, a person known to have supported peace moves, told her: "It must have been pukka because of Kent's involvement. Kent (King George V's fourth son Prince George Duke of Kent) was the youngest and brightest so it clearly came from him to give the royal blessing."

The authors of *Double Standards*[7] interviewed a woman who served with the Auxiliary Territorial Service and was at Dungavel on the night of Hess' arrival. She claims that the landing lights at the Dungavel airstrip were switched on ready to receive an incoming aircraft but were later switched off after Hess' forced parachute landing.

This information ties in with the evident fact that Hess must have received an expected signal from Dungavel. On his own map Hess drew a line on a bearing of 250 degrees. The line has no relevance as a navigation aid but the spot where he drew the line is the point where he would have had his first sighting of Dungavel House. The line extended passes precisely through RAF Aldergrove in Northern Ireland. Picknett and her colleagues believe that this was the 'abort point' from which Hess would head for Aldergrove (Plan B) were he not to receive the Dungavel signal.

This explains why two Hurricanes were scrambled from Aldergrove but turned back when Hess, having received the signal, turned his plane towards Dungavel House and its illuminated runway.

The personal logbooks of two Czech pilots who flew for the RAF 245 Squadron during the Battle of Britain, Sergeants Vaclav Bauman

---

[7] Picknett L, Prince C., Prior S., *Double Standards: the Rudolf Hess Cover Up*, Time Warner, 2001

and Leopold Sroom, make for interesting reading. They record details of a flight in the early evening of 10 May 1941 when they were scrambled in a pair of Hurricanes to attack a German aircraft over southern Scotland. As they were closing in on a Messerschmitt Bf110, Fighter Command suddenly called them off. Apart from the pilots' logbooks no official record of their mission exists.

This account, though disputed in some quarters, is supported by the content of an article published in the *American Mercury* in 1943, which said that the "two Hurricanes took off to trail the mystery plane with orders to force it down but under no conditions to shoot at it."

An interesting feature of Dungavel House was that in 1941 it served as a Red Cross centre—mutual territory and an ideal place for a peace meeting. Perhaps unsurprisingly, the Red Cross theme runs right through the Hess affair. A few days before Hess' flight Albrecht Haushofer had meetings with Carl Jacob Burckhardt, a member and later President of the International Committee of the Red Cross. Burckhardt was an influential middleman for peace negotiations and played a key role in co-ordinating Hess' mission arrangements.

Prior to his Red Cross position Burckhardt had served as High Commissioner to the Port of Danzig, a post for which Hess had recommended him. Hess told his aunt Emma Rothaker that if all went well she would receive a message from the Red Cross.

Otto Rahn, too, was no stranger in high-level Red Cross circles. From the mid-thirties Rahn was on social terms with André François-Poncet, French Ambassador to Germany (1931-1938), Vice President and, like Burckhardt, later President of the Red Cross International Committee. During the war François-Poncet provided papers and passports to Nazis fleeing Allied justice along the Vatican's infamous 'Ratlines' escape channels. François-Poncet was also an agent for the notorious Klaus Barbie, the 'Butcher of Lyons.'

During a series of lectures given in Glasgow in June 1941 Sir Patrick Dollan, a former editor of the *Glasgow Daily Herald* and the then Lord Provost of Glasgow, conveyed to his audiences remarks that were summarised on 20 June in the *Bulletin and Scots Pictorial*, viz: "Hess came here an unrepentant Nazi. He believed he could remain in Scotland for two days, discuss his peace proposals and be given petrol and maps to return to Germany." Evidently privy to inside information, Dollan's remarks were clumsily missed by the censor.

Why did Hess hold this belief? Because he felt protected by guardians at the very highest level in Britain—the Royal Family.

Edward VIII succeeded his father, George V, to the British throne on 20 January 1936. Since the Great War the monarchy had been at pains to redact its German lineage, changing the family surname in 1917 from Saxe-Coburg-Gotha to Windsor as a part of the family's efforts to re-invent itself as British to the core. Edward had little or no empathy with these efforts, regarding himself at least as much of a German as an Englishman. He was so comfortable with the German language that he would refer to it as his mother tongue. After Edward's accession he quickly became the most controversial king in modern British history.

Edward did little to disguise his admiration for Hitler and his pro-Nazi beliefs. Around the time of his accession Edward broke with protocol by speaking directly to the German ambassador to the Court of St. James, Joachim von Ribbentrop, who later became Foreign Minister in Hitler's Nazi administration. He expressed his determination to avoid conflict with Germany. This was passed on to Hitler who taking these remarks to heart forged ahead with his first step on the road to war: the conquest of the Rhineland.

In 1936 von Ribbentrop's links with the British Establishment were not limited to exalted contact with Royal circles. By then he had enjoyed warm relations with key security figures for at least three years, including MI5 operative Guy Liddell. In 1933, the year Hitler came to power, MI5, in one of its murkier operations, despatched Liddell to Berlin to cooperate with the Gestapo as part of a crackdown on communists. Liddell forged sympathetic contacts with von Ribbentrop while developing close working relationships with a number of Gestapo officers. Between 1947 and 1952 Liddell went on to become Deputy Director-General of MI5. The Ribbentrop-Liddell collaboration illustrates the depth of the shared and unsavoury far-right sentiments described by Cecil Williamson as commonplace within the British security services before and during the war.

For years prior to the accession the FBI had been keeping a close eye on the heir to the throne. Recently opened files report that Prime Minister Stanley Baldwin and his Cabinet regarded Edward as dangerously pro-Nazi. When Alan Lascelles, one of Baldwin's Private Secretaries, confided that he thought it would be best for the country if Edward fell off his point-to-point horse and broke his neck, the Prime Minister replied: "God forgive me, so do I."

Edward's affair with Wallis Simpson, a twice-married American with a racy past, provoked a constitutional crisis and the King's position quickly became untenable. In December 1936 Edward abdicated and was succeeded by his younger brother Albert (George

VI). After the abdication the British secret service watched Edward and Simpson closely, reporting on their every movement. The couple married as the Duke and Duchess of Windsor in 1937 and continued to cause trouble.

In October 1937 the Duke and Duchess visited Nazi Germany against the advice of the British government and met Adolf Hitler at his Obersalzberg retreat. The visit was much publicised by the German media. During the visit the Duke gave full Nazi salutes as a mark of respect to his hosts. They dined with Rudolf Hess and even visited a concentration camp where the guard towers were explained away as meat stores for the inmates.

According to Charles Higham,[8] in the early stages of war the Duke of Windsor met secretly with Hess in the Hotel Meurice in Paris.

Wallis Simpson had had numerous affairs, including a liaison with von Ribbentrop. According to files released in 2003 by the British Public Records Office, there were rumours that Simpson had been passing information to Germany via Ribbentrop. Edward was renowned for extraordinary laxity in his careless handling of top-secret files, often leaving them lying around in his Berkshire Fort Belvedere residence for anyone to see.

Ribbentrop tried to curry Edward's favour by using the latter's cousin, Charles Edward Duke of Saxe-Coburg and Gotha, as an emissary. A Nazi Party member, Charles Edward brazenly attended the funeral of George V in his Sturmabteilung (SA) uniform. Ernst Röhm's SA stormtroopers (the "brownshirts") functioned as a paramilitary organization of the Nazi Party and played a key role in Adolf Hitler's rise to power in the 1920s and 1930s.

When hostilities commenced Edward was assigned an army job in France with limited access to military intelligence because of Churchill's deep distrust of the Duke.

Historians suspect that Windsor leaked vital information to the Germans, ensuring that their invasion of France succeeded. He then fled to Spain where he continued to make pro-German statements.

In February 1940 the German Minister in The Hague, Count Julius von Zech-Burkersroda, claimed that the Duke of Windsor had leaked the Allied war plans for the defence of Belgium.

Hitler's plan to install Edward as puppet king after a German invasion of Britain came to light in 2002 in newly found Nazi documents. The Duke of Windsor and Mrs Simpson were to be paid the then staggering sum of £5m—in excess of £300m today—to return to

---

[8] Higham C., *Trading with the Enemy*, Dell Publishing Company, 1984

Britain in the autumn of 1940. At Balmoral Hitler would bestow upon the couple the titles of Prince and Princess Regent. Hitler planned to enlist the support of Neville Chamberlain who always favoured negotiation and Lord Halifax, a known Nazi sympathiser.

Halifax, the British Foreign Secretary from 1937 to 1940, was a close friend of Hitler's confidant Lord Brocket who owned Knoydart Estate in the West Highlands where Nazi sympathisers met in secret in the run up to the war. Together with Anglo-German Fellowship members the Duke of Buccleuch and Major-General "Boney" Fuller (a leading member of the British Union of Fascists), Brocket was Hitler's personal guest at his fiftieth birthday celebrations in April 1939.

MI5 officer Anthony Blunt, named in 1979 by then Prime Minister Margaret Thatcher as the "Fourth Man" in the infamous Cambridge spy ring, was sent to Germany in 1945 as a personal emissary of King George VI. His task was to retrieve papers written between the Duke of Windsor and Nazi officials that, had they been made public would, it is claimed, have destroyed the Royal family.

There is a further, little know dimension to Edward VIII's abdication and its aftermath that connects it with Scotland. Archbishop of Canterbury, Dr. Cosmo Lang, vehemently opposed Edward's affair with Simpson. He stated on film that he had the gravest doubts about the sanctity of the proposed marriage, thereby clearly emphasising that he believed it to be an issue of such constitutional enormity that it would only be resolved if the King stepped down.

William Cosmo Gordon Lang (1864-1945) was born in Fyvie in Aberdeenshire and underwent his schooling at Park School in Glasgow. He matriculated to study at Glasgow University at the age of fourteen. Lang graduated MA in 1884 and went to Balliol College, Oxford, where he graduated with a first in History 1886 and was President of the Oxford Union.

Abandoning his earlier plans to become a barrister, Lang was ordained a priest in the Church of England in 1891. He was consecrated Bishop of Stepney in 1901, Archbishop of York in 1908 and Archbishop of Canterbury in 1928. He retired in 1942 when he was created a baronet.

Both George VI and the Prime Minister Stanley Baldwin were aware of Lang's views and it was widely assumed that he had played a leading role in forcing Edward out. The Archbishop unwisely made a radio broadcast after the abdication, which was seen as kicking Edward when he was down. The broadcast helped to cement the public belief that Lang was the key figure in the abdication crisis.

Interestingly, recent historical research has shone new light upon Cosmo Lang's concern about the Nazis' racial policies. He supported moves to assist refugees. He backed Bishop George Bell who supported anti-Nazi clergy in Germany against Bishop Arthur Headlam who wanted to emphasize good relations with Germany. On the other hand, as reported in *The Times Online* on 23 April 2004 based on extracts from the Archbishop's newly released diaries, Lang said shortly before the war that he believed German Jews had brought upon themselves the hatred of Hitler.

The High Commissioner for Refugees, James Grover McDonald, met the Archbishop and recorded in his diary Lang's comment that "the Jews themselves" might be responsible for the "excesses of the Nazis." It would appear that in expressing his anti-racist views Lang was acting more than a little disingenuously and was, in fact, more concerned about stopping harsh treatment of clergy rather than protecting racial groups.

During the war stories were circulating that "Nazi Pope" Pius XII and Archbishop Cosmo Lang had fallen out. A subject that connected them both was Edward's abdication—Hitler held Edward in high regard while Lang had done nothing to conceal his wrath. This is a likely explanation for the tension between the two leading prelates.

Files still classified top secret under the British Official Secrets Act include those that link Pius XII both to Cosmo Lang and to Oswald Mosley (the British fascist leader of the Black Shirts movement).

Six days before Edward VIII's abdication on 10 December 1936 a report reached Archbishop Lang that Dr. Alexander Cannon, a qualified psychiatrist, had hypnotised the King by using spirit mediums. So seriously did Lang take the information that he immediately questioned a Harley Street doctor to find out about Dr. Cannon. He also briefed Downing Street. It was discovered that another of Dr. Cannon's patients was George Drummond, a banker who subsidised Oswald Mosley and his British Union movement. Cosmo Lang was beginning to make powerful enemies.

It appears that Dr. Lang's anti-fascist views were not appreciated either within Hitler's circle or in Rome, an ironical state of affairs considering the Archbishop's unkind and intemperate remarks about the culpability of the Jews in forcing Hitler's hand against them in Germany.

In 1945, while hurrying to Kew Gardens Station to get to a meeting at the British Museum, Cosmo Lang fell to the pavement and died quickly. At eighty-one years of age was it Lang's natural time to make his exit from life…or were there more sinister forces at work?

Edward was not the only sibling of George V to support a policy of appeasement. His younger brother Prince George Duke of Kent had strong pro-German sentiments.

A report written by Alfred Rosenberg for Adolf Hitler in October 1935 stated that the Duke of Kent was working behind the scenes "in strengthening the pressure for a reconstruction of the Cabinet and mainly towards beginning the movement in the direction of Germany."

In February 1937 it was reported that the Duke of Kent had met the Duke of Windsor in Austria. Later that year a Foreign Office document pointed out that the Duke of Kent, like his brother and notorious sister-in-law, had developed a close relationship with Ambassador von Ribbentrop.

The Duke of Kent, widely regarded as the head of the Anglo-German Fellowship, took part in secret talks with his cousin Prince Philip of Hesse in early 1939 in order to avoid a war with Nazi Germany.

In July 1939 the Duke of Kent approached George VI with a plan to negotiate directly with Adolf Hitler. The King, who supported the idea, spoke with Neville Chamberlain and Lord Halifax about the plan.

On the outbreak of war the Duke of Kent and his family moved to Scotland, living in Pitliver House near Rosyth in Fife. He returned to active military service with the rank of Rear Admiral, briefly serving in the Intelligence Division of the Admiralty. In April 1940 he transferred to the Royal Air Force. He took the post of Staff Officer in the RAF Training Command with rank of Air Commodore. At the time of Hess' arrival, therefore, the Duke of Kent was living in Scotland.

Martin Allen maintains that both the Dukes of Kent and of Bucccleuch were at the Duke of Hamilton's Dungavel Estate on the night when Hess arrived.

The Duke of Buccleuch was very pro-German but nevertheless George VI appointed him as Keeper of the Royal Household, a prestigious appointment that automatically made him a Privy Councillor, one of the King's handpicked advisers.

A member of the women's wartime services stationed at Dungavel on 10 May claimed that the Duke and "his people" were at the Kennels (a small house close to the airstrip), together with "some Poles." She clarified that she was not speaking about the Duke of Hamilton but about the Duke of Kent.

As the Duke of Kent's papers are embargoed it is impossible to confirm the story that he was at Dungavel on the 10th. However, it is known from other sources that he was at RAF Sumburgh in the Shetlands on the 9th and at Balmoral in Scotland on the 11th. The following day he was at RAF Wick at Caithness. He was ideally positioned geographically to be on hand to visit Dungavel during this period.

The Duke of Hamilton's diary records several meetings with the Duke of Kent during the early months of 1941. Elizabeth Byrd worked as a secretary for Hamilton's brother. She claims that Lord Malcolm told her that the Duke of Hamilton took the "flak for the whole Hess affair in order to protect others even higher up the social scale." Byrd added that: "he had strongly hinted that the cover-up was necessary to protect the reputations of members of the Royal Family."

Picknett *et al* [9] similarly concluded from their investigations that the Duke of Kent was with Hamilton at his home on that night. The first-hand testimony for this statement comes from the Duke of Hamilton's housekeeper. But were these highborn Britons alone?

The housekeeper told the authors that also present at Dungavel House was a man with a foreign accent. This was almost certainly journalist Baron William de Ropp, who was involved in the German-British peace talks. A second German present was an Intelligence operative named Voigt.

Baron Wilhelm de Ropp was born in the Baltic States. He moved to Britain in 1910 and later served in the Royal Flying Corp in World War One under the command of Major R.F. Winterbotham. De Ropp relocated to Germany in 1920 and became an associate of Nazi enthusiast Alfred Rosenberg, a fellow son of the Baltics (Rosenberg was Estonian) whose task was to establish links with elevated figures in Britain for the Nazis in the 1930's. In the 1920s and early 1930s de Ropp worked as a freelance journalist.

Through Rosenberg de Ropp met Hitler and Hess. Winterbotham became head of Air Intelligence, part of MI6. Between de Ropp and Winterbotham lines of communications were opened between Rosenberg and the King's youngest son, the Duke of Kent. Author Ladislas Farago wrote[10] that Baron de Ropp, used by Hitler as his confidental consultant about British affairs, was a British double agent who penetrated the Nazi echelons in pre-World War II days.

John Simkin, author of a dozen books on various historical themes and co-founder with Andy Walker of the online International Education

---

[9] Ibid
[10] Farago L, *The Game of the Foxes: The Untold Story of German Espionage in the United States and Great Britain during World War II.*, New York, 1971

Forum,[11] has researched the Hess story extensively. His findings indicate that on the morning of 11 May the Dukes of Kent and of Buccleuch were involved in a car crash while driving along the Douglas to Lanark road. The Duke of Kent's car hit a coal lorry. The scene of the accident was very close to Dungavel House.

Other sources have expanded on this incident, claiming that on the following day, the 12th, Voigt despatched a memorandum: "I can confirm that neither the Duke nor his passenger Buccleuch were injured and in view of Lanark's close proximity to the events of last weekend (*Hess' flight*) steps have been taken to ensure the accident remains unreported by the press."

William de Ropp and Voigt—a Baltic journalist who was spying for Germany and a German intelligence spook—how had they travelled to Scotland during wartime?

They would have hardly hopped onto a handy commercial flight into Glasgow or Edinburgh or boarded a Continental train with all of the precarious stops and ferry crossings and the prolonged risk of discovery. Had they been brought to Scotland by ship…by submarine even?

Were they intelligence runners from the same spy stable as Albrecht and Klinger? By virtue of their need to maintain high security and low visibility the probability that de Ropp and Voigt came to Scotland by U-boat has to rank highly compared with other means of transportation. Had they been among the personnel dropped off by U-33 in November 1939 on Islay and Carradale?

The Hess-Duke of Kent story does not end on 10 May 1941. At 13:10 on 25 August 1942 the Duke took off from Invergordon in northeast Scotland in an S-25 Sunderland Mk III Flying Boat carrying 15 passsengers and crew. A short time later (official reports give the timing as 13:30) it crashed on Eagle's Rock in Caithness killing all on board, save one.

The official story is that the Duke was on a morale-boosting visit to RAF personnel stationed in Iceland. The crew had been carefully selected. The captain, Flight Lieutenant Frank Goyen, was considered to be the most proficient Sunderland flyer in the RAF and had flown some of Britain's politicians during the war. The co-pilot was Wing Commander Thomas Lawton Mosley, the commanding officer of 228 Squadron. Mosley was one of the RAF's most experienced pilots

---

[11]

http://educationforum.ipbhost.com/index.php?showtopic=9208&pid=120478&st=15&#entry120478

having completed 1,449 flying hours. He was also a navigation specialist and a former instructor at the School of Navigation.

The Duke of Kent was accompanied by his Private Secretary John Lowther, his equerry Michael Strutt and his valet John Hales.

Being a flying boat, standing orders stipulated that it must fly over water, only crossing land when absolutely unavoidable. The route was to follow the coastline to Duncansby Head, the northernmost tip of Scotland, and then turn northwest over the Pentland Firth towards Iceland.

The S-25 Sunderland Mk III crashed into Eagle's Rock, having descended for reasons never officially clarified from its normal operational altitude to a height of approximately 650 feet. The flying boat was well off course when the accident happened. Its 2,500 gallons of fuel, carried in the wings, exploded.

The crash was heard by a number of local people who reached the scene about ninety minutes after the explosion. They included seventy-year old local GP Dr. John Kennedy and two policemen: Will Bethune and James Sutherland. The arrivals found 15 bodies, including that of the Duke of Kent.

Bethune gave a radio interview in 1985 where he described finding Prince George's body. He said that handcuffed to the Duke's wrist was an attaché case that had burst open, scattering a large number of 100-Kroner notes over the hillside.

The Duchess of Kent collapsed in shock when she heard the news. The following morning the newspapers reported that *everyone* (author's italics) on board the Sunderland had been killed. Telegrams were sent to the next of kin of all members of the crew.

But here's the rub. Later that day Andy Jack, the tail-gunner, was found alive in a crofter's cottage at Ramscraigs. When the flying boat exploded the tail section was thrown over the brow of the hill, coming to rest in the peat bog on the other side. Andy Jack only had superficial injuries.

What he did next was one of the most curious aspects of the Sunderland flying boat event. Instead of going to the wreckage to see what had happened to his colleagues and waiting for rescuers to arrive he ran away in the opposite direction. Jack's inexplicable action was contrary to standard procedure, which was always to remain with the wreck.

The cottage owner Elsie Sutherland telephoned Dr. Kennedy. It was some time later before the authorities were told of Sutherland's communication with Dr. Kennedy, by which time Andy Jack's sister

Jean had already received a telegram saying that her brother had been killed in the accident.

Winston Churchill made a statement in the House of Commons where he described the Duke of Kent as "a gallant and handsome prince." Of the many tributes and messages of condolence received from other countries the most significant was from General Władysław Sikorski, the head of the Polish government in exile. The two men were very close and Sikorski sent a special dispatch to all Polish troops in Britain in which he described the Duke as "a proven friend of Poland and the Polish armed forces."

(It had been proposed in 1937 that Prince George be made King of Poland in a move to restore the Polish monarchy, much as the Greek monarchy had been restored using imported royals. In August 1937 the Duke and his wife visited Poland and were well received. However, the plan was called off due to the invasion of Poland in 1939.)

The Duchess of Kent visited Andy Jack several times after the death of her husband. It is believed that the information he provided to her influenced what the Duchess subsequently had inscribed on Prince George's memorial, which included: *"In memory of....the Duke of Kent... and his companions who lost their lives on active service during a flight to Iceland on a special mission on 25th August 1942."*

The use of the words "special mission" is interesting. They echo those used by Pilot Officer George Saunders who a few days before joining the crew of the Sunderland told his mother: "I'm just on leave for a couple of days. I'm going on a most important mission, very secret. I can't say any more."

The circumstances of the Sunderland disaster raise some very pertinent questions. Why did the pilot take the flying boat off course? It was a clear day and he would have been fully aware that he was flying over land rather than the sea. Why, when the aircraft included four experienced navigators, did the aircraft drift a huge 15 degrees off course from its point of departure? Why did the pilot descend to 650 feet when he was flying over high land? This is especially puzzling when one considers that the S-25 Sunderland Mk III had one major defect—it was sluggish when climbing, especially when heavily laden with personnel as it was on the Duke of Kent's flight.

The craft took off at 13:10 and crashed 60 miles from its departure point, a journey of no more than 20 minutes. However, contemporary local newspaper reports and the Prime Minister's official papers lodged with the Public Records Office (PRO) confirm that the crash actually took place at 14:30, one hour later than reported. Where had it been in the meantime?

A court of inquiry was held. Details of its findings were presented to the House of Commons by the Secretary of State for Air, Sir Archibald Sinclair, on 7 October 1942. The conclusion of the report was: "Accident due to aircraft being on wrong track at too low altitude to clear rising ground on track. Captain of aircraft changed flight-plan for reasons unknown and descended through cloud without making sure he was over water and crashed." Sinclair confirmed that weather conditions were fine and there was no evidence of mechanical failure. He added: "the responsibility for this serious mistake in airmanship lies with the captain of the aircraft."

It was therefore suggested that the reason for the crash was that the team of four (highly experienced) pilot/navigators drifted off course and then failed to reach the necessary height to clear Eagle's Rock. The problem is that the documents that would enable researchers to re-examine the evidence have vanished. This includes the flight plan filed by Goyen before take-off.

The secret court of inquiry should have been made available after 15 years. When researchers asked the PRO in 1990 for a copy of the report it was discovered that it had gone missing. The PRO suggested it might have been transferred to the royal archives at Windsor Castle. However, the registrar of the royal archives said they did not have it and never had done.

Andy Jack was forced to sign the Official Secrets Act while still in hospital. He later told his sister that he could not talk about the crash because he had been "sworn to secrecy." Jean Jack did provide researchers with one piece of interesting information. Frank Goyen gave Andy Jack a signed photograph of himself just before take-off on which he had written: "With memories of happier days." Was this a reference to the mission they were about to undertake? Does it suggest that Goyen disapproved of the mission?

On 17th May 1961 the Duchess of Kent brought the case to national attention when she visited the scene of her husband's death. This created a discussion about the crash in the media. Andy Jack then came forward to give an interview to the Scottish *Daily Express*. He was still serving with the RAF and, not surprisingly, he went along with the conclusions of the official inquiry.

An important witness to the crash was Captain E.E. Fresson. He piloted an aircraft over the same area around the same time as the crashed Flying Boat. The following day he took the only aerial photographs of the wreckage. In 1963 Fresson published his autobiography *Air Road to the Isles*. Amazingly, the book does not refer to the death of the Duke of Kent. According to his son, Richard, the book originally did include a full chapter that covered his investigation into the crash. However, the book's publisher removed this material at the last moment.

15 men set off from Invergordon; 15 bodies were found; 1 man survived. The arithmetic is unarguable. There were 16 persons on board. The King clearly recognised this fact when he asked specifically about the finding of *all* 15 victims of the crash, aware of course that gunner Andy Jack had survived.

The weekly *John o' Groat Journal* of 28 August carried the unequivocal headline:

DUKE OF KENT KILLED IN AIR CRASH
TRAGEDY IN THE NORTH OF SCOTLAND
FIFTEEN DEAD IN WRECKED PLANE
SURVIVOR DISCOVERED ON FOLLOWING DAY

A local history book published in Wick in 1948, *Caithness and the War 1939-1945,* by Norman M. Glass, compiled from local newspaper archives, states that the Duke of Kent "set out for Iceland on the afternoon of Tuesday August 25 1942 in a Sunderland Flying Boat carrying 16 in all," and that when the search parties arrived at the crash site "all the occupants (15) were dead."

Who was the 16th man? The Picknett team[12] argue that the probable cause of the Sunderland's deviation from its planned route was to put down on Loch More to pick up Rudolf Hess at Lochmore Cottage, which belonged to Sir Archibald Sinclair. Loch More is about 8 miles from the crash site.

The two cottages mentioned by Lord Thurso as locations for Hess' concealment by the British government—Braemore Lodge and Lochmore Cottage—are on the same road nine miles apart as the crow flies. The received wisdom is that Hess was kept at Braemore Lodge and removed later to Lochmore Cottage while waiting to be picked up by the Flying Boat.

The authors posit that the flight was a peace mission bound for Sweden where Prince George was going to sign a treaty with Hitler to join forces and attack Stalin. Seeing that in May 1941 the Iceland Kroner was almost worthless, it is suggested that it was actually Swedish Kroners which the Duke was carrying in his attaché case.

---

[12] Ibid

This theory has drawn considerable interest, particularly as the last person to see Prince George alive was Prince Bernhart of the Netherlands. The Prussian Prince Bernhart von Lippe joined the Nazis while studying at the University of Berlin in 1934 and worked openly in the motorised SS. According to *Newsweek* (5 April 1976) Prince Bernhart was a member of a special SS intelligence unit in I.G. Farben (the wartime patentholder for concentration camp gas Zyklon B) and that this came out in testimony at the Nuremberg trials. Bernhart resigned from the SS in 1937 when he married the future Queen Juliana of the Netherlands. Adolf Hitler forwarded a congratulatory message through Bernhart who became a naturalised Dutchman.

A destination in Sweden makes sense, too, for a take-off from Invergordon on the east coast, instead of from Oban (where the plane was based), which would have been the logical departure point for Iceland.

Andy Jack took his sister, Jean, to see the plane the Saturday before the crash. She saw it was being painted white "like a white bird," odd because the usual paint scheme for a Sunderland was camouflage olive and brown. The white colour makes more sense for a flight to Sweden because flights between Britain and Sweden were painted white to highlight the markings so that German patrols would not attack a plane en route to a neutral country. Wartime aviator Hughie Green (later to become a British television personality) described making a diplomatic flight to Sweden in a white-painted Catalina flying boat.

Strong arguments have been put forward to support the theory that the Sunderland failed to gain sufficient height by the crash site because of engineering failure caused deliberately—that the occupants were murdered.

There are precedents and parallels that support this opinion. Kent's great friend General Sikorski was killed in July 1943 when his plane crashed into the sea after taking off from a refuelling stop at Gibraltar. The Czech pilot, the only survivor, had donned his life jacket before setting off but not his parachute as if he knew before take-off that he would be coming down in the water. Although an RAF court of enquiry could find no reason for the craft's elevator controls having jammed (the mechanical cause of the accident) Summer Welles, the U.S. Under-Secretary of State, explicitly called Sikorski's death "assassination."

A similar incident, not made public until 1967, happened with General de Gaulle in the spring of 1943. He was persuaded by the Air Ministry (Sir Archibald Sinclair's ministry) to make his trip to Glasgow by plane even though he hated flying. On take-off the elevators failed, just as in the Sikorski crash, but this time the flight was straightaway aborted. A secret RAF investigation found that the control rods had been eaten through by acid. This happened at a time when Churchill regarded de Gaulle as a nuisance "to be eliminated" (John Lichfield writing in *The Independent* 5 January 2000).

Picknett et al conclude that the British—presumably elements within the SOE—were responsible for the Sikorski assassination and for the attempt on de Gaulle's life, thereby establishing that the Establishment's preferred mode for getting rid of unwelcome VIPs was "air accident."

It is fact that on the day of the Sunderland crash there was a team of army sabotage experts known as an Oxen Unit in the area at Berriedale near Braemore. These units were linked with the SOE. Were these a part of the team of 'military personnel' at Braemore who joined the locals in the search party after the crash?

The 'Special Mission' that the Duke of Kent's wife Marina referenced on the commemoration stone could have been one of peace, which would have made the plane a target for the Soviet Union and the U.S.A., as well as those in Britain opposed to peace with Germany. Was Kent, acting on behalf of his brother George VI, doing the decent thing by allowing Hess to return to Germany under the rules of the Geneva Convention?

There is another intriguing aspect to this story. Just ten days after the death of the Duke of Kent another flying boat, also from 228 Squadron, crashed in the Scottish Highlands. The official explanation was that the plane had run out of fuel. Everyone on board was killed, including passenger Fred Nancarrow, a journalist from Glasgow. Nancarrow was investigating the Eagle's Rock crash. Naturally, when he died he could no longer continue with those enquiries.

U-33 was ordered to undertake its February 1940 voyage to Scotland by Adolf Hitler. The evidence reveals that among its deceased were high-level emissaries. We know, too, that in the first few weeks of the war U-33 was vigorously active in and around the Firth of Clyde, dropping off personnel in west of Scotland island locations before fulfilling its near-suicidal the entry into the Clyde Anchorage together with one, possibly more special submarines. It can only have made sense to take these tremendous risks if they were carrying Hitler's envoys and were mandated to deliver them safely to pre-arranged disembarkation points.

This clandestine political activity, facilitated at terrible risk by U-33, took place when Hitler was desperate to reach an accord with

Britain, primarily necessary in his view so that Germany could focus on attacking a common enemy—the Soviet Union.

Based on what is known about the make-up and motives of the peace faction in Britain, many members of which were Scottish (the Dukes of Hamilton and of Buccleuch *inter alia*) or Scotland based (Prince George Duke of Kent), it is beyond question that U-33 was expected on both of its Firth of Clyde excursions. German agents—Wilhelm de Ropp, Voigt, perhaps others—were in place to ensure that the wheels of secret diplomacy remained greased and free from obstacles barring successful progress.

U-33's role as peace facilitator helped lay the groundwork for all subsequent steps along the unofficial peace trail. Rudolf Hess' flight and the ill-fated Sunderland flying boat journey, Sweden-bound for covert peace discussions, were the principal waymarkers along that pathway, interventions not sanctioned by the British Government of the day.

The U-boat went to the bottom in February 1940 unaware and uncaring of all the scheming that would follow to encourage Churchill to agree to the ending of hostilities with Hitler.

But did U-33 sink into the silt of the Clyde quite so unfulfilled? Is the real mystery of U-33 truly concerned with issues as 'mundane' as furtive peace politics and Allied operational deceptions? No, I believe the objectives of U-33's mission were intended to achieve so much more than that.

Remarkably, had U-33 successfully delivered, or at least laid the essential groundwork, for a second altogether more sensational component of its agenda, one that was wholly unconcerned with anything as vulgar as matters of war?

Had U-33, in fact, expedited a journey of discovery in which the prize sought was the seriously valuable cargo of items reportedly brought to Scotland by the surving Knights Templar after the enforced dissolution of their Order in 1307? Lead on Macduff.

Chapter TWENTY-ONE

U-33: Argo of the Grail

Our revels now are ended. These our actors,
As I foretold you, were all spirits, and
Are melted into air, into thin air

According to Andrew Sinclair,[1] Hitler approached Walter Johannes Stein through Rudolf Hess to help find the Grail. The belief entertained among the Hitler circle that the Grail was in Scotland, Stein suggested, was another powerful inducement for Hess to make his flight.

Hans Fuchs, an intimate of Hess and a member of the Thule society, visited Rosslyn Chapel in May 1930 and signed the Visitors' Book. He told members of the Edinburgh Theosophical Society that Hess identified with Parsifal and believed that Rosslyn was a Grail Chapel or even *the* Grail Chapel. Remarkably, it has been alleged that Churchill availed Hess of the services of the fledgling Special Air Service (created in August 1941) to help in his searches at Rosslyn.

Adolf Hitler shared Otto Rahn's belief in the existence of a "second" Grail, which comprises stone tablets inscribed with an indecipherable language revealing the combined wisdom of the ages— 'Ultimate Truth.' Rahn based his belief on an interpretation of the writings of Wolfram von Eschenbach who wrote in *Parsifal* that:

Guyot, the master of high renown,
Found, in confused pagan writing,
The legend which reaches back to the prime source of
(All) legends.

Hitler arrogated Rahn's scholarly conclusions and then embellished them to insist that this Second Grail was no less than the Sacred Book of the Aryans. Convinced of this lofty but entirely spurious

---

[1] Sinclair A., *Sword and the Grail: The Story of the Grail, the Templars and the True Discovery of America.* Edinburgh: Birlinn Limited, 2002

interpretation, Hitler made every effort to locate this record of the secret genesis of the world to revive the ancient Germanic myths and draw on their provenance to justify the Nazis' extreme political theories.

Otto Rahn in the "cathedral" of Lombrives in the French Pyrenees

Accordingly, popular wisdom has it that Rahn was sent into Europe's ancient places of power, most notably into sacred locations such as Ornolac in the French Pyrenees and Externsteine in Germany, to find the Grail tablets described by Eschenbach. Once found, the all-powerful talisman would be wielded by the Führer to re-awaken the German deities and to re-present Cathar solar symbology as the swastika of the Third Reich.

In reality, there is no evidence that Rahn found a single thing of value in the caves and grottoes of Continental Europe. From an analysis of his writings one arrives at the conclusion that Rahn never expected to make any such sensational discoveries in those locations; that what he sought lay elsewhere. There is a powerful argument that Rahn believed Scotland to be this place of concealment.

In 2003 *The Greenock Telegraph* published a story about the activities of U-33. The article explored the theory that the submarine carried Nazi language specialist Otto Rahn, a man closely associated with the Third Reich's search for the Grail treasures.

There is no evidence that Rahn was a passenger on U-33. However, we do have the accounts of men dropped off by U-33 in various locations and also the implied position from an analysis of the NHB's figures that there was a third unrecorded person on board U-33—one whose absence in the burial lists suggests survival. Any one of these mysterious travellers could have been Otto Rahn. The difficulty with this scenario is that by the time U-33 was sunk off Pladda Rahn had been reported dead for eleven months.

By all accounts the *Telegraph*'s storyline was pure flight of fancy but, surprisingly, it elicited a keen response from local history experts. The Scottish heritage group, Magic Torch, supported the newspaper's proposition on the Rahn visit and set out the sound historical basis as to why the west of Scotland can lay claim to be the Grail's place of concealment. Personally, I do not believe in the story that Rahn killed himself in March 1939 in the Tyrol's Wilder-Kaiser Mountains. I have argued[2] strongly that there is abundant, albeit circumstantial evidence that he lived on. Consequently, I am open to the possibility that there were those among the Magic Torch membership who had personal knowledge, through family or friends, of the young German explorer's arrival in Scotland in 1939-1940.

Equally, they could have had access to the same documents said by reliable sources to have been in the possession of British researcher and Cathar authority Alex Closs (a relation of Hannah Closs, author of the acclaimed Tarn trilogy Cathar novels) in the 1990s, which allegedly prove that Rahn lived on past 1945. If there is substance to this latter report then Sikh Hidtalla, buried at Greenock in January 1940, is ruled out as a cover identity for Rahn.

If Otto Rahn had travelled "*post-mortem*" to Scotland in U-33 what would have been his likely chief objective? Rahn's overriding subject of research from his teenage years was concerned with deconstructing the writings of Wolfram von Eschenbach, author of *Parsifal*, to unravel a code said to identify the hiding place of the Holy Grail.

Rahn knew also that in the closing hours of the infamous ten-month

---

[2] Ibid

siege of Montségur in 1244, which culminated in the mass burning by the Church of Rome of more than two hundred so-called "heretical" Cathar Christians and their supporters, four Knights abseiled down the Pyrenean Mountain under the cover of darkness. The treasure in their care was said to include the Oriflamme (Grâl or Mani) of the Cathar faith and, it is rumoured, the Ark of the Covenant and the Grail Cup.

The Knights handed over the treasures to a "Son of Belissena" (Son of the Moon), Pons-Arnaud de Castella Verdunam, who then re-concealed the items in the caverns of Ornolac in the Sabarthès region of the Pyrenees.

Eschenbach wrote *Parsifal* in the first quarter of the thirteenth century. The Cathars entrusted the safety of the Grail treasures into the Knights' friendly hands around twenty-five years later. In the early 1930s Otto Rahn set himself the task of learning the complete picture of the movements of the Grail cache including the post-Montségur efforts to conceal it from the Catholic Church, which Rahn in the twentieth century distrusted intensely and vice versa.

It is understood that both Otto Rahn and Rudolf Hess believed that the Grail was removed from France post-1244 and that sometime thereafter was concealed at Rosslyn Chapel. Startlingly, both men believed that this Grail was not in the form of a chalice or cup but was a Head—the so-called "Head of God."

One of the principal charges levelled against the Knights Templar in 1307 was that they worshipped a head or a heathen idol of some kind. The name Baphomet spilled out in confessions wrung under torture. Many Templars denied having heard of it. Others described it variously as a severed head, a cat or a head with three faces.

Hess at least partly derived his theories about Rosslyn and the Grail from his love of the Wagnerian cycle, undertaking an interpretative process of the works very similar in context to Otto Rahn's philological studies of Eschenbach's *Parsifal* (the basis for a substantial part of Wagner's Ring Cycle), which led him to commence his own Grail quest. For Hess and Rahn to have held identical, highly unconventional beliefs about Grail lore suggests that they were at least aware of each other. They may have had meetings, in light of which one cannot rule out a scenario, for example, in which Rahn, while attending the Berlin Olympics in 1936, was present when Hamilton and Hess met at the Games.

Whatever the physical characteristics of the Grail object, if Rahn, an extraordinarily able scholar and researcher, believed it to be located in Scotland what might have led him to this conclusion?

En route to Iceland in 1936 on a study-commission for the SS-Führen, the ship bearing Rahn and his colleagues docked briefly at Leith to take on more coal. In the following hours Rahn visited Arthur's Seat in Edinburgh. Arthur's Seat is the highest of a series of ancient volcanic peaks, which take the form of a crouched lion. Rahn described the visit in his second book.[3]

More accurately, in his description Rahn skips over the Edinburgh sights and instead writes enthusiastically about finding himself on British soil and its cultural significance. He states that for British heretics an Arthur figure has a lot more meaning than an Abraham or a David, a Parsifal-Perceval figure more than a Christ.

The Arthur figure that Rahn draws on in his essay is Sir John Oldcastle, one of the most renowned among British heretics and a chief member of the fourteenth-century Lollard movement. Rahn quotes a ballad composed by one of Oldcastle's contemporaries, Thomas Occleve, which states that Oldcastle preferred to read the stories of chivalry rather than the Bible.

John Oldcastle burning at the stake

Elaborating on this observation, Rahn likened Oldcastle to Don Quixote who, fired with zeal after consuming stories about the legendary Amadis de Gaul and other fabled knights-errant, rode off on Rossinante (his Pegasus) to do battle with windmills and imaginary foes. In Cervantes's master work, though, we come to understand that far from being a madman Don Quixote was the greatest Knight of them all.

Rahn's researches indicated that the principles of Lollardy had arisen firstly in the Netherlands and in Germany before reaching England where its Continental adherents merged with the followers of John Wycliffe (1320s-1384), an English theologian and early dissident in the Roman Catholic Church.

In describing the fate of English heretics from 1160 onwards, most commonly by burning at the stake, Rahn said that they died with a *dietrich* in their heart and the key of St. Peter on their tunic. In Rahn's philosophy a *dietrich* is a personalised symbolic passe-partout or

---

[3] Rahn O., *Luzifers Hofgesind: Eine Reise zu den guten Gelstern Europas*, Schwarzhaupter Verlag, Leipzig, 1937

skeleton key with which the determined student may seek to access the greater mysteries.

After a period of imprisonment in the Tower of London Sir John Oldcastle in 1419 was wrapped around with a heavy iron chain and, like Templar leader Jacques Molay a century earlier, suspended over a raging fire and roasted to death. His last words were recorded by monk Thomas Elmham. Oldcastle affirmed that he would ascend to heaven in a chariot and rise again on the third day.

Rahn emphasises this remarkable statement of Oldcastle's amidst his endearing remarks about Don Quixote, aware that the knight's most extraordinary adventure was his initiation in the Caves of Montesinos. In the space of an earthly thirty-minute period Quixote spent three days in the crystal caves where his wondrous experience "admits of neither reply nor question" and culminates in his seeing a vision of his beloved Dulcinea del Toboso in her enchanted Goddess form. In this fantastical adventure the mysteries of the Grail are revealed to the valorous knight and, thus, he is made immortal.

Here we begin to get an insight into the possibility of a very powerful prize, which may have more relevance to Scotland's longstanding reputation as a source of great spiritual riches rather than to myths that proclaim the concealment of fabulous physical items thereabouts.

Having made this brief introduction to the topic of the Lollards, Rahn simply adds that the 12th century English heretics belonged heart and soul to the Court of Lucifer, meaning that they were a flaming torch (Lucifer meaning "Lightbringer") in the universal darkness of Catholic repression.

Rahn then embarks upon a commentary on the connection between Sir John Falstaff in *Henry IV* and *Henry V* and Oldcastle. He refers to the Epilogue to *Henry IV Part 2* in which a Dancer says in the last lines of the play that: "*Oldcastle died a martyr, and this (Falstaff) is not the man...My tongue is weary; when my legs are too, I will bid you goodnight: and so kneel down before you; but, indeed, to pray for the queen.*" In this passage Shakespeare emphasises the courageous qualities of Oldcastle compared with the character of Falstaff's puffed-up, cowardly buffoon. Moreover, in mentioning the queen Shakespeare introduces a matriarchal element, which was a key constituent of ancient esoteric philosophies that over the centuries shaped the evolution of Gnostic and "heretical" thinking into the Common Era.

Mistress Nell Quickly (Dame Hurtig in German translation), hostess of the London Eastcheap lodgings where Falstaff dies states that he is not in (heretic) hell but in Arthur's bosom. Rahn, likening Oldcastle to the Norse thunder-god Thor and his magical chariot, declares that the Lollard martyr is no more in hell than old Falstaff.

What were these Lollard beliefs and what connection might they have to Scotland? Its followers rejected the majority of the sacraments of the established Church including marriage, baptism ceremonies and confession. A personal commitment to love for Jesus Christ was the only sacrament required. Much to the fury of the Church Lollards also rejected all clerical intermediaries, not only priests but elders who administered the ordinances commanded in the New Testament such as baptism and communion. This latter stricture was widely perceived to threaten State as well as Church authority since it encouraged all people to access God directly through the scriptures and, by extension, to practice self-government in the mundane world of day-to-day life.

In these respects, Lollardy promoted ideals and beliefs very similar to those of Catharism, which was most popularly practised in the Languedoc region of France. From 1209 up to the massacre at Montségur in 1244 the Church of Rome attempted with great ferocity during the Albigensian Crusade to eradicate all traces of heretical practices as exemplified in the eyes of the Church by the Cathar faithful.

King Richard II employed leading Lollards as Knights of the Crown. The King's mother, Joan Plantagenet, was among Wycliffe's chief advocates. She intervened in his trial at Lambeth in 1378, securing his release before he could be formally sentenced.

In 1399 John of Gaunt's son Henry of Bolingbroke deposed Richard and was crowned Henry IV. On Henry's orders Richard was imprisoned and it is rumoured that his death in 1400 was an assassination ordered by the new King. The Lollards plotted to overthrow Henry for some time after Richard's death.

Sir John Oldcastle became the Lollards' military leader and led the knights in various failed *coups d'état*. In these ultimately abortive operations Oldcastle intrigued with sympathisers in Scotland, which was already "infected" by Lollard thinking.

Over time Lollardy in Scotland was absorbed into the Celtic Church of Scotland, which derives its origins from the work of Saint Columbanus who came to the Scottish Island of Iona in 563 CE and established a Bible College. For the next 700 years this was the source of much of the non-Catholic evangelical Bible teaching in Scotland. Its students were called "Culdees," which has been translated as meaning 'certain strangers.' Others maintain that the term is a corruption of

Chaldee (Chaldeans) but the most probable origin is the Irish term Céile Dé, a general term applied to monks and hermits.

The Culdees were an outgrowth from British druidism. Like the Druids and the Essenes the Culdees wore white robes. They were a secret society dedicated to safeguarding the tenets and beliefs of the "old religions" and their evolvement into aspects of mystical Christianity.

In *The Pre-Reformation History of the Bible*, a chronological history of the English Bible, one reads that the Culdees asked John Wycliffe to "lead the world out of the Dark Ages," hence the occasional description of him as the "Morning Star of the Reformation."

On a deeper level of interpretation one sees here a direct identification with the ancient tradition of the Mother Goddess, personified by Venus the Morning Star, a powerful theme of veneration that would have been wholly familiar to the druid faithful in past millennia. By this account we are asked to consider that the philosophy behind Lollardy originated in Scotland, not in England; that Wycliffe was actually a secret agent of the mysterious Culdees, guardians of the druidic traditions of Albion. An ancient verse sums up the position:

Peace to their shades. The pure Culdees
Were Albyn's earliest priests of God
Ere yet an island of her seas
By foot of Saxon monk was trod.

Similarly, scholars argue that the Cathars of the Languedoc and the closely linked Bogomils of Eastern Europe enjoyed, at least in part, druidic beginnings. In this picture one sees developing in both Western and Eastern Europe a powerfully interlinked network of guardians of the old beliefs, working quietly over the centuries to achieve their unseen incorporation into "mainstream" Christian dogma. Otto Rahn's conclusions that Lollardy spread from outside of Britain are confirmed in this model of scholarly thinking.

The early fourteenth century purge of the Templars by the combined forces of Pope Clement V and French King Phillipe le Bel occurred when the Pope and his curia were setting up their new headquarters in Avignon. John Wycliffe, a Culdee 'agent,' entered the political scene around 1376 at the close of the Avignon Papacy and at the onset of the Great Schism, a thirty-nine year period of intense flux characterised by multiple claimants (Antipopes) to the throne of St. Peter.

In this sequence of events commentators have observed the hand of Wycliffe at work as an agent of the secret societies which Henry Sinclair, Earl of Orkney, is said to have established on the British Isles. Henry was the grandfather of William Sinclair, 1st Earl of Caithness and the builder of Rosslyn Chapel.

The objective of these societies was to achieve the infiltration into the Christian Church of Gnostic-Cathar beliefs, a programme of endeavour which formed an integral part of wider contemporary European efforts to ensure the constancy of ancient esoteric traditions.

In this venture the remnants of the Knights Templar, having found refuge in Scotland under the protection of Sinclair, were free to establish "heretical" bodies such as the Order of the Rose Croix and, later, Freemasonry.

Two adjacent areas where the Lollard movement gained a strong foothold were Kyle and Cunninghame in Ayrshire, a county whose sea-coast runs for more than fifty miles alongside the Firth of Clyde. The Lollard movement was so deep-rooted in these parts that it was claimed to be the forerunner of the Scottish Reformation.

Among the parishes bounded by Kyle and Cunninghame were Kilbirnie, West Kilbride, Kilmarnock, Kilmaurs and Kilwinning, all places prefixed with Kil and evidence of the existence of 'Kils' or cells of the Culdee or Celtic Church. These are the same places where the Knights Templar survivors from the 1307-1314 *putsch* were most closely grouped.

The Magic Torch group is not the only source to promote the theory that the Grail treasures reside in western Scotland. The *Scottish Sun* of 23 August 2009 carried a story about the conclusions reached by historian A.J. Morton that the most likely place of concealment of the Grail Chalice used by Jesus at The Last Supper is in Kilwinning. Morton has discovered in ancient records that there are more than two hundred Templar properties in the west of Scotland, the highest concentration being in Kilwinning and nearby Irvine.

The Masonic lodge at Kilwinning is known as the Mother Lodge of Scotland. It dates back to the building of Kilwinning Abbey around 1140 whose ruins are at the rear of the Lodge premises. It has a unique history in the Masonic world. Mother Kilwinning, as it is proudly termed, is placed at the head of the roll of the Grand Lodge of Scotland and bears the famous and distinctive Number 0. Morton is particularly drawn to the old Abbey on the site of the Mother Lodge as the most probable hiding place for the Grail Cup. His research findings have drawn considerable support from other influential historians in Scotland

and in the U.S.A.

It is fact that here has been a religious house in the area occupied by Kilwinning Abbey since the early part of the seventh century. Saint Winin was the holy father of the first house of Culdee monks. Winin has been identified by some scholars with Saint Finnan of Moville, an Irish Saint of much earlier date.

Otto Rahn's remarks made while in Edinburgh about the greater relevance of an Arthur figure than an Abraham to Britons also highlight Scotland's claims as the geographical site of Camelot. We have already learned of the claim of Arran (Emain Ablach—meaning "the place of apples" and "the sleeping lord") to be the location of the fabled Enchanted Isle of Avalon where King Arthur lies sleeping. In Chapter 17 we read, too, of various Scottish locations where historians have made a link with the supposed physical location of Camelot. To these we may add Dumbarton Rock, ancient court for Rhydderch Hael, King of Strathclyde. Like Arthur, King Rhydderch was a king to the Britons. The Welsh histories portray him as a warrior king who wielded a magical sword.

Interestingly, a number of pagan worship sites near Dumbarton are attributed to Lailoken, more commonly known as Merlin. Several medieval texts describe the protection that King Rhydderch gave to Lailoken. He was allowed the freedom of the surrounding lands and forests. Walter Bower's 15th century epic chronicle, the *Scotichronicon*, also details a meeting near Dumbarton of Merlin and Saint Mungo (an early Celtic Christian Church father).

In the course of researches I learned that Sax Rohmer (Arthur Henry Sarsfield Ward), author of the famous Fu Manchu tales of evil Tibetan sorcerers and a member of the Hermetic Order of the Golden Dawn, wrote a foreward for John William Brodie-Innes' book *The Devil's Mistress*.[4] The book is a powerful story of witchcraft in Scotland in which the chief focus of attention is King Arthur. Notably, Brodie-Innes was the founder member of the Golden Dawn's Amen-Ra Temple in Edinburgh and was a member of the Theosophical Society.

At the site of the "Golden Triangle" of Houston, Kilbarchan and Kilmalcolm is a yew grove more than six hundred years old. The yew tree was of significant religious significance to druids, especially in connection with prophecy. As we have seen, the town of Johnstone, two miles southeast of Houston, lies on the sacred line of latitude *55 50* while Roslin village, 60 miles to the east along the Roseline meridian,

---

[4] Brodie-Innes, John W. *The Devil's Mistress*. London: William Rider and Son, 1915

lies at *55 51 15.*

We read in Chapter 10 of local newspaper reports that the Knights Templar had cached the Ark of the Covenant on high ground in Ayrshire among twelve guardian villages beginning with Kil, signifying their importance within the old Culdee communities of Scotland. Otto Rahn's close friend Gabriele Winckler-Dechend told me in 1999 that Rahn believed the Ark of the Covenant was included in the horde of ancient artefacts cached by the Cathars in the Pyrenees during the 12th-13th century Albigeois inquisition.

In any substantial investigation into the stories of Scotland as the prime location for legendary treasures, Rossyln Chapel is invariably at its epicentre. Scottish legend speaks of at least three temples built on the Rosslyn site in past millennia, a clear indication of the site's longstanding sacred provenance. In *Rosslyn: Guardian of the Secrets of the Holy Grail*[5] the authors state that French Masonic ritual indicates that Scotland was destined to be the repository of the Templar treasures. They add that almost immediately after the dissolution of the Templars the fortunes of the Sinclair family of Roslin improved dramatically.

The National Library in Edinburgh has a letter dated 1546 from Mary of Guise, Queen Regent, to Lord William Sinclair in which she swears to be a "true mistress" to him, and to protect him and his servants for the rest of his life in gratitude for being shown "a great secret within Rosslyn."

Stories circulate, too, about secret societies established one hundred and fifty years earlier by Henry Sinclair whose objectives were the continuing integration into mainstream Christianity in Britain of ancient esoteric beliefs.

But does Rosslyn wholly deserve its reputation as Scotland's treasure repository without equal? In these descriptions and local histories we see numerous references to tales of treasure in Scotland, most of which in fact centre upon Scotland's *western* regions.

At their root lies the evolution of the Celtic Church of Scotland, itself an outgrowth from earlier mystical traditions dating back to the druids and to the far older cults of the Mother Goddess.

St. Columbus' Culdees shared common purpose with the European Cathars, a Gnostic Christian movement long held to have been the custodians of both spiritual and physical treasures jealously coveted by the Church of Rome. The Elders of the Cathar faith entrusted their legacy to the Knights Templar at the time of the fall of Montségur in

---

[5] Wallace-Murphy T. & Hopkins M., *Rosslyn: Guardian of the Secrets of the Holy Grail*, Thorsons, 2002

1244. It is claimed that seventy years later the Cathar trove, including the Ark of the Covenant, was brought by Templar survivors to a place of safety in Scotland. It is argued that the precise spot chosen was the high ground of the Golden Triangle, which incorporates twelve sentinel "Kil" villages.

This area was an important power centre for the druids (guardians of the secrets of the ancient Goddess cults), then for the Culdees, next for the associated Lollards movement through the work of the 'Morning Star' John Wycliffe and then, finally, for Scottish freemasonry which established at Kilwinning Mother Lodge # 0.

We learn also of enduring legends that the secrets of Arthur and Camelot have a strong west of Scotland focus, illustrated by the stories of Arran as the location of the Isle of Apples and the place of the Sleeping Lord. These traditions, built upon Scotland's western geography, appear to relegate Rosslyn Chapel situated 63 miles east of the centre of the Golden Triangle to a far less significant location for the hidden cache of Grail treasures.

Unquestionably, Rosslyn does occupy an important position in Scottish legend. But perhaps its relevance does not relate so much to its reputation as the hiding place of the physical Grail but to its purported location as an extraordinary confluence of powerful, global earth energies (commonly called ley lines), a subject briefly aired in Chapter 17.

Students of Grail lore make reference to the supposed existence of an invisible pan-world energy grid. The story goes that prior to the Biblical Flood there lay an island known as Ruta or Alta-Ru. Among its inhabitants was a priesthood that constructed a temple network in accordance with an energy pattern called the 'Reshel Grid.' The grid system extended several thousand miles into an area that is now geographical Europe. Supporters of this theory claim that there are many hundreds of similar grids all over the earth.

The energy system in Britain is said to comprise a number of matrices or nodes. We have already noted Roslin's location upon the Roseline meridian at latitude *55 51 15.* Within the Scottish grid system Rosslyn Chapel is said to control the 28-mile radius Edinburgh matrix. In turn, Edinburgh (actually Arthur's Seat) is the apex of all British grids. The grid within Rosslyn Chapel is the same geometric construction as Edinburgh's but to scale.

Baphomet, the Skull, is represented in the Rosslyn grid geometry at a location in the Sacristy, the small room sometimes called the Monk's Cell in the north part of the lower chapel's crypt. The Sacristy gives the crypt its distinct L-shape. It is referenced in the Bible as the Chief Head Stone of God (Psalms 188: 19-23), which "the builders refused" (to non-believers) in the "gates of righteousness" where the faithful will pass and meet the Lord.

There are elements in this description which support opinion that the energy grid and Rosslyn's strategic placement within it constitute a "gateway" characterised by an L-shaped 90° energy flowing in the directions of both time and space. The right-angled direction of moves made by the Knight on a chessboard symbolises this process. In the same way that the Rosslyn grid is a microcosm of the larger Edinburgh network, the L-Gate in the crypt is itself a fully formed grid in perfect reflection of the Chapel grid.

Those who study the grid claim that the Rosslyn gateway is accessible to those who possess a certain belief or knowledge, which enables one to fashion a key (Jules Verne's cryptic *passe-partout* and Otto Rahn's folktale *dietrich*) to the "many mansions" in the worlds beyond. In Chapter 17 we noted the claim extracted from Templars under torture that 6th Century Grail Knights found their way to a "dimensional" Camelot along pathways navigated by a sense of "inner sight" rather than on physical trails drawn on map or parchment.

Accounts passed down have it that Saint Columbus re-established the Reshel Grid system in the Hebrides and in Edinburgh. He did this as an essential step in a quest to incorporate and protect ancient esoteric wisdoms under the guise of establishing his fledgling Celtic (Culdee) Christian Church of Scotland. Eight hundred years later, it is claimed, Henry Sinclair and the survivor Knights Templars, aware not only of the interlacing geometry around the British Isles but of the prime position of Arthur's Seat at its epicentre, "rebooted" it to ensure the continuance of Columbus' work to safeguard Scotland's metaphysical heritage.

In these descriptions we begin to dig deeper into the background behind Otto Rahn's rhapsodic remarks in 1936 about Arthur's Seat and its apparently incongruous connections with Lord John Oldcastle, Shakespeare's Falstaff and English Lollardy.

Rahn evidently had a deep interest in earth energies and sacred geometry. He was sufficiently immersed in the subject to ensure that if he visited just one place during his brief stopover in Scotland that it should be the volcanic mound famously known as Arthur's Seat. But Rahn's involvement went beyond that of a casual enthusiast. In correspondence with French mathematician and 20th century alchemist Gaston de Mengel in June 1937 they conversed about an "axis" (northeast of Paris) and a "big triangle" with a "black centre" in western Mongolia.

De Mengel provided Rahn and Himmler with calculations concerning the origin of the geometric forces. Some years ago I asked renowned UFO and Antigravity expert Bruce Cathie to analyse de Mengel's coordinates. Cathie's analysis of the Frenchman's calculations was astonishing. Disarmingly, he confirmed that: *"It appears that the SS did have some knowledge of the grid and harmonic maths. The latitude and longitude...has connections with the harmonic 288 (twice the speed of light) and also the answer to one of the unified equations. They were getting close to the truth. Much is being kept hidden."*

The main thrust of Bruce Cathie's work underlines his theory that all major changes of physical state are caused by harmonic interactions of light, gravity and the mass of electrical and magnetic forces. The controlled manipulation of these resonant factors makes it possible to move mass from one point to another in space-time. Similarly, time can also be controlled by these manipulations of harmonic pulsations due to time's relationship to the speed of light. Cathie's investigations revealed that the grid's lines of force correspond to the paths of UFO flight patterns. His studies also indicate that atomic disruption (nuclear bomb blasts), volcanic and earthquake activities are connected to the grid structure.

Were German physicists, even as early as the 1930s, achieving successes at the quantum level in harnessing the power of the global energy grid? Was local access to the Scottish grid in some way important to this work?

Otto Rahn was an unwilling conscript into the SS but he entered that nightmare environment with a vital duty to perform. In my book I reviewed evidence that suggests he was one of a small group working secretly and at terrible risk in Nazi inner circles to create a degree of positive balance against Hitler's policies and actions. I wrote, too, about the reputed work of a Dr. Karl Obermayer and his team, which had become increasingly concerned about space-time experiments being conducted by Nazi scientists. The story goes that with the aid of Rudolph Steiner and inventor Nikola Tesla, Obermayer set up a project in the Ural Mountains under the auspices of his Prometheus Foundation. This location was in the geographical area bounded by Gaston de Mengel's triangle coordinates. Between 1923 and 1933 Obermayer's Prometheus Foundation attempted to counter Hitler's plans to use grid technology to manipulate the laws of space-time and even to open pathways to other dimensions of existence.

Cathie's analysis confirms that Obermayer had cause to be concerned. It appears that Hitler's scientists were making advances ahead of capability elsewhere in particle physics and associated fields of space-time technologies. These advances had to be stopped and the technologies secured. In an interesting side-note to the Hess story Vatican insiders confided to Editor Jim Keith[6] that their sources indicated that Hess travelled to Scotland to deliver to the British Germany's atomic research secrets.

Did U-33 or its sister special submarine(s) carry personnel into the Firth of Clyde who had the knowledge to divine and, thereafter, to manipulate the local grid's properties in furtherence of Germany's technology interests? And is there something in the Magic Torch group's position that U-33 was carrying anti-Hitler language scholar Otto Rahn to become an expert advisor to the British? Alex Closs' reported documentation that Rahn lived on past 1945 would suggest that his activities from 1939 to 1945 were concentrated in Britain itself. An advisor role fits this profile.

Are there, though, other aspects to the earth's invisible geometry, which offer a different, more startling perspective on its Scottish component centred upon Arthur's Seat and Rosslyn?

Once more we look to the distant past for guidance. Philosophers such as Pythagoras and Plato believed that the universe was composed of geometrical figures. The most interesting of these was the dodecahedron, a regular solid with twelve pentagonal faces. It is one of the five regular polyhedra or Platonic solids. The ancients identified the dodecahedron as the "hull of the sphere." In the *Phaedo* Plato addresses the notion that the construction of the world is likened to the building of a ship using geometric shapes. It was not until the twentieth century that physicists confirmed the philosophers' findings. Research undertaken since 1950 has indicated that the earth resembles a gigantic crystal reinforced beneath its surface by a rigid skeletal structure. In his 1952 *Die Welt der geheimen Mächte* (The World of the Secret Force) Siegfried Wittman and his study team concluded that the earth is overlaid with a checkerboard pattern of positive and negative poles.

Twenty-three years later Russians Vyacheslav Marazov and Valery Makarov wrote a paper: *Is the Earth a Giant Crystal?* They posited that the earth projects from within itself a dual geometrically regularised grid. The first grid layer consists of twelve pentagonal slabs over the surface of the earth, while the second is formed by twenty equilateral

---

[6] Keith J., *Secret and Suppressed*, Feral House, 1993

triangles making up an icosohedron. The Russsians stated that by superimposing the two grids over the earth's surface a pattern of the earth's energy grid can be identified. In accordance with the ancient maxim: "*as above as below*" do the twelve sentinel 'Kil' villages on high ground in North Ayrshire and their leyline connections reflect this complex global geometry and energy grid?

Ancient teachings refer to the zones described by Marazov and Makarov as etheric web points. These points form the crystal apices of the earth's master geometry. If one had the "second sight" the geometry's nodes, lines and vertices would appear as shifting, vivid brilliant kaleidoscopes of colour. Wise men from Pythagoras to Lovelock have described our planet as a vibrant, intelligent living organism, its physical structure surrounded by increasingly finer fields of energy much in the same manner as the human body radiates outwards its invisible multi-coloured aura. These fields comprise an integral part of the fabric of the earth but, equally, each is a discrete dimension of conscious awareness.

Perhaps the concept of dimensions is not so hard to understand. Humans possess the respective dimensions of the physical, the emotional, the mental, the philosophical and the spiritual, each being whole and distinct but at the same time each is an essential component of the complete human experience. Stories handed down are full of tales about different dimensions. Writers, for example, have described Camelot as the 'Dream Dimension' of Merlin; that when Arthur used Excalibur in anger the dream was dissipated and the doorway to a wondrous realm of knightly initiation closed.

In reflection of the human model the physical earth and its etheric bodies constitute its Gaia consciousness, at the heart of which resides the all-loving beauty of the maternal Goddess—the Holy Mother. Perhaps the most potent personification of the Mother Goddess in myth and legend is Isis whom "no mortal man hath unveiled," which brings us once more to the unmourned Sikh Hidtalla. The name is an obvious fabrication, which makes no sense whatsoever unless someone wanted to draw attention to it for reasons which at first are wholly unclear. I mentioned earlier that a thorough search had elicited no trace of the specific term Sikh Hidtalla in any field of enquiry…with one exception.

The whole name appeared fleetingly in a web source connected with the Voynich Manuscript. I say fleetingly because the next time I accessed the site (hours later) the name had disappeared. The Voynich Manuscript (named after Wilfrid M. Voynich who acquired it in 1912) is a mysterious, undeciphered illustrated book. The author, script and language of the manuscript remain unknown although a strong contender for authorship lies with thirteenth century Franciscan friar Roger Bacon. It has also been speculated that Queen Elizabeth I's astrologer Dr. John Dee (the model for Shakespeare's Prospero) wrote it. The manuscript has been the object of intense study by many professional and amateur cryptographers, including top Second World War American and British codebreakers, each of whom failed to decrypt any portion of the text. These failures have turned the Voynich Manuscript into a famous subject of historical cryptology. On the other hand, many believe it to be no more than an elaborate hoax.

Author Leo Levitov stirred up the Voynich Manuscript research community when he wrote[7] that it is an encoded instruction handbook for undertaking the ritual suicide ceremony of Endura. The act of Endura is closely associated with the Cathar faith. Some who claim that Otto Rahn killed himself in the Austrian Tyrol in March 1939 believe that he chose to die by performing the Cathar ritual of Endura.

Levitov explains that the intricate plant illustrations in the manuscript are secret symbols of the faith and that its unidentifiable heavenly constellations are representative of the stars in Isis' mantle. He is the only researcher to have linked the evolution of the Cathar faith with the Egyptian cult of Isis. He appears to have arrived at his conclusions via a tortuous process of deduction, largely unsupported by fact. Certainly, there does not appear to be any evidence in the particulars of Cathar history to suggest an obvious connection with Isis. But are there any less obvious signposts?

There are numerous stories that Mary Magdalene fled to France after the Crucifixion. In French legend the exiled "Magdal-eder" who seeks asylum on the southern coast of France is Mary of Bethany, otherwise known as Mary Magdalene. Other strands of the legend state that Mary, accompanied by her brother Lazarus, sailed from Judah in an unmanned black rudderless boat; that it was purely by God's grace that it landed safely off the coast of Provence.

Mary's arrival in France was momentous because she was bearing the "sangraal," the sacred vessel reputed to have contained the blood of Jesus—the Holy Grail. However, it is now accepted that the translation of sangraal into "Holy Grail" was misleading because the term had been broken incorrectly after the 'n' into san graal. Gradually, it became clear that sangraal was more accurately a composite of 'sang raal,' which in old French means "blood royal"—the blood of a King. In this

---

[7] Levitov L., *Solution of the Voynich Manuscript: A liturgical Manual for the Endura Rite of the Cathari Heresy, the Cult of Isis,* Aegean Park Press, California, c1987

Mary Magdalene wearing the Girdle of
Isis worn only by her Priestesses

El Greco's 'Mary Magdalene with Skull'

more evolved interpretation of the legend the vessel that contained the "sang raal" was Mary Magdalene herself. How could this be?

Legend has it that in Jesus' day Mary was the High Priestess of the Temple of Ishtar (the Babylonian counterpart of Isis) in Jerusalem, an ancient sisterhood of Sacred Prostitutes. Mary had fulfilled her allotted term in the Temple and was free to remain in the service of the Goddess or to leave and marry if she wished. Esoteric Christianity teaches that Mary chose to leave the Temple of Isis and marry Jesus. Not long afterwards Mary gave birth to a child. This child, a boy, was the First Grail, the holy vessel through which flows the blood and genes of Jesus Christ.

The story of the "second" Grail is filled with mystery. In this account the "hidden" histories describe an extraordinary event that took place after the Crucifixion on Golgotha (the Place of the Skull). Jesus had fulfilled the old prophecies that the Messiah would suffer and then rise from the dead after three days. Having made His appearances, Jesus returned to the tomb cave and met with His wife Mary one last time before His ascension. He stood at its entrance, stretched out His arms and a bolt of lightning struck Him from head to toe. It is claimed that the Biblical description of the curtain of the Temple being rent asunder is a coded allusion to this scene. The Temple is Jesus' physical body, torn by the lightning. What the legends speak of as occurring next is spine chilling.

The life force of Jesus, liberated by the lightning encounter, was channeled into a large crystal, some speak of a Skull, which in moments became the most potent and magical spiritual artefact in existence. Mary Magdalene then took the Head of God—the Second Grail that Otto Rahn sought so avidly—to France with her son.

It is in the corresponding details of a separate account that one is offered many startling points of corroboration with the legendary crystal skull episode. There is emerging study investigating the premise that in addition to the child, Mary Magdalene was also carrying in her escape from Judah an extraordinary artefact that dated back to the Magdalenian Era (15000 BCE to 9500 BCE)—an item handed down from one High Priestess to the next. The Magdalenian Era is linked powerfully with the symbology of the Mother (Triple) Goddess, including the mysterious Bird Goddess. Sumerian texts describe the actions of the Goddesses at the time of the Flood:

"Even the gods became afraid of the flood;
They retreated, they went off (to) the heaven of Anu....
Ishtar screams like a woman in labour"

The Magdalenian Goddess wore a many horned crown, a design that evolved into the cone shape favoured by the Zoroastrians and, later, by Merlin. Hundreds of crowns found at Goddess sites over the centuries bear the image of a female wearing a diadem with a crescent shape at the forehead.

Traces of Magdalenian civilisation are predominant in Northern Spain and Southern France. This latter location is the area where, successively, Mary Magdalene arrived with the Grail, the Merovingian monarchy appeared and the Cathar faith took root. In fact, the Magdalenian Era saw a settlement explosion in which the population of France increased from about 15,000 persons in the preceding Solutrean Era to more than 50,000.

One of the principle areas where similar Magdalenian cave art and artefacts have been found is at Niaux in the Pyrenean grottoes, precisely where Otto Rahn first began to excavate when he arrived in the South of France in November 1931. He also wrote about a headpiece and diadem falling from the heavens and landing on the Pog (peak) of Montségur. By all appearances, Rahn was hot on the trail.

The Sumerian texts also record that Goddess Queen Anu sent to Earth the gift of seeds, which were lowered to earth from the House of Offerings in her heaven world. Cave glyphs of Anu and her subjects depict strange, oval-eyed ET-like figures.

In my Rahn study I demonstrated that the character of *Indiana Jones* was based on Otto Rahn's Grailseeking activities in the South of France. In Lucas and Spielberg's fourth outing in the series, *Indiana Jones and the Kingdom of the Crystal Skull*, we see them drawing on the story of the alien-like Anu race, whose home was a dimension beyond our own, and the tremendously powerful crystal energy it created in the distant Magdalenian Era.

In his first book[8] Rahn writes of an ancient lake of dark green waters in the Montségur region where the druids threw gold, silver and precious stones. These valuables were said to be the fabled treasure of the Temple of Delphi, which was stolen from Mount Parnassus in 279 BCE by Celtic Chief Brennus and a force of two hundred thousand soldiers. The Oracle told the townsfolk of Delphi that Apollo would not allow them to suffer distress because of the theft of the treasure nor would he let the heinous act go unavenged. Brennus brought the spoils to Montségur. Subsequently, Celtic settlers began dying of a devestating ailment. Those who fell ill in the morning were dead by

---

[8] Rahn O., *Kreuzzug gegen den Gral,* Urban Verlag Freiburg i/Breisgau, 1933

nightfall. The druids divined by the flight of birds that the only remedy was to throw Delphi's treasure into the lake. They traced a magical circle around its shores whereupon all the fish perished and the green waters turned to black. At this moment the people were cured of their terrible affliction. The legend says that all the gold and silver will belong to one who can break the magic circle. However, as soon as the finder touches the treasures they will succumb to the same malady as the old mountain folk.

Within the stories of Anu's otherworldly gifts and Brennus' theft of Apollo's treasures from Parnassus and its dreadful consequences described by Otto Rahn, we are reminded that something very precious and very holy was brought to France by Mary Magdalene in the distant past.

It is a just a small step in reasoning to conclude that the artefact Mary Magdalene brought to Jesus' tomb was an item of skull-shaped crystal, similar to the exquisitely carved heads discovered in relatively recent times in Central and South America such as the famous 'Mitchell-Hedges' skull, which ten thousand years earlier had been a highly valued talisman of veneration among the Goddess-worshipping tribes of the Magdalenian Era. Could this special object have been the source for all subsequent Grail stories?

We have established that items of incalculable value were protected by the Cathars for approximately one hundred and fifty years and then passed into the custodianship of the Knights Templar in 1244. These items were subsequently conveyed to Scotland by surviving Templars to protect them from the Pope and the French king.

None of these remarkable legends, fables and histories is remote from the ulterior objectives of U-33's missions in the Firth of Clyde in November 1939 and February 1940.

The "*legend which reaches back to the prime source of All legends*"—the great secret—the wisdom of the ages about which Wolfram von Eschenbach composed *Parsifal* so cryptically and later deciphered by the brilliant Otto Rahn—was guarded for millennia by one generation of disciples ("Sikhs") of the Grail after another. Mary Magdalene, a devotee of the Goddess Isis-Ishtar, practised and protected these secret principles in the time of Jesus. By coming to France, Mary introduced them into Gaul. Nothing had changed in fifteen thousand years; the will, reach and influence of the Goddess prevailed.

In the centuries after the arrival of Mary in Provence the dynasty of Kings known as the Merovingians gained power in France. Legends associate the origins of the Merovingian kings with the royal bloodline of Jesus and Mary Magdalene. The term Merovingian is said to derive from its founding leader Merovée, meaning "one from over the sea," Jesus' son.

Merovée was the living seed by which the beginnings of a powerful new thread of mystical Christianity would grow in Europe. Those drawn to its teachings learned that to experience a personal relationship with God did not require priestly intermediaries. As the Cathars and Lollards were to discover centuries later what was required to enjoy a lasting, personal interconnectedness with God was an enduring belief in and love for self and one's fellow man.

Jesus had taught that the Kingdom is within; that humankind has all that it needs to build and sustain a personal earthly paradise in everyday life. Men and women had only to compose their own personal doxology in praise of God within to enjoy the beauty of this life before joining Jesus and the Holy Mother and Father in the next. The Church of Rome naturally saw this process as a direct and extremely subversive challenge to its authority. Knowing that this battle for the souls of men and women would be a drawn out struggle waged over a period of centuries, the Church settled in for the long haul.

In 751 Pepin the Short, the father of Charlemagne, defeated Childeric III, the last Merovingian king. Under Charlemagne's rule the strength and influence of the Catholic Church grew quickly. But the Church's actions in bringing down the Merovingians failed to secure for it two critical objectives. It did not staunch heretical practices nor did it secure control and possession of either of the two Grails—the direct descendants of Jesus and Mary Magdalene and the magical Head of God.

Guardianship of these powerful expressions of mystical Christianity remained in the hands of small groups of men and women, among them the Scottish Culdees and the later Lollards. Often these custodians were priests or nuns of the Catholic Church who, secretly, were dedicated to the higher ideal of the Gnosis—direct knowledge of God through personal experience—rather than through rule-bound ecclesiastical Roman ritual. Three hundred years later it fell to the Cathars to safeguard the things of great value to the esoteric strand of Christianity. In 1209 Innocent III launched the Church's ferocious Albigensian Crusade against the Cathars and other Gnostic faithful during which approximately one million people were killed.

By 1244 and the infamous siege of Montségur the powers in Rome must have felt as if the "Grail" prizes they had sought for twelve centuries were within their grasp. But once again they were denied ownership. The treasures were spirited away under the cover of darkness by Templar sympathisers (faidits) and, sixty years later, were carried to the west of Scotland after the Pope and Phillip the Fair had made another desperate attempt to seize possession.

Jesus and Mary Magdalene bequeathed their unique respective powers and legacies to their child who was the seed from which quietly flowed a strong current of mystical Christianity by which the Church of Rome felt increasingly threatened over the centuries.

'Hidtalla' offers additional clues into the mindset of the unknown person(s) who chose both this obscure name for Greenock Cemetery's burial records and, just as certainly, the coded names Haryog and Handy assigned to the *Maillé Brézé* fatalities.

The prefix "talla" tells a story that speaks of the Goddess legends of old. Thalia (or Talia) was one of the Nine Muses on Mount Parnassus in the Temple of Apollo at Delphi. Cervantes described them in *Journey to Parnassus*. Talia was a rustic goddess, the Muse of comedy and idyllic poetry. The late 15th century saw the appearance of a unique tarot deck—the Tarocchi di Mantegna. Albrecht Dürer created illustrations for twenty-two of the fifty cards. Talia is card XVI.

Albrecht Dürer's *Talia* card

The term Talla was part of a Roman taxation system. The English word tally comes from the Latin talea meaning a "method of payment." The Talla system worked by using notched tablets of wood called tessere. In the Welsh language 'taliad' means payment or charge.

Another meaning of tessere is password (Otto Rahn's "*dietrich*"). Rahn wrote a fictional story about Jehan Tessenre, a synonym for the Huguenot weavers, the Tisserands, who were associated with the Cathar faith. Tessera also had the particular meaning of a tally or token which was divided among friends in order that they or their descendants would always recognise each other. This is an especially appropriate interpretation in connection with the handing down from priestess to priestess of the highly prized crystal artefact from the Magdalenian Era via Mary Magdalene and its likely arrival in Scotland in the fourteenth century. This particular meaning of talla is the basis, too, for the prayer card of the Legion of Mary, a family organization of lay Catholics who "become instruments of the Holy Spirit through prayer and work."

Moreover, it is a telling fact that 'Taliahad' is the Hebrew angel of the element of water, thereby making it the *de facto* protector of U-33, succeeding in this capacity in November 1939 but not in February 1940. Curiously, Taliahad is also invoked in the ritual magic of the Order of the Golden Dawn.

Read together, these variances suggest that the sardonic tease who created the composite name 'Hid-talla' was indicating that U-33 was involved in seeking out concealed bounty collected in the past under some form of taxation or seizure. This is a precise description of Brennus' plunder by force of the Delphic spoils from Mount Parnassus in the third century BCE and also of the Visigoth king Alaric's theft of the Treasures of the Temple of Solomon and the Ark of the Covenant during his sack of Rome seven hundred years later.

Legend records that both of these sources of treasure were brought to the South of France, all or in part eventually coming into the safe hands of the Cathars and, thereafter, to the Knights Templar who included them among the valuables brought out of France in their subsequent flight to Scotland. Moreover, in undertaking its political and treasure-seeking activities U-33 deployed passwords ("tessere"), like those constructed for Albrecht, Klinger, Hidtalla, Haryog and Handy—men whose identities and roles were truly not what they seemed.

The cryptic term "Sikh Hidtalla" thus reveals a powerful symbology underling a vast history of conflict between the established Christian Church and the esoteric line founded upon two very powerful teachings. One concerns insights into the ancient Hermetic wisdoms, which Jesus shared with his disciples in private. The other, arguably at least as profound, was Mary Magdalene's knowledge and practice of the cults of the Goddess that even in Mary's day were many thousands of years old but none the less powerful in the ageing.

It was the mission of U-33 to seek not only wise heads in Britain who could help shorten the war but also to seek the miraculous Head of God. This Second Grail, cached in Scotland in the fourteenth century, was an almighty prize for the Nazis in the twentieth.

Chapter TWENTY-TWO

The Female Pope

What's past is prologue

Did U-33 come up trumps in discharging its twin covert objectives? The turn of the card from the Tarocchi di Mantegna deck for the fortunes of U-33's political agenda reveals The Hanged Man. U-33 was sunk with the loss of 27 men. King George VI's brother Prince George Duke of Kent, a top-level protagonist of the unofficial peace discussions between Britain and Germany, was killed as a result of the S-25 Sunderland Mk III seaplane crash on Eagle's Rock in 1942. A compelling argument also places Deputy Führer Rudolf Hess among the 15 deceased from this accident. The war did not end in 1940 nor at any time soon after. By all appearances U-33's actions in seeking to expedite an early political solution to war were undertaken without success.

The upturned card for the esoteric agenda may tell a different story. Perhaps The Hermit was induced from his forest cave to guide the search.

Controversy rages today about the keenly anticipated prospect of unearthing extraordinary finds at Rosslyn Chapel. If anything of legendary or religious value was recovered in Scotland by those on U-33 or was done so subsequently as a consequence or by-product of its Firth of Clyde activities the success has not been publicly acknowledged. Nor has continuing intense speculation that artefacts such as the Head of God remain to be discovered by determined Grail seekers been dampened.

On the other hand, there has long been considerable suspicion that Heinrich Himmler was given something of spectacularly significant value and that the gift to the Reichsführer-SS was connected with finds achieved at Rosslyn. Many describe the talisman of power gifted to Himmler as the Spear of Destiny while others claim it was an artefact from among the Treasures of the Temple of Solomon cached in the Pyrenees by one-time Holy Lance possessor Alaric I in the 5th Century, safeguarded by the Cathars in the 12th and brought to Scotland by the Templars early in the 14th. Assuming that there is an ember of light in all the smoke of rumour and dissemblance there is one intriguing possibility to consider.

We noted in Chapter 10 inconsistencies connected with the actual dates of exhumation for Klinger and, by extension, for Albrecht. The CWGC requested the exhumation of the deceased from U-33. However, there are sufficient pointers to suggest that it never received these two bodies.

The authoritative and globally connected U-boat network, Sharkhunters, told me in writing in 2003 that "these two men were exhumed shortly after burial" but its representative later claimed that he could not remember making the statement despite being sent a copy of his email to refresh his memory, viz:

From: HC <mailto:sharkhunters@earthlink.net>
To: Nigel Graddon <mailto:ruedamboise@enterprise.net>
Sent: Wednesday, January 01, 2003 12:58 PM
Subject: RE: U-33: new and critical research findings

Hello Nigel,
Nice to hear from you...

This is a difficult question. We work closely with Horst Bredow, founder of the Cuxhaven Archive, and he has great records. It is easy to understand your extreme curiosity, as these two men were exhumed shortly after burial, and that would indicate that the authorities thought there was more to these two and their possible individual missions than just submarine crews. Let me look into our files and see what we can come up with.

January 2003 email from Sharkhunters (sender anomymised by author) confirming that Albrecht and Klinger were "exhumed shortly after burial."

An analysis of burial papers of 1940 and exhumation records and correspondence from Greenock Cemetery, CWGC and Greenock Town Council in 1962 throws up significant areas of doubt upon the circumstances relating to the handling of the remains for U-33's 'Mystery Men.'

Taken together, the gaps and questions support the contention that the Sharkhunters representative's intemperate remarks might be far closer to home than is comfortable for those in the know about the events in the Clyde in 1940.

In the course of my researches I learned of a fascinating and little known practice in Nazi circles. A longstanding friend overseas was an undergraduate at an American University in the 1950s. One of his Professors had escaped Nazi Germany because his brother was in the SS. The Professor revealed to his students that during the war there had been a "re-burial unit," which was established by German patriots for the benefit of members of the armed forces secretly opposed to Hitler who died in active service, persons such as those who supported General Ludwig Beck's resistance undertakings. After the first official burial the special unit would exhume or commission the exhumation of their resistance colleague and cremate the body in a secret ceremony of honour.

The putative existence of this special unit squares with the controversial claim examined in my book on Otto Rahn that there were those among the inner cadre of Himmler's SS, Rahn included, who were working with like-minded brethren in Nazi Intelligence with links to British security services to thwart Hitler's policies. Top Nazis suggested to have been allied to this group include Abwehr Chief Admiral Wilhelm Canaris who was named as a British Agent by author Ian Colvin in 1951.

It has been suggested that the special unit collaborated with friendly, highly placed Britons to bring home Albrecht and Klinger. The unit's intervention in this matter would have indicated that the two men, ostensibly envoys acting on behalf of Hitler, were associated with the 'Secret Germany' resistance movement. A plan was therefore made to repatriate the bodies for ceremonial cremation on home soil.

In Chapter 10 we briefly reviewed the irregular burial and exhumation circumstances of Charles Haryog and Modiste Handy, two alleged victims of the 30 April 1940 *Maillé Brézé* disaster. Officially, 6 of the 27 killed were recovered but only 4 can be traced in the GRO Scotland register of deaths; Haryog and Handy are off the radar. According to Greenock Cemetery records the 6 were buried on 3 May 1940 and exhumed 12 October 1949.

In the absence of the complete facts about Albrecht and Klinger a powerful and seriously credible scenario arises nevertheless—that, in reality, there were only *four* men who died in Greenock Infirmary after being recovered alive from the scene of the *Maillé Brézé* explosion— Bolard, Albrand, Coucherat and Alleon.

We have learned of correspondence headed '*Greenock Cemetery, Renfrew, Exhumation of German War Dead*' in October 1962 from the Regional Director of the CWGC to the Greenock Town Clerk in connection with the exhumation that month of 27 bodies (the deceased from U-33 plus "unknowns"). The letter confirmed that the German

War Grave Commission had exhumed the burials annotated on an attached list and that the corresponding 7 graves (lairs) should be deleted from the "Agreement signed in December 1947 by the (Greenock) Deputy Town Clerk."

However, in the letter's appendix details are provided for just 5 occupied lairs—CCC-931A, CCC-932 A through D, CCC-933 A through D, CCC-934 A through D and CCC-935 A through C. The Remarks column states that Lair 930 was not used.

The next two numerically consecutive lairs deployed after this batch of five—936 and 937—were used for the fatalities from the *Maillé Brézé*. Bolard, Coucherat and Alleon were buried in lair 936 while Albrand, Haryog and Handy were put into lair 937. The latter pair is described in the cemetery ledger as occupying 1st and 2nd upper positions while Albrand is on the bottom.

Could either of these lairs have become commingled in the CWGC's reference to the deployment of seven graves?

If there was a connection how could it have come about that the exhumation of "German War Dead" became linked to the deaths of French sailors?

Greenock Cemetery's records explain the deployment of just 5 of the 7 graves requested for deletion by the CWGC. Might lairs 936 and 937 have been the 6th and 7th lairs that required deletion from the 1947 Agreement?

A connecting thread would have to tie back to Albrecht and Klinger and, in particular, to the Sharkhunters' authoritative statement that they were exhumed not long after burial. Their unequivocal claim appears to indicate access to privileged information. However, the difficulty with this scenario is that Greenock Cemetery has no public record of any exhumations, foreign nationals or Scots, undertaken in or around this period. Lack of public record cannot of course rule out undertakings carried out or overseen under cover of secrecy.

Recall that the names of Albrecht and Klinger were the only ones among the U-33 deceased on the Greenock Cemetery hand-written burial list with an added hyphen as if to denote something different about the pair or to flag up some form of impending or temporary action. They were to be returned to Germany at the earliest appropriate opportunity for ceremonial re-burial with help from well-placed Britons sympathetic to Germany, firmly allied to the unofficial peace process. Quite how the pair was going to be spirited out of Greenock and away from Scotland was not something that could be determined quickly or easily.

In the meantime, what to do? An unfolding scenario along the following lines is well within the bounds of credible speculation.

Burying Albrecht and Klinger with the twenty-one Kriegsmarine casualties from U-33, thereby necessitating a subsequent and visible exhumation was not a smart option. However, it was appreciated that with the high volume of shipping traffic coming into and out of the Clyde Anchorage it would not be long before an opportunity arose to transfer the bodies for repatriation; perhaps a matter of days, a few weeks at most.

As an interim measure the bodies would have to be preserved as effectively as possible. Professionals would have to be brought into the operation and strict confidences secured. I contacted a source in the undertaker fraternity in Greenock for advice. By coincidence, he said he had been reading about wartime embalming practice in this part of Scotland. He confirmed that in the war years Greenock undertakers seldom used deep freezing for preservation (between -15°C and -25°C), especially in circumstances when the frozen body had to be moved any distance because decomposition would start to set in rapidly. Instead, local practice was to preserve bodies by either submerging them in an arsenic solution or by injecting them with the solution. (In the American Civil War the medical department of the Union Army set up battlefield arsenic-embalming stations to enable the bodies of Union dead to be returned home quickly.)

Embalming by arsenic is a high-risk business. The substance is toxic and elemental arsenic will never degrade into harmless by-products. The leaching of arsenic into the soil poses very serious health risks to people such as cemetery workers and archaeologists. Consequently, its use as an embalming agent began to drop off in the U.S.A. in the early 20th century. The use of arsenic in the United Kingdom, at least in Scotland, continued a while longer.

The scenario supposes that the two bodies were subjected to arsenic preservation and carefully stored. One may picture a situation where as time went on certain pressures accumulated—top down—and an order was issued to get the bodies out of Scotland without delay. But how was this to be achieved precisely?

Suddenly, 77 days after the death of Albrecht and Klinger, the *Maillé Brézé* explodes in the Clyde Anchorage, the opportunity for the transfer of the pair ("shortly after burial") arising like the wave of a wand by accident and virtue of the terrible explosion.

Of the 51 wounded sailors from the *Maillé Brézé* recovered from the scene, 4 are recorded as dying in Greenock Infirmary but 6 are recorded as buried. In this irrational arithmetic one sees the basis of contrivance to provide secret cover for repatriating Albrecht and Klinger.

The deaths from the *Maillé Brézé* required the digging of two new lairs—936 and 937, three men to a lair, Haryog and Handy listed as occupying the top two positions in 937.

A plausible description of subsequent events is that on 2 May, after Coucherat's death, undertakers collected from Greenock Infirmary mortuary 6 bodies—Bolard, Alleon, Albrand and Coucherat plus Abrecht and Klinger labelled as 'Haryog' and 'Handy.' When inevitable exclamations of surprise were expressed about the preserved state of the latter pair an official hand was clamped tight upon curious lips.

Prior to burial, probably in the small hours of the 3rd under strict security, the Haryog and Handy caskets were removed and replaced by identically labelled coffins each containing something of corresponding respective weight.

The burial ceremony later that day for six "genuine" deceased was then performed with the hapless Albrand serving as a mattress for, literally or metaphorically, two coffins of stones or other such ballast.

Greenock Cemetery entry No. 11,706, French Admiralty, notes in the Remarks column: "These lairs 936-937 are full." No one, therefore, was going to be re-opening these lairs at any time after 3 May 1940 to add more bodies and thereby chance upon the ruse.

Horace Oakes' diary entries for May 1940 refer to the arrival in the Clyde Anchorage of vessels from Norway, Poland and France. Any one of these boats, for example, could have quietly taken aboard two caskets for removal to mainland Europe.

One must stress that the foregoing has no firm basis in recorded fact but it does serve as a wholly plausible train of events, built on facts as they are known and upon insights developed by deduction.

If the pair was exhumed at this time and in this manner for secret repatriation to Germany into the hands of the special re-burial unit what else may have been concealed in their coffins? The story that something of immeasurable value was taken to Himmler's SS-castle at Wewelsburg, for example, has not diluted over the years.

In this regard some speak of the stone tablets of 'Ultimate Truth' described by Wolfram von Eschenbach in Parsifal as conferring immortality. Otto Rahn's exhaustive studies of Parsifal convinced him, too, that there was a real possibility that such an artefact, inscribed in "confused pagan writing," remained to be discovered. Many persist in a belief that he did so.

Parallel legends also speak of the fabled *lapsit exillis*—the Grail stone that fell from Lucifer's Diadem upon the Pog (summit) of Montségur in the French Pyrenees—which the Cathars, the Pure Ones, sought so avidly aeons later. It is evident that an item so described is not sculpted in giant proportions and could conceivably be accommodated in a coffin. A crystal skull would also have been small enough to be so concealed.

But, then again, maybe the card of fate that fell from the Tarocchi di Mantegna pack was The Female Pope, the symbol and High Priestess of the Goddess. Somehow one cannot believe that the disciples of the old matriarchal religion who had successfully protected the Grail treasures for tens of thousands of years were ready to hand them to "Klingsor's" envoys without a fight.

If the defences at their command were anything like that available to the all-powerful and otherworldly Grail guardians in the closing scenes of *Indiana Jones and the Kingdom of the Crystal Skull* the battle was shortlived!

U-boat pen at Lorient (photographed by the author)

*I long
To hear the story of your life, which must
Take the ear strangely.*

Appendix

U-33's Technical Specifications[1]

> *Hull*: double. Surface displacement: 626-tons
> *U/Dt*: 745-tons
> *LBD*: 64.51m × 5.85m × 4.4m × 9.50m
> *Machinery*: 2 × 1155ps Maschinefabrik-Augsburg-Nürnberg (MAN) diesels, without turbo-charger, giving 1050ps each @470 rev/min continuously or 1155ps @485 rev/min for half an hour in an emergency
> *S/Sp*: 16kt
> *Props*: 2-bronze
> *U/Power*: 2 × Siemens-Schkert-Werke electric motors, which gave 375ps each at 322 rev/min, with full battery gave 8kts
> *Battery*: 2 × 62-cell lead/acid by Accumulatoren-Fabrik-Aktiengesellshcaft, Berlin
> *Op/R*: 4,300-n.miles @ 12kt, 8,790-n.m. @ 8kts
> *Sub/R*: 90-n.m @ 5kt
> *Fuel/ cap*: 67-tons
> *Armament*: 4-bow × 1-stern torpedo tubes
> *Torpedoes*: 11
> *Gun:* 1 × 88 mm (3.46 in) Quick-firing deck gun
> *Ammo*: 160-rounds of 88 mm
> *Mines*: 33-TMB but only carried on special order in exchange for torpedoes
> *Diving*: max-op-depth 100m (328 ft) and 200m (656 ft) crush-depth and 50-sec to crash-dive
> *Complement*: about 44 normally

---

[1] Courtesy of Pamela Armstrong

Crew of U-33 with details of ranks

Anger, Paul	Master Petty Officer & 3rd Watch Officer
Becker, Johannes	Sub-Lieutenant (or Ensign) & 2nd Watch Officer
Bergfeld, Hans-Georg	Seaman 1st Class (Machinist)
Braun, Friedrich	Petty Officer Mechanic/Engineer
Dresky von, Hans W.	Lieutenant Commander (Captain)
Ehrhardt, Hans-Joachim	Able Seaman 2nd Class
Enders, Werner	Senior Chief Petty Officer (Machinist)
Galileia, Paul	Petty Officer (Boatswain)
Gross, Karl	Seaman 1st Class (Machinist)
Heckerodt, Adalbert	Seaman 1st Class (Machinist)
Henneberg, Gustav	Petty Officer (Boatswain)
Johne, Johannes	Leading Seaman 2nd Class
Kampert, Heinrich	Able Seaman 2nd Class (Mechanic/Engineer)
Keller, Werner	Leading Seaman 1st class
Krampe, Manfred	Seaman 1st Class (Machinist)
Krink, Heinz	Seaman 2nd Class (Machinist)
Kumpf, Friedrich	Master Petty Officer
Kunick, Walter	Able Seaman 2nd Class
Kursiefen, Heinrich	Leading Seaman 1st class
Liebert, Heinrich	Seaman 2nd Class (Machinist)
Lingscheidt, Peter	Leading Seaman 1st class
Marticke, Heinz	Petty Officer 1st Class (Machinist)
Masanek, Ernst	Petty Officer 2nd Class (Machinist)

Mohr, Heinz	Petty Officer (Boatswain)
Patten, Erich	Petty Officer 2nd Class (Radio Operator)
Peters, Karl-Heinz	Seaman 1st Class (Machinist)
Pöppel, Leopold	Able Seaman 2nd Class (Radio Operator)
Puchta, Robert	Seaman 2nd Class (Machinist)
Raath, Herbert	Petty Officer 2nd Class (Machinist)
Rausch, Paul	Petty Officer 2nd Class (Machinist)
Rottmann, Heinz	Senior Lieutenant Engineer
Scherer, Ernst	Seaman 2nd Class (Machinist)
Schiller, Max	Ordinary Seaman
Schilling, Friedrich-Ernst	Lieutenant Commander Engineer
Schmid, Christian	Petty Officer 2nd Class (Machinist)
Siegert, Werner	Leading Seaman 2nd Class (Machinist)
Steiner, Willibald	Seaman 2nd Class (Machinist)
Vietor, Karl	Senior Ensign and 1st Watch Officer
Wagner, Ludwig	Petty Officer 1st Class (Machinist)
Weber, Heinrich	Leading Seaman 1st class
Wilden, Wilhelm	Seaman 2nd Class (Machinist)
Winterhoff, August	Able Seaman 2nd Class

The crews of all Kriegsmarine ships were essentially divided into two categories:
➤ naval personnel i.e. sailors trained in seamanship
➤ technical personnel trained in running machinery and other technical equipment aboard.

There were three broad levels of rankings:
➤ Seamen (Matrosen)
➤ Petty Officers (Unteroffiziere ohne Portepee)
➤ Senior NCOs (Unteroffiziere mit Portepee)

U-33 Deceased

Die Gefallenen von U 33

v.Dresky, Hans Wilhelm	Kptlt	Kommandant	27.01.08
Anger, Paul	StObStrm		12.07.05
Enders, Werner	ObMasch		26.12.11
Petten, Erich	ObMt		11.11.14
Rath, Herbert	ObMt		22.12.13
Rausch, Paul	ObMt		14.10.13
Schmid, Christian	ObMt		01.09.14
Braun, Friedrich	Mt		29.11.17
Henneberg, Gustav	Mt		24.06.14
Mohr, Heinz	Mt		25.02.14
Wagner, Ludwig	Mt		03.02.16
Johne, Johannes	HptGfr		13.06.16
Keller, Werner	ObGfr		07.09.15
Kursiefen, Heinrich	ObGfr		21.03.13
Liebert, Heinrich	ObGfr		08.11.15
Steiner Willibald	ObGfr		14.08.18
Wilden, Wilhelm	ObGfr		
Bergfeld, Hans G	Gfr		26.11.19
Gross, Karl	Gfr		20.07.18
Heckerodt, Adelbert	Gfr		21.12.16
Kampert, Heinrich	Gfr		18.10.18
Kunick, Walter	Gfr		20.09.19
Peters, Karl Heinz	Gfr		28.12.19
Pöppel, Leopold	Gfr		22.09.20
Winterhoff, August	Gfr		28.10.19

U-33 Survivors

Die Überlebenden von U 33

Schilling, Fritz	Kptlt(Ing)	LI	nach dem Krieg verstorben	
Rottmann, Heinz	Olt(Ing)	LI-Schüler	03.09.14	
Vietor, Karl	OltzSee	I.WO	10.11.13	23.03.86
Becker, Johannes	LtzSee	II.WO	29.04.17	
Kumpf, Fritz	StObMasch	Techn.Nr.I	28.12.10	
Galileis, Paul	Btsm	Seem.Nr.I	03.09.13	11.02.77
Msaanek, Ernst	ObMaschMt	E-Masch	24.10.13	
Marticke, Heinz	ObMaschMt	Diesel	14.12.12	
Lingscheidt, Peter	OGfr	Seemann	17.06.14	
Weber, Heinrich	OGfr	Torpedo	17.09.17	21.01.85
Puchta, Robert	OGfr	Masch	02.10.14	
Siegert, Werner	OGfr	Masch	16.12.15	
Krempe, Manfred	Gfr	Funk	07.04.19	
Schiller, Max	Matr	Seemann	17.07.21	nach Schottland verheiratet
Scherer, Ernst			24.03.15	lt.Ordnungsamt Worms verstorben
Krink, Heinz			27.12.18	wahrsch.wohnh. in der DDR
Ehrhardt, Hans	keine Unterlagen			wahrsch. wohnh. in der DDR

Out & About with John McCreadie

U-Boat Dramas in the Clyde

MR. Douglas McKillop of 17 Kilruskin Drive, West Kilbride, writes as follows: "I have read with great interest your two reports on the U-Boat dramas in the Firth of Clyde. The U-Boat sunk off Pladda was confirmed after the war. With regard to the U-Boat sinking at the Boom, as reported by Mr Gavin Crawford, I wish to state that I was a sapper with the Fort Matilda Fortress R.E.'s Searchlight Company Territorials at the start of the war in 1939.

"one evening in 1940 while stationed at Fort Matilda, Greenock, there was a telephone call from the searchlight station emplacement at the Cloch that flares had gone off at the Boom; and that a U-Boat had been sighted.

The destroyer stationed at the Boom had tried to ram the submarine and consequenity ran aground. Owing to censorship then in force no confirmation of this sinking was confirmed. The Admiralty at that time denied any sinking. What Mr Crawford reported was true; a U-Boat tried to force the Boom at the Cloch".

Mr McKillop adds: "Just after Dunkirk when I was serving in the Burns-Laird vessel, Royal Scotsman, as a radio officer, we had just come into Liverpool from Bordeaux with a Polish division rescued from France.

I picked up a radio broadcast from USA which stated that the Germans had tried to invade Britain. When I got home to Gourock, where I stayed at that time, some pals of mine who wereserving in destroyers confirmed that the German invasion barges had been cut to ribbons by destroyers led by Lord Louis Mountbatten. Again, this was denied in Parliament, just as the Cloch U-Boat sinking was denied."

A pivotal article published in the *Largs and Millport Weekly News* in 1985 that renewed public interest in the Tail of the Bank U-boat event.

Greenock Cemetery burial record of 3 May 1940 for reported *Maillé Brézé* fatalities Haryog, Handy, Bollard (sic), Alleon, Albrand and Coucherat.

Page 91

19__. DEATHS in the WEST DISTRICT of GREENOCK in the COUNTY of RENFREW

No.	Name and Surname. Rank or Profession, and whether Single, Married, or Widowed.	When and Where Died.	Sex.	Age.	Name, Surname, and Rank or Profession of Father. Name, and Maiden Surname of Mother.	Cause of Death, Duration of Disease, and Medical Attendant by whom certified.	Signature and Qualification of Informant, and Residence, if out of the House in which the Death occurred.	When and Where Registered, and Signature of Registrar.
271	Lucy Helen Crawford Widow of John Crawford Grocer (Master) Tyne Place Inverkip	1940 May Seventh 11h.30m AM Royal Infirmary Greenock Usual Residence Tyne Place Inverkip	F	74 years	Archibald McIven Customs Officer (deceased) Beatrice McIven m.s. McIven (deceased)	Pleurisy Pneumonia Lobar. as cert. by R.K. Wilton M.D.	B. Plunkett Daughter Tyne Place Inverkip	1940 May 8th At Greenock Rockie Registrar
272	Gaston Bolard Premier Maitre Mechanic Marine Française Married	1940 April Thirtieth 2h.P.M Royal Infirmary Greenock Usual Residence Destroyer Maillé-Brézé	M	36 years		Fractured Skull as cert. by R.C. Mathieson M.B.	[signature] Medical Officer Destroyer Maillé-Brézé F. GAUFFRIAUD	1940 May 9th At Greenock Rockie Registrar
273	Félicien Alleon Seaman Marine Française Single	1940 April Thirtieth 1h.30m P.M Royal Infirmary Greenock Usual Residence Destroyer Maillé-Brézé	M	26 years		Multiple Burns Fractured Skull as cert. by R.C. Mathieson M.B.	[signature] Medical Officer Destroyer Maillé-Brézé	1940 May 9th At Greenock Rockie Registrar
274	Marcel Albrand Seaman Marine Française Single	1940 May First 1h.am Royal Infirmary Greenock Usual Residence Destroyer Maillé-Brézé	M	24 years		Compound Fracture Both Legs as cert. by R.C. Mathieson M.B.	[signature] Medical Officer Destroyer Maillé-Brézé F. GAUFFRIAUD	1940 May 9th At Greenock Rockie Registrar
275	Jean Coucherat 2nd Mate Marine Française Married to	1940 May Second 8h.30m PM Royal Infirmary Greenock Usual Residence Destroyer Maillé-Brézé	M	29 years		Multiple Burns as cert. by R.C. Mathieson M.B.	[signature] Medical Officer Destroyer Maillé-Brézé F. GAUFFRIAUD	1940 May 9th At Greenock Rockie Registrar
276	Leo Morrison Harkins	1940 May Seventh 11h.30m PM Number d St Michael and All Saints Royal Infirmary Greenock Usual Residence School Street Greenock	M	6 years	Thomas Harkins Welder-Iron Margaret Harkins m.s. Mooney	Premature of Skull Post traumatic decapitation born after death by W. Elder M.D.	Thomas Harkins Father 10 East Shaw Street Greenock	1940 May 9 At Greenock Rockie Registrar

Rockie Registrar

The corresponding death registration records for *Maillé Brézé* fatalities after the event. However, only the deaths of Bolard, Alleon, Albrand and Coucherat were registered. There is no trace of a death registration record for either 'Charles Haryog' or 'Modiste Handy.'

INTERMENTS, November, 1939.

NAME.	Age.	LAIR.	Class.	Section.	PROPRIETOR.	Fees.		
Nov								
16 John Clabby	1 day	3/14	C.G.	Yr.			3	6
17 Frank P. Kernan	13 days	3/14	C.G.	Yr.		'	3	6
" Mrs Janet Corrigano	S.B.C.	3/14	C.G.	Yr.		'	3	6
21 Margt I. J. or Montgomery	65	137	8 jun	T	Margret B. Henderson Montgomery	4	4	1
23 Mrs Wilson	ADC	3/14	C.G.	m	John Gordon		3	6
23 Archibald A. H. Gordon	69	A/94	20 jun	T	John Gordon	4	4	1
24 Mrs Helen Pollock	ADC	3/14	C.G.	m			3	6
Jan 1940								
Robert Macpherson	85	C/10	7 jun	W	Robert Macpherson	3	7	6
Sikh Hiddtalla	Adult	315	C.G.	Yr.			5	6
John Gallacher	2 days	315	6 y	m		3	3	6
David Millar	82	215	6 y	m		6	6	6
James Barclay	66	269	8 jun	I	True Jane Speirs or Barclay	4	4	1

Extract from Greenock Cemetery Interments Day Book entries for November 1939 to February 1940 showing 'Sikh Hiddtalla' (sic). Out of almost 500 entries for the period Hidtalla's name is the only one written in pencil, suggesting that the entry was hurried or was temporary.

Greenock Cemetery site plan

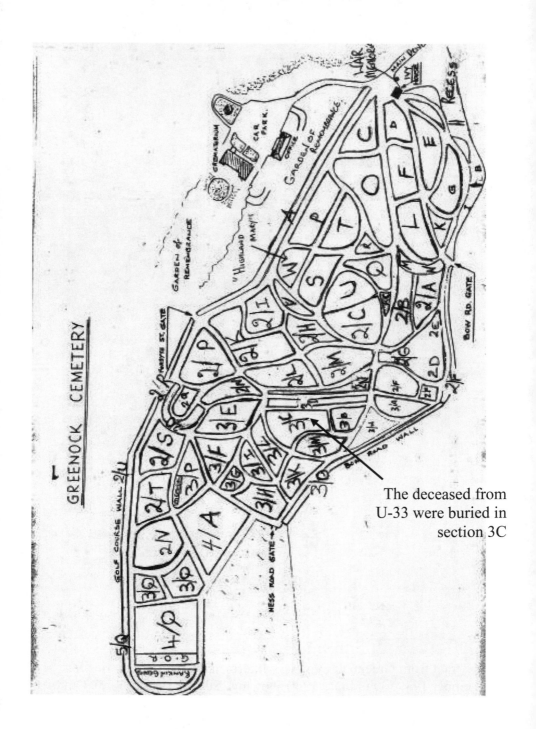

The deceased from U-33 were buried in section 3C

Greenock

Cem.

Name:	Christian Name:	Born:	Date of Death:	Grave Location:
Unknown	?	?	?	CCC-931 A
Unknown	?	?	?	CCC-931 A
Unknown	?	?	?	CCC-931 A
Unknown	?	?	?	CCC-931 A
Henneberg	Gustav	24.6. 14	12. 2.40	CCC-932 D
Liebert	Heinrich,E.	8.11.15	12. 2.40	CCC-932 C
Mohr	Heinz Karl	25. 2.14	12. 2.40	CCC-932 B
Raath	Herbert	22.12.13	12. 2.40	CCC-932 A
Steiner	Willibald	4. 8.18	12. 2.40	CCC-933 D
Kampert	Heinrich	18.10.18	12. 2.40	CCC-933 C
Kunick	Walter	20. 9.19	12. 2.40	CCC-933 B
Unknown	?	?	12. 2.40	CCC-933 A
Patten	Erich	11.11.14	12. 2.40	CCC-933 D
Wilden	Wilhelm	10.10.16	12. 2.40	CCC-933 C
Keller	Werner	7. 9.15	12. 2.40	CCC-933 B
Schmid	Christian	1. 9.14	12. 2.40	CCC-933 A
Wagner	Ludwig	3. 2.16	12. 2.40	CCC-934 D
Pöppel	Leopold	22. 9.20	12. 2.40	CCC-934 C
Gross	Karl	20. 7.18	12. 2.40	CCC-934 B
Heckerodt	Adalbert	21.12.16	12. 2.40	CCC-934 A
Anger	Paul	12. 7.05	12. 2.40	CCC-934 D
Albrecht	-	-	12. 2.40	CCC-934 C
Kursiefen	Heinrich	21. 3.13	12. 2.40	CCC-934 B
Reusch	Paul, Amand	14.10.13	12. 2.40	CCC-934 A
Peters	Karl-Heinz	28.12.19	12. 2.40	CCC-935 C
Bergfeld	Hans	26.11.19	12. 2.40	CCC-935 B
Enders	Werner Paul	26.12.11	12. 2.40	CCC-935 A

Greenock Cemetery's 1962 exhumation list for the Commonwealth
War Graves Commission. It lists details of lairs 931 A through 935 C
and their occupants—22 from U-33 and 5 "unknowns." Note Albrecht.
One of the unknowns is Klinger.

U-Boot-Archiv

U 33

Weitere Angaben zum Boot :

1936 bis 1938 dreimaliger Einsatz im Spanien-Krieg

1.) Mai-Juli 1937
2.) Dez.37 - Febr.38
3.) Sept.-Okt.38

Unternehmungen :

1.) September 1939 Ein Wilhelmshaven 27.09.1939 - Reparatur-Arb. Werft.
   Erfolge :

Datum	Planqu.	Schiff	BRT	
07.09.1939	Planqu.BE 29	br.D. OLIVEGROVE	4060 BRT	+
16.	BF 41	br.D ARKLESIDE	1467 BRT	+
24.	AM 32	br.DF CALDEW	287 BRT	+

   Boot wurde zweimal von Flugzeugen angegriffen.
   10 Besatzungsmitglieder wurden mit dem EK ausgezeichnet.

2.) November 1939   Op.-Gebiet Bristol Kanal - Minen legen. Ausl.29.10.1939
   Erfolge :
   05.11. Im Bristol-Kanal zwölf Minen gelegt.
   16.11. Angriff auf SS 'Hope Star' - bei Lands End

Datum	Planqu.	Schiff	BRT	
20.11.	AM 56	br.Df THOMAS HANKINS	276 BRT	+
20.	AM 56	br.Df DELPHINE	250 BRT	+
20.	AM 55	br.Df SEA SWEEPER	329 BRT	+
21.	AM 53	br.Df SULBY	287 BRT	+
21.	AM 53	br.Df WILLIAM HUMPHRIES	276 BRT	+
23.	AN 13	dt D BORKUM	3670 BRT	+

   BORKUM war von den Engländern als Prise genommen,- U 33 konnte
   das Schiff noch vor Erreichen eines engl.Hafens versenken

Datum	Planqu.	Schiff	BRT	
24.11.	AM 65	br.M SUSSEX	13647 BRT=	(M 05.11.)
25.12.	AM 65	br.D. STANHOLME	2473 BRT	+(M 05.11.)
16.01.1940	AM 65	br.MT INVERDARGLE	9456 BRT	+(M 05.11.)

   26.11.1939 Einlaufen Wilhelmshaven

3.) 05.02.1940 Auslaufen Wilhelmshaven - Helgoland für kleinere Reparaturen
   07.02   Auslaufen Helgoland
   10.02.   im Atlantik - drei Flugzeuge werden gesichtet - tauchen
   12.02.   Versenkung des Bootes,- es liegt englischer Bericht dar-
              über vor.

   Bei der Versenkung fielen den Engländern 3 Enigma-Walzen in die Hände
   (s. Brief Jak P. Mallmann-Showell vom 05.10.1984

U-Boot-Archiv list of boats sunk or damaged by U-33

U-Boot-Archiv — U 33

Kiellegung	:	01.09.1935	Typ : VII A
Stapellauf	:	11.06.1936	
Indienststellung	:	25.07.1936	
Bauwerft	:	Germania-Werft Kiel	

Verbleib des Bootes :

Am 12.02.1940 im Firth of Clyde durch Wasserbomben des brit. Minen-räumers GLEANER versenkt.

25 Gefallene   17 Überlebende - in Gefangenschaft

Versenkungsort : 55°25'N 05°07'W   Feldpost Nr. M - 28 962

Flottillenzugehörigkeit :
U-Flottille Saltzwedel bis 12.39
2.U-Flottille (fb) 01.40 - 02.40

Kommandanten :

Kptl Otto-Heinrich JUNKER   07.36 - 10.38

Kptl Hans-Wilhelm v. DRESKY   11.38 - 02.40   +

Wachoffiziere :
OlzS Wilhelm ZAHN   07.36 - 09.37
OlzS Georg-Heinz MICHEL   1937 f.3 Monate
OlzS Georg-Wilhelm SCHULZ ab 10.37
LzS Ernst v.BERGEN-WINDELS 12.37 - 02.38 (lt.Brief Junker v.17.03.1982)
OlzS Hans HEIDTMANN   09.38 - 01.40
LzS Paul-Karl LOESER   1938
OlzS Karl VIETOR   1WO bei Untergang
LzS Johannes BECKER 2WO bei Untergang

Leitende Ing. :   StOMasch Fritz KUMPF
1.) Kptl(Ing) Karl SCHEEL   OMasch Werner ENDERS   +
2.) Kptl(Ing) Fritz SCHILLING
               LI-Schüler bei Untergang : Ol(Ing) Heinz ROTTMANN

Bordarzt :

Obersteuerleute :
StOStrm Paul ANGER   +

U-Boot-Archiv list of U-33's officers for its three patrols and other key facts

Two pictures of language scholar, Grail historian, author and explorer Otto Wilhelm Rahn 1904-1939 (reproduced courtesy of Hans Jurgen-Lange and Arun Verlag)

"Fertig!"

Bibliography

Aarons, Mark; Loftus, John, *Ratlines*, Heinemann, London, 1991

Angebert, Jean-Michel, *The Occult and the Third Reich*, Macmillan N.Y., 1971

Buechner, Col. Howard; Bernhart, Capt. Wilhelm, *Adolf Hitler and the Secrets of the Holy Lance*, Thunderbird Press, 1988

Buechner, Col. Howard; Bernhart, Capt. Wilhelm, *Emerald Cup-Ark of Gold: the Quest of Lt. Col. Otto Rahn*, Thunderbird Press, 1991

Buechner, Col. Howard; Bernhart, Capt. Wilhelm, *Hitler's Ashes*, Thunderbird Press, 1989

Busch, Harald, *U-boats at War*, Putnam, 1955

Cathie, Bruce L., *The Energy Grid: Harmonic 695 The Pulse of the Universe*, Adventures Unlimited Press, 1997

Cornwell, John, *Hitler's Pope*, Penguin, 1999

Crawford, Ian and Moir, Peter, *Clyde Shipwrecks*, Urban Fox Press, 1997

Dasman, Peter, *The Third Reich Day by Day*, Zenith Press, 2001

Dönitz, Admiral Karl, *Memoirs: Ten Years and Twenty Days,* London, Weidenfeld and Nicolson, 1958

Drummond, John, *A River Runs to War*, W.H. Allen, 1960

Gannon, Michael, *Black May*, Dell, 1999

Graddon, Nigel, *Otto Rahn and the Quest for the Holy Grail: the Amazing Story of the Real "Indiana Jones,"* Adventures Unlimited Press, 2008

Haskin, Susan, *Mary Magdalene: Myth and Metaphor*, Harper Collins, 1993

Jamieson D.D., John, *An Historical Account of the Ancient Culdees of Iona and of their Settlements in Scotland, England and Ireland*, John Ballantyne and Co., 1811

Laidler, Keith, *The Head of God: the Lost Treasure of the Templars*,

Weidenfeld & Nicolson, 1998

Lange, Hans-Jürgen, *Otto Rahn und die Suche nach dem Gral*, Arun Verlag, 1999

Leasor, James, *Rudolf Hess: the Uninvited Envoy*, George Allen and Unwin Ltd, London, 1962

Macintyre, Ben, *Operation Mincemeat*, Bloomsbury Publishing, London, 2010

Mallmann Showell, Jak P., *U-boats at War: Landings on Hostile Shores*, Ian Allan Publishing, 2000

Miller, David, *U-boats' History, Development & Equipment 1914-45*, Conway Maritime Press, 2000

Picknett, Lynn; Prince, Clive; Prior, Stephen, *Double Standards: the Rudolf Hess Cover Up*, Time Warner, 2001

Qualls-Corbett, Nancy, *The Sacred Prostitute*, Inner City Books, 1988

Rahn, Otto, *Kreuzzug gegen den Gral,* Urban Verlag, 1933

Rahn, Otto *Luzifers Hofgesind: Eine Reise zu den guten Gelstern Europas,* Schwarzhaupter Verlag, 1937

Ravenscroft, Trevor, *The Spear of Destiny*, Sphere Books Ltd, 1983

Sampietro, Luciano, *Nostradamus: the Final Prophecies*, Souvenir Press, 1999

Sebag-Montefiore, Hugh, *Enigma*, Weidenfeld and Nicholson, 2000

Sinclair, Andrew, *Discovery of the Grail*, Arrow, 1999

Sinclair, Andrew, *Sword and the Grail: The Story of the Grail, the Templars and the Discovery of America*, Crown, 1992

Sinclair, Andrew, *The Secret Scroll*, Sinclair-Stevenson, 2001

Stem, Robert, *Type VII U-boats*, Arms and Armour, London, 1991

Thomas, Hugh, *The Unlikely Death of Heinrich Himmler*, Fourth Estate, London, 2002

Von Lang, Jochen, *Top Nazi SS General Karl Wolff—the Man between Himmler and Hitler*, Enigma Books, New York, 2005

Wallace-Murphy, Tim; Hopkins, Marilyn, *Rosslyn: Guardian of the Secrets of the Holy Grail*, Thorsons, 2002

Wynn, Kenneth, *U-boat Operations of the Second World War*, Caxton Editions, 2004

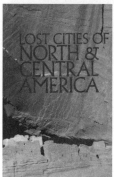

MAPS OF THE ANCIENT SEA KINGS
Evidence of Advanced Civilization in the Ice Age
by Charles H. Hapgood

Charles Hapgood has found the evidence in the Piri Reis Map that shows Antarctica, the Hadji Ahmed map, the Oronteus Finaeus and other amazing maps. Hapgood concluded that these maps were made from more ancient maps from the various ancient archives around the world, now lost. Not only were these unknown people more advanced in mapmaking than any people prior to the 18th century, it appears they mapped all the continents. The Americas were mapped thousands of years before Columbus. Antarctica was mapped when its coasts were free of ice!

316 PAGES. 7x10 PAPERBACK. ILLUSTRATED. BIBLIOGRAPHY & INDEX. $19.95. CODE: MASK

PATH OF THE POLE
Cataclysmic Pole Shift Geology
by Charles H. Hapgood

Maps of the Ancient Sea Kings author Hapgood's classic book *Path of the Pole* is back in print! Hapgood researched Antarctica, ancient maps and the geological record to conclude that the Earth's crust has slipped on the inner core many times in the past, changing the position of the pole. *Path of the Pole* discusses the various "pole shifts" in Earth's past, giving evidence for each one, and moves on to possible future pole shifts.

356 PAGES. 6x9 PAPERBACK. ILLUSTRATED. $16.95. CODE: POP

SECRETS OF THE HOLY LANCE
The Spear of Destiny in History & Legend
by Jerry E. Smith

Secrets of the Holy Lance traces the Spear from its possession by Constantine, Rome's first Christian Caesar, to Charlemagne's claim that with it he ruled the Holy Roman Empire by Divine Right, and on through two thousand years of kings and emperors, until it came within Hitler's grasp—and beyond! Did it rest for a while in Antarctic ice? Is it now hidden in Europe, awaiting the next person to claim its awesome power? Neither debunking nor worshiping, *Secrets of the Holy Lance* seeks to pierce the veil of myth and mystery around the Spear. Mere belief that it was infused with magic by virtue of its shedding the Savior's blood has made men kings. But what if it's more? What are "the powers it serves"?

312 PAGES. 6x9 PAPERBACK. ILLUSTRATED. BIBLIOGRAPHY. $16.95. CODE: SOHL

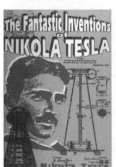

THE FANTASTIC INVENTIONS OF NIKOLA TESLA
by Nikola Tesla with additional material by
David Hatcher Childress

This book is a readable compendium of patents, diagrams, photos and explanations of the many incredible inventions of the originator of the modern era of electrification. In Tesla's own words are such topics as wireless transmission of power, death rays, and radio-controlled airships. In addition, rare material on a secret city built at a remote jungle site in South America by one of Tesla's students, Guglielmo Marconi. Marconi's secret group claims to have built flying saucers in the 1940s and to have gone to Mars in the early 1950s! Incredible photos of these Tesla craft are included. •His plan to transmit free electricity into the atmosphere. •How electrical devices would work using only small antennas. •Why unlimited power could be utilized anywhere on earth. •How radio and radar technology can be used as death-ray weapons in Star Wars.

342 PAGES. 6x9 PAPERBACK. ILLUSTRATED. $16.95. CODE: FINT

OTTO RAHN & THE QUEST FOR THE HOLY GRAIL
The Amazing Life of the Real "Indiana Jones"
by Nigel Graddon

Otto Rahn led a life of adventure in southern France in the early 1930s. The Hessian language scholar is said to have found runic Grail tablets in the Pyrenean grottoes, and decoded hidden messages within the medieval Grail masterwork *Parsifal*. The fabulous artifacts identified by Rahn were believed by Himmler to include the Grail Cup, the Spear of Destiny, the Tablets of Moses, the Ark of the Covenant, the Sword and Harp of David, the Sacred Candelabra and the Golden Urn of Manna. Some believe that Rahn was a Nazi guru who wielded immense influence on his elders and "betters" within the Hitler regime, persuading them that the Grail was the Sacred Book of the Aryans, which, once obtained, would justify their extreme political theories and revivify the ancient Germanic myths. But things are never as they seem, and as new facts emerge about Otto Rahn a far more extraordinary story unfolds.
450 pages. 6x9 Paperback. Illustrated. Index. $18.95. Code: ORQG

TECHNOLOGY OF THE GODS
The Incredible Sciences of the Ancients
by David Hatcher Childress

Childress looks at the technology that was allegedly used in Atlantis and the theory that the Great Pyramid of Egypt was originally a gigantic power station. He examines tales of ancient flight and the technology that it involved; how the ancients used electricity; megalithic building techniques; the use of crystal lenses and the fire from the gods; evidence of various high tech weapons in the past, including atomic weapons; ancient metallurgy and heavy machinery; the role of modern inventors such as Nikola Tesla in bringing ancient technology back into modern use; impossible artifacts; and more.
356 PAGES. 6x9 PAPERBACK. ILLUSTRATED. BIBLIOGRAPHY. $16.95. CODE: TGOD

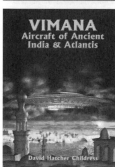

VIMANA AIRCRAFT OF ANCIENT INDIA & ATLANTIS
by David Hatcher Childress, introduction by Ivan T. Sanderson

In this incredible volume on ancient India, authentic Indian texts such as the *Ramayana* and the *Mahabharata* are used to prove that ancient aircraft were in use more than four thousand years ago. Included in this book is the entire Fourth Century BC manuscript *Vimaanika Shastra* by the ancient author Maharishi Bharadwaaja. Also included are chapters on Atlantean technology, the incredible Rama Empire of India and the devastating wars that destroyed it.
334 PAGES. 6x9 PAPERBACK. ILLUSTRATED. $15.95. CODE: VAA

LOST CONTINENTS & THE HOLLOW EARTH
I Remember Lemuria and the Shaver Mystery
by David Hatcher Childress & Richard Shaver

Shaver's rare 1948 book *I Remember Lemuria* is reprinted in its entirety, and the book is packed with illustrations from Ray Palmer's *Amazing Stories* magazine of the 1940s. Palmer and Shaver told of tunnels running through the earth—tunnels inhabited by the Deros and Teros, humanoids from an ancient spacefaring race that had inhabited the earth, eventually going underground, hundreds of thousands of years ago. Childress discusses the famous hollow earth books and delves deep into whatever reality may be behind the stories of tunnels in the earth. Operation High Jump to Antarctica in 1947 and Admiral Byrd's bizarre statements, tunnel systems in South America and Tibet, the underground world of Agartha, the belief of UFOs coming from the South Pole, more.
344 PAGES. 6x9 PAPERBACK. ILLUSTRATED. $16.95. CODE: LCHE

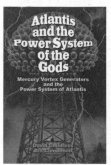

ATLANTIS & THE POWER SYSTEM OF THE GODS
by David Hatcher Childress and Bill Clendenon
Childress' fascinating analysis of Nikola Tesla's broadcast system in light of Edgar Cayce's "Terrible Crystal" and the obelisks of ancient Egypt and Ethiopia. Includes: Atlantis and its crystal power towers that broadcast energy; how these incredible power stations may still exist today; inventor Nikola Tesla's nearly identical system of power transmission; Mercury Proton Gyros and mercury vortex propulsion; more. Richly illustrated, and packed with evidence that Atlantis not only existed—it had a world-wide energy system more sophisticated than ours today.
246 PAGES. 6x9 PAPERBACK. ILLUSTRATED. $15.95. CODE: APSG

THE ANTI-GRAVITY HANDBOOK
edited by David Hatcher Childress

The new expanded compilation of material on Anti-Gravity, Free Energy, Flying Saucer Propulsion, UFOs, Suppressed Technology, NASA Cover-ups and more. Highly illustrated with patents, technical illustrations and photos. This revised and expanded edition has more material, including photos of Area 51, Nevada, the government's secret testing facility. This classic on weird science is back in a new format!
230 PAGES. 7x10 PAPERBACK. ILLUSTRATED. $16.95. CODE: AGH

ANTI-GRAVITY & THE WORLD GRID
Is the earth surrounded by an intricate electromagnetic grid network offering free energy? This compilation of material on ley lines and world power points contains chapters on the geography, mathematics, and light harmonics of the earth grid. Learn the purpose of ley lines and ancient megalithic structures located on the grid. Discover how the grid made the Philadelphia Experiment possible. Explore the Coral Castle and many other mysteries, including acoustic levitation, Tesla Shields and scalar wave weaponry. Browse through the section on anti-gravity patents, and research resources.
274 PAGES. 7x10 PAPERBACK. ILLUSTRATED. $14.95. CODE: AGW

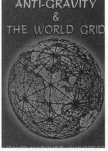

ANTI-GRAVITY & THE UNIFIED FIELD
edited by David Hatcher Childress
Is Einstein's Unified Field Theory the answer to all of our energy problems? Explored in this compilation of material is how gravity, electricity and magnetism manifest from a unified field around us. Why artificial gravity is possible; secrets of UFO propulsion; free energy; Nikola Tesla and anti-gravity airships of the 20s and 30s; flying saucers as superconducting whirls of plasma; anti-mass generators; vortex propulsion; suppressed technology; government cover-ups; gravitational pulse drive; spacecraft & more.
240 PAGES. 7x10 PAPERBACK. ILLUSTRATED. $14.95. CODE: AGU

THE TIME TRAVEL HANDBOOK
A Manual of Practical Teleportation & Time Travel
edited by David Hatcher Childress
The Time Travel Handbook takes the reader beyond the government experiments and deep into the uncharted territory of early time travellers such as Nikola Tesla and Guglielmo Marconi and their alleged time travel experiments, as well as the Wilson Brothers of EMI and their connection to the Philadelphia Experiment—the U.S. Navy's forays into invisibility, time travel, and teleportation. Childress looks into the claims of time travelling individuals, and investigates the unusual claim that the pyramids on Mars were built in the future and sent back in time. A highly visual, large format book, with patents, photos and schematics. Be the first on your block to build your own time travel device!
316 PAGES. 7x10 PAPERBACK. ILLUSTRATED. $16.95. CODE: TTH

ORDER FORM

**10% Discount
When You Order
3 or More Items!**

One Adventure Place
P.O. Box 74
Kempton, Illinois 60946
United States of America
Tel.: 815-253-6390 • Fax: 815-253-6300
Email: auphq@frontiernet.net
http://www.adventuresunlimitedpress.com

ORDERING INSTRUCTIONS

✓ Remit by USD$ Check, Money Order or Credit Card

✓ Visa, Master Card, Discover & AmEx Accepted

✓ Paypal Payments Can Be Made To:

   info@wexclub.com

✓ Prices May Change Without Notice

✓ 10% Discount for 3 or more Items

SHIPPING CHARGES

United States

✓ Postal Book Rate { $4.00 First Item
                     50¢ Each Additional Item

✓ POSTAL BOOK RATE Cannot Be Tracked!

✓ Priority Mail { $5.00 First Item
                 $2.00 Each Additional Item

✓ UPS { $6.00 First Item
        $1.50 Each Additional Item

NOTE: UPS Delivery Available to Mainland USA Only

Canada

✓ Postal Air Mail { $10.00 First Item
                    $2.50 Each Additional Item

✓ Personal Checks or Bank Drafts MUST BE

  US$ and Drawn on a US Bank

✓ Canadian Postal Money Orders OK

✓ Payment MUST BE US$

All Other Countries

✓ Sorry, No Surface Delivery!

✓ Postal Air Mail { $16.00 First Item
                    $6.00 Each Additional Item

✓ Checks and Money Orders MUST BE US$
   and Drawn on a US Bank or branch.

✓ Paypal Payments Can Be Made in US$ To:
   info@wexclub.com

SPECIAL NOTES

✓ RETAILERS: Standard Discounts Available

✓ BACKORDERS: We Backorder all Out-of-
  Stock Items Unless Otherwise Requested

✓ PRO FORMA INVOICES: Available on Request

ORDER ONLINE AT: www.adventuresunlimitedpress.com

Please check: ☑

☐ This is my first order   ☐ I have ordered before

Name			
Address			
City			
State/Province		Postal Code	
Country			
Phone day		Evening	
Fax		Email	

Item Code	Item Description	Qty	Total

Please check: ☑

	Subtotal ▶	
	Less Discount-10% for 3 or more items ▶	
☐ Postal-Surface	Balance ▶	
☐ Postal-Air Mail Illinois Residents 6.25% Sales Tax ▶		
(Priority in USA) Previous Credit ▶		
☐ UPS Shipping ▶		
(Mainland USA only) Total (check/MO in USD$ only) ▶		
☐ Visa/MasterCard/Discover/American Express		

Card Number

Expiration Date

10% Discount When You Order 3 or More Items!